Thresholds of Change in African Literature

D0081730

STUDIES IN AFRICAN LITERATURE
▼▼▼▼▼▼▼▼▼▼▼▼▼▼▼▼▼▼▼▼▼▼▼▼▼

Thresholds of Change in African Literature

The Emergence of a Tradition

KENNETH W. HARROW
Michigan State University

HEINEMANN
Portsmouth, NH

JAMES CURREY
London

Heinemann
A division of Reed Publishing (USA) Inc.
361 Hanover Street   Portsmouth, NH 03801–3912
Offices and agents throughout the world

James Currey Ltd
54b Thornhill Square, Islington
London N1 1BE

ISBN 0-435-08082-2 (Heinemann)
ISBN 0-85255-532-6 (James Currey)

Acknowledgments for borrowed material are on page vi.

Library of Congress Cataloging-in-Publication Data
Thresholds of change in African literature : the emergence of a
    tradition / Kenneth W. Harrow.
        p.   cm. — (Studies in African literature)
    Includes bibliographical references and index.
    ISBN 0–435–08082–2
    1. African literature (French)—History and criticism.   2. African
literature (English)—History and criticism.   3. Influence
(Literary, artistic, etc.)   I. Harrow, Kenneth W.   II. Series.
PQ3980.T47   1993   93–13478
809'.8896—dc20   CIP

British Library Cataloguing in Publication Data
Thresholds of Change in African
Literature:Emergence of a Tradition.—
(Studies in African Literature)
I. Harrow, Kenneth W.   II. Series
809.8896

ISBN 0–85255–532–6

Designed by Jenny Jensen Greenleaf
Cover illustration is a composite of photographs from the National Archives of Zimbabwe
and the Killie Campbell Africana Library
Printed in the Unites States of America on acid-free paper
98   97   96   95   94   EB   7   6   5   4   3   2   1

28066991

To
A. H., Budding Architect
S. H., Budding Scholar

The author and publisher are grateful to the following for permission to reprint previously published material:

"Change on the Margins" also appeared in similar form in *Callaloo* 16(2). Published by Johns Hopkins University Press, 1993.

"Literature of the Oxymoron—The Crossed Lovers" also appeared in similar form in *Callaloo* 14(4) as "*Le Bel Immonde:* African Literature at the Crossing." Published by Johns Hopkins University Press, 1991.

Excerpts from *The Structure of Scientific Revolutions* by Thomas Kuhn. Published 1962, 1970 by The University of Chicago Press. Reprinted by permission.

"Death in the Dawn" and excerpts from "Around Us, Dawning" from *Idanre and Other Poems* by Wole Soyinka. Copyright © 1967 Wole Soyinka. Published by Methuen London. Reprinted by permission.

"Primer for Blacks" from the book of the same name, published by Third World Press, Chicago, 1991. Copyright by Gwendolyn Brooks © 1991. Reprinted by permission of the author.

Contents

Preface
▼▼▼▼▼▼▼

Conventional critical models are often utilized as if they were universally valid for all literatures—this is Eustace Palmer's (1972, 1979) argument in favor of using New Critical approaches. The same assumption is made when a critic attempts to place a work within its cultural and historical parameters. A theory that calls for the treatment of each text in isolation, and that utilizes "universal" archetypes, models, or codes, is no less allegorical than one that focuses on extraliterary—sociological, historical—criteria: both are grounded in the same logocentrism. None of this is to deny the value of close reading. Nor of the pleasing allegories of deconstruction.

Languages are not mutually incomprehensible. Translation from one language to another is always possible; the nuances of the translation can be understood by one who speaks both tongues. The same should apply to the utilization of critical methods when reading texts from differing times and traditions. We need a critical language informed by Northrop Frye, but that is also cognizant of literatures, peoples, and cultural codes about which Frye or Carl Jung, for that matter, knew absolutely nothing (which did not prevent them from making pronouncements about universal literary modes or psychological archetypes)—a critical language cognizant of widespread proverbs, tales, and epics, of the role of ancestors and elders, and of the invisible forces and their discourses, all of which have contributed to patterns of perceiving and ways of living in the world. Dennis Duerden has begun this task in his admirable study *African Art and Literature: The Invisible Present* (1975), in which he avoids the "Bolekaja" fallacy that would have us look to oral literature as an answer to all the questions of sources and influences on written literature. As a body of texts, orature is joined with other influences in the process of weaving the fibers of tradition that influence an author's discourse. The revival of a more sophisticated treatment of ethnographic context can be found in the solid work of Christopher Miller (1990) and Jacques Bourgeacq (1984, 1991), among others.

Wilfred Cartey (1969) has done a great service to the fundament of African criticism in establishing a typology based upon themes. To a certain extent he has elaborated on Franz Fanon's charting of the reactions of the colonized, beginning with the failures of assimilation, followed by the individual revolt against a particular condition of oppression—these reactions often degenerating into nostalgic forms of escapism, autobiography, and ethnographic literature—and concluding with the awakening of a national consciousness, the ultimate form of revolt against the conditions and ideology of oppression (Fanon 1965, 188). The literature of exile, homecoming, revolt, and return that Cartey presents is analyzed largely in terms of a hermeneutics based upon theme and image. The sensitive readings Cartey gives to the texts shows how far this typology can take us.

Our approach here will be to elaborate a model of African literature, addressing first the critical issue of change itself: How does change come about in literature, and especially in a body of works that belong to a common tradition? How do the texts represent the process of change and thus suggest models by which their own relationships to earlier and later works make sense within the larger perspective of the corpus of African literature? Finally, what forms do change and African literature begin to assume as a written tradition emerges? What are the thresholds of that change?

Our examination of the literature begins with the works of the generation of novelists of the 1950s and early 1960s, which we are calling the literature of *témoignage,* a literature that bears witness to individual lives and to social, cultural, and historical realities. The general tendencies of this literature provide subsequent generations of novelists with a springboard as well as a target for their own efforts at fiction. The period from the 1960s to the 1990s saw changes in the major trends, giving rise to new "literatures of revolt" and eventually to literatures expressive of postindependence contradictions and frustrations—"literatures of the oxymoron." Alternatively, we might use the term "postrevolt" writing to signal the passage to texts that we sense have gone past the exigencies of political commitment as conceived in the era of anticolonialism, just as we might employ the term "postoxymoron" writing for those works of the most recent period in which the paradoxes of contemporary life do not lead inevitably to the blockage of an unsynthesized, endless dialectical struggle.

Despite the risks entailed in periodization, it seems necessary to maintain these categories so as to accommodate the concept of defamiliarization that marks the changes that occurred from the 1950s to the present period.

Close analyses of representative, key texts best demonstrate the traits of their respective "literatures." We can see this in the works by Camara Laye and Chinua Achebe that are examined as part of the literature of *témoignage*; in those of Ferdinand Oyono, Yambo Ouologuem, Bessie Head, and Ahmadou Kourouma (especially in *Les Soleils des indépendances*), which are part of the literature of revolt; in the works of Wole Soyinka, V. Y. Mudimbe, and Henri Lopes, which are part of the literature of the oxymoron; in the recent efforts by Lopes and Kourouma, which are postrevolt writing; and in the postoxymoron works of Sony Labou Tansi, whose corpus might be labeled a literature of the threshold itself.

The approaches I employ deal with how the process of change works within the development of a new literary tradition. The contradiction between Formalist and deconstructionist viewpoints should be apparent. However, this does not invalidate the insights gained by proceeding as if a structured periodization of the literature could be elaborated, or as if the bases for such structures rest upon qualities intrinsic to the literature. The theoretical assumptions about change, which do indeed form the basis of this study, appear to me as *brouillons,* sketches drafted in a fog of uncertainties. I would be pleased in thinking that these sketches invade each detail of the subsequent analyses and cause them to turn an inquisitive eye back on themselves.

Acknowledgments
▼▼▼▼▼▼▼▼▼▼▼▼▼▼▼▼▼▼▼▼▼

It was my ambition to write a poetics of African literature not grounded in Western theory but in the works themselves, and I began work on this project in 1982, a sabbatical year spent in Dakar. In the course of the following decade I wrote the chapters that make up this volume, reconciling myself more and more to the necessity of relying upon theory, and eventually taking inspiration from Henry Louis Gates, whose defense of the empowering intellectual practices of theory won me over. I wish the texts to speak for themselves but in my analyses must lend them my voice, and I have none other than that which is informed with the language of literary analysis and theory.

I began with the belief that the texts contain the essential clues to their meaning and significance, and with the notion that a systematic investigation of the structure of African literature would reveal its underlying patterns. I still adhere to the former belief, while I feel more ambivalent about the latter. All systematizing entails a certain degree of falsehood, whatever the truths it may also embrace. We may learn a great deal about African literature by seeing its patterning as a series of stages, but we may also be turning a blind eye to that which stands outside the pattern. I would like to think of all the systematic structuring that I posit in this study as being bounded by supplements that overtake the structures without negating them. A hedge may be an enclosure from one point of view; from another it may be turned inside out, so to speak, and give us the more indefinite shape of a Möbius strip, my preferred image for the boundaries that give definition to the structures of African literature.

I am grateful to the Fulbright program for providing me with that year in Dakar, and to Michigan State University for granting me sabbatical leaves in 1982 and 1990. I am grateful to the English Department at MSU for granting me a research term off in 1991, permitting me to finish the rough draft of the study.

Much of this book was written during the six months of 1990 I spent in the home of Jean Sévry in France, living with my family and that of Stephen Arnold—a wonderful and most productive time. Jean Sévry's library was a marvelous resource for me.

I am grateful to Richard Bjornson for his warmth and friendship, and for his skillful editing of those portions that appeared in *Research in African*

Literatures. I am grateful to Jonathan Ngaté for his kindness and thoughtful exploration of issues that concerned me in this volume.

My wife patiently sustained me in this work over a long period, and she provided skillful help in translating many of the passages from French into English. Where it is marked "my translation" it should read "our translation." When I needed to examine a thought, to find a means of expressing an idea, she was there to help.

I thank Joan Howard for her skillful editing, and Angelleta Gourdine and Marcella Kirk for their assistance in preparing the manuscript.

Finally, at Heinemann, I am grateful for the encouragement from John Watson and the wonderful support of Alan Huisman.

Part One
▼▼▼▼▼▼▼▼▼

Chapter 1

▼▼▼▼▼▼▼▼▼

Thresholds of Change in African Literature— The Emergence of a Tradition

There is one overriding issue facing African literature now, as at the time of its inception in Europhonic writing, and that is change. The issue of change appears in the preoccupations of authors faced with the struggle of a society to adapt to, as well as to create, a new social and cultural order; it appears in the predominance of characters forced to face the dynamics of their own processes of transformation; and most of all, for the poetics of African literature, it exists in the relationship between texts that have commented on each other, have grown on each other, have been formed on each other's words, and have collectively forged the processes of constituting a literary tradition. The subject of this book is the elaboration of the process whereby that tradition has been formed, including the delineation of the stages that have been created and the dynamics of change from stage to stage. The problematic term here is *stage*.

What is a stage? Not an advanced evolutionary phase. Not a product of progress, nor an improvement over a lower level. The emergence or succession of stages will not imply a hierarchy of values, nor the growth, maturity, or advance of African literature, any more than its coming into its own entails the passage from childhood to adulthood, the preeminent imperialist metaphor. Stage does imply a relationship to what occurred in a prior time period, and to a body of past works that bear on present ones. But how do they bear on them, and which works are the pertinent ones? Do all the works of a period belong to a given stage? Do some reflect the effect of earlier ones in some significant way that others do not? What is the relationship among works that coexist in the same period? These are all issues confronted by the Formalists before Roman Jakobson and Claude Lévi-Strauss discovered that the answer to all questions about diachronic change as well as synchronic structure could be discovered in the model of linguistics.

What is a stage? also poses the problem of temporality. Are we bound to consider the question as a diachronic one? Does Barthes's question regarding the authorship of the readerly (*lisible*) text oppose the concept of discontinuity that is implied by "stage"? Once the author is abandoned can we still retain notions of a coherent periods or movements? Does it make sense to place works in relation to earlier or later ones? Does the writerly (*scriptible*) text likewise annul traditional models of influence, of impact, of change? If the writerly text is already written, or being written as it is read, is there not also a pre-text that must be preinscribed before the text can come into existence?

It seems altogether natural to suppose that that a pre-text, or pretextual work, can occur at a period later than the actual writing of the book (just as El Greco's paintings required three centuries of change before their pre-texts had been positioned). But the relationship between the text and its predecessors still obtains, still appears as a necessary condition for the text to exist and to have an impact. Though the text is always already written, the sense of a community of works that share certain values, certain attitudes, must emerge with time, and likewise the perception of a change that explains that emergence is always potentially present as each work appears, as each text is read/written.

Change and a literary tradition are inextricably bound. To deny African literature the emergence of its own tradition is to deny it the power to differ from "world" literature, or European literature. And to accept that difference without also accepting the process of emergence is to impute a stagnation to one corner of literature while generally accepting the power of writers to create traditions elsewhere. Other conventional denials of African literature are now all too familiar and need no rehearsal, though one, perhaps, bears mentioning.

Whereas it is understood that "il n'y a pas de hors texte" challenges the reductive fragmentation and classification of "text" by period, with diachronic continuities and pre- and posttext positions—that is, that "trace" is coterminous with text—it is also true that the effacement of temporal or cultural distinctions or periods brings us back to the conventional effacement of Africa, back to the old centers of Western literature and its history. We can't hold to notions of a literary tradition without some frame, however uncertain its basis. In the end, we are willing to accept a radical calling into question of "traditions" but not that of a particular tradition. The reason is simple. The question of the existence of an identifiable tradition is bound to issues of presence, of centers, of existence. The question of an African literary tradition shifts the inquiry to the level of culture, and indirectly, to society, while putting into abeyance its ontological base. Only after having elaborated the tradition, can one move on to the issue of its ground in order for the question to escape the trap of abstraction.

The related issue, the effacement of the tradition of African literature, is raised when one insists upon the pertinence of interaction and change as occurring within the corpus of African writing, and not merely as a consequence of external social developments. I will argue this point later, specifically in terms of the rapport between periods, between texts like *L'Enfant noir* (1953) and *Une Vie de boy* (1956). For now let me agree with Bakhtin that the text exists in the world, is "worldly" as Edward Said insists, and yet still hold to the notion that paradigms for texts are transmitted when previous texts are heard or read, that if all texts are always already written, then it is specifically those paradigms that bear upon the writer and to which she responds that must primarily account for emergence and for change. If I say "primarily" it is because it seems to me essential that we recognize the reality of literary creation in Africa as entailing the transmission of literary lineages along with each language, and the reality of previous literary traditions, along with previous literary texts, that also have borne on all African writers. The languages and the texts to which African writers were exposed entailed complex cultural transmissions—literary as well as social—for the African writer as for the European. How can we reduce the primacy of textual influence to social impact, the substance of literary change and of the emergence of tradition to social change, without denying Africans a literary heritage or making the dynamics of their literary production a special (and by inference, less developed) case? Without denying the presence of social ideology in language, I would still wish to stress the existence of literary paradigms, their impact upon texts, and the importance of accounting for change in relation to them.

At the outset, then, change itself needs to be defined. We will consider it under the rubric of Thomas Kuhn's theory of paradigm change, of Formalism, and of deconstruction.

(I) Change and Kuhn's Theory of Paradigms

We are constantly led to wonder whether the factors involving change in science do not resemble those of change in literature. That what leads to the acceptance of a scientific theory is congruent with what leads to the acceptance of a style or genre in a given period, and what leads to the discarding or modification of a scientific theory is what leads to the discarding or modification of a literary style. The following propositions bear on this theory.

1. *That change occurs around points of destabilization.* Within *L'Enfant noir*'s certainties about the past and tradition, there exists a destabilizing reference point, the present, which is without certainties. Camara Laye's attempt to make the past and tradition prevail implies (a) the existence of a struggle between the past and the present; (b) the sense of operating from a lost position (as in *L'Aventure ambiguë* [1961], in which we are presented, in Part 2, with a sense of loss that is unmotivated, unexplained, and yet, paradoxically, overdetermined); (c) the lack of fullness (the need for supplement) of the past/tradition; (d) the centrifugal direction of success, leading toward the present, and, simultaneously, the centripetal direction of individual introspection and nostalgia, leading toward the past; (e) the search for the self in the past, along with the present demand to carry out this search; thus implying (f) the attempt of a fractured self or subject to recuperate a unified self.

The terms are reversed with Ferdinand Oyono and Mongo Beti, with new certainties (of youth, rebellion) set against tradition, the elders, and the past, as much as against colonialism. As for the ironic fractured subject in their texts, it is located, alternatively, on the levels of the protagonist, the narrator, and the implied author. At the last point the regression comes to an apparent halt with the reader's sense of the author's certainty of a revolt that supplies the basis for the ironic vision.

Unlike the Formalists, Bakhtin sees in the unresolved nature of opposition that which is life-furthering. Change is possible only when opposites are present to each other. While Bakhtin suggests the first terms of a dialectical movement here, we are in fact not far from Derrida's notions of trace and *différance*. Gayatri Spivak (1982) likens this pattern to that engendered by the metaphor of economy in Freud: "Economy is a metaphor of energy—where two opposed forces playing against each other constitute the so-called identity of a phenomenon" (xlii). For us, change is the consequence of this play of energy engendered by opposing forces.

2. *That paradigms must become visible* (Kuhn's theory of paradigms). Between the invisible unreality of phlogiston and the invisible reality of oxygen came the change in paradigms.

> What the work on oxygen did was to give much additional form and structure to Lavoisier's earlier sense that something was amiss. It told him a thing he was already prepared to discover—the nature of the substance that combustion removes from the atmosphere. That advance awareness of difficulties must be a significant part of what enabled Lavoisier to see in experiments like Priestley's a gas that Priestley had been unable to see there himself. Conversely, the fact that a major paradigm revision was needed to see what Lavoisier saw must be the principal reason why Priestley was, to the end of his long life, unable to see it. (Kuhn [1962] 1970, 56)

In literature that ability to see or not to see, the visibility of the text, also depends upon a paradigm—usually designated as the reader's horizon of expectations, or, as with Bakhtin, the conceptual horizon.

3. *That texts, like discoveries in science, do not suddenly come into being.* The key question for us will be, How does the change in horizon or paradigm come about? Here is where Kuhn's model becomes useful:

> Clearly we need a new vocabulary and concepts for analyzing events like the discovery of oxygen. Though undoubtedly correct, the sentence, "Oxygen was discovered," misleads by suggesting that discovering something is a single simple act assimilable to our usual (and also questionable) concept of seeing. That is why we so readily assume that discovering, like seeing or touching, should be unequivocally attributable to an individual and to a moment in time. *But the latter attribution is always impossible, and the former often is as well.* (55)

The same is true of texts, of movements, of stages, of traditions: the moment of their advent can never be reduced to a precise time and place, though they can nonetheless be said to exist. We duplicate the falsifications of science textbooks by assigning such precision to moments and movements in literature in our studies of literary history.

4. *That discoveries, like texts, have no signature.* "Discovery is not the sort of process about which the question [Who first discovered oxygen?] is appropriately asked. The fact that it is asked—the priority for oxygen has repeatedly been contested since the 1780s—is a symptom of something askew in the image of science that gives discovery so fundamental a role" (Kuhn [1962] 1970, 54) The same applies to the text, and to the existence of something askew in the image of literature that gives authorship and innovation so fundamental a role. Roland Barthes has given us the definitive statement on the problematical, patriarchal status of the author:

> The author is regarded as father and owner of his work. . . . The Text, on the other hand, is read without the father's signature. The metaphor that describes the Text is also distinct from that describing the work. The latter refers to the image of an *organism* that grows by vital expansion, by "development" (a significantly ambiguous word, both biological and rhetorical). The Text's metaphor is that of the *network* [*réseau*]: if the Text expands, it is under the effect of a *combinatorial,* a *systematics* (an image that comes close to modern biology's view on the living being).
>
> Therefore no vital "respect" is owed to the Text: it can be broken. . . . The Text can be read without its father's guarantee; the restitution of the intertext paradoxically abolishes the concept of filiation. (Barthes 1981a, 78)

Clearly in passing from work to text we have gone through a change in paradigm, a change radical enough to call into question the very process by which the paradigm or the text itself is formulated. That equivalent gesture needs now to be extended to the full range of the literary system, both diachronically across its history and synchronically across the spectrum of its definitions and categories.

5. *That change in literature can occur only when the conditions have been prepared—only when there is a prior text and a prior reading can there be a next text and a next reading.*

> But if both observation and conceptualization, fact and assimilation to theory, are inseparably linked in discovery, then discovery is a process and must take time. Only when all the relevant conceptual categories are prepared in advance, in which case the phenomenon would not be of a new sort, can discovering *that* and discovering *what* occur effortlessly, together, and in an instant. (Kuhn [1962] 1970, 55–56)

This is also true of defamiliarization, as it is of change in literary history. Jakobson succinctly summarizes how this process of preparation permitted Velimir Chlebnikov's works to be "discovered": "Despite the fact that Chlebnikov's poetic personality crystallized prior to Majakovskij's and, in turn, Majakovskij's before Pasternak's . . . the reader brought up on Symbolism was willing to accept Pasternak first, then he stumbled over Majakovskij, and only after conquering him was he ready to begin the strenuous siege of Chlebnikov's fortress" (quoted in Steiner 1984, 222). Peter Steiner completes the logic of Jakobson's observation:

> Chlebnikov's critical recognition, eloquently described by Jakobson, is a function of what might be called the dialogic nature of the literary process: the spaciotemporal gap between the author and reader. Here we reach a crucial contradiction, for to conceive of the poetic utterance as dialogic is utterly inconsistent with Husserl's or Saussure's semiotic concept underlying the expressionist model. (222–23)

Further, it is utterly inconsistent with any system that assigns a transcendental presence to the work or to the author's inspiration in its creation. In place of the transcendental subject we find the dialogic text. Finally, we see that the paradigm itself is also dialogic in terms of its response and responsiveness to past and to future models (texts). This dissemination of texts and origins is dizzying. This is not because it eliminates origins, stages, literary works, but because it problematizes all these terms that we cannot dispense with and that we cannot continue to use as before.

6. *That the process by which the paradigm takes hold resembles the rise of a literary movement.* Kuhn lists three classes of problems for normal science that follow from the development of a paradigm, presenting us with the same pattern found in Jurij Tinjanov's formulation of the development of

a literary movement. First, Kuhn's list: "determination of significant fact, matching of facts with theory, and articulation of theory" ([1962] 1970, 34). Substitute "dominant style" or "literary movement" for "theory"—both being paradigms—and substitute "dominant works/factors" for "significant fact," and you have Tinjanov:

> The connection between the principle of construction ["a special relation between the dominant constructive factor and the subordinate material"] and the literary system is especially apparent from a developmental perspective. As soon as an automatized "principle" is negated by a new principle, its systemic existence becomes clear. For only if we conceive of the new principle as a dialectic negation of the old literary system can we perceive its implementation as a literary fact and not merely a mistake. On the other hand, the new principle must be system-creating, must be implemented in more than a single "accidental" speech construction. Tinjanov's model of literary change thus contains four stages: "(1) the contrastive principle of construction dialectically rises in respect to the automatized principle of construction; (2) it is applied—the constructive principle seeks the easiest application; (3) it spreads over the maximal number of phenomena; (4) it is automatized and gives rise to a contrastive principle of construction." (Steiner 1984, 121)

It is not accidental that this system is based on a constructive principle which becomes "dominant" and which reduces the former dominant factors to "subordinate material." The spread of a constructive principle, like a dialectical term, entails the conquest of territory, no less than the prevalence of a scientific paradigm represents a conquest. We might well wonder if this pattern is not intrinsic to the very systems under consideration; that it is not simply a point of view or a quality of a single text that accounts for the roles of domination/subordination, but a combination of both over time, that is, the inherited workings, the practice that implies particular values and thus gives rise to its "reception."

7. *That anomaly is the key to change.* For Kuhn, the essential factor that leads to the substitution of one paradigm for another is the presence of an anomaly. In fact, the anomalies must reach crisis proportions for a paradigm to be discarded, and when it is, a new one must be invented before the old can be replaced. No observations or experiments are possible without the preexistence of a paradigm to provide the framework and logic for the observations, and it is inconsistencies in those observations that lead to the modification or discarding of a paradigm. "Once a first paradigm through which to view nature has been found, there is no such thing as research in the absence of any paradigm. To reject one paradigm without simultaneously substituting another is to reject science itself" (Kuhn [1962] 1970, 79). Similarly, there is no such thing as writing in the

absence of literature; once the first text appears, all subsequent texts must either carry the work forward or seek to replace it. For African literature, "patriarchal texts" can be located in the colonial novels—travelogues and their fictional counterparts, exotic literature or ethnography, adventure concoctions, or testimonials by expatriots: *Le Roman d'un Spahi, Mr. Johnson, The Heart of Darkness,* the journals of Speke, Livingstone, Stanley, Griaule's reportage, Frobenius's ethnography . . . the entire Africanist discourse, traced by Mohamadou Kane (1982) and Jonathan Ngaté (1988) to its direct sources; traced indirectly through the European line by Christopher Miller (1985) and V. Y. Mudimbe (1988).

In literature there are several filiations to be detected. Each work is written or spoken in a particular language, which we can call the immediate language of expression. One can imagine within the language of a text a multitude of related linguistic ties and discourses. Simultaneously, there must be another level of language which is not direct expression. The African literary text is refracted through several languages. Thus, Chinua Achebe writes in English, but also lives within the linguistic systems of Ibo and pidgin. Both Ibo and pidgin emerge, but always within an English-language universe.

The same pattern applies to genre, mode, and style, which "write" the text on the basis of preexistent codes. The notion of a story is always already given whenever a story is told, and stories told in Ibo abound through translation or transliteration within the text, just as stories, jokes, mannerisms of speech and behavior, are conveyed through pidgin in all of Achebe's texts. This corresponds to Kuhn's observation that no "fact" can be recorded without there being a preexisting paradigm.

What does it mean, then, to reject a paradigm? First, a crisis must be generated by the application of the "initial" paradigm; second, the crisis must lead to the spawning of multiple theories, "preparadigms," which function to save the previous paradigm; third, a substitute model must be posited before the old paradigm can be discarded.

If this theory posits radical changes—discoveries, inventions—it also recognizes that the moment of discovery cannot be identified, that there is always already a previous model that provides the explanation for the existence of the problems that gave rise to the substitute paradigm. The theory implies what the Hegelian model makes explicit—that the change into the new always entails a retention of the old, that the dialectic is a passage from an already existent potential to an actual—that the new is an actualization of what is inherent in the old. This is what is meant in literature when the new is described in terms of defamiliarization of automatized literature, or when Henry Louis Gates, Jr., (1988) describes the role of *signifyin'* in the black literary tradition as a black vernacular discourse within white discursive models. If no new paradigm can arise without two comparisons—that of the anomaly to the paradigm and that of the old to the new paradigm—so, too, does signifyin' entail the play of one set of new words on another old set, while simultaneously setting multiple works against each other.

Every work in literature must be set against its predecessors: it first must set an inherited model *for* itself, as well as ultimately *against* itself, in the form of a self-consciously constructed opponent. The point of change that is provoked by the anomaly or crisis arises when the inherited model cannot serve the needs of the text, when the text struggles to free itself, and in the struggle succeeds in elaborating something new.

That new literary paradigm arose in Africa when the colonial and Africanist discourse of the 1920s and 1930s failed to serve the goals of a new generation of authors. The literature grounded in ethnological purpose was intended to explain the unknown and remote life of Africans to a European audience. The literature of the African oral tradition served as the basis for a local performance in which the artist, the artist's words, and the audience all shared a common set of understandings. The novels of Laye, Achebe, and Kane, to take three "fathers" of African literature, or of Emecheta, Aidoo, and Nwapa, to take three "mothers," are unmistakably different from both the works of ethnography and of orature, though owing something to both.

The image of a science built around paradigms and crises is what allows us to speak of concrete or discrete moments in its history; similarly we can speak of different styles, models, or phases in literature. If an entirely new branch of science can be developed, so, too, can an entire literary movement or even a literary tradition emerge. African literature has such a tradition; it emerged from the ashes of Africanist discourse and was nourished by orature; it experienced the crisis of failure to which trivial works of imitation led; it elaborated new paradigms through *L'Enfant noir* and *Things Fall Apart* that bore comparison with Loti's, Cary's, or Greene's novels; in short, it behaved very much as the paradigms of Kuhn and the Russian Formalists would have us expect.

We cannot read the Formalists or Kuhn without simultaneously dealing with notions of the text as developed by Barthes, or with Derrida's notions of *différance*. The Formalists must be read "as if" or against, and not as literal truth. However, the Formalists provide a space for dialogue, so that Bakhtin's dialogical approach can be sustained without closing off their models for change. Kuhn's theory of how crisis affects science corresponds to the Formalists' theory on defamiliarization, which is the starting point for the investigation of the problem of change and its role in the emergence of African literature.

8. *A discourse of change, or a change of discourse.* "The children sang, without any pauses, in a language which was not their own or French but the strange gibberish which village people suppose is French and Frenchmen suppose is the vernacular" (Oyono 1982, 40).*

9. *That the suppression of* différance *in science and in literature led to the same blindness in accounting for change.*

(a) For Derrida the privileging of presence, of logocentrism, is achieved by the suppression of *différance.* This is replicated in Kuhn when he describes how scientific textbooks present the current state of scientific knowledge as being the result of a rational accretion of knowledge, an evolving process of accumulation, and not of discontinuous steps forced forward by anomalies. For Kuhn, the crises lead to competing paradigms, resulting in revolutions, in the elimination of old paradigms and their replacement by new ones. Instead of replicating the old paradigms, textbooks either do not mention them along with their advocates or recast them into the patterns established by the accepted paradigms, falsifying their actual epistemology. "The depreciation of historical fact is deeply, and probably functionally, ingrained in the ideology of the scientific profession, the same profession that places the highest of all values upon factual details of other sorts" (Kuhn [1962] 1970, 138). Whereas Kuhn sees a contradiction here, Derrida would posit the prevalence of logocentrism, along with the need to validate presence as if it were unitary, and the need to render scientific truth monological. "The result is a persistent tendency to make the history of science look linear or cumulative, a tendency that even affects scientists looking back at their own research" (Kuhn, 139).

But the monologism cannot prevail. As long as scientists verify the parameters of a paradigm, they remain within a single world. But when the results are anomalous, and the paradigm is then called into question, a crisis—and invariably dialogism—arises:

> Therefore, paradigm-testing occurs only after persistent failure to solve a noteworthy puzzle has given rise to crisis. And even then it occurs only after the sense of crisis has evoked an alternative candidate for paradigm. In the sciences the testing situation never consists, as puzzle-solving

---

* "Les élèves chantèrent d'une traite dans une langue qui n'était ni le français ni la leur. C'était un étrange baragouin que les villageois prenaient pour du français et les Français pour la langue indigène" (Oyono 1956a, 63). Published translations are provided when available. In some instances no published translations have been made, or the translations are inadequate, in which case the translations are by Kenneth Wettroth Harrow and Elizabeth Wettroth Harrow.

does, simply in the comparison of a single paradigm with nature. Instead, testing occurs as part of the competition between two rival paradigms for the allegiance of the scientific community. (Kuhn, 145)

Similarly, the dialogic struggle between competing voices, languages, discourses, fits the Formalist sense of "the contrastive principle of construction [that] dialectically arises in respect to the automatized principle of construction" (Tinjanov, quoted in Steiner 1984, 121). Scientists view the crisis as arising from the failure of a paradigm to explain nature adequately, as if "nature" were an objective reality and not a construct; Formalists explain the crisis as arising from the automatization of the old, as if the pressures to create the new did not arise out of the need to respond adequately to objective reality. But what if both were, in fact, a response to the same: for instance, a response to the need for the development and acquisition of knowledge, of language, to respond dialogically; or to the competing needs on the one hand to suppress *différance* in favor of logocentrism, and on the other to promote *différance* in favor of change.

(b) In the course of the development of his theories, Tinjanov eventually changed the notion of function:

> In 1928 Tinjanov replaced the principle of construction with the "literary function" in a wholesale revision of his terminology. He conceptualized . . . three literary levels . . . as three sets of functions: the constructive function corresponding to the infraliterary level, the literary function to the intraliterary level, and the social function to the extraliterary level. (Steiner 1984, 121)

Before this change, Tinjanov conceived of literary evolution as "a struggle for domination of different elements, [in which] the 'dialectical' play of devices in parody becomes an important vehicle of change" (Steiner, 119–20). This change led to the opening of Formalist theory outward to the sphere of social realities, as well as to fuller concepts of intertextuality.

> As Tinjanov elaborated the systemic metaphor, his view of the intraliterary level broadened and he eventually transcended the mechanistic model. He realized that not only parodies and stylizations but all literary texts are directed toward other works. The identity of a work in respect to genre, style, or school, indeed its very identity as literature, is based on its relations to other literary works through the underlying literary system. The principle of construction—a special relation between the dominant constructive factor and the subordinate material—was the means Tinjanov used to link the internal organization of a work to the appurtenant literary system. Tinjanov even went so far as to identify the principle of construction with the literary system itself. . . . The connection between the principle of construction and the literary system is especially apparent from a developmental perspective. As soon as an automatized "principle"

is negated by a new principle, its systemic existence becomes clear. For only if we conceive of the new principle as a dialectic negation of the old literary system can we perceive its implementation as a literary fact and not merely a mistake. (Steiner, 121)

The "new principle" for Tinjanov is what Kuhn calls the paradigm, which otherwise behaves the same as the literary principle, and which participates in the same process. "[T]he new principle must be system-creating, must be implemented in more than a single 'accidental' speech construction" (Steiner, 121). So, too, must the explanation of a scientific anomaly be more than an isolated explanation to become a new paradigm, and to evolve into a new theory, a new system.

The ground is thus set for the structuralists' systemization of the linguistic model, as one of the paradigmatic possibilities that followed Formalism; for Harold Bloom's (1973) theory of psychotropological influences; and for the fully developed semiotic analyses of transposed codes and the idea of intertextuality as elaborated by Julia Kristeva (1984). If Tinjanov and the Formalists seemed to be groping for a systemic or analytical explanation in the form of a quasi-scientific "principle of construction" without having arrived at this goal, then we seem to have come full circle with the postmodernist deconstruction of the logocentric systems of structuralism and semiotics.

As for the problem of whether change arises due to internal developments within the literary system or due to external social changes, Barthes's definition of text, as well as Bakhtin's principle of the dialogic, nullifies the distinction between internal and external influences, replacing both with endless chains of discourse formation for the one, and equally indefinite acts of refraction or dispersion of the word for the other. Barthes's fracturing of subjectivity best conveys this: "The 'I' which approaches the text is itself already a plurality of other texts, of infinite, or more precisely, lost codes (whose origins are lost) . . . (Barthes 1974, 10).*
The model for change, however, can remain. And it is here that the Formalists' originary conception of defamiliarization plays a crucial role.

(II) Change and Formalism

1. *That change can be perceived at the level of the device.* If we are to consider change, it has to be in reference to a point from which change can be measured. The literary device provides us with such a point. However, for African literature the devices for oral literature contain configurations that

---

* "Ce 'moi' qui s'approche du texte est déjà lui-même une pluralité d'autres textes, de codes infinis, ou plus exactement: perdus (dont l'origine se perd) . . . " (Barthes 1970, 16–17).

often differ from those of written literature. This opposition is all the more marked by the fact that oral literature has been misunderstood as a frozen body of works, unchanged from generation to generation, whereas recent theory about the written text has emphasized its instability and its continual revisions.[1] In light of this, the following definitions of device and defamiliarization must be taken as naive but necessary points of departure.

> Everything in literature—from the choice of thematic materials, the various motifs and their use together, to systematic pronouncements about language, diction, etc.—may be made into a conventional device. The use of one word and the proscription of another, and so on, may be subject to regulation. Conventional devices originate because they are convenient technically; their repetition becomes traditional, and, falling into the area of normative poetics, they are codified as compulsory rules. But no convention can exhaust all possibilities and foresee all the devices necessary for the creation of an entire work, so that along with the conventional devices there are always free devices—devices peculiar to individual writers, works, genres, movements, etc.
>
> Conventional devices usually destroy themselves. One value of literature is its novelty and originality. In the struggle for regeneration, the orthodox, the traditional, the stereotyped devices are most attacked, and the obligatory becomes the prohibited. The creation of new traditions and techniques does not, however, prevent the revival of prohibited devices after the passing of two or three literary generations. (Tomashevsky 1965, 93)

What is a literary generation? When does it start and end? Every answer that might fit written literature might also not apply to oral literature, for which the transmission of conventional plots, phrasings, proverbs, values, praises, truths, requires a restraint on originality and places a value on inherited traditions or conventions. Instead of conventional devices destroying themselves, they are the basis that must be retained, while novel ones provide the supplement and not the framework. Conversely, perversely, we can see in the free space of creativity that characterizes oral literature (more in tales, less in epics or proverbs) the room for a supplement that becomes the "archiwriting" of orature. This is because it is in this less obvious free space that the project of the work is realized, while the dutiful transmission of conventionalized truths takes place on the obvious level of the work. That is, the dimension of a tale or proverb that functions as a lesson becomes a vehicle for permitting the fuller act of signification to take place as if within its interstices. The devices then consist of both the conventional and the novel, and reaction against them must be complicated by the intention of the new author who might be responding to the basic framework of the work or to its subtler, implied qualities. The key in all cases is a complicated relationship of subversion that accompanies the act of transmission.

2. *That art is created when devices become perceptible.* For the Formalists, devices become perceptible because they are either very old or very new. The present ones, in contrast to the new, are by definition invisible.

3. *That art is created by the domination of old devices by new ones.* For Tinjanov art is produced when the constructive factor subordinates the other factors that characterize the text (he even speaks of words themselves being made of these subordinating and subordinated components). Literature is automatized when these various components are not arranged into subordinating and subordinated parts, and art arises out of the struggle between components:

> The advancing factor deforms those which are subordinated to it. One can then say that form is always perceived in the course of the evolution of the relationship between the subordinating and constructive factor and the subordinated factors. We are not obliged to introduce the *temporal* dimension into the concept of evolution. One can consider the evolution, the dynamic itself, outside of time, as a pure movement. Art lives in this interaction, this conflict. The artistic fact does not exist outside the sensation of submission, the deformation of all factors by the constructive factor (the *coordination* of factors is a negative characteristic of the principle of construction [V. Shklovsky]). But if the sensation of *interaction* of factors disappears (and this presupposes the necessary presence of *two* elements, the subordinating and the subordinated), the artistic fact is effaced; art becomes automatism.
> . . . What is important here is the issue of a new interaction and not a simple introduction of just any factor. (My trans.)*

> Given that the system isn't a form of cooperation founded on the equality of all the elements, but that it presupposes the advancement of a group of elements (dominant) and the deformation of others, the work enters into literature and acquires its literary function thanks to this dominance. (My trans.)†

---

* Le facteur promu déforme ceux qui lui sont subordonnés. On peut donc dire que l'on perçoit toujours la forme au cours de l'évolution du rapport entre le facteur subordonnant et constructif et les facteurs subordonnés. Nous ne sommes point obligés d'introduire la dimension *temporelle* dans le concept d'évolution. On peut considérer l'évolution, la dynamique en elle-même, hors du temps, comme un mouvement pur. L'art vit de cette interaction, de ce conflit. Le fait artistique n'existe pas hors de la sensation de soumission, de déformation de tous les facteurs par le facteur constructif (la *coordination* des facteurs est une caractéristique négative du principe de construction—V. Shklovsky). Mais, si la sensation d'*interaction* des facteurs disparaît (et elle suppose la présence nécessaire de *deux* éléments, le subordonnant et le subordonné), le fait artistique s'efface; l'art devient automatisme.
. . . Ce qui importe ici, c'est qu'il s'agit d'une nouvelle interaction et non de la simple introduction d'un facteur quelconque. (Tinjanov 1965b, 118)

† Etant donné que le système n'est pas une coopération fondée sur l'égalité de tous les élé-

The question that insists on being asked is, What is the dominant and what the subordinated terms? Can we escape the conclusion that these relative positions are read into the constructive factors, and are not intrinsic in the literature? It is a small step from that quandry to the basic deconstructive move that would metamorphose the subordinated term, once subordinated, into the general term of which the dominant is a subjoined element. If struggle between these terms makes the oppositions art/*byt* [everyday life], perceptible/imperceptible, possible, and if these oppositions belong to the familiar categories of logocentric systems, then the deconstruction of logocentrism must extend to the familiar concepts of art and of its dialectical bases. This is why, without any irony intended, Tinjanov can entitle his article "On Literary Evolution" while at the same time he identifies the colonial status of his discipline: "Among all the cultural disciplines, literary history retains the status of a colonial territory" (my trans.).* For us the leap of faith is not grounded in a system based on domination, but in the existence of the system itself as the product of a process of change.

　　4. *That defamiliarization can occur on all the levels of the literary experience.* Defamiliarization (*ostranénie*)—making strange; making perceptible what has become automatized; creating art—can occur with respect to:

a. Devices themselves, such as images or figures of speech or constructions. The language of the text is the immediate site for this, as in the strange wording employed by Amos Tutuola. ("I, as Ajaiyi by name, was fifteen years of age, my junior sister, Aina by name, was twelve" [Tutuola 1967, 11].)

b. Inherited conventions, rules for the sonnet, for the folktale, for the novel, for plot—conventions of genre, mode, style. (*Ajaiyi*: a novel? a series of tales? an oral novel? a novel of oral tales? a story?) This is defamiliarization measured in terms of patterns created by earlier texts. ("This story happened about two hundred years ago when I first came to this world through another father and mother" [Tutuola 1967, 11].)

c. Social patterns, expectations, rules, behavior. Defamiliarization occurs in terms of the centrifugal elements, pointing away from the text; it is less a reaction to other texts, than to expected social patterns. ("By that time I was a boy and not a girl, by that time I was the poorest farmer and not a storyteller, by that time I was the most wicked gentile and the strongest worshipper of all kings of the false gods and not a christian, by that time

---

ments, mais qu'il suppose la mise en avant d'un groupe d'éléments ("dominante") et la déformation des autres, l'oeuvre entre dans la littérature et acquiert sa fonction littéraire grâce à cette dominance. (Tinjanov 1965a, 130)

★ "Parmi toutes les disciplines culturelles, l'histoire littéraire conserve le statut d'un territoire colonial." (Tinjanov 1965a, 120)

I was the poorest among the people of my village and not the richest, by that time there were no cars on the roads or the aeroplanes on the sky but to trek from village to village and to cross large rivers by hand-made canoes and not by steam-ships" [Tutuola 1967, 11].) It is motif, theme, content rather than the language of the text which is considered.

d. Prevailing critical practice. Derrida's text *Glas* (1974) as a text that provides its own critical reading, and that deconstructs the critical reading conventionally applied to such a text; Ouologuem providing a reading, through *Devoir* (1968), that undoes the conventional reading of the text—undoing, for example, propriety/plagiarism in relation to the texts/traditions of "Literature." ("'My son and daughter, remember the day after tomorrow because it will come back to you soon or later after my death!' Alas! Aina and I were too young this time to understand this our father's warning and we were so very stupid to ask for the meaning of it from our father" [Tutuola 1967, 12].)

Jakobson's warning reminds us that the concept of defamiliarization itself, especially when reduced to the modernist impulse, can become conventionalized:

> One would be equally wrong to identify the discovery, even the essence of "formalist" thought, with debased platitudes concerning the professional secret of art, which would be to have things appear when they are disautomatized and rendered surprising ("ostranénie"), whereas, in fact, the issue at stake in poetic language is an essential change in the relationship between the signifier and the signifed, as well as between the sign and the concept. (My trans.)*

5. *That every level of defamiliarization corresponds to a level of naturalization of a text.* Naturalization is a process involved either in making a text appear real, to have *vraisemblance,* or to work naturally within a code or discursive system, like a genre, or like a social code. In other words, there is naturalization that corresponds to centripetal readings directed towards the text, or to centrifugal readings directed outward towards the external world. Tzvetan Todorov (1968) defines three conventions of naturalization as the relation of a particular text to (1) public opinion, (2) to a particular genre, and (3) to the convention of disguising its own literariness (1–2).

---

* On aurait également tort d'identifier la découverte, voire l'essence de la pensée "formaliste", aux platitudes galvaudées sur le secret professionnel de l'art, qui serait de faire voir les choses en les désautomatisant et en les rendant surprenantes ("ostranénie"), tandis qu'en fait il s'agit dans le langage poétique d'un changement essentiel du rapport entre le signifiant et le signifié, ainsi qu'entre le signe et le concept. (Jakobsen 1965, 10–11)

If the world and its conventions can be conceived as a text, then the relationship between any particular work and the "real" world is an intertextual one, which Jonathan Culler (1975) has defined on five levels, the text's relationship with (1) the "real" world, the socially given text; (2) a cultural text, recognized by participants of a given culture as naturally belonging; (3) genre conventions, that is, specifically literary *vraisemblance*; (4) "the natural attitude to the artificial," in which a text makes explicit its use of genre conventions, implying a natural presence on the metatextual level, and thus reinforcing its own authority; and (5) another, specific work, which becomes a "basis and point of departure and [which] must be assimilated in relation to [the work]" (140). Thus there is defamiliarization with respect to the norms and the forms of expression of a society, of a culture, of a literary genre; defamiliarization of the relation between an implied author and the narrator, or, correspondingly, between a metatext and a text; and defamiliarization of the norms of intertextuality, as in the open use of deliberate plagiarisms. Defamiliarization spreads like irony, onto social levels, within textual levels, between texts, within narrative points of view, until it turns against itself and like postmodernism becomes a permanent condition of self-consciousness. Rather than worry whether the compilation of self-conscious gestures is complete, it might be more fruitful to adhere to the general concept that the tendency to naturalize a text is as inevitable as is the process that eventually flows from that naturalization, which is to defamiliarize the naturalized.

The deconstructive consequence of this pattern is obvious: the act of defamiliarization, which would seem to be the appendage and supplement to naturalization, would be, in fact, the condition of possibility for naturalization—that nothing can appear naturalized unless set against a frame of the unfamiliar, which must already be there, and even more against the act of differentiation of the familiar from the unfamiliar. If naturalization is the basis for the literary work, and if defamiliarization is the condition of possibility for naturalization, then it would appear that the very act that sets itself against the natural is fundamental to the existence of the literary work.

6. *That defamiliarization takes us, in the end, to the limits of self-referentiality of the text.* At the limits, the problem of change (with respect to what? at the locus of whose subjectivity?) becomes that of self-referentiality, of a text that provides its own strategies for interpretation.

7. "If a text's description of its own procedures is always a graft that adds something to those procedures, there is a related graft whereby the analyst applies the text's statements to its own processes of enunciation. Asking how what the text does relates to what it says, he often discovers an

uncanny repetition" (Culler 1982, 137). Each level of first-person subjective discourse in a novel like *L'Enfant noir* provides a graft for reading the narrative as embedded within that level: the protagonist, Laye, as a persona for the narrator Laye; the narrator, himself, in turn a persona for the author Laye; and so on. Further, the novel *L'Enfant noir* can be read as a persona to be grafted onto the African literature of its period. An endless series can be generated in which each new reading recasts the entire pattern of changes, just as each institutionalized pattern attempts to freeze it.

8. *That defamiliarization is a form of intertextuality that "limps."*

> Whatever we call it, we should beware of assuming that in exploiting the potential self-referentiality of the text Derrida is repeating the now familiar critical move in which the text is shown to describe its own signifying processes and thus said to stand free as a self-contained, self-explanatory aesthetic object that enacts what it asserts. The possibility of including the text's own procedures among the objects it describes does not, Derrida shows, lead to a presentational coherence and transparency. On the contrary, such self-inclusion blurs the boundaries of the text and renders its procedures highly problematical."Alors," writes Derrida," à propos of Freud's own procedures in *Beyond the Pleasure Principle* "ça boite et ça ferme mal." ("It limps and closes badly.") (Culler 1982, 139)

9. *That classical Formalist change, like classical Oedipal change, like classical revolutionary change, enables us to read African literature from* L'Enfant noir *to* Une Vie de boy *to* Entre les eaux. The classical Africanist model leads us to *L'Odeur du père,* while the classical Formalist model for this definition of change is provided by Shklovsky:

> When literary schools change, the succession passes not from father to son, but from uncle to nephew. . . . In every literary period there exists not one but several literary schools. They exist simultaneously in literature but one of them represents the canonized peak. The others exist in uncanonized obscurity. . . . [O]ld forms, being no more perceptible than are grammatical forms in speech, cease to be elements of artistic set and become subservient, imperceptible. The younger line then bursts in to take the place of the elder. . . . Every literary school is a revolution, something like the emergence of a new class. (Shklovsky, quoted in O'Toole and Shukman 1977, 42–43)

Bloom's distinction between the strong and the weak poet enables him to construct a model of literary history grounded in a similar struggle between generations: "Poetic history . . . is held to be indistinguishable from poetic influence, since strong poets make that history by misreading one another, so as to clear imaginative space for themselves. . . . Weaker talents idealize; figures of capable imagination appropriate for themselves" (Bloom 1981, 5). If we return to Shklovsky's term for those strong figures, they are, interestingly, nephews and not sons. Bloom would appreciate this notion of an heir whose poem represents a veering off from the main branch, a "clinamen." But in Africa the relationships are more complicated. This is not simply because of different social relations—deriving from extended families, matrilineages, and polygamy—but because of Africa's particular, we might say unique, historical rapports which have borne upon the paternities and maternities of every text.

Shklovsky's figure of the revolutionary nephew obliges us to ask, Whose nephew? In the matrilineage where the maternal uncle is head of the lineage, the nephew's right to acquire authority derives from his mother. Conversely, in a patriarchal system, a man's sister's sons will belong to a different lineage. Finally, without overly romanticizing the pattern, it will not be a simple question of the individual subject—be he nephew of a slave or of a king—but of the lineage and the clan that is at issue. The paradox will then be to establish a line, a lineage, whose works enable a tradition to emerge, taking into account all the languages, all the false and true fathers, all the loving and smothering mothers, all the enthroned uncles, the independent aunts, the alienated and distant cousins—Laye's paternal uncle Mamdou, who took him in when he pursued his studies at Conakry, as well as his maternal uncle Lansana, who looked after him in the fields of Tindican. Whereas Bloom centers his attention upon the dominant figure of influence, and Shklovsky centers his on the "canonized peak," we might do better to consider the figure in the shadow, the author whose "trace" is left invisibly on the palimpsest—the nameless uncle, the younger twin brother of Uncle Lansana, Uncle "Bo":

> I saw him only once. He had returned to Tindican, and though he had been there only a few days, he thought of nothing but leaving it. I remember him as a most attractive man who talked a great deal. Indeed, he never stopped talking, and I never wearied of listening to him. He told me about his adventures, which were strange and bewildering, but which opened undreamed of vistas to me. (Laye 1978a, 49)*

This is the only one of his uncles whose name Laye cannot recall ("What was his name? I don't remember"† [49]); and yet of all the elder relatives whom he had known, this uncle was clearly his predecessor as storyteller.

---

* "Pour moi, je ne l'ai rencontré qu'une fois: il était revenu à Tindican; il y était de quelques jours et déjà ne songeait qu'à repartir. J'ai conservé le souvenir d'un homme extrêmement séduisant et qui parlait beaucoup, qui n'arrêtait pas de parler, et qu'on ne se lassait pas d'écouter. Il racontait ses aventures qui étaient étranges, qui dépaysaient, qui m'ouvraient des horizons surprenants." (Laye 1953, 41).

† "Quel était son nom? Je ne m'en souviens plus."(42)

The nephew rebaptized the uncle "Bo" ("The few days he was at Tindican, I called him Bo . . . "*), and this generic sobriquet becomes his patronymic (" . . . but this was also the name by which I called my uncle Lansana. Twins are always called 'Bo,' *and this nickname often makes people forget their proper names*" [49, my stress]†). None of the marvelous stories of Uncle Bo are retained, any more than his name, yet they must have traced the outlines for a map whose contours would be appropriated, misread, in that particular reading of the nephew that it pleased Bloom to call the misprision: " . . . really strong poets can read only themselves" (Bloom 1981, 19).

10. *That a literary system can become visible only by virtue of* différance.

> Here we encounter another interesting fact from the point of view of evolution. One puts forward a correlation between a work and a given literary series to measure the gap between it and the same literary series to which it belongs. . . . The more the gap with a given literary series is evident, the more the system from which it is distanced becomes visible. (My trans.)‡

We reach the end of the Formalist endeavor with the deconstructive principle of *différance*. If the system becomes visible only by virtue of the distance between it and a work that belongs to it, where is one to place the element that defines the work as belonging to a given system? Derrida's point here is that that what defines a genre, for example, within a given text cannot coincide with the elements in the text itself that are being subject to the definition ("Ča boite et ça ferme mal"). Formalism ends with deconstruction because instead of presence supplying the basis for the device, for the literary system, and for the change, it is *différance,* it is defamiliarization as deferring, it is trace and that elusive texture of weaving that constitutes text. Yet we cannot avoid the language of Formalism and of paradigms because to speak of change is to imply change from something to something. If we can dispense with Tinjanov's "evolution" and Shklovsky's "domination," we still can adhere to their insistence on seeking the explanation of literary change in the relationships between texts. And if we are to approach the question of literary change with the advantage of

---

* "Je l'avais appelé Bo, durant les quelques jours qu'il était demeuré à Tindican." (42)

† " . . . et c'était le nom aussi que je donnais à mon oncle Lansana, car ainsi surnomme-t-on habituellement les jumeaux, et *ce surnom efface le plus souvent leur véritable nom.*" (42; my stress)

‡ *Nous nous heurtons ici à un autre fait intéressant du point de vue de l'évolution. On met une oeuvre en corrélation avec telle série littéraire pour mesurer l'écart qui existe entre elle et cette même série littéraire à laquelle elle appartient. . . . Plus l'écart avec telle ou telle série littéraire est net, plus le système duquel on s'écart est mis en évidence. (Tinjanov 1965a, 130)

hindsight, then we must begin with the excavation of theory. For us that originary point is with the Formalists.

(III) Change and Deconstruction

1. *That the strategy of using a text to formulate the critical analysis of the text leads to an infinite regress and the critical problem of boundaries or frames.* The complications of using the model of self-analysis are analyzed by Culler (1982) in his discussion of Cleanth Brooks's *The Well Wrought Urn* in which the neat organic technique of using the text to formulate the strategy for analysis of the text is shown to generate a second text, the text that contains the analysis, and that stands in a relation of self-referentiality to the original text. Instead of closure a kind of infinite regress is created. The pattern of the regress can be seen in the model of the frame, which is not only a margin to the text, separating its inside from the outside, but is also part of the text. Invagination is Derrida's term for the outside folded in, creating a pocket of the outside at the center of the inside of the text. Another term utilized for the frame is *parergon*; Kant's term for those accessories or supplements to a work of art like the frame, or drapery on statues. An alternative figure for this external/internal element is the signature of the author. "A *parergon* is *against,* beside, and above and beyond the *ergon,* the work accomplished, the accomplishment, the work, but it is not incidental; it is connected to and cooperates in its inside operation from the outside" (Derrida 1979b, 20). It is easy to see why Derrida focuses on this variety of figures, all of which pose the same problem of framing. It leads to the central concern of deconstruction: "The logic of the *parergon* is, as one can see, quite similar to the logic of the supplement, in which the marginal becomes central by virtue of its very marginality" (Culler 1982, 196).

The issue is also posed in terms of paradoxes, in which the problem of the relationship of the frame to the text is one of both belonging and not belonging:

> Another example might be what Derrida calls "the law of genre," or rather, "the law of the law of genre . . . a principle of contamination, a law of impurity, a parasitical economy" ("La Loi du genre," p. 179/206). Though it always participates in genre, a text belongs to no genre, because the frame or trait that marks its belonging does not itself belong. The title "Ode" is not a part of the genre it designates, and when a text identifies itself as a *récit* by discussing its *récit,* this mark of genre is about, not of, the genre. The paradox of parergonality is that a framing device which asserts or manifests class membership is not itself a member of that class. (Culler 1982, 196)

Thus, interpretive statements construed as self-referential within the African literary text are metaliterary and yet literary at the same time. This is a perfect description of the status of African literature as marginal to European literature, and yet Europhonic/meta-European; as both belonging to a textual body and as commenting on it from without; as having as its center that space of the outside folded within the text. The subjective space of a Medza, for example, in Mongo Beti's *Mission terminée* fits this description. In two centripetal movements, he returns first to his village, where he carries the burden of his scholastic failures at the European school home to his father. Secondly, he carries the false allure of the *"civilisé"* to the country village, Kala, where he is both outsider and witness to his marginality. Finally, he returns at the end to the marginality of the prodigal son as he is chased from his home village by his father. He turns outward toward the world, inward toward himself, and in a simultaneous metanarrative observation toward his narration of the events:

> Yet I remain proud of my mission to Kala—that mission which formed the original subject of my story, though I must apologize for wandering fairly far afield from it at times. . . .
>
> The more I think about it, the more certain I am that it is I who owe him [Niam] a debt of gratitude for sending me on a journey which enabled me to discover many truths. Not least among these was the discovery—made by contact with the country folk of Kala, those quintessential caricatures of the "colonized" African—that the tragedy which our nation is suffering today is that of a man left to his own devices in a world which does not belong to him, which he has not made and does not understand. (Beti 1970, 181)[*]

In fact the European space that occupies the text of African literature is invaginated space. In contrast to European literature, it is the problem of that invagination that is central to African literature because, for Africans, European space, not African space, poses the problem of marginality. Like the *parergon,* European space is both marginal and necessary. This is perfectly given as the image of the frame:

> An external frame may function as the most intrinsic element of a work, folding itself in; conversely, what seems the most inner or central aspect of a work will acquire this role through qualities that fold it back outside of and against the work. The secret center that appears to explain everything folds back on the work, incorporating an external position from which to elucidate the whole in which it also figures. (Culler 1982, 198)

---

[*] Je suis tout de même fier de la mission que j'ai rempli à Kala et qui, primitivement, devait être l'objet de ce récit (je vous demande pardon si je me suis laissé aller). . . . Plus j'y pense et plus je me dis que c'est certainement moi qui devrais lui [Niam] savoir gré de ce voyage qui m'a permis entre autres choses de découvrir au contact des péquenots de Kala, ces sortes de caricatures de l'Africain colonisé, que le drame dont souffre notre peuple, c'est celui d'un homme laissé à lui-même dans un monde qui ne lui appartient pas, un monde qu'il n'a pas fait, un monde où il ne comprend rien. (Beti 1957, 250–51)

This is a paradoxical situation, especially for the critic of African literature who utilizes a Eurocentric critical discourse.

> [Critics] are outside when their discourse prolongs and develops a discourse authorized by the text, a pocket of externality folded in, whose external authority derives from its place inside. But if the best examples of metalinguistic discourse appear within the work, then their authority, which depends on a relation to externality, is highly questionable: they can always be read as part of the work rather than a description of it. In denying their externality we subvert the metalinguistic authority of the critic, whose externality had depended on the folds that created this internal metalanguage or pocket of externality. (199)

This is the situation of Mudimbe's African, endlessly riding an elevator (*L'Odeur du père*), like Sisyphus, both inside and outside at the same time; it is the problem of an African discourse framed within a European discursive tradition and language; it is the issue of the locus of the subject in African fiction, at once narrator and protagonist of the conquistador's adventure, as Medza put it; of the ambiguous adventurers, Camara Laye and Samba Diallo; and especially those figures trapped inside and outside themselves, Oyono's three heroes: the Boy, Joseph Toundi; the Old Man, Meka; and the cynical Barnabas of *Chemin d'Europe*. Richard Bjornson (1986) aptly describes Barnabas as having the corrupt mentality of one whose "calculated individualism permanently isolates him from any genuine human contact with Europeans or fellow Africans" (1); what better figure for that locus of ambivalent subjectivity than the circle within which the old Meka stood, waiting in the hot sun for the medal to be pinned on his chest?

2. *That African literature is a generalized literature with respect to which European literature is the special case.*

(a) The marginality of a term is determined by its placement in a binary opposition, e.g., good/bad, rational/emotional, civilized/uncivilized. Conventional Western philosophic discourse has always assumed the priority of the first term over the second. Derrida's basic strategy, however, has been to show that the first term of the "logocentric" series of oppositions has always been dependent upon the second, in the same fashion that any system could be said to depend upon what is marginal or supplementary to it for its own completion. Derrida extends the logic of that dependency so as to show that, in fact, the second terms, or the marginalized or supplementary terms, are generalized, or archi-forms of the first terms. The classical case is the opposition between the spoken and the written word. Derrida claims that from Plato to Rousseau the "natural" spoken word has been privileged over the written. In *On Grammatology* (1982) he sets out to demonstrate that the spoken word is but a special case of that larger pattern of inscription that he terms "archi-writing" or "generalized writing."

As long as the relationship between Europe and Africa has been defined through European eyes, European literature has been the central body and African literature marginal to it. By what logic could one then assert that this marginal body is central? For Derrida archi-writing is to be located in the condition of possibility for the oral text. General literature, then, as the condition of possibility for European literature, would be a literature of *métissage,* at the very least; a literature of heteroglossia, as dreamed of by Bakhtin, in which the refraction of languages, of semiotic systems, would multiply the possibilities of textual interplay. For such an archi-literature, the longstanding monophonic and relatively monocultural nature of European literature would lead to a relatively monological text.

Culler employs the term generalized literature for archi-literature. After demonstrating that the opposition serious/nonserious literature is based on "ordinary language"/nonserious utterances, and that the latter term indicates the general category of which the former is the special case, he then argues for a concept of literature in general: "If serious language is a special case of the nonserious, if truths are fictions whose fictionality has been forgotten, then literature is not a deviant, parasitical instance of language. On the contrary, other discourses can be seen as cases of a generalized literature, or archi-literature" (1982, 181). By the same token, the discourse of the other can be seen as the generalized discourse in which all literature about oneself, given within the framework of one's own world, is a special instance of the larger pattern of discourse. African literature began as a discourse of the other—in its Europeanized incarnation—while at the same time being also a literature of the self, an autobiographical literature. If we consider Dennis Duerden's (1975) caution that the ego or subject in traditional African society encompasses the larger social units of lineage and clan, then it is possible to identify oral literature with autobiographical forms, and therefore to see in those forms already the bases for the written literary forms, which had developed in Europe at an earlier time, as well as being the bases for oral transmission, performance, community values, etc. The first radical alteration of the African's literary base came with the advent of writing, and thus with the models, paradigms, discourses, and even words that established the conditions of possibility for written expression. But the oral components never disappeared, and even when not directly transcribed, existed as discourses whose effects were felt as those of an interlocutor who may or may not necessarily vocalize a response, but who is continually affecting the discourse.

(b) No more than any other literature can African literature be said to have a beginning. All texts are grounded in discourse and words that are either equally ancient or whose origins are lost in time. Bakhtin provides us with the image of words as bearing the traces of all the previous usages, as if each instance of uttering a word, as well as each utterance, adds to the totality of the inheritance we receive when first hearing that word. Our utterances do not so much change the words as add to that tradition, and in the broader sense the same thing happens not only with larger utterances and even discourses, but with literature itself. All literature is thus the inherited verbal practice of the ancestors. But all literature is characterized also as a differentiated practice. Literature is composed of words within a language, a language whose traits are given not only on a diachronic axis of unlimited duration, but also within the present moment on a synchronic axis, in which the comprehensible and current practice of the language is the only one immediately used or understood. This text, for example, is in the English of our times, whatever the burdens of history of the language.

African literature is likewise the heir of multiple traditions, each with its own diachronic thread of immeasurable longevity. But in the present moment one can identify a current practice and a current understanding that represent a radical departure from past practice. That departure occurred when African literature underwent the transition to a written literature. Even that, of course, was not enough to effect the total change into the African literature of our time. The beginning of that change was limited—depending on the genre under question—by the pressures and by the potentialities of the times. By the mid-twentieth century, the novels that were appearing represented themselves as (1) a new literature, (2) explicitly indebted to the traditions inherent in the European languages and their past written expression, and (3) implicitly indebted to the oral traditions inherent in the maternal languages of the writer, languages denied explicit expression in the written text, yet continually dialoguing with the implicit text.

Even this scenario doesn't approach the complexity of the textuality informed by the linguistic elements. Each writer, of course, was affected differently. Thus a Serer, like Léopold Senghor, attending school in French and living, after his early years, in a Wolof speaking environment, could not but feel the impress of at least three languages. Berber speakers, like Kateb Yacine, underwent the same triple language experiences when they underwent French schooling in Arabic speaking environments. In Africa this pattern is typical. In a country like Cameroon hundreds of languages are spoken (by one count, 240), yet there were, and still are, a small number of lycées, and only one university. Invariably, a large percentage of those attending high school or university will be taking classes in English or French, and living in a region where their mother tongue is not spoken.

Cameroon is officially bilingual: in fact, French is a sine qua non for official communications throughout the country, English is officially required in the west, and at the same time the most widespread language in the country is pidgin English. Thus there are official languages, trade languages (such as Swahili in East Africa, Bambara in the Sahel, or pidgin English in West Africa), home languages, and the languages commonly spoken in the region in which one lives. And all these languages are no less subject to dialect formations than any other: thus we recognize that there are significant varieties of pidgin—Nigerian, Cameroonian, Sierra Leonean Creole, etc.—that are also factors. Thus the inadequacy of the simple observation that Ibo and pidgin English act as palimpsests for Achebe's fiction.[2]

These languages are all as richly inhabited by the weight of their words, discourses, and traditional texts (oral or written) as those chosen by the author to be the written vehicle of expression. Their importance does not reside in the notion that African literature is a variety of polyglossia, a special case of multilinguistic synchretism. Neither is it the case that African literature is a special, peripheral branch of European-language literature. Rather, two points need to be emphasized. The first is that the conditions that made possible the development of Europhonic written African literature were framed by the colonial context, so that the use of various languages in the texts also implied the awareness of the use of another's language, discourse, and literary tradition. The subjective sense of otherness in the text was a preliminary given. The second is that this sense of the self, which was expressed in languages and traditions enmeshed in a politics of domination and subordination, was not marginal or unique. African literature typifies the general condition of all textual creation, and only the special kind of blindness of the dominant culture, unconstrained in its monolinguistic practice, could embolden European critics and audiences to think that African literature was a marginal branch of their own mainstream.

In order to be convinced of this fact, the Europeans had to deny the African literary components of African literature—easy enough to do, when the prevailing colonial politics denied to Africans so much of their culture, language, and traditions. In other words, the novels were judged entirely as products of the European discursive traditions, while the reality of an African discursive tradition wasn't even acknowledged. Having made these denials, it was easy enough then to regard African literature as the product of a "young" culture, or even of children, debutantes, and dilettantes. And the ancestors were entirely othered. This was why the issue of being other was at the heart of this literature.

3. *That the Möbius strip defines the frame for the stages of African literature.*
The final model that deconstruction suggests for analysis of the relationship between African and European literature is also derived from Derrida's concept of invagination, of the outer space folded in to create a pocket
of the external within an enclosed space. What Derrida is reaching for is an
image of an external element that is shown to be the basis of the central,
enclosed object; or an image of an outside that cannot be maintained on
the margin. But the context of his discussion of this point in "Living On:
Border Lines" (1979a) takes us in the direction of the problematics of borders or edges: notably the edge that demarcates a beginning or an ending,
as well as an inside or outside, a major or minor term, a privileged or subordinated term. All these distinctions bear on Formalist notions of dominant and subordinated factors, of periodization marked by the beginnings
of new stages and endings of old ones, of texts that lie outside of groups
that are made visible by what they exclude. They bear equally on notions
of old and new paradigms—with crises and revolutions that set off one
body of beliefs or practices from another; and they especially bear on the
unstated assumptions of any dominant, patriarchal process of canoniza-
tion. All these distinctions are put under erasure by Derrida when
described by invagination, or, alternatively, by the hymen (both border
and *alliance* at the same time).

If all texts are condemned to use or to comment on already-existing
textual practices or discourses, then already, according to Derrida, "You
lose sight of any line of demarcation between text and what is outside it"
(1979a, 82). The boundaries, the frame, the margins become fluid: "What
has happened, if it has happened, is a sort of overrun [*débordement*]" (83).
All starting points, all quotations that are quotations of earlier requota-
tions, *fold back* on themselves—*pli* and *repli*—creating an endless regress.
Derrida uses the term *hymen* to designate the infolded edge, and *double
invagination* to designate the narrative that contains its own self-defining
qualities, qualities that are external to any narration qua narration ("double invagination constitutes the story of stories, the narrative of narrative,
the *narrative of deconstruction in deconstruction*"[100]). He extends the effect
of this folding in to include the relationship with the other implied by the
image of closure:

> [T]he apparently outer edge of an enclosure (*clôture*), far from being sim-
> ple, simply external and circular, in accordance with the philosophical
> representation of philosophy, makes no sign beyond itself, toward what
> is utterly *other,* without becoming double or dual, without making itself
> be "represented," refolded, superposed, *re-marked* within the enclosure.
> (100–101)

We might recast this figure of an exteriority folded in on itself so as to create a space without definite beginning or end, inside or outside, higher or lower, as a Möbius strip. Although the strip might appear to be a simple ring on first sight, a closer look reveals the impossibility of such a reduction. In other words, the one who looks is instrumental in establishing the identity of the strip. It is an object whose essential quality depends on being folded in on itself and in losing all definiteness of inner/outer. It becomes an endless boundary without bounded space. Whereas Derrida uses the figure of invagination specifically to demolish the closure of the text, we might equally apply the Möbius strip to our several levels of analysis. For example, we might analyze a text in terms of the Formalist concept of the device. Such a device might be the technique of embedding used by Sembène Ousmane in *Les Bouts de bois de Dieu,* or the employment of a dominant trope, like metaphor or proverb in *Things Fall Apart.* When the Möbius strip becomes the border of such devices, their role as dominant elements of definition is inverted: the values they enclose, ideologically, culturally, are folded back against all that they are intended to exclude. Like any absolute figure, any ideologically closed system, they posit terms outside the system that could be distinguished as different only by an unfolded and impermeable strip. The Möbius strip cannot maintain that clear-cut division of space.

The same thing happens when the text divides its effects against itself by the employment of a metatextual narrative level, as in the case of Birago Diop's collections of tales. This might be seen as an extension of the problematics of the autobiography in which there are, to begin with, three clear levels: that of the one described in the action, the protagonist; that of the one doing the describing, the narrator; that of the one who created the narrator, and who is presumably the one with the same name as the narrator and the protagonist, namely, the author.

If the texts are to be regarded as containing an imaginary fictional world, set off by the devices of fiction from the reality it imitates, the Möbius strip returns the ambiguity to the act of mirroring that lies at the foundation of the techniques, and deceptions, of realism.

The Möbius strip is the figure of the erasure of absolute distinctions; yet is still demarcates space, still maintains the boundariness of the ring. If cut along one axis it collapses into a flat strip, and loses its capacity to enclose; cut along the other axis (perpendicular to the first), it is first extended into a thinner, doubly twisted Möbius strip, and if cut again, magically turns into two interlocked Möbius rings. We can regard African literary history as being similarly divisible. On the one hand the divisions collapse when any ground for the periodization or the typology is taken as prescriptive and definitive. However, when the rules of definition are replaced by infinite flowing lines, as of discourses, of their origins and their dispersions into literary space, the resultant freedom permits a reorganization of textual patterns along provisional lines. Let us elaborate such a reorganization, not so as to limit African literature, but to free it from the oppressive containers of "Francophone," "Commonwealth," or "traditional" literature. The logic of the Möbius strip should then enable us to recast all the terms of exclusion and inclusion, recognizing that while we cannot do away with the terms, we can now predicate them on the basis of a boundary that repeatedly calls itself into question.

Chapter 2

▼▼▼▼▼▼▼▼▼

Literatures of Témoignage and the Foundations for Change

Lévi-Strauss and Bricolage:
In fact the Bororo myth which will from now on be designated by the name reference-myth *is, as I shall try to show, nothing other than a more or less forced transformation of other myths originating either in the same society or in societies more or less far removed. It would therefore have been legitimate to choose as my point of departure any representative of the group whatsoever. From this point of view, the interest of the reference-myth does not depend on its typical character, but rather on its irregular position in the midst of a group.*
— Claude Lévi-Strauss, *The Raw and the Cooked*

Literatures of *Témoignage*: An Introduction
V. Y. Mudimbe (1982) has located the basic problem for us:

> Really to escape from the West presupposes an exact assessment of what it costs to become detached from it: that presupposes knowing how far the West, insidiously perhaps, has become close to us; that presupposes knowing, in what is permitted us to think against the West, what is still Western; and to measure the extent to which our recourse against it is still perhaps a ruse that it uses against us and at the end of which it awaits us, unmoving and distant. (My trans.)*

In the 1950s a body of fictional works emerged in Africa that served to establish the place of the African novel and to give a presence to African

---

* [E]chapper réellement à l'Occident suppose d'apprécier exactement ce qu'il en coûte de se détacher de lui; cela suppose de savoir jusqu'où l'Occident, insidieusement peut-être, s'est approché de nous; cela suppose de savoir, dans ce qui nous permet de penser contre l'Occident ce qui est encore occidental; et de mesurer en quoi notre recours contre lui est encore peut-être une ruse qu'il nous oppose et au terme de laquelle il nous attend, immobile et ailleurs. (44)

literature that would provide a basis for its future developments. The point at which a literature finds its own referents primarily in itself is where the traditions, and not merely the influences upon a literature begin. I take the appearance of *L'Enfant noir* in 1953 to be one of the key moments because of its seminal influence on much subsequent African fiction. Other early works that appeared around that time included both literatures of *témoignage* and, a bit later, works of a second stage, what might be termed literatures of revolt. Logically, if not always chronologically, literatures of *témoignage* came first. Jonathan Ngaté (1988) makes this point when discussing the place of Aké Loba's *Kocoumba, l'étudiant noir* and Cyriaque Yavoucko's *Crépuscule et défi, kité na kité* in the formulation of a tradition of Francophone African fiction, echoing Jakobson's remarks on Chlebnikov and Pasternak:

> Published in 1960 and 1979, [these books] serve to demonstrate that the three stages . . . [that form the tradition of African literature in French] do not occur in rigid chronological order. Instead, each one of them represents different points of emphases in the history of francophone African fiction. It is fair to say, however, that the first stage clearly dominated the literary scene from the beginnings to the early sixties, when memories of colonial experiences were still very clear in most people's minds. (75)

Francophone Africa produced the first literary movement with the publications of the Negritude poets in the 1930s and 1940s. For the novel the early trends were established in the 1950s with authors whose educational experience during the colonial period had had a decisive impact on their lives. Many were students in France, including, among the first generation, Léopold Senghor, Birago Diop, Bernard Dadié, and the writers who came to be associated with *Présence africaine.* Those who followed in the 1950s included Camara Laye, Mongo Beti, Cheikh Hamidou Kane, and others whose schooling in France included lycée as well as university studies, such as Ferdinand Oyono and Tchicaya U Tam'si. If a formal Metropolitan education was not available to all, others like Sembène were no less influenced by French language and culture. For some a European diploma offered the gateway to a successful career, but for most authors the acculturation was more problematic. The reality to which African authors were to bear witness almost always began with their own personal experience, while parallel efforts at cultural valorization were being undertaken with the publication of *contes* and collections of African tales and stories by Birago Diop, Bernard Dadié, Maximilien Quenum, Fily Dabo Sissoko, Julien Alapini and others.

These authors stand apart from the well-known Anglophone authors, most of whom published works tending to take a somewhat different direction a decade after their Francophone counterparts. Amos Tutuola was one of the rare Anglophone authors who appeared far less profoundly marked by acculturation.[1] Others, like Chinua Achebe and Cyprian Ekwensi in Nigeria, and Okot p'Bitek and Ngugi wa Thiong'o in East Africa, were to respond with various forms of historical and social fiction. For all these writers the discourses on Africa that had prevailed before them were inadequate at best, and essentially false in many ways. Anglophone as well as Francophone writers lived through colonialism, underwent schooling in European languages and literatures, and in most instances left Africa for work or to attend universities abroad. For all, the experiences seemed best summed up in the words of Cheikh Hamidou Kane's title, "une aventure ambiguë." A new urgency to bear witness drove them to write, resulting primarily in four narrative types of literature of *témoignage: autobiographical, folkloric, social, and historical.*

Autobiographical Literature of *Témoignage*

Laye's *L'Enfant noir* remains the ur-text for this kind of fiction. Other autobiographies may have appeared earlier, but they generally did not seek to validate African tradition.[2] If Laye has been faulted, it was not for succumbing to the pitfalls of facile imitative forms, but because of his sins of omission: there is almost no mention of the burdens of colonialism in his account, and Mongo Beti finds his depiction of life in colonial Guinea too idealized (1954b, 419–20). Still, for a number of reasons, *L'Enfant noir* has become a kind of prototype for many African authors who turned, like Laye, to their own culture for inspiration. The choice of autobiographical form is central to the inspiration of literatures of *témoignage* and also presents us with the classical situation developed in early African literature, the European impact on African culture, highlighted in *L'Enfant noir* through Laye's dilemma over choosing to complete his education rather than become a goldsmith like his father.

Other early key examples, often characterized by cultural validation and political revolt, include *L'Aventure ambiguë* (1961), *Dramouss* (1966), *L'Harmattan* (1964), *Ville cruelle* (1954), *Climbié* (1956), and more recently Amadou Koné's *Jusqu'au seuil de l'irréel* (1976), Ken Bugel's *Le Baobab fou* (1982), Mariama Bâ's *Une si longue lettre* (1980), as well as Nafissa Diallo's *De Tilène au plateau* (1975) (one of the Nouvelles Editions Africaines series of autobiographical narratives). Correspondingly, in North African fiction the classic example of this mode is Mouloud Feraoun's *Le Fils du pauvre,* to which one might add Driss Chraïbi's *Le Passé simple.* In works written in English, examples abound, including works by Robert Cole (1960), Peter Abrahams (1954), William Conton (1960), and Ezekiel

Mphahlele (1959). Gerald Moser (1991) has made a thorough study of Lusophone autobiographical writing, noting especially works focusing upon childhood.

The affirmation made by these authors across the continent gives voice to a new cogito, "me voici," with the community voice simultaneously echoing "nous voici," forging with their voices the basic building blocks of Third World literature.

Folkloric Literature of *Témoignage*

The forms taken by *témoignage* may turn on broader cultural or social issues without the close-up portrait of a narrator. Collections of folktales were published at an early point by major African authors, including Birago Diop (*Les Contes d'Amadou Koumba,* 1947) and Bernard Dadié (*Le Pagne noir,* 1955). The need for cultural validation leads to the search for and recuperation of tradition, a common subtext of the oral literature that is mediated through these authors and their French renditions. The *contes* are not mere ethnographic transcriptions, though they may be modestly presented as such. The "contract," as Philippe Lejeune (1982) would put it, is with a reconstructed model, not an original document of orature. Indeed, the tales are skillful reconstructions, framed by the authors' personalities in such a way as to complete the underlying project of cultural validation. At the same time they both praise and preserve the heritage of the ancestors ("the dead who are not dead"[*]). The personality of the collector, as with that of the narrator, is not effaced: it is simply shifted out of the text, onto the level of the metatext, often given in the form of an introduction, an epigraph, or an epilogue to a tale. These "supplements" are what reveal the underlying design of the texts as congruent with that of the autobiographical literature of *témoignage.*

Social Literature of *Témoignage*

Here the narrative is focalized through the larger social group instead of through the personality of the individual narrator or protagonist. Usually the emphasis is placed upon village life, or on life in the African *quartiers* of the city instead of the European neighborhoods. The prototype for this might best be seen in *Things Fall Apart* (1958) and the flood of imitators that followed it, as well as in popular market literature or its offshoots, as in *Jagua Nana* (Ekwensi 1961). Although it was Achebe's intention to restore the historical image of Africa distorted by colonialist ideology, in fact the first half of his novel presents the best known literary portrait of traditional Ibo society.

---

[*] "les morts [qui] ne sont pas morts" (Birago Diop, "Souffles")

After Laye's and Achebe's endeavors, many were inspired to depict their own culture, including John Munonye, Elechi Amadi, Flora Nwapa, and T. M. Aluko. Though not simply limited to this category, Ngugi's early novels and the principal works of Okot p'Bitek also fit here. In French writing, one finds powerful examples of this mode in Sembène Ousmane's *Vehi Ciosane* (1965), *Voltaïque* (1962), or *O pays, mon beau peuple* (1957); novels written in French that follow the model include those of Mbella Sonne Dipoko, Francis Bebey, and René Philombe.

At the limit we can approach "ethnographic" literature of *témoignage* as being the reverse of the folktale literature of *témoignage*. In the folktale the story is mythic or takes the form of a romance—as far removed from realism and mimesis as possible—while the metastory or container, the tradition and those recounting it, are presented as real, authentic, believable. Lesser efforts were often thinly disguised ethnologies, such as Onuora Nzekwu's *Wand of a Noble Wood* (1961), little more than an exposition of traditional Ibo customs in which the characters lose all plausibility. In Birago Diop's tales the content is "fabulous," unreal, while the container is the locus of the realism.

Wand of a Noble Wood is an extreme case, and most African novels avoid the pitfall it gets caught in by successfully informing credible situations and believable characters with ethnographic information. The earlier forerunners of this approach, *Karim* (1935) or *Maïmouna* (1953), are relatively sentimentalized examples of expressive realism, but they still retain much of the project of presenting, and therefore validating, African ways to a non-African audience. Sembène moves beyond them, and stands at the opposite extreme from Diop.

Historical Literature of *Témoignage*

Although the line between social and historical texts is not absolute, the focus becomes important, especially when specific historical episodes, like strikes or wars, are at stake. Thus, though Ngugi portrays Kikuyu society in *A Grain of Wheat* (1967), it is always under the impress of the historical moment. The split between the first half of *Things Fall Apart* and the last also reflects this division of focus. The primary concern of the African author has been to reconstruct an historical period or episode from an Afrocentric point of view. Thus Sembène develops the picture of the strike of railroad workers along the Dakar-Niger line in *Les Bouts de bois de Dieu* from the perspective of the workers, their families, the beggars—impoverished and struggling people whose lives were caught up in the historical moment. The whites were peripheral to the story, though necessarily present. A good deal of Sembène's subsequent work, including especially his films, is of this nature (e.g., *Ceddo, Emitai, Camp de Thiaroye*).

In a sense all of Ngugi's works bear witness to the historical struggle in Kenya, while Achebe's historical novels—that is, the two that are set in the late nineteenth and early twentieth centuries, *Things Fall Apart* and *Arrow of God* (1964), also set the stage for later Nigerian successors like Amadi.

Although trends are to be found that lie outside these four narrative types of *témoignage,* they are peripheral to these main tendencies. Readings of Amos Tutuola or of popular market literature might well be used to rewrite the tradition of African literature—indeed, these categories are not absolute straightjackets but rather provisional points of departure whose primary usefulness can be adduced from the relationships of defamiliarization to which they give rise. And even those relationships are provisional points of departure. Bakhtin's notion that all discourse is a product of the inherited discourses of speech applies equally well to traditions of literature. But instead of deconstructing African literature on the basis of its own putative supplements, I prefer to offer African literature itself as the margin which refuses marginality, as the point of departure for a tradition.

This approach then demands a basis for the defamiliarization that follows, a basis to be found in the original predominant narrative traits. The changes that then followed do not indicate a point-by-point development, but a shift away from the general tendency, eventually giving rise to parodic or ironic forms elaborated in the fiction of Ferdinand Oyono, Mongo Beti, Yambo Ouologuem, Ahmadou Kourouma, and Wole Soyinka's early plays. Much of the writing by women writers in the 1960s and 1970s is also informed by a refusal of canonical centering, and though less given to parody is no less informed by revolt: Ama Ata Aidoo, Buchi Emecheta, Bessie Head, Micere Mugo, and Mariama Ba are major authors of literatures of revolt. Eventually, the same process continues with respect to their work as well, giving us the subsequent literatures of the oxymoron, heralded by the later works of Wole Soyinka, and those of V. Y. Mudimbe and Tchicaya U Tam'si, along with what we might now call the postrevolt and postoxymoron writing of Sony Labou Tansi, Henri Lopes, and most recently Werewere Liking, Calixthe Beyala, Christopher Hove, and Ben Okri.

A Poetics of the Literatures of *Témoignage*

At the center of the range of narrative modes within which the novel can be situated, Roberts Scholes (1974) places history, defining the midpoint of his narrative schema as the place where characters are situated neither above nor below us, where the world is depicted as neither better nor worse than our perception of the world of experience. The inadequacy of this definition is apparent from a quick glance at both historical and autobiographical narrative. Unless Scholes meant to redefine the common usage of the term history, it is clear that the changes in historical modes in many ways corresponded to and were coterminous with the changes in the novel itself.[3] In any event, African *témoignage* writing presents a vision of the world as variable as the point of view of each individual author. For some, like Peter Abrahams, the world was filled with struggle, with pain and injustices to which the inquiring mind of the creative artist slowly awoke. Most African literatures of *témoignage* tend not to exhibit such negative features, as seen in the success stories of Laye or Conton. Other works are more mixed.[4] Nonetheless, a tradition struggled to emerge with the novels that appeared in the 1950s and early 1960s, and that gave definition to a dominant practice that we call literature of *témoignage*. Eight of its traits will be examined. The first four define the parameters of mimesis; the second four are aspects of discourse, based on four codes: those of mode, form, theme, and language. The mimetic devices employed in the first group, as well as the mediating qualities in the second, are subsumed under the categories of two principal projects that underlie the sense of purpose we discern in literatures of *témoignage*.

1. *Point of departure.* Beginning with "I was born," or a brief genealogy leading to the protagonist's entry onto the scene, the narrative opens with a clearly defined point of departure rather than starting in medias res. In some cases this point of departure is deferred, but not omitted. In sociothematic terms we might note the concern that origins be clearly defined and, at the limit, validated by the establishment of the narrator's patrimony or patent. Precisions of time and place, Bakhtin's "chronospace," correspond to those of identity.

Mohamadou Kane (1974) shows how the pattern of rational, linear development, starting with definite origins, characterizes this literature:

> We note that almost all African novels employ a single narrative line. [Outside of Paul Hazoumé's *Doguicimi* and Yambo Ouologuem's *Le Devoir de violence*] the other novels are built around a single narrative line, with a central character through whom the author focalizes so as to present his or her current concerns. (My trans.)*

Action becomes "unique et linéaire." Kane draws upon the influence of oral tales in proposing the following traits: a simple plot line to aid comprehension; the avoidance of composite character story lines before and after the occurrence of events; an orientation intended for a collective

---

* On relève dans presque tous les romans africains le recours à une action unique … les autres romans sont bâtis sur une action unique, sur un personnage centrale par le biais duquel l'auteur dévoile ses préoccupations du moment. (21, 23)

audience; didacticism; and the defense of group values. The direct unrolling of plot, without the temporal density engendered by multiple, simultaneous actions, and by polyphonic voices, results in a strong sense of order and coherence.[5]

Kane seems to discount the element of authorial choice here—as if the writers had no control over their style. Further, his examples of exceptions—Williams Sassine or Beti (*Perpétué ou l'habitude du malheur* [1974])—fail to include notable Anglophone authors, Ngugi (*A Grain of Wheat*), Soyinka (*The Interpreters* [1965]), whose works deviate from this rule from a relatively early date. Finally, Kane's thesis is that this predominance of linear emplotment is due to the influence of oral literature, or to the desire to display tradition and custom rather than to investigate psychological states. "The foremost issue of the novel resides in the presentation of traditions which are revalorized for the edification of the French and African publics" (my trans.)* In fact, Kane's focus upon the "présentation des traditions" might be thought to apply best to the examples he chose—Hazoumé and Socé—whose works in my view led less to the establishment of dominant traits than did *L'Enfant noir* and *Things Fall Apart*.

2. *The protagonist is situated in a space defined by his or her relations with others.* Usually the protagonist is surrounded, virtually from the outset, by a host of figures whose relationship to him or her is immediately supplied. Sometimes an opening episode might precede these definitions, but in all events we quickly learn about the people around the protagonist including the family and those who live in the compound or the home environment. Eventually we are acquainted with the extended family with whom precise ties are drawn. Typically the child's relationship with the mother, or occasionally the grandmother, is shown to be strongest, while the relationship with the father is usually more problematic. Communities of siblings, schoolmates, or simply friends are formed, while within the circles of community relationships, privileged ties are established, setting the stage for potential conflict—as between mother and girlfriend or father and lover.

3. *The narrative point of view is usually focalized through the protagonist's subjectivity,* so that the coordinates of reality—time and space—are given relative to the protagonist's subjectivity. This sense of time and space, like that of the relations to others, is generally developed in ever-widening circles, so that the narrative line first encompasses a familiar world, which then grows, pushing back the limits of the unfamiliar. The world becomes partitioned into mine and others'. The movement outward, as seen clearly

---

* "L'intérêt premier du roman réside dans la présentation des traditions que l'on revalorise pour l'édification des publics français et africain" (64).

in Amadi's *The Great Ponds* (1969), carries from home to village or town, city, country, and even to mother Africa. When the protagonist is a child, the broadening of the horizon matches the child's growth. Unlike the urban settings of European or North African novels that might center on the street (with equivalent settings to be found in South African literature, as in the works of Laguma, Abrahams, or Mphahlele), a large proportion of works of black African literature have rural settings, giving us village or compound, wherein the home is often a metaphor for the extended family. Even if not an actual village compound, the home conveys the same qualities of security as the family. Thus Laye links the two at the outset of *L'Enfant noir,* evoking what appears to be his earliest memory: "My mother was in the workshop, near my father, and I could hear their reassuring, tranquil voices . . . " (my trans.).* The openness onto a series of worlds, all unified within a central circle, with its locus of security, gives the "chronospace" its most definitive quality—that of being encompassed by the boundary. The line between the interior and the exterior of the circle serves as the model for a range of boundaries delineating security/insecurity, safety/danger, familiar/foreign, self/others.

As the narrator often portrays himself or herself as simply a prototype of the community, the act of remembering serves to establish the portrait of reality for all who are contained within the boundaries. For literatures of *témoignage* this usually takes the form of a positive act of validation: "Ah! How happy we were in those days" (*L'Enfant noir,* my trans.).† For literatures of revolt, the same communal gesture is made, but the affirmation has turned to revolt or rejection: The refrain of *Une Vie de boy* now becomes "poor us."‡[6]

4. *Use of the first person.* In autobiographical literature of *témoignage* three illusions of mimesis are associated with the use of the first person. Todorov's analysis (1981) serves as the best starting point.

> [T]here is an impassible barrier between the narrative in which the narrator sees everything his character sees but does not appear on stage, and the narrative in which a character-narrator says "I." . . . Once the subject of the speech-act [conventionally the narrator, or subject of the enunciation] becomes the subject of the discourse [or *énoncé*] as the protagonist, it is no longer the same subject who discourses. To speak of oneself signifies no longer being the same "oneself." The author is unnameable: if

---

* "Ma mère était dans l'atelier, près de mon père, et leurs voix me parvenaient, rassurantes, tranquilles . . . " (1972, 9).

† "Ah! que nous étions heureux, ces jours-là" (Laye 1972, 59).

‡ "pauvre de nous" (Oyono [1956a] 1970)

we want to give him a name, he leaves us the name but is not to be discovered behind it; he takes eternal refuge in anonymity. He is quite as fugitive as any subject of the speech-act, who by definition cannot be represented. In "He runs," there is "he," subject of the discourse, and "I," subject of the speech-act. In "I run," a spoken *subject of the speech-act* is intercalated between the two, taking from each a part of its preceding content but without making them disappear altogether: it merely hides them. For "he" and "I" still exist: this "I" who runs is not the same as the one who discourses. "I" does not reduce two to one, but out of the two makes three. (39)

What is reduced to one is what Lejeune (1982) calls "identity in name," a function of the autobiographical contract, as he terms it: "The autobiography, a narration of the life of the author, presupposes *identity in name* between the author, as represented by his name on the cover, the narrator, and the one being spoken of" (200). From this situation we can see how three "fictions" arise with respect to the three subjects represented by the same name or pronoun, "I":

a. *The illusion that the subject of the discourse is identical with the subject of the speech act,* or, to simplify, that the protagonist is the same as the narrator. This is the fiction engendered by the use of "I" for both.

b. *The illusion generated by the identity of the narrator with the implied author, that the life of the three subjects extends outside the text,* opening onto the "real" world, or onto the real mind of the author. This can lead to a body of True Life Stories that not only "tell all" (cf. Bugel 1982), but that stand as models for "The African," for "l'enfant noir," for all those of the author's generation generally represented as prototypes for success. Even Mezda in *Mission terminee* (Beti 1957a) is presented to us in this fashion, carrying on the pattern into the later literature of revolt. We see this in the prologue addressed to "vous," to those who have shared Mezda's experiences, representing the typical African youth: "But you who have traveled the same road as I; you who have made the same journey . . . " (my trans.).*
This assumption of complicity leads to what Ngaté (1988) identifies as "the poetics of the 'hypocrite lecteur, mon semblable, mon frère'" (38) in which, paradoxically, the African writer typically appears as "an outsider who is defined by his in-betweenness" (39).

However, the fictions of confession are different from those of parody. The more that is "revealed," the more the disguise of revelation works to complete the concealment. The frankness is, then, even if unintentionally, that of the con artist whose first line is always, let me tell you

---

* "Mais vous qui avez parcouru le même chemin que moi; vous qui avez accompli le même voyage . . . " (10).

all about myself, implying, you can trust me, and these are my secrets. The self-conscious utilization of this device in literature, when designed to unmask the disguise, to reveal the con man, is also a literary technique. Yet it rests upon a natural "contract" with the reader generated by the author's name, supposing that "an author is not just a person, he is a person who writes and publishes. With one foot in the text, and one outside, he is the point of contact between the two" (Lejeune 1982, 200). This assumption, not only about the one named as the author but also about the world he or she inhabits, leads us away from the figure of the creator to that of the text that is generated—to the text of reality. It is here that Lejeune identifies the most ambivalent moment in the presentation of a first person narrative, that in which the unstated assumptions about reality are seen to depend not only upon a given set of experiences and memories, but also upon the conventions of the genre: "But this is where we begin to feel dizzy, for even the most naive among us is tempted to ask whether it is not the person [i.e., the person of the author] who defines the 'I', but rather the 'I' which defines the person—that is, whether there is no person except within the discourse" (198).

c. The dizziness is fought off by the third illusion, that *the events narrated are not a created text based on an individual's own particular verbal construction of events, constituting a discourse, but merely recordings of actual past events,* as faithful as the narrator's abilities and memory permit— recordings and not constructions; transcriptions and not interpretations; translations and not inventions. The dissimulation of the literary code lies in the unspoken assumption that there is no artifice, no style or literariness, no higher order of meaning, no subtext, no nameless mind, structuring or shaping the events. This parallels Todorov's statements on the concealments implicit in this kind of narrative:

> The true narrator, the subject of the speech-act of the text in which a character says "I," is only the more disguised thereby. A narrative in the first person does not make the image of its narrator explicit, but on the contrary renders it still more implicit. And every effort at such explication can lead to only more nearly perfect dissimulation of the subject of the speech-act; this discourse that acknowledges itself to be discourse merely conceals its property as discourse. (1981, 39)

All three levels of disguise operate effectively in *L'Enfant noir.* The continuity between the child and the narrator looking back on his childhood is stressed in the opening lines with the narrator entering sympathetically into the events of his past, and in the process projecting outward as a protagonist. The continuity enhances the illusion of validating the account by showing how the author's success was brought about by overcoming a

and Greene's indifferent gaps, to cite only two of the more influential sources of "African" texts.

No text is ever completely new or without forebears—only new in relation to its predecessors. And the language and literary conventions of *témoignage* were far less visibly written "in the teeth" of their predecessors: if Joyce Cary's *Mr. Johnson* had served as a target for a generation of readers, there was also Zola's *Germinal,* to which Sembène's *Les Bouts de bois de Dieu* was clearly indebted. Lying between these two positions, the early African text found itself in an impossible set of circumstances: its vehicle for delivery, its language, its genre, were well-established in European codes and models; its sense of identity, of authentic presence, was grounded in relations to parents, family, friends, and extended relatives whose prerogatives and filiations were totally African, totally demanding, totally "real." Each emplacement—text and experience—was naturalized and each laid claims to opposing statements concerning the natural, the real. Only the voice that attempted to evoke that ambiguity could claim to speak faithfully to the demand for realism; and the moment such a claim was established, its claimant entered once again into the field of deception by concealing its own naturalizing convention, the all too familiar act of concealing one's own artifices. Literatures of *témoignage* move to their limits when this approach is taken, as with Kane's *L'Aventure ambiguë,* the classical case.

Yet defamiliarization never seems to remain immobilized for long. If Cheikh Hamidou Kane's and Kateb Yacine's anguished response to acculturation sounded familiar notes during the high days of existentialism, the force that was to move African literature in the years that followed was to come from the last of the forms of naturalization defined by Culler—parody. Culler's focus is appropriately structuralist: "When a text cites or parodies the conventions of a genre one interprets it by moving to another level of interpretation where both terms of the opposition can be held together by the theme of literature itself" (1975, 152). In Africa, this focus on the closure of the theme of literature appears ill-placed when one considers texts so deliberately oriented toward political or social action. The closure of a system of naturalization itself calls for deconstruction, a method inspired less by literatures of revolt than by their successors of the 1970s and 1980s.

The last four traits of literatures of *témoignage* reflect the opening toward the exterior—the centrifugal force that, for Bakhtin, gives the novel's discourse all the power of dialogism.

5. *The mode of most African literatures of* témoignage *can be described as falling between comedy and the novel of sentiment,* generally typed as expressive

realism, and, at the limit, approaching the point lying between the picaresque and the tragic where naturalism can be located (Scholes 1974, 136ff). The schematization shown in Figure 1, which represents the overall pattern literary modes generally form, is drawn from Scholes.

Satire		!		Romance
\		!		/
Picaresque		Naturalism		Tragedy
\		!		/
Comedy		Realism		Sentiment
\		!	/	
		History		

FIGURE 1

Adapted from the work of Northrop Frye, Scholes's V-shaped schema represents a refined version of both a historical patterning and an organization of fictional representation based on what Frye (1957) calls a "conventional power of action assumed about the chief characters" (366). That power of action is relevant to the world inhabited by the character. Thus we have one pattern established by the degree to which the world may be seen as ordered, another as chaotic. Beginning with the attempt to represent the world as it is commonly experienced—through history or nonfictional autobiography—fiction can move either in the direction of a world romanticized as better or more orderly, more coherent than ours, peopled by figures who rise above our level, or it can move toward a world of chaos, disorder, peopled by those recognizably worse than what we expect common sense or experience to record (Scholes 1974, 135–37). The lower the degree of conflict and tension, the closer the work lies to the midpoint between comedy and works of sentiment. The greater the tension, the more the characters move from feeling emotional to feeling deeply emotional, from a fiction of sentiment to tragedy. On the other arm of Scholes's V, the world becomes more chaotic as the tensions lead to greater

Lejeune's "autobiographical space," that extends beyond the bounds of its closed universe, inviting us to join in the action of liberation—an unending struggle onto which the universe of the novel is opened.

In the final analysis, it is the comforting recourse to ideological categories of class and struggle that give much of Sembène's work the closure of classical realism. This is the type of closure defined by Catherine Belsey (1981) as "disclosure," that is, the ultimate revelation of the solution to the problem, the answer to the questions posed by the novel: "The dissolution of enigma through the reestablishment of order, recognizable as a reinstatement or a development of the order which is understood to have preceded the events in the story itself" (70). Here it is not a social order that is reinstated, but an intellectual and ethical one made clear through the revelation of truths based on ideological codes.

7. *African literatures of* témoignage *thematize the conflicts and tensions between African and European culture:* Samba Diallo's personal dilemma in dealing with Muslim values in the context of French society and Camara Laye's choice of schooling over an apprenticeship in his father's workshop are two well-known examples. The theme of conflict is repeatedly invoked in popular literature; ironically Market literature takes a sympathetic position on "modernism" in contrast to the more thoughtful repudiation of crass Westernization in "serious" literature. The conflict appears central to feminist concerns: Issues of polygamy, arranged marriages, the woman's social role, are all crossed with style and culture, and appear frequently in the early work of Sembène, Mariama Bâ, Ngugi, and a host of others. Languages, cultures, and discourses meet, and shape such banal questions as whether Laye would marry Marie or Fanta. For Aidoo the conflict is often put in terms of the single woman's choice to remain unmarried.

The encounter with European culture generated a set of social and personal patterns that diverged from African conventions. Instead of widening circles circumscribing and defining the self—the African norm—the very substance of European identity is perceived as unique. Attitudes toward authority, community, and hierarchical structures reveal how the European topoi function outside the generally accepted African framework. This apartness is visible in the representation of space: from the compound one moves to the forbidden regions of the Evil Forest, from the *quartier* to the European neighborhoods, to the commandant's house. Difference is marked, accentuated, exaggerated. The two sets of values enter into conflict: the European presence is scrutinized, setting the signification of "civilization" against that of conquest.

The result is not a dialectical transcendence or resolution, but, as Jonathan Ngaté so perceptively indicates in *Francophone African Literature,* a range of *mentalités* always marked by dualism. Initially the mark is presented as innocuous: as Ngaté states (1988), writers like Paul Hazoumé entered into relations with colonial literary texts as if they were twins of their European counterparts. "Not identical twins, to be sure, since the gulf separating colonized Black from White colonizer was thought to be unbridgeable" (30). With the advent of literatures of *témoignage,* the gulf itself became the key to the relationship—indeed, for African literature generally, according to Ngaté, the dialectically opposed terms always render problematic the cultural opposition, bringing into the conflict not only the tension between cultures, but that implied between reader and text. Thus, Toundi, in *Une Vie de boy,* arrives at "a lucid understanding of both his inclusion and exclusion from the colonial society in which he has to live." Similarly, authors from Senghor to Mudimbe are aware of addressing two sets of audiences at the same time, thus generating a dialectic binding text and reader with both "intimacy and distance" (Ngaté 1988, 37). The tension is generated only because there is a closeness that borders on "seduction" and a rejection that resembles an "exorcism," without the possibility of the one term dismissing the other. For Ngaté this is a consequence of the African author's being obliged to "count on European narratees while at the same time having to rail against them" (40). However, the tension goes beyond the narrator-narratee relationship, marking all discursive formations with a fundamental diglossia.

8. *Heteroglossia is a characteristic feature of African literature.* In *The Dialogic Imagination* (1983), Bakhtin asserts that a discourse "orchestrates" voices on many levels: "authorial speech, the speech of narrators, inserted genres, and the speech of characters." Each voice he mentions "permits a multiplicity of social voices" whose diffuse movement, whose "dispersion into rivulets and droplets of social heteroglossia," whose "dialogization" defines the novel in its richest aspect, endowing it with the "basic distinguishing feature of the stylistics of the novel" (263). But in focusing on this social component, the linguistic basis is depressed, and in Africa this basis is what is most heavily overlaid with palimpsests and echoes, voices that are forcefully unspoken.

The example of Achebe is typical. Schooled in English, speaking Ibo at home and pidgin English in common social intercourse, he sprinkles his texts with multiple linguistic registers. The most common voice in his fiction is conveyed in the narrator's congenial tones as that of a moderately ironic, educated Nigerian speaker. But the countervoice of the cultivated English colonialist is also always evoked. Those who serve the colonial system speak in pidgin in *Things Fall Apart* and *Arrow of God*; in *Anthills of the Savannah* (1967) pidgin reflects contemporary Nigerian speech patterns and is presented as the language spoken informally between friends. Ibo is at times untranslated and is frequently associated with village life and its culture and religion; it is used by figures of authority and in oral expressions. The listing of language usages, however, fails to indicate the potency in the deployment of these languages and of their registers, and even less does it reveal the space occupied by the silent interlocutors—with implied unenunciated responses to the ubiquitous English presence. The pressure of Ibo speech is silently exerted on the text—not just when "chi" is mentioned, with or without explanations—and not just in the edifice of the plot, in the conception of the characters, in the setting or in the tempo of narration. It is woven intertextually as the echo of one language against and within another, at times appearing through pinholes.

As each language has its social components, it is impossible to eliminate the social context from the consideration of language and voice. Given this situation, duplicated in various forms throughout Africa and common to most African authors, it is inevitable that any literary discourse will begin with a complex weave of voices and registers, with full heteroglossia. Added to this, as Mohamadou Kane has stressed, is an equally widespread exposure to oral literature, usually in African languages, combined with schooling in written European literatures. The archeology of the African text must reveal that each word is overlaid with traditions and structures that are repositaries of long-standing usages in several languages. One finds, thus, that the word for money order in Cameroonian pidgin English is the French term, *mandat,* while the Wolof term used in Senegal is *mandabi* (*bi* serving as the definite article). Wolof in Dakar is now increasingly incorporating French terms, thus setting it apart from its forms outside the capital. Each creolized term must be linked to the previous multitudinous usages recorded over the years. The result cannot be reduced to a simple binary opposition, to a clear ambivalence, or to a contradiction reduced to a simple term. Rather, at its best the effect is that of a concerto, often with one voice given prominence, but always with a polyphonic accompaniment.

Synthesis of the Traits of the Literatures of *Témoignage*

The literary expression of these various linguistic, social, and cultural encounters can be constructed around the same V-type pattern utilized by Scholes in describing the principal literary modes. We can overlay three patterns onto the basic model (see Figure 2).

The relative relationships of oral African-language discourses versus written European-language discourses may also be organized into the V pattern (see Figure 3).

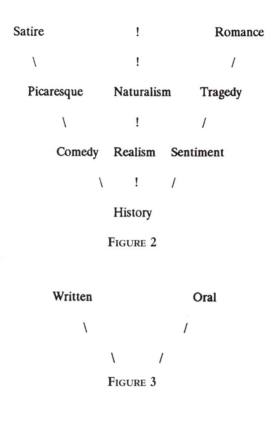

FIGURE 2

FIGURE 3

Conventionally associated with the European discursive patterns, the written literature approaches more closely the ironic modes. According to Lukàcs and de Man this association is natural: "The tie between irony and the novel seems to be so strong that one feels tempted to follow Lukàcs in making the novel into the equivalent, in the history of literary genres, of irony itself" (de Man 1983, 210). Despite de Man's reservations that the connections between the novel and irony are not simple, the fundamental orientation of the novel as a demystifying mode of literature is particularly fitting for African literatures of *témoignage*, in which the function of demystifying colonial half-truths was implicitly or explicitly assumed.

Irony, and generally the left axis of our V, is associated with a destabilized order. The rupture with and within traditional society, the chaotic consequences of colonialism, and finally the corrupt, anomalous world of post-Independence Africa have all served to provide appropriate settings for this ironic purview, from the 1950s on. Thus the dominant trait would be the ironic gaze cast upon an overinflated order. However, the project of demystifying is not merely a dialectical negative, despite Sartre's views, expressed in "Orphée noir."[11] Where Sartre saw in blacks an antibourgeois revolutionary force, Negritude writers viewed revolution as a vehicle to affirm a threatened existence. At its limit, the affirmation can take a straightforward, dogmatic form, as we see in David Diop's reservations about Mongo Beti's *Mission terminée,* complaining essentially that it was not adequately anticolonialist. For Diop, Beti's humor and irony were not enough: "But does all that count when around us in Africa so many major events cry out for our attention?" (my trans.)*

In contrast to the challenges to order, oral forms have radically different conventions grounded in the affirmation of a stable world order, with characters who are either epical heroes, mystical beings, or folk types. The overt messages of proverbs, tales, and epics are usually educative and celebratory, not subversive. The order is associated with clan and lineage, with structures of village society, or of royal rule. It is this penchant for order, and the presumed close association of the performer and the audience, that accounts for Bakhtin's dismissal of oral literature as monologic.

> The epic past is called the "absolute past" for good reason: it is both monochronic and valorized (hierarchical); it lacks any relativity, that is, any gradual, purely temporal progressions that might connect it with the present. It is walled off absolutely from all subsequent times, and above all from those times in which the singer and his listeners are located. . . . The epic past is absolute and complete. It is as closed as a circle; inside it everything is finished, already over. There is no place in the epic world for any openendedness, indecision, indeterminacy. There are no loopholes in it through which we glimpse the future; it suffices unto itself, neither supposing any continuation nor requiring it. . . . Everything incorporated into this past was simultaneously incorporated into a condition of authentic essence and significance, but therefore also took on conclusiveness and finality, depriving itself, to so speak, of all rights and potential for a real continuation. Absolute conclusiveness and closedness is the outstanding feature of the temporally valorized epic past. (Bakhtin 1983, 15–16).

Our contention is that this same view of a closed discourse would be applied by Bakhtin to other oral forms—proverbs, tales, and myths. As all serve to valorize tradition, and as "the epic relies entirely on this tradition," it follows that tradition is the force that encloses the space of oral literature: "The epic past, walled off from subsequent times by an impenetrable boundary, is preserved and revealed only in the form of national tradition" (16).

---

* "Mais tout cela fait-il poids quand autour de nous en Afrique tant d'événements majeurs sollicitent notre attention?" (1957, 187).

The problem with Bakhtin's formulation is that he places the wall inside of itself: The closed universe includes its own boundary, tradition being placed not only on the periphery of that which expresses it, but also being placed beyond what it excludes. This suggests that the enclosed space is immured against change, as is tradition itself. We are forced to ask, Where did this tradition come from? recognizing all too well that the obvious violence of change in the cities is only a foil to the realities of change in all cultures, including the villages that are now threatened with final closure and destruction by those very urban forces. However, though this monological reading of epic and tradition is inadequate, it is not entirely false. In fact, the surface message of the oral work generally supports an established order, which is only natural when one considers that oral literature is invariably performed and therefore engenders a close relationship between the performer and the audience. Ruth Finnegan (1970) signals this in her discussion of lyrical poetry: "In such cases the close connection between artist and audience can almost turn into an identity, the chorus directly participating in at least certain parts of the performance" (10). It is this necessary connection that has led Bakhtin and others astray into thinking that the text itself is frozen into an unchangeable form.

Just as tradition is an expression of a living culture, always in the process of formation, so, too, are its literary expressions, and especially oral ones. Thus we can say that if the surface message of oral literature leads one to suppose a monological base, then on the subtextual level it is, rather, the contrary. This fact is signaled by the constant process of constructing the walls of tradition. Thus Finnegan begins with a cautionary claim:

> The scope of the artist to improvise or create may vary, but there is almost always *some* opportunity for "composition." It comes out in the exact choice of word and phrase, the stylistic devices like the use of ideophones, asides or repetitions, the ordering of episodes or verses, new twists to familiar plots or the introduction of completely new ones, improvisation or variation. (9)

Indeed, the very factor that generates stability, the audience, may be responsible for the mutability in the performance: "This possibility of both clarification and challenge for members of the audience and their effect on the performance is indeed one of the main distinctions between oral and written literary pieces" (11). Finnegan goes on to question those very assumptions upon which Bakhtin relied in his definition of the epic as a closed universe: the principal mistakes are in thinking

> that "oral tradition" (including what we should now call oral literature) is passed down word for word from generation to generation and thus reproduced verbatim from memory throughout the centuries; or

alternatively, that oral literature is something that arises communally, from the people or the "folk" as a whole, so that there can be no question of individual authorship or originality. (14)[12]

In breaking down these reductive assumptions, Finnegan tackles the very distinction between oral and written forms themselves, asserting that there is no absolute boundary:

> Oral and written [forms] are not so mutually exclusive as is sometimes imagined. Even if we picture them as two independent extremes we can see that in practice there are many possibilities and many different stages between the two poles and that the facile assumption of a profound and unbridgeable chasm between oral and written forms is a misleading one. (20)

We can see this specifically in the meeting of oral and written forms—chronicles, epics, *tarikha*—that celebrate and record the rule of Askia Mohammed (Hale 1990).

The subtext of oral tales is all too often a subversive one. It is no accident that the trickster rabbit of West Africa, along with a host of other ostensibly weak or foolish characters in African oral literature, passed into figures of resistance and subversion, on the formal level of the narrative, in African-American tales, as with the character Wiley in "Wiley, His Momma and the Hairy Man" (cf. Hamilton 1985). However, Robert Cancel (1989) and others have shown that even conventional stories are usually given to various social and political ends according to the performer's intentions. The subtext must be considered dialogic, then, just as the surface message is often the opposite.

Lastly, on both surface-textual and subtextual levels, oral literature conveys its messages by analogy, rather than by direct reportage. If the novel is given to irony as its dominant figure, the corresponding trope for oral literature, following Jakobson, is metaphor. Our V then is more nuanced (see Figure 4).

What is left to complete the V at the bottom is the meeting place of a world imaged as ordered on one hand and unordered on the other. That meeting place we assign to a world without preconditions, a world subject to our actions and intentions. In literature that is the place occupied by the least fantastic forms of realism—chronicle, history, or autobiography; in short, "unreconstructed" *témoignage*. On the oral side, the *griot* is the repository of historical events, chiefly biographical ones, and master of the epic; on the written side we have, strictly speaking, autobiographical literature of *témoignage*. The trope Jakobson assigns to realism, and sets in distinction to the dominance of metaphor in romanticism and symbolism, is metonymy. This completes the base of the V (see Figure 5).

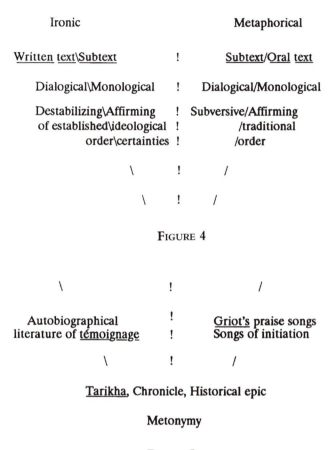

Ironic   Metaphorical

Written text\Subtext   !   Subtext/Oral text

Dialogical\Monological   !   Dialogical/Monological

Destabilizing\Affirming   !   Subversive/Affirming
of established\ideological   !   /traditional
order\certainties   !   /order

        \   !   /

          \   !   /

FIGURE 4

    \   !   /

Autobiographical   !   Griot's praise songs
literature of témoignage   !   Songs of initiation
        \   !   /

Tarikha, Chronicle, Historical epic

Metonymy

FIGURE 5

The schematization in Figures 4 and 5 is not intended to reduce what Finnegan has warned us against, that is, the need to preserve the space between oral and written forms, but rather to identify dominant features in a discourse. We might accomplish the same goal by constructing a new V, comparable to those above, based not on tropes, modes, or oral/written forms, but on values assigned to reality. These values are implicit in the work of Camara Laye, and are made explicit in Wole Soyinka's *Myth, Literature and the African World* when he speaks of reality as existing on either a mundane or a mystical level. The two levels would seem to correspond to Jakobson's figures of metonymy and metaphor, or to de Man's opposition of irony to symbol. A series of analogical terms that correspond roughly to

the opposing discourses of African and European *mentalités* could be constructed along these lines, with the dialogue between these two discourses
resulting in what Barthes calls plural literary texts. Yet an explicitly philo-
sophical treatment of this encounter is relatively uncommon. In *L'Aventure
ambiguë* the two spokesmen for the opposing positions are represented by
Samba Diallo's father, "le Chevalier," and the French colonial administrator, Paul Lacroix. More typically one finds the clash of cultural ways represented thematically, as in much of the work of Sembène, Ngugi, Aidoo,
Head, and Soyinka. If one were to seek a base for this contrast in values, one
could refer to Laye's appeal to "les profondeurs cachées" (1978b, 16),
which is intended to reflect a fundamental African openness to spiritual
dimensions of reality foreclosed by Western materialism.

Significantly, this clear-cut binary opposition of mystical and material
leaves out the possibility of subtextual nuances, and is fundamentally as
closed and monological as the critical apparatus upon which it is constructed. In order to move beyond it, the third element of the V is needed,
what Bakhtin valorizes as essential to the spirit of the dialogic imagination,
and that is parody, or what we have identified with irony and satire. It is
inconceivable that African literature can be constructed around a monologic discourse that valorizes hidden spiritual depths, ignoring the fact that
the vehicle for conveying that discourse is grounded in the language and
culture of the colonialists. The bad faith entailed in ignoring an English
presence while utilizing the English language and English literary forms
could only subvert any eventual attempt to construct an enduring tradition. Thus it is necessary to add a third element to Soyinka's basically conservative binary structure, and that is demystification. Conveniently, this
allows us to schematize a V structure along the lines developed above, permitting an overall classification of the broad lines of African literature (see
Figure 6).

Though Figure 6 is a schematization, one may think of the poles and
divisions as representing general tendencies. Any novel that engages us is
apt to do so on levels that encompass much of what is given in Figure 6,
and indeed through cracks and distortions that escape any charting. But
we can discern the movement of a crowd however idiosyncratic the individuals, and we can chart a tradition and its changes despite the resistance
of its components. Each mode provides a marker for change, from the
early expressive realism to the increasingly dark tones of irony. Sembène
and Ngugi are pulled from their broad adherence to an anticolonial rhetoric, located on the left pole, in the direction of a more stable center due to
their ideological certitudes, their grounding in a logocentric order. Their
more cynical counterparts, Aidoo, Oyono, Kourouma, and especially

DEMYSTIFICATION   MYSTICAL

Irony   Metaphor

Unstable order   !   Stable order

Impotent characters   Empowered characters

<u>Satire & literature of</u>   !   <u>Romance & quest literature</u>
<u>subversion & disorder</u>

\   /

\   !   /

<u>Picaresque</u>   !   <u>Tragedy</u>

\   !   /

\   <u>Realism</u>   /

\   !   /

<u>Comedy</u>   !   <u>Sentiment</u>

\   !   /

\ ! /

Mundane

Metonymy

<u>Autobiographical</u>, <u>Historical</u>

FIGURE 6

Ouologuem, are far less drawn to the center, and give a strong foundation for a literature of demystification that is eventually developed in the writings of Sony Labou Tansi, V. Y. Mudimbe and Wole Soyinka. This development represents the major trend in contemporary African literature.

Coming from the opposite side, that is, the right-hand pole, closer to order, is a world peopled by those who walk with a heavier step and breathe with louder breath than ordinary folk, identified with the work of Achebe. However, he, too, is pulled toward the direction of demystification, although in none of his works, including his latest, *Anthills of the Savannah,* does he abandon the basic certainties of the humanist. J. P. Clark, John Munonye, and Elechi Amadi fall roughly into the same category.

At the reasonable center, approached on the right side by Robert Cole or Cyprian Ekwensi, and on the left by Francis Bebey, we find the convergence of traits characteristic of literatures of *témoignage,* with the plot constructed in a linear, open form, and with a well-defined point of departure. The trope that corresponds to the deep narrative structure of this type of fiction is metonymy. The broad lines of realism are never very distant from the work of writers like Sembène, Achebe, or Laguma, and are usually only modified by the tendencies that extend toward irony or metaphor. The tension created by moving up the V, as Scholes would have it for twentieth-century Western literature (1974, 138), is equally compelling for African literature. Beginning with a relatively harmonious interpenetration of the two poles, as *Things Fall Apart* and many works of early literatures of *témoignage* so well demonstrate, late developments in African literature have foregrounded the complexity, tension, and anxiety involved in attempting to maintain this creative dualism, as Makombo Bamboté's fiction, Soyinka's "difficult" plays, and the recent works of the school of Congolese writers, Sylvain Bemba, Tchicaya U Tam'si, Henri Lopes, V. Y. Mudimbe, and Sony Labou Tansi, as well as the more distant works of Nuruddin Farah, Werewere Liking, and Calixthe Beyala, have shown.

We are now in a position to take a more global look at the main features of this literature and hazard an assessment of the larger projects that it aims to fulfill—projects generally characteristic of African literature as a whole.

Recuperation and Education

In the first stage of African literature we see the narrator's relationship to himself or herself as a subject governed by the need for *récupération*—in the French sense of salvaging. In broader terms, we can see this when Cheikh Hamidou Kane reconstructs the features of a Sufi Muslim identity, and earlier when the Negritude poets reclaimed a threatened sense of worth and dignity by recouping an aesthetic based on black values. Laye reclaims the lost beauty of youth and culture by reconstructing the past. The key to the literature is the act of recalling, and the *témoignage* "salvages" four foyers of identity: (1) the individual's personal experience, (2) the individual who reclaims a social or cultural loss, (3) the culture and the race, and (4) the past and the heritage.

The project of *récupération* is achieved through the use of devices of mimetism, intended to serve the need for education or social meliorism. The essence of this mimesis of the world of immediate experience is conveyed through a transparent style, presented with metonymic, "mundane" terms—in short, truth given the form of the Real.

Correspondingly, for Senghor, the project served by even the least realistic of African literary forms, the folktale, is advocative: "The fable and even the tale are gnomic genres; they are intended to be educational" (my trans.).* Similarly, Achebe underlines the instructional purposes that African literature must serve: "Many of [my readers] look to me as a kind of teacher" (1973, 2). Achebe's goal is to hold a mirror up to reality, that of today and yesterday, so as to ameliorate his society: "[T]he past needs to be created not only for the enlightenment of our detractors but even more for our own education" (9).

In his *Studies in European Realism* (1964), Lukàcs shows how for the Russian Democratic Literary Critics, Bielinski, Chernyshevski, and Dobrolyubov, "life itself was the criterion for artistic beauty; art grew out of life and creatively reproduced it; the fidelity and depth of this reproduction was the true measure of artistic perfection." Closely related to this conception is their basic idea that life itself, "deeply conceived and faithfully reproduced in literature, is the most effective means of throwing light on the problems of social life and an excellent weapon in the ideological preparation of the democratic revolution they expected and desired" (107). The materialist basis for this approach, corresponding to the right-hand axis of the V of our schemata, is thus linked by Lukàcs to realism: "The essence of [their] critical method is therefore to juxtapose life and literature, the original and the reflection. This conception of art as a mirror of reality is a common trait of all aesthetic theory based on a materialist philosophy" (111).

The curious assumption that reality is best evoked for educational purposes by the use of realist techniques dates to the nineteenh century when such fiction was intended to serve the instructional needs of the

---

* "La fable et même le conte sont des genres *gnomiques*; ils visent à l'éducation" (9).

newly literate bourgeoisie. Prior to then, a certain deference to stylization—in art as in literature—was not thought to be incompatible with the ameliorationist goals of the Enlightenment. For Barthes (1982a), "reality" is an effect, achieved by the use of artifice and convention no less than any other literary effect; but the line of this argument runs counter to Achebe for whom there is a necessary connection between a transparent prose style and the project of "enlightened" realism. Only the awareness of the literary conventions of the discourse, the self-consciousness of the choice, seems to have escaped him. Thus, Achebe writes:

> When white light hits glass one of two things can happen. Either you have an image which is faithful if somewhat unexciting or you have a glorious spectrum which though beautiful is really a distortion. Light from the past passes through a kind of glass to reach us. We can look for the accurate though somewhat unexciting image or we can look for the glorious technicolor. . . . [In the latter case,] the credibility of the world [the artist] is attempting to re-create will be called into question. . . . (1973, 9)

For Achebe the artist serves the goals of the teacher by constructing a mimetic art.

The appearance of literatures of *témoignage* at their particular historical juncture, with the stress upon realism, is based on the certainty that art can and should serve life. No questions about the integrity of social action arise, or if they do, it is not in the form of an ironic disjunction, which would cast the future into doubt, or refuse to view the past as beyond critical inquiry. In short, ironic distance and temporality were put under erasure. Nonetheless, they reappear in the sentiments that color this literature. Nostalgia and even anger are based upon certain refusals of the present. The choice of classical realism could not be made without suppressing the distance evoked by say a Léon Damas in "Solde" ("Pigments"), in the repetition of the word *their* ("leur"):

> I feel like an awful fool
> in their shoes
> in their dinner-jacket
> in their shirt front
> in their collar
> in their monocle
> in their derby hat (1970, 41) *

---

* J'ai l'impression d'être ridicule
  dans leurs souliers
  dans leur smoking

In contrast, the quiet tones employed by Laye when he thinks of his mother reach across the distance of space and time, to escape the cold situation of the present and its negation of the tender effect of the past. "Education" is more than a pure view of events: it recovers what was rejected, rejects what was put in its place, and asserts a rightful place in the present. It cannot afford to suppress irony.

Reality is more than a springboard: it is, in fact, the surface of being—de Man's empirical self—for the ironist. Achebe's mimetic fiction lies between two temporal zones: the past, cut off from the present, which provides the mode of allegory; and the immediate present moment in which the ironic effect of the narrator is achieved. The latter depends upon the visibility of the narrator to give irony presence, turning the vision away from the allegorical past. Mimesis pretends to a vision without that ironic presence—a narration without a narrator. It is the play between this pretence and the ironic act of demystification that moves literary history forward (de Man 1983, 226). In our scheme, it is precisely in this play that African literature passes from literatures of *témoignage* to literatures of revolt.

Achebe's goal of education is achieved by classical realism. His image of light and glass conveys the desire for transparence or clarity—an essential feature also of French classical writing as it developed in the period of the ascendancy of the bourgeoisie, giving rise to "the novel [as] the predominant art form of the modern bourgeois culture" (Lukàcs 1964, 2). For de Man, the trajectory that led to the dominance of realism in the novel represented a decline: "The regression in critical insight found in the transition from an allegorical to a symbolic theory of poetry would find its historical equivalent in the regression from the eighteenth-century ironic novel ... to nineteenth-century realism" (1983, 222). There are two levels on which this regression is to be measured: the absence of irony in the seriousness of realist business—attested to in David Diop's review of Mongo Beti's *Mission terminée*—which calls into question the entire project of demystification. The project of *récupération* depends upon a clear reading of colonial distortions, yet remains blind to insights into the self because its rhetoric is grounded in absolute certitudes. Secondly, and more to the point, the subject whose gaze through the clear glass provides the basis of the narrative discourse, the truthful witness who can see the road and its windings in fog and mist as in sunlight, pretends to a wisdom

---

dans leur plastron
dans leur faux-col
dans leur monocle
dans leur melon (1937, 39)

because he is both free and free from irony. This is the Wordsworth of the Lucy Gray poems whose subject de Man analyzes. His analysis could apply word for word to the writings of Achebe or Ngugi:

> The stance of the speaker, who exists in the "now," is that of a subject whose insight is no longer in doubt, and who is no longer vulnerable to irony. It could be called, if one so wished, a stance from the point of view of a unified subject that fully recognizes a past condition as one of error and stands in a present that, however, sees things as they actually are. (224)

It need hardly be added that the past condition of error is attributed first to those who accepted the colonial ideology, and second to those who chose an associative Eurocentric mystification in revolutionary or surrealistic stances of defiance. In reaction to both rhetorics of colonialism and Negritude, literatures of *témoignage* chose clarity. It remained for Barthes to chart the limited vision of that choice: "In actual fact, clarity is a purely *rhetorical* attribute, not a quality of language in general, which is possible at all times and in all places, but only the ideal appendage to a certain kind of discourse, that which is given over to a permanent intention to persuade" (1981b, 58; my stress).

This desire to persuade, rather than merely to present, may be realized as a natural consequence of the commitment to social meliorism. Barthes analyzes the larger program of the language of classicism—its world, its horizons—in terms of ideological goals: "Political authority, spiritual dogmaticism, and unity in the language of classicism are therefore various aspects of the same historical movement" (58). The conventional dogmatism in African literature and criticism is found in the advocacy of meliorism, to be realized through the unity of language, and given as a realist portrayal of the past and the present. Inherent in this approach is a certain reticence or even hostility to romance or allegory, which stand at opposite extremes from realism, perhaps explaining some of the negative reactions toward the quintessentially romantic African author, Amos Tutuola, or toward the extreme ironist, Yambo Ouologuem. By extension, as romance or allegory is associated with the unreal world of imagination, the privileging of realism is seen as involving the sacrifice of Art for education (or for the bare truth in history, reality, experience, or ideology). "Perhaps what I write is applied art as distinct from pure. But who cares? Art is important but so is education of the kind I have in mind" (Achebe 1973, 6).

It is ironic that this choice of mode is at odds with that employed in traditional oral narratives—epics, folktales, or myths.[13] It appears that the most direct influence on almost all African novelists came from the European realist tradition. The problem faced by the African heirs of this tradition is precisely one of freedom, of moving forward from the visions already formed and ossified. The issue is compounded, as Mudimbe has shown in *L'Odeur du père,* by the innate hostility of the European discourse to African culture. Barthes shows how this problem of change is inherent in all literature:

> A modern masterpiece is impossible, since the writer is forced by his writing into a cleft stick: either the object of the work is naively attuned to the conventions of its form, Literature remaining deaf to our present History, and not going beyond the literary myth; or else the writer acknowledges the vast novelty of the present world, but finds that in order to express it he has at his disposal only a language which is splendid but lifeless. In front of the virgin piece of paper, at the moment of choosing the words which must frankly signify his place in History, and testify that he assumes its data, he observes a tragic disparity between what he does and what he sees. Before his eyes, the world of society now exists as a veritable Nature, and this Nature speaks, elaborating living languages from which the writer is excluded: on the contrary, *History puts in his hands a decorative and compromising instrument, a writing inherited from a previous and different History, for which he is not responsible and yet which is the only one he can use. Thus is born a tragic element in writing, since the conscious writer must henceforth fight against ancestral and all-powerful signs which, from the depths of a past foreign to him, impose Literature on him like some ritual, not like a reconciliation.* (1981b, 86; my stress)

When one considers that for the African author the language placed at the writer's disposal is not only splendid and lifeless but that of the conqueror, one can appreciate the degree to which writing poses the problem of alienation in African circumstances. For literature as for history, Africa is faced with the dilemma of having to invent the new when trapped by the necessity of utilizing the tools of the old employed in her own oppression. This is the same dilemma Barthes sees as characteristic of all revolutions: "Revolution must of necessity borrow, from what it wants to destroy, the very image of what it wants to possess" (1981, 87). Here we see the fundamental limit to the program set for itself by African literature. If it is to persuade, to educate, and to do so using classical realism as its device, it limits its own horizons to those defined by its own value-laden instrument.

If the only way out of this dilemma for a Ngugi is writing in Kikuyu, for most other African writers it is to be found in the possibilities afforded by the interstices of the text through which the Afrophonic subtext emerges. Despite the calls for a committed, socially relevant realism, early African novels contained details that we might compare to those analyzed by Barthes in what he calls the reality effect. For Barthes, when Flaubert evokes a barometer on the wall over a piano, it is an irrelevant detail—one not needed to drive the plot forward, not assimilable into any pattern of meaning, except for the general project of evoking reality. It is the generality of this project that strips the detail of meaning: "It is the category of the 'real,' and not its various contents, which is being signified: in other words, the very absence of the signified, to the advantage of the referent, standing alone, becomes the true signifier of realism" (Barthes 1981, 16). This Barthes calls "l'effet de réel."

In Achebe's novels this effect of the signifier evoked for its own sake is most visible in the discourse of the women, the tales they tell, the extraneous gossip or quarrels that fill in the space of the compound. These interventions do not move the story forward, do not reflect that linear structure that Mohamadou Kane posits as a quasi-universal trait of oral and written African literature, do not signify outside of the closed space they inhabit. Yet I would not identify them as marginalized discursive spaces as much as signifiers of "le réel africain." To a certain extent, this same effect is achieved by the use of African proverbs by the male speakers, by the intercalation of Ibo phrases, and, more emphatically, by the structuring of the narration along lines that are parallel to those of a folktale, especially when this lends emphasis to the thematic development, as in Part 1 of *Things Fall Apart*. But these qualities, which give Achebe's, or even Ngugi's, fiction their distinctive style, are best regarded primarily as intertextual, and not thematic, qualities.

It is significant that these intertextual elements are precisely the areas in which the African literary heritage makes its presence felt. That is, the principal plot lines, dialogue, and characterization are constructed along familiar realist patterns, primarily influenced by European traditions; but the subtext, intervening intertextually, is African. As Barthes has shown in *Writing Degree Zero,* the signifying system employed in realism is anything but neutral. We can then conclude that the subtextual and intertextual African systems are also not neutral, but constitute both a counterdiscourse, to the extent that they validate repressed African or feminine values, and an affirmative discourse, to the extent that they further the assumptions about power that undergird African social structures.

As the genuinely intertextual African elements assert themselves, the straightforward act of bearing witness cracks. The story of Okonkwo yields to that of Eneke the bird who flies without perching, and then to stories for "foolish women and children" (Achebe 1972, 53) like that of the clever tortoise called "All of you" who tricked the birds out of their heavenly repast. The weight of the tales bears down on the important central plot, displacing its originary signifying system by the effect of its transposition: Okonkwo shifts from being an insecure bully whose personal

life takes on special meaning because of the impact of colonialism, to a figure in a tale, lending shape to proverbs warning the unwary against taking
too-rigid stances. The European form and humanitarian pre-texts shift,
like the language of the text, from clear and open narrations to multiple
texts that eventually compel the reader's complaisance to give way:

> Intertextuality pushed to its most extreme consequences results in the
> disintegration not only of the narrative but also of the discourse. The
> narrative disappears, syntax explodes, the signifier itself begins to show
> cracks, when the assembling of texts is no longer guided by a desire to
> save at any cost a monologic meaning and an aesthetic unity. (Jenny
> 1982, 48)

With each chapter, Achebe seeks to return from the brink of such chaos,
restoring the linear development. But the foolish women's tales persist,
and, at the limit, can be seen exploding in all their glory. Such a moment,
typical of a writer like Tutuola (1967), is to be found with the appearance
of the spirit of fire:

> We managed to look at this fearful creature and we saw clearly that his
> head was three times bigger than his body and it was about six feet long
> and tapered towards the end. The whole head was curved a little bit
> towards his back. As it was a little bit curved towards his back, it was so
> both edges of it had many long and wide feathers which were also curved
> together with the head. His nose was thicker than a round pillar of about
> three feet diameter and it was so much curved like a sickle that it was
> touching his chest. Each of his ears was as big as a big hat. Both his eyes
> were at the point where his curved head started. Each was seeing faintly
> in his skull and it was sparking out fire continuously to all directions to
> which he was turning his head. (44)

At this point we could say that Tutuola has reversed the situation of
Achebe, so that now the principal text is essentially a stitched fabric of
Yoruba tales, while the European subtext persists in preserving the pres-
sures of the novel form.

Intertextuality, the reading of the novel as a weaving of dominant and
subdominant traits, the meeting of discursive traditions and texts through
both form and word, leads in two contrary directions. On the one hand,
the intercalated material, the surreptitious women's talk, enters into a dialectic with the visibly constructed male narrative—a normative pattern is
established. Whether the intertextual transformation of the original source
involves embedding, whether it has a negative, contrastive, passive, or distorted nature, as Michel Arrivé has defined it, the ultimate effect is for it to
be "normalized" by its "insertion in a new textual whole" (Jenny 1982,
50).[14] On the other hand, its presence represents a continual disturbance

to the established norm of the principal text: it disturbs, defamiliarizes, demystifies, regardless of the mystifications upon which it may have originally rested itself. Thus, "[i]ntertextuality is a mechanism of perturbation. Its function is to prevent meaning from becoming lethargic—to avert the triumph of the cliché by a process of transformation" (59).

When African authors first began along the path of imitative fiction in the early years of Europhonic writing, acceptance of this heritage of lethargy was the great risk they incurred—much more than that of being co-opted by a moribund system that was inherently closed and coercive. When African writing became independent it was not because a revolutionary goal was substituted for one that domesticated opposition, but, despite itself and its borrowed humanist rationalizations, because of its foolish stories, which refused to disappear. Like Nwoye's mother, African authors who recounted such tales in their novels knew that they were not the "serious substance," but like Nwoye, they persisted in their enjoyment of them: "Nwoye knew it was right to be masculine and to be violent, but somehow he still preferred the stories that his mother used to tell, and which she no doubt still told to her younger children" (Achebe 1972, 52). By themselves these tales could not defamiliarize European fiction; but in an intertextual context, transposed into embedded, disruptive digressions, they provided the substance for further intertextual development to occur. What began as a project of educative mimesis and as an "effect of the real" became a literature with a tradition in its own right.

Achebe's success as a leading voice in the establishment of this new literature follows from his intuitive sense in creating a language flavored with palm oil, not from his own conventional critical views. Barthes underlines the key role of such language in the creation of a new literature: "The proliferation of modes of writing brings a new Literature into being in so far as the latter invents its language only in order to be a project: Literature becomes the Utopia of language" (1981, 88).

Chapter 3

From Témoignage *to Revolt*

The present must become invisible.

—Dennis Duerden, *African Art and Literature*

Mediation at the Crossroads of Culture

The historical experience of the Europhone African author virtually ensures the need for a mediation process to take place with each act of writing. Instead of a single project of mediation between conflicting cultural values, one may speak of a complex network of mediations that occur with African literature. But the African-European encounter has all the qualities of the Hollywood star system: it vies for our attention, announces its unique importance, attempts to reduce all other participants to supporting roles, to states of dependency. It masks the productive relationships which generate it, disguises the interests that go into its promotion, disguises its own status as a superstructure. At best we can accord it the same status as that of the overinflated role of culture itself in shaping the forces of history, that of a relative autonomy, reflecting the dual roles of participant and product, the subject and the object of the mediating process.

The African author is engaged in the struggle for power with each act of literary expression. This can be seen, in part, in the direct political call for action, or with the broad *engagement* called forth by any historical period when style and subject are deliberately chosen and joined in a common cause. Basic conflicts may be found in every social order, often resembling those delineated by Dennis Duerden (1975) in his paradigm of traditional African societies. There he identifies elements of individual self-assertion that bring change and innovation, and that compete with more rigid and conservative forces that seek to preserve the existing order.[1] These overall forces are basic to African society, and provide us with a useful model with which to consider the mediating role of the African artist.

The value of Duerden's model for us is that of a useful paradigm; it is not intended as an anthropological explanation for literary behavior. As it is based upon traditional societies (what Duerden calls nonindustrial societies), it is questionable how relevant it would be to those individuals who spend a large portion of their lives, including their formative years of schooling, in African or European cities. It would also be too reductive and behaviorist to view the paradigm as demonstrating the existence of absolute causative factors in literary production. However, the struggle for power in society does occur within concrete circumstances that are shaped by inherited relationships and their accompanying values. Traditional values may not determine literary qualities, but they can bear upon the nature of the mediations in which an author is engaged as well as upon the context within which the subject of a discourse is to be located. Literary change can then be viewed, following Tinjanov, as part of a larger pattern within which literary production occurs (its "social function" corresponding to the extraliterary level).

Duerden develops the notion of a society with a series of age grades that resolve the population into three or four groups. Each group has its own roles and responsibilities, each is related to the other groups. Additionally, there is a hierarchical configuration of authority, often encompassing the spiritual and political orders: a supreme god, lesser gods or spirits; kings, chiefs, ancestors, elders, priests—each fitting into structures that vary throughout Africa. A common feature, however, is reflected in the tensions between generations, specifically between elder son and father, corresponding to those between the age grades of mature men and of elders. Duerden is categoric in assigning different social roles to these grades: adult men, those initiated into manhood, are the ones who press for change. They are the generation of sons to have attained maturity; they are going through the process of marrying and having children, and yet, like the elder children of Achebe's Ezeulu, are still strictly bound by the authority of their father, where they will remain until his death. The advent of an urban society, and changing gender roles, will have modified some of the absoluteness of this regimen, but will not have fundamentally changed it.

In much of West Africa, the spirit of the elder must be treated with care when death comes. There are specific ceremonies of burial and especially second burial that are intended to ensure the passage of an honored member of society to an appropriate afterlife. The patterns are complicated, and need not be recapitulated. Suffice it to say that generally it is esteemed elders with children who are deemed worthy of the full passage to ancesterhood. There are several spiritual components to one's being and each has its own appropriate destiny, including the possibility of rein-carnation in one's descendants. Those without children cannot expect the same degrees of fulfillment.

Except for hunting-gathering peoples, traditional African societies are generally ruled by institutions that admit some degree of leadership. In addition to the obvious forms of kingships, even acephalous groups have, or had, means of recognizing prestige in outstanding individuals, and in according them ways of influencing public decisions commensurate with their weight. The pressure of the individual voice, then, is two-sided. On the one hand there are figures like "the Man" in Armah's *The Beautyful Ones Are Not Yet Born* or Okolo in Okara's *The Voice* whose individuality reflects an original ethical impulse—corresponding to those sons who have attained the age of maturity, like Edogo in Achebe's *Arrow of God,* but who chafe at the authority of their elders because they are still under the tutelage of the social decision makers; and there are rulers whose individual power is circumscribed by councils of elders who assure the continuation of traditional custom and law, and who can dethrone or even put to death an unsatisfactory ruler.

The social structure is marked by role divisions, with the pressures for change emanating from the children, especially from the sons, who find a natural ally in the rulers who tend to resist the elders' authority to maintain social order. To be sure, every individual must meet the desire for change and the need to maintain order in his or her own way. The exceptions to the pattern show that it is not monolithic or absolute. Duerden (1975) postulates that some of these exceptions are reflected in social structures, but ultimately admits that the final determinant is aleatory:

> It might be suggested that in matrilineal societies, matrilineal male ancestors represent rigidity and the patrilineal dead represent innovation and disorder and that conversely in patrilineal societies the male ancestors of the patrilineage represent the ordering, rule-making principle, the dead of the matrilineage the opposing principle of change working against the established order. However, we have seen that in the Edo society described by Bradbury the patrilineal ancestors can remain "ghosts" in the bush and opposed to established order if they have no children to "plant" them [i.e., to insure their complete passage through a second burial]. Consequently, there is ambiguity inherent in every man's position until he has a grown-up son to "plant" him. Until that happens he does not know whether he is on the side of order or change. (63)

Duerden goes on to explain that the various age grades, including men who died without children, will respond differently at the time of the burial of an elder: the elders will seek to ensure the passage by presenting gifts to the younger or childless men who might otherwise seek to obstruct that passage. In the case of the Nigeria Edo, the age grades of warriors or of youths are in the service of the Oba, thus reinforcing his position as an agent of change. Edo society is thus not strictly hierarchical, but rather is marked by "a state of uneasy equilibrium poised between the elders of the village on the one side and the king and those chiefs he had chosen to represent him on the other" (63).

This ambiguity in status is reflected on generational levels associated with political power and its dependencies, and can vary depending on whether one has married and had children, often especially male children. All of these determinants of status apply to the women as well, with the same ambiguities for women as for men stemming from the differences between matrilineal and patrilineal societies. In short, the multiple roles and allegiances inherent in the various relationships generated in African societies—to which urban life may often add new dimensions without entirely eliminating the old—will ensure the existence of patterns responsible for change and continuity, while simultaneously the ambiguities built into the systems create the possibility for each individual to respond to either demand according to his or her predilections.

These are the social parameters that give substance to basic attitudes toward time and permanence, which are of critical importance for the act of mediation and of literary expression. The most striking claims made by Duerden arise from his deconstruction of conventional truths concerning permanence in African culture. Duerden asserts that the absence of a long-standing tradition of writing in Africa is in general due to a choice and not to the failure of historical circumstances. That is, Africans either invented scripts or systems of notation, or were exposed to Arabic or other written languages, and chose to restrict the knowledge and development of such systems to outsiders, foreigners, or specialists, or not to use them at all. The reason was that writing preserved in permanent form the laws or beliefs that inhered in the existent power structure, such as the expressed will of a monarch, or the credos pertaining to a religious belief system. It was not so much that change had to be ensured, but that the static immobility of a permanent system ran counter to the needs of social structures built upon harmony and balance. The striking conclusion Duerden reaches is that this hostility to an irreversible institutionalization of power extended to the images of authority, to statues and masks, to all the present forms of expression of power. The past needed to be retained in the living memory, the future prepared for by the continuation of the balancing forces, but the present could not be enshrined in a rigid and unalterable state without unbalancing society. The present could enjoy the polysemic richness of the spoken word, the word that was received from the elders and preserved in the living memory; the image of authority given conventional form. But the word was always to be transmitted, to be refracted in subsequent generations; the masks to be discarded after the ceremonies, recast in new wood after the termites had had their way. In the face of an impermanent past and a potential future, the present could not suffer being reified: it became "invisible."

This leads Duerden to go so far as to assert that in traditional Africa, the permanent preservation of stored memories constituted a "sacrilege" (7). The masks and statues were hidden precisely "to prevent [them] from becoming a stored memory" (8). The careful isolation of the powers and knowledge of the older groups—the men and women as opposed to the children, the elders as opposed to the adult men and women, the priests or kings as opposed to the common people—not only enshrined and assured the protection of this knowledge in the proper repositories, it meant that it too was no more permanent than those who carried the knowledge, and, rather than being indefinitely enshrined in a social institution was inevitably consigned to loss and death with the departure of each elder. The loss of an elder was not irreparable, as each new generation would eventually come into its own, but its accession was always carefully limited and controlled so that the special status of the knowledge would be preserved— thus preserving the status without freezing the knowledge into a rigid canon. The status could be derived only from the individuals who embodied the newly acquired positions, and to acquire those positions they had to have access to the mechanisms of change. The dynamics of change were, in fact, all that were inscribed as permanent in the system, and to ensure this "the old men were encouraged to take their memories with them to their ancestors. They may not impose them on their heirs who wish to be free to fulfill their own destinies" (8).

This explains the refusal to accord a fixed symbolic meaning to objects, to masks or statues, or to social roles. The extension of this concept to the whole society leads to the extraordinary devaluation of the present. The clan and the lineage cannot afford the totalizing pressures of a permanent authority; the cult and the diviner, as well, cannot function on their own authority if they become mere repositories and instruments of an inherited rule: the symbolism cannot function as symbolism if given a fixed and inhering signification; it cannot be permitted to freeze into a permanent sign: "the art must never become a frozen symbolism, must never make the structure of the present into a lasting and visible structure which takes too long to destroy" (24). African art, normally hidden from view, is to be used only in the present, and values that might be associated with some immortal quality are never imputed to it. By the same token, paradoxically, the forces of change, closest to the earth (a permanent locus of impermanence?) cannot tolerate domination from the sun; the gods that are lodged in the sky suffer correction from an earthbound presence that insists upon its right to infuse temporality into the instruments of rule. Thus the objects that consecrate the values of a lineage, hidden away and invisible, are held in the same check as are the kings, priests, elders, and gods: "[Members of lineages] have understood that the fear of dominating, powerful and lasting constants is a permanent fear of the human individual living in a group" (25).

This model reverses the usual portrayal of Africa as subject to a strict hierarchical pattern; it restores a priority to elements of change in a society burdened with stereotypical images of frozen symbology and a limitless transmission of permanent values, of a society incapable of creativity. Further, it not only provides a place for the sons and daughters in the kingdom of the fathers—something that stopped with the intrusion of colonial rule—it rationalizes the mediations that inhere in the social structures. The artist, or *griot,* as Sembène likes to call himself, can easily be situated into these patterns. As praise singer and oral historian, she or he freezes into memory, and learns to recite, the chronology of the important families, rulers, or social events passed down from an elder *griot.* Yet, as Ruth Finnegan (1970) has shown, this does not prevent the *griot* from adding a creative element to the recitation. It is not only the demands of performance that inspire the *griot*'s innovations, but the spirit of the sons and daughters who become, one day, more than students of another's discipline, to be honored as "maîtres de la parole" in their own right.

The development of written literature in Africa was grounded in a series of "*griot* struggles" between visible and invisible values. First came mastery over the word, and then acceptance of an opposition to texts received from the earlier generation, followed by the struggle between a newly emergent subordinated factor against the dominant factor. With defamiliarization and the spread of the new dominant factor creating in turn newly subordinated factors, the revolt of the sons and daughters came full circle. The early African authors of the 1950s and 1960s would seem to have played the role assigned by Duerden to those mature adults impatient to assume the authority of the elders. Against the sun and its permanence, they inscribed a new discourse of opposition and demystification. The project of *récupération* elaborated by authors of *témoignage* literature turned into one of ironic revolt, and the rebel sons became the primary agents of this change. By the time full-blown literatures of revolt had emerged, an entire generation of youthful rebels was claiming its place, including Ngugi, Armah, Oyono, Beti, Ouologuem, Soyinka, Sembène, and shortly thereafter women authors like Head, Aidoo, and Emecheta.

But if the writers of the late 1950s and early 1960s are mostly sons, mostly advocates of change, mostly rebels, they are also mediators of a new power, also instruments of the new kings who introduce the new order of the "sun." Just as *Arrow of God* ends with the foreseeing of the new age, the new dispensation of independence, beginning with the Nkrumahs and Lumumbas, brings a new generation of university-educated graduates who are placed in charge of the country, rather than the traditional chiefs whose power had devolved from colonial rule. The mediation that begins with the struggle between colonialism and traditional African values, that continues with the Africanists, with the Negritude writers, and that is carried into the literatures of *témoignage* and literatures of revolt, is one in which the role and nature of the subject of the novel's discourse is inextricably bound. We can identify an entire spectrum of writings that extends from moderate expressions of acceptance, as with Laye or Birago Diop, to clear-eyed calls for change and reform, as with Achebe or Oyono, to more radical movements of rejection with the latest works of Armah and Ngugi. Yet these thematic positions are only surface ones. The pattern of change, underlying the literature of a youth that is attempting to assert its own rightful position, echoes the larger dynamic of generational struggle and equilibrium in which no single individual can be said to be free from the pressures of both conformism and individualism. The ambiguity of the adventure for Samba Diallo only surfaces with the encounter with Europe. It is more centrally located in the struggle between the *parole* of the Diallobé, which is inscribed by his *maître*—as though permanently carved into his mind—and the letters of a new alphabet that form the unique discourse of the prodigal son. Its ambiguity stems less from the conflict between Europe and Africa and their respective values than from the position of the mediating artist who is both the initiated man and the intended candidate for the position of new *maître*.

The locus of this ambiguity resides in a basic literary conflict. On the one hand, the conventions of a committed discourse in the 1950s were to valorize symbols of revolt and change typically given in works of mimetic realism. This installs permanency upon the present moment that is the focus of the discourse, whether it is set in the past or the present, whether it is thematically concerned with folktales or with contemporary social problems. This is because the project of the narrator-cum-author as a unified subject is consistently put forward. The insistence upon inserting truth into contemporary reality imposes a rigidity upon the discourse that the discourse itself resists. The author can play devil and his advocate in the narrative of the novel, but not on its metatextual levels where the commitment is de rigueur, and where the values of integrity and unified identity are basic assumptions—the same assumptions posed by classical realism.

Yet the ambiguity urged by waves of defamiliarized writing, of polysemic texts, eventually intrudes upon the certitudes of the age. As Laurent Jenny (1982) puts it, the intertextuality inevitably has a perturbing effect. The serious fiction of Laye is followed by the ironic humor of Oyono. And the permanent fixtures of the present dissolve before irony.

If we shift the focus from thematics and society to mode and narrative voice, the nature of the change from literatures of *témoignage* to literatures of revolt becomes clearer. As the former is grounded in the recovery or reaffirmation of values, it subordinates all images of the past, all relationships and all structures, to an elucidation of the vision that presents the recovered values. The present is privileged because it is the time frame within which the narrator presents the narration. It is a centered discourse, corresponding to the unity of the subject that presents it. And it is a logocentric discourse, corresponding to the system of values, of oppositions, that it puts forth. The contrast between Laye and Oyono is crucial here. Laye's nostalgia never turns against the narrator's final vision: it is clearly presented as a portrait of a past whose relationship to the narrator in the present is determined.

Oyono, however, calls that very relationship into question at the outset of *Une Vie de boy* with the ambivalent position of the author of the notebooks when he asks, "Brother, what are we? What are we blackmen who are called French?" (1982, 4).* Ngaté is right to pose the question of the narratee when one considers the development of the literature. However, it is no less significant to consider what happens when the voice that addresses that narratee returns its own demystifying gaze on itself—and when, indeed, the complaisant narratee is subtly included in that apparently self-conscious gesture. We are in the presence of a shift in the conditions of possibility that occurs when the allegorizing mode of *Le Regard du roi* is succeeded by the "irony of ironies" (de Man 1983, 221) in a work like *Le Vieux nègre et la médaille,* where the safe position of the narratee's laughter at Meka at the beginning of the novel is undermined by the end when the self-conscious voice turns its irony inward. The unstated difference between an ostensible authorial voice and that of the narrator, hidden in the fictions of literatures of *témoignage,* no longer remains invisible, and it is the moment of this proclaimed self-consciousness that separates the narrative

---

* "Mon frère, mon frère, que sommes-nous? Que sont tous les nègres qu'on dit français?" (1956a, 12–3).

self from the present, from the world: "The moment when this difference is asserted is precisely the moment when the author does not return to the world. He asserts instead the ironic necessity of not becoming the dupe of his own irony and discovers that there is no way back from his fictional self to his actual self"(de Man 1983, 219). This *blick* suffices to unravel the thread of certainties upon which the pattern of demystification was based, because once the irony becomes turned on the self, it is permanently ungrounded and the unraveling cannot be stopped. De Man calls it madness, vertigo, and dizziness—absolute comedy, in citing Baudelaire. It is described as though the mind itself free-falls into an uncontrollable spiral.

> It may start as a casual bit of play with a stray loose end of the fabric, but before long the entire texture of the self is unraveled and comes apart. The whole process happens at an unsettling speed. Irony possesses an inherent tendency to gain momentum and not to stop until it has run its full course; from the small and apparently innocuous exposure of a small self-deception it soon reaches the dimensions of the absolute. (de Man 1983, 213)

The fractured self positioned by irony cannot construct a reality based upon the present, cannot erect a contemporary scene that is comprehensible in terms of its continuities with past patterns of production, with social relationships, with controlling forces that underlie existence and account for its motion, nor even with its own personal history. "Irony divides the flow of temporal experience into a past that is pure mystification and a future that remains harnassed forever by a relapse within the inauthentic. It can know this inauthenticity but can never overcome it" (de Man 1983, 222). The fractured self sees its own fall, and as that stems from an ironic stance, it is what separates its consciousness from the object of its regard, even when it is itself that object. The moment of separation is that of the instantaneous present: "Irony comes closer to the pattern of factual experience and recaptures some of the factitiousness of human existence as a succession of isolated moments lived by a divided self. Essentially the mode of the present, it knows neither memory nor prefigurative duration" (226). Both allegory, in which the past is the point of reference, and irony, which cannot construct continuities with the past, are distinct from the realist mode of temporality: "Both are determined by an authentic experience of temporality which, seen from the point of view of the self engaged in the world, is a negative one" (226).

It is precisely this negative experience of temporality when seen from the realist point of view that informs the mediating role of the African artist for whom the present has become invisible. This is because the act of demystification that is fundamental to irony is what drives the irrepressible demands for change and for full being made by the initiates into the age grade of adulthood. And perhaps it is also because allegory, unlike symbolism, refers present experience back to another level of temporality that does not depend upon contemporary values for its authenticity. Thus the moment in which the present becomes invisible corresponds to that in which the divided self of the subject becomes aware of itself and simultaneously becomes aware of the impossibility of taking hold of that self, feeling that "there is no way back," and that, paradoxically, it is the allegorical appeal to the past that is the condition of possibility for the initiate's own new grade of being.

As with De Man's (1983) reading of Stendahl (227–28), so, too, can we see in the generation of Oyono and Beti a thematization of ironic distance that succeeds, despite the vision of inauthenticity and despair, in allegorizing that irony so as to construct a new literature of revolt.

From Declarative to Interrogative Text:
The Passage to Revolt and Postrevolt Literatures

The passage from literatures of *témoignage* to literatures of revolt, literatures of the oxymoron, and postrevolt literatures can be measured by the ways in which the subject is presented to us and by the ways in which we, in turn, are interpellated as subjects. For Catherine Belsey it is possible to define literature along the linguistic lines defined by Emile Benveniste when he analyzed the three possible types of sentences as declarative, interrogative and imperative (Belsey 1981, 90). For Belsey, classic realist literature corresponds to the declarative type—it states without seeking to elicit questions and without posing any. The assumptions of the declarative statement rest on the unstated assertion that this is how things are: The declarative statement conveys a portrait of "the real world," without imposing the imperative demand to change things or to question or challenge the basis of its own vision. Its assumptions are broad: that there exists and can be known such things as the truth, as a preexistent and prevailing order, as a subject who stands behind these assumptions at the moment they are enunciated, a subject Louis Althusser appropriately calls the Absolute Subject, the "authority of the social formation" (Belsey 1981, 62).

In general, literature is multifaceted, multilayered. It is no doubt possible to read perversely: to come at Dickens and Brecht, to use Belsey's examples, or Laye and Soyinka to use our own, as if the texts written by the first author in these pairs conveyed interrogation marks and as if Brecht or Soyinka were purveyors of humanist truths and answers. But inasmuch as the text participates in its own interpellation of the reading subject, it must be possible to define the dominant reading as fitting the patterns of a declarative or interrogative rhetoric. This is clearly made visible when we consider the role of the subject in the text.

Following Lacan, Belsey states that the subject is constituted through language: that it is through the use of language that we acquire consciousness of ourselves and of our difference from what is not ourselves. We both recognize and constitute ourselves as subjects when we use language, and we express our sense of ourselves primarily through language as well. But this recognition and this expression is split. When I use "I" in a sentence, I am constructing a discourse within which I fit my sense of myself. The "I" in the discourse, the subject of the *énoncé*, is thus different from the one who is constructing the discourse, the "I" of the enunciation. For Lacan the subject whom one recognizes (one's image of oneself) differs from the subject who recognizes that image of the self that is conveyed, as in a mirror, from without. These split subjects, like the split discursive first-person voices, are divided between the one who expresses him/herself (and is only partially conscious of what is being expressed), and the one who is created (the subject of the *énoncé*). The gap between the two is crucial. The voice that expresses itself, the I that tries to give voice to its vision of the world and of itself, is seen only partially in the "I" that it constructs. The unconscious lies as a vast buried repository of subjective reality, not expressed through the visible subject.

With Laye, as in classic realism, that gap is made unproblematic through the conventional assumption that the subject must assume an identity between the speaking voice and the actor, that is, between the consciousness of the narrator and that of the protagonist. The unaddressed, invisible third subject, that of the implied author, is never evoked. The way in which this bridging of identities is accomplished is by turning the gaze of the reader away from the literariness of the text—to construct a world of words so that the world can be seen without the words being noticed.

The reader becomes witness, *témoin,* to the world not as stage or staged but as real. The words become, in Barthes's phrase, invisible, the text "lisible." For this to happen gaps and contradictions that normally arise must be smoothed over. Thus, when contradictory ideological positions interpellate the subject, the classic realist texts assume a higher position of resolution. If Laye is torn between the various directions indicated by his mother and his father, in the end he decides on a course that appears to be not only inevitable and natural, but that accounts for his mother's dismay in such a way as to incorporate it into a larger synthesis. His going out into the wide world is easily assimilable to the traditional patterns of initiation and of meaning that inevitably accompany the passage to adulthood. The direct interpellation of the reader—"Do we have any secrets any more!" (1978, 109)* —joins us to this larger sense of an Absolute Subject for whom the negative answer to the question appears to have been provided as a foregone conclusion. This is the function of ideology as given by Althusser: "Ideology obscures the real conditions of existence by presenting partial truths. It is a set of omissions, of gaps rather than lies, smoothing over contradictions, appearing to provide answers to questions which in reality it evades, and masquerading as coherence in the interests of the social relations . . . " (quoted in Belsey 1981, 57).

The key to this approach to ideology lies in the role of the subject: just as we can say that language constitutes the subject, so, too, is it true that language is constructed along ideological lines. Language comes along in no more neutral a fashion than the individuals who employ it. It is spoken so as to be put to some use, and that sense of a direction or purpose is what determines its character as a discourse. Discourse is grounded in assumptions, "truths," normalized and naturalized beliefs—a system of representations that give form to ideology. Once ideology is expressed, it is constitutive of the subject, just as the subject constitutes ideology through the expression or discourse he or she frames. Now, this framing, as we have seen, involves the division of the subject into the one who expresses him/herself and the one being expressed, the one who recognizes and the one being recognized. Thus, whereas ideology seeks to totalize and to harmonize contradictions, its very means of coming into being, that is, its expression, is by nature divided. The fundamental basis of realism lies in this pattern of ideology, in its project of "'constituting' concrete individuals as subjects" (Althusser 1971, 160). Thus realism, like its ideological frame, is grounded in the need to smooth over contradictions.

Once constituted by the project of ideology, the subject is shaped by two assumptions. The first is that the act of being recognized (of recognizing oneself) as a subject implies/implicates the notion of subjective individuality. One bears witness, ultimately and always, to oneself. Even if it is a question of a real world with real problems, like the one Sembène is so concerned with, the consciousness—the subject—that both constructs and recognizes that world must do so by constructing and assenting to a discourse about that world. The declarative statement never appears by itself—someone must construct it, but it always acts as though it were not a construct, but rather a mere reflection. And that is the second trait of this literature—its pretension not to recognize the role of language:

---

* "Avons-nous encore des secrets!"(1972, 108)

> The ideology of liberal humanism [and of classic realism] assumes a
> world of non-contradictory . . . individuals whose unfettered conscious-
> ness is the origin of meaning, knowledge and action. It is in the interest
> of this ideology above all to suppress the role of language in the con-
> struction of the subject, its own role in the interpellation of the subject,
> and to preserve the individual as free, unified, autonomous subjectivity.
> (Belsey 1981, 67)

Laye's use of a "limpid" classical French was completely conventional, completely invisible in the sea of francophone prose, as though he
were completely oblivious to the actual spoken languages that swirled
around him in Kouroussa, Conakry, and Paris. He refrains from calling
out his own name—it is almost never mentioned in *L'Enfant noir*. Yet the
unnamed one is always assumed to share the name given to the voice that
addresses us. His dilemmas always involve choices of action: we share
with him the unproblematic assumption that he is an autonomous subject
capable of deciding between options, and, in fact, as he is from the outset
continuously faced with options, we deduce that being an autonomous
subject entails being free to choose between different options. The unity
of the subject is all the stronger for being assumed, for never being the
object of inquiry, and for being the basis for the act of choice.

Oyono breaks with all these patterns, setting the stage for the new literatures of revolt. The image of the unified subject is strangely mirrored.
If Toundi is the protagonist of *Une Vie de boy,* the subject of the *énoncé* in
the Notebooks, there is the other unnamed Cameroonian, also a
"Français," who shares his fate and whose sympathies strangely resonate
with those of Toundi. He is the secret sharer. As we shall see, Engamba
has a similar function of doubling Meka in *Vieux Nègre,* whereas Barnabas
can be described as divided against himself in *Chemin d'Europe.* This doubling is reflected in the narrative structure, especially in *Une Vie de boy,*
which presents us with the metanarrative of the fugitive Cameroonian that
encases that of Toundi's Notebooks. This structural parenthesis is
stretched out into a linear sequence with the double narrative concerning
Meka and Engamba in *Vieux Nègre.* In contrast, *L'Enfant noir* is constructed as a conventional unilinear story that unfolds in time directly.

If choosing is the act of the autonomous subject, we can say that characters like Toundi and Meka are chosen, rather than that they choose. Indeed, their drama consists in coming to an awareness of having submitted
to outside choice, an awareness that the one being chosen, a "boy," a dog, a
recipient of a medal, is a dupe as much as a lucky winner—"le chien du roi
[et] le roi des chiens" (Oyono 1956a, 32). Seduction, the weakness for
sweets, supplants free choice. In *Chemin* Barnabas is clearly both dog and

winner of a scholarship—and if not a dupe, he is, as Richard Bjornson (1989) puts it, "victimized in a more profound sense than either Toundi or Meka.... [H]is calculated individualism permanently isolates him from any genuinely human contact with Europeans or fellow Africans" (1).

The act of interpellation places us and the protagonist in radically different places. Whereas we witness with Laye (as narrator) the triumphs, fears, struggles, separations, anguish, and praise singing experienced by Laye (as character), the "location" occupied by Toundi and Engamba and the reader's perspective on them are much more problematic. Where are we when Toundi has fled up the tree to escape M. Janopoulos's dogs—what is the place where laughter, embarrassment, fear, and anger emerge? Where are we when Toundi's invisibility disappears as he stands in his accustomed spot next to the refrigerator while the Commandant and Madame squirm before Toundi's averted gaze? Where are we when Meka appears on the stage of the community center, or when he stands in the circle, agonizing under the broiling sun, as Kerala comes to the difficult realization that they have been duped? These are more than painful scenes—they are stage sets for divided feelings, for multiple vantages, for multiple names.

Toundi Ondoua is equally divided: though he is baptized, and wears a St. Christopher medal to signal his allegiance, only his African names are employed, the Joseph going practically unnoticed. Son of Toundi, he becomes M. Toundi. But as son of Zama, his Maka mother, he tells us he comes from a "race" known as "people eaters" (Oyono 1982, 16),* that is, Maka. He identifies himself as Maka, and yet also as "Français" from Cameroon (12). No less dramatic is the scene in prison where Meka is forced to give his legal name, Laurence, which he can pronounce only as "Roron." And no less complicated is the given name Barnabas for the educated, cynical, and ambitious student. These names call out, demanding a person, a persona, to wear them. They are indeed ideological interpellations: "People recognize (misrecognize) themselves in the way ideology interpellates them, or in other words, addresses them as subjects, *calls them by their names* and in turn 'recognizes' their autonomy" (Belsey 1981, 61). Once this recognition is accomplished, the subject acquires a double relationship to ideology—both passive and active. As an active subject, the individual, according to Althusser, recognizes his/herself as a center from which action can emanate: "a center of initiatives, author of and responsible for its actions" (quoted in Belsey 1981, 62). But by passively submitting to the ideology, the subject acquiesces in and acknowledges the

---

* "mangeurs d'hommes" (Oyono, 1956a,16)

authority represented in ideology as "the Absolute Subject." The free subject freely accepts subjugation. This is never questioned by Laye. Oyono's novels are either explicitly (*Boy, Vieux Nègre*) or implicitly (*Chemin*) about the moment in which the divided consciousness develops, coming to an awareness of the negative side to one's former acquiescence. Finally, we can anticipate the later works of Soyinka, Aidoo, Mudimbe, and Sony Labou Tansi, for whom the assurance of "consciencization" is never easy, indeed, is no longer possible.

The passage from Laye to Oyono to Mudimbe, from *témoignage* to revolt and thence to oxymoron, takes us from the classic realism of the declarative text to the openness and heteroglossia of the interrogative text. This is made clear if we employ Belsey's analysis of the subject in the classic realist text. Her conclusions concerning the subject bring together both the role of the subject within the text and that of the reader with respect to the text:

> The reader is invited to perceive and judge the "truth" of the text, the coherent, non-contradictory interpretation of the world as it is perceived by an author whose autonomy is the source and evidence of the truth of the interpretation. This model of intersubjective communication, of shared understanding of a text which re-presents the world, is the guarantee not only of the truth of the text but of the reader's existence as an autonomous and knowing subject in a world of knowing subjects. In this way classic realism constitutes an ideological practice in addressing itself to readers as subjects, interpellating them in order that they freely accept their subjectivity and their subjection. (1981, 69)

Along with identifying the role of the subject, Belsey identifies three fundamental traits of classic realism: (1) illusionism, what we have identified as its mimetic properties; (2) closure, the sense that enigmas are solved at the end, in a process whereby truth is disclosed, order reestablished—an order "recognizable as a reinstatement or a development of the order which is understood to have preceded the events of the story itself" (70); and (3) a hierarchy of discourses in which a privileged discourse subordinates all other forms of discourse in the text—a familiar Formalist position.

The *interrogative* text does not subject the text to the illusionism of classic realism, but indirectly calls attention to its literariness. The magical realism of Sony Labou Tansi, the Brechtian breakdown of illusion with Soyinka, mark their distance from Achebe and Laye. Instead of the assurance of closure, of answers, of a reinstated order, the interrogative text leaves us with Toundi in flight, Meka turning away from an established colonial order, with Soyinka's Eman, Professor, and Elesin dying ambivalent deaths—with the reader displaced along with the subject inter-pellated by the text. "Now I don't care any more" (my trans.),* Meka blithely states, as he spits at the end of *Le Vieux Nègre.* The gesture and the tone complete the act of turning away. For Belsey, "the interrogative text invites an answer or answers to the questions it poses" (1981, 92). "I'm just an old man" (my trans.)† may suggest closure, an answer to the ques-tions of identity, the realization of bitter truths, but it is also the answer of the tortoise[2] —a return to the African tradition of reticence associated with old age and wisdom. The hidden, unspoken statement of identity is not for quick and easy banter—it is left open behind the mask that Meka has now learned to assume, as in the final scene at prison with Gosier d'Oiseau. It leaves the façade of the story closed, but the subtext restored to its appropriate position of openness. Oyono moves the declaration for-ward to the full interrogation of a time and its ideologies.

In biographical literature of the first stage, as with Laye, the narrator's re-lationship to his earlier self is governed by the need for *récupération.* The literature that follows *témoignage* does not seek to recuperate, nor aim at writing degree zero. The past and its heroes are not idealized, nor held as a standard by which to judge the present. The narrator does not justify him/herself, his culture, or her people by asserting, "Look how far I (we) have come." Instead, there is a gap between the narrator-subject and the protagonist-subject. In post*témoignage* writings, instead of a past, a family, and a cultural background being reconstructed in positive terms, exemplary of African culture, the past is often viewed negatively, as something from which the protagonist has escaped, as in *Mission Terminée,* as well as other early Beti novels, where youth is betrayed by the collusion between mis-guided parents and colonialists. Similarly, Oyono gives voice to youth's rejection in the prostitutes' negative judgments in *Chemin d'Europe;* Ouo-loguem broadly condemns the past; Kourouma mocks Fama's pretensions to former Malinke glory and power; Head and Aidoo extend this struggle to gendered oppression inherent in traditional Tswana or Fante cultures; and Okara condemns oppressive traditional authority in *The Voice.* These form the voices of a new generation of writers.

In their early works, Oyono and Beti construct similar relationships within their central family structures. Power plays a decisive role: the father typically exercises power unjustly over children and wife. Usually

---

* "A présent, je m'en moque" (1956b,187).

† "Je ne suis qu'un vieil homme" (1956b, 187).

the only children mentioned are sons, although there is also a daughter in Beti's *Le Roi miraculé*. Usually the story is told from the son's point of view, so that the oppressed mother and son share a common fate. They are further drawn together by a close mother-son relationship that counterbalances the father-son struggle. Typically, the son revolts while the mother suffers silently or, at best, silently rebels. Further, Oyono carries this set of relationships into the colonial situation and into race relations. He is often interested in depicting the interaction between European and African cultures rather than in creating a world that remains enclosed within African society. Thus, what is problematic in the family relationships is carried over, in *Une Vie de boy,* to Toundi's submission/silent-revolt against the Commandant and his love/hate for Madame.

In general the pattern is set for a revolt in which family relations provide the model. On the one hand we see the heritage of this revolt passed on in a broad range of parent-child relationships. The rebellious child is represented in Sembène's work by such characters as Rama, El Hadj's daughter in *Xala*; by Nyambura in Ngugi's *The River Between*; and in Soyinka's works by Eman in *The Strong Breed,* Igwezu in *The Swamp Dwellers,* and Lakunle in *The Lion and the Jewel.* Similar figures may be found in the generation of the "interpreters," continuing through Olunde, the son of Soyinka's King's Horseman. On the other hand, the "odeur du père" carries the revolt to the level of the surrogate fathers, "les pères blancs," and eventually to their surrogate rule, with Mudimbe and Ouologuem providing the models. In the end, the comforting line of classic realist literature, begun with literatures of *témoignage,* yields to protest and revolt, even deviance and madness, as political and psychological rebels give voice to their acts of refusal in texts that insist upon hard lines of interrogation rather than upon the directness of straight declaration. By the end of the 1960s this new direction in the dominant discourse was established. And it has provided the foundation for the new directions of "postrevolt" writings that define the current trend.

Part Two
▼▼▼▼▼▼▼▼▼▼

Chapter 4

The Margins of Autobiographical Literature of Témoignage

CAMARA LAYE, *L'Enfant noir*

Though chronological priority lies with the lesser works, like Bakary Diallo's *Force Bonté* (1926), Ousmane Socé's *Karim* (1935), or Abdoulaye Sadji's *Maïmouna* (1953), Camara Laye's *L'Enfant noir* has played a more important role in establishing a tradition of works of *témoignage*. First published in 1953, it was written by Laye while he lived in lonely and impoverished conditions in Paris, completing a *stage* in auto mechanics. The *récit* might best be regarded as an effort to recapture a distant home and fading memories of youth under conditions of *dépaysement*.

The epigraphs that precede the *récit* praising Laye's mother—"Femme noire, femme africaine, ô toi ma mère"—echo Senghor's "Femme nue, femme noire" and lead us to expect a Negritudinist theme. Instead, the basic European/African dialectic of Negritude is absent, and the novel takes the form of a series of episodes, expanding like concentric circles. Their radiation outward suggests the movement of alienation as Laye progressively experiences success as a student, which leads him farther and farther from home.

Throughout the novel Laye maintains a double point of view: that of the child as protagonist experiencing the events, usually employing for this point of view the imperfect past tense, and that of the narrator using the present tense to comment on the action. To musings such as, "Was it the ovenlike heat or the oil . . . which attracted the snakes?"* the narrator

---

* "Est-ce cette chaleur de four ou est-ce l'huile . . . qui attirait les serpents?" (Laye [1953]

responds, "I don't know."* Derrida situates this present moment of the narration in a timeless twilight zone. Using Maurice Blanchot's terminology, he contrasts the "narrative voice," which is neutral and which utters the work "from the placeless place where the work is silent," to the "narratorial voice," which is the voice of a subject "recounting something, remembering an event or a historical sequence, knowing who he is, where he is, and what he is talking about" (Derrida 1979a, 105). The distance between the two temporal zones of the narration gives Laye's novel its distinctive air of sentimentality and nostalgia. "I was a little boy playing around my father's hut. How old would I have been at that time? I can not remember exactly" (Laye 1978a, 17).†

The line between the continuous past—"My father was openhanded; in fact, a lavish giver" (Laye 1978a, 20)‡ —and a specific action— " 'There is a snake!' I cried out"** —is effaced by the same kind of movement, from continuous or habitual action to specific event, that characterizes the shift from the narrator's to the protagonist's point of view. For example, when the black snake appears in the courtyard that defined the limits of the child's world, the voice that presents us with the rule against playing with the snake approaches us with the neutrality of the third person "il" ("not an 'I,' not an ego" [Derrida 1979a, 105]), and "atopically" ("It takes place placelessly, being both *atopical,* mad, extravagant, and *hypertopical,* both placeless and overplaced" (105): "[D]epuis qu'on m'avait défendu de jouer avec les serpents, sitôt que j'en *apercevais* un, j'*accourais* chez ma mère" (13; my stress) [Since I had been forbidden to play with snakes, as soon as I saw one I would run to my mother]. Once this "natural," neutral perspective is established, Laye enters into the person of the narrator, playing the past against the present with perfect ease. The zero-degree narration slides commentary into action as if the narration itself were invisible ("a silent voice, then, withdrawn into its 'voicelessness' " [Derrida 1979a, 104]): "Et moi, je serrais ma mère contre moi, j'essuyais ses larmes, je disais . . . que disais-je? Tout et n'importe quoi, mais c'était sans importance" (188) [I held my mother close, I wiped her

---

1972, 13). All page references to this text are to the 1972 edition. Unless otherwise indicated by reference to the 1978 translation by James Kirkup and Ernest Jones, all translations are my own.

★ "Je ne sais pas" (13).

† "J'étais enfant et je jouais près de la case de mon père. Quel âge avais-je en ce temps-là? Je ne me rappelle pas exactement" (9).

‡ "Mon père donnait facilement et même avec prodigalité" (12).

★★ "Il y a un serpent! criais-je" (13).

tears, I said . . . what did I say? Everything and anything that came to mind, but nothing of importance.] The phrase "c'était sans importance" is clearly part of the process of recollection, a metatextual commentary, but as the course of events in the novel brings the reader closer to the implied present moment of the act of narration, the sense of judgment and understanding of past events is gradually grafted onto the character, "l'enfant noir," whose earlier naiveté is replaced by the dry-eyed, tight-lipped vision of the self-exiled narrator. The continuity is reinforced by the use of the conditional, as we see toward the end of the novel when Laye uses this mood to enhance the suggestion of an actual occurrence in his life, implying an existence for the narrator outside the narrative: "Marie . . . would accompany me to Dakar. . . ." *

In *L'Enfant noir* the reader is continually led beyond the events to the perspective of the implied author. We are left wondering, as in any autobiography of youth, about Laye's ultimate fate, and not unnaturally we look for the sequel that will satisfy our craving. The apparently open form, reinforced by the open-ended conclusion, is part of the autobiographical "contract," in which the author's life is presented as if extending beyond the events given at the end of the novel. This belies the uncontractual dimension of autobiography, specifically its structure, which in this case is built on a series of expanding concentric rings or circles. The best model for describing this progressive action of distancing or removing oneself from a center is found, appropriately enough, in the focal episode of the novel, the initiation.

Like the autobiographical narrative itself, initiation is inscribed within a double perspective; it inhabits a dual realm contextualized simultaneously by its realistic appearance and its symbolic subtext, creating a discourse that is both literally what it states and figuratively suggestive of hidden meanings. In his introduction to *Le Maître de la parole,* Laye (1978b) evokes this discourse by referring to "des profondeurs cachées" that underlie the realities of the world as seen by the African. In *L'Enfant noir,* when Laye's father describes the dream in which the black snake comes to him, or when he gives his son advice on religious or moral values, he stays within the conventions of realism. By describing an event as if the narrator were an objective witness, as if the conventional line between the plausible and the implausible were obvious and natural—so that even when describing his own parents' magical powers the narrator feels compelled to call those events inexplicable—Laye remains well within the logic and

---

* "Marie . . . m'accompagnerait jusqu'à Dakar. . . " (189).

linear continuities of realism. The figurative reading, however, lacks these clear-cut contours. This oscillation is manifested when Laye recounts his reaction to the sight of his father's hand caressing the black serpent: "Each caress and responding tremor invariably threw me into an inexpressible confusion. I thought of I know not what mysterious conversation—the hand inquired and the tremor answered."* The silence before the mystery, a suggestive attitude of questioning and waiting, asking and answering, feeling and responding, discretion and desire, adumbrate the fuller exposition of the mystery in the scene between the old woman, Dioki, and her serpents in *Le Regard du roi* (Laye [1954] 1982) where the dominant position of the realist reading over the figurative is reversed.

For Laye's generation, the sense of one overriding question and answer pose a particular problem, as we see in the allusions that follow this scene with the serpent:

> Yes. It was like a conversation. Would I too converse that way some day?
> No. I would continue to attend school. Yet I should have liked so much to place my hand, my own hand, on that snake, and to understand and listen to that tremor too; but I did not know whether the snake would have accepted my hand, and I felt now that he would have nothing to tell me. I was afraid that he would never have anything to tell me. (Laye 1978a, 29)†

Laye's success as a student obliged him to travel farther and farther from home and to suffer the pain of rupture, which was linked to the student's newly defined success and growth. His creative response was to turn alienation into a simulation of the self-abnegation, self-immolation, and "death" that precede the initiation and full incorporation into society. The novel of initiation that resulted gives particular weight to the role of the community, even if, as is the case here, Laye's path leads away from the knowledge of his fellow initiates, from their traditional way of life. We never lose sight of the unstated premise that his ascension and successes are desirable goals, that the alienation and sadness are merely part of the price to be paid, and that, no matter how poignant the feeling of loss, the

---

* "Chaque caresse et le frémissement qui y répondait—me jetaient chaque fois dans un inexprimable confusion: je pensais à je ne sais quelle mystérieuse conversation; la main interrogeait, le frémissement répondait . . . " (Laye [1953] 1973, 20).

† "Oui, c'était comme une conversation. Est-ce que moi, aussi, un jour, je converserais de cette sorte? Mais non: je continuais d'aller à l'école! Pourtant j'aurais voulu, j'aurais tant voulu poser à mon tour ma main sur le serpent, comprendre, écouter à mon tour ce frémissement, mais j'ignorais comment le serpent eût accueilli ma main et je ne pensais pas qu'il eût maintenant rien à me confier, je craignais bien qu'il n'eût rien à me confier jamais. . . . " (20–21)

grounds for his decisions are never questioned: the new community he joins, *its* secrets, knowledge, customs, rituals, good or bad points, are ignored—as if this silence were part of the oath of membership.

The act of initiation bears upon the question of identity because of the particular relationship between the individual and the group involved. In his discussion of the ego in African society, Dennis Duerden indicates the nature of this relationship:

> [T]he ego is not found in the separate human body but exists in the group in which a man lives.
>
> A man's ego cannot exist on its own. It is this principle which explains why the present is never visible. What is happening to me now is not just happening to me. It is happening to the whole group in relation to its environment, but the properties of the group are vague and shadowy. Its boundaries fade away to a distant horizon, extending from the family to the lineage, from the lineage to the clan, from the clan to the linguistic and territorial grouping. However, each man somehow constructs his own universe of such wider relationships, and this is what is meant by his personal destiny. (Duerden 1975, 10)[1]

The act of circumcision or excision, and the mental equivalents of these incisions into the flesh, are felt deeply within the individual as a coming to terms with his or her own being. The space of the African who is alone—in the hut like Eman in *The Strong Breed* (Soyinka 1973), inscribed in the circle like Meka in *Le Vieux nègre et la médaille* (Oyono [1956b] 1979), grotesquely trapped in a latrine like the Man in *The Beautyful Ones* (Armah 1968), standing before the threshold of the initiation house like Laye separated from his mother, or even among one's fellow villagers (as when Laye participated in the dance celebrating the boys' impending initiation)—is complemented in each case by communal and social dimensions of identity. Though Laye joined in the circle of dancers, and though the entire village shared in the celebration, each boy still felt something of his own special place. Laye paints his image of isolation in the midst of the crowd by highlighting his embarrassed reactions to his second mother's act of flourishing of a pen in proud display of his educational accomplishments.

For the contemporary African novelist, the close relationship between the community and the individual subject is represented in images that emphasize the unease of isolated figures who stand not as marginalized outcasts but as protagonists of a new social order. This unease should be attached to *any* definition of the subject that attempts to delimit the subject within a given locus. The same "shadowy" set of boundaries that give definition to the group are best seen as fundamental to the concept of the ego itself. This provides us with the best approach to African literary discourse, and despite the reservations voiced by Jonathan Ngaté, I would apply his definition of Francophone African literature to *all* African discourses: "Unlike, say, Bambara or Xhosa literature then, francophone African literature is not an Afrocentric given. It is best appreciated as being *the site of intersections between different traditions*" (Ngaté 1988, 21; my stress).

While Ngaté is referring to the encounter of African and European literary traditions, we might equally evoke the intersections *within* a given discursive tradition. A beginning might be made with the dimensions of discourse corresponding to Wole Soyinka's binary opposition of mystic/mundane. The hidden/open meaning, especially in oral African literature, is reflected in the pair metaphor/metonymy. The literal level of the narration, constructed typically along realist lines, is characterized by metonymy, or contiguity, as Roman Jakobson applied the term to narrative. Jakobson associates metaphor, or similarity, more with poetry than prose. He evokes the presence of both poles in examples of language usage, but, like the Formalists, pronounces one to be dominant:

> Since on any verbal level—morphemic, lexical, syntactic, and phraseological—either of these two relationships (similarity and contiguity) can appear—and each in either of two aspects—an impressive range of possible configurations is created. Either of the two gravitational poles may prevail. In Russian lyrical songs, for example, metaphoric constructions predominate, while in the heroic epics the metonymic way is predominant. (Jakobson 1971, 255)

For Jakobson this bipolarity reflects the nature of language. Although he speaks of language as being constructed along the two lines defined by contiguity or similarity—thus implying an indefiniteness—in the end he always asserts the presence of a dominant feature, as though the aphasiacal troubles of speech provide definiteness to language as to all sign systems ("[t]he alternative predominance of one or the other of these two processes is by no means confined to verbal art" [Jakobson 1971, 256]).

This basic bipolarity of speech is particularly applicable to African literature, especially as it is viewed by such major authors as Laye, Senghor, and Soyinka. For Laye the quality of truth, in Africa, is distinct from what it appears to be in Europe. Whereas spiritual reality is experienced both rarely and transcendentally in the European context, in Africa it is a frequent companion of life. Yet its essence remains aloof from everyday reality, whence the phrase, "profondeurs cachées".[2]

Laye's work reflects Soyinka's dualism of mystic and mundane. If metonymy and realism dominate *L'Enfant noir,* metaphor and symbolism, or religious allegory, prevail in Laye's *Regard du roi,* complementing the autobiography. Both ends of the narrative spectrum are uneasily juxtaposed in *Dramouss* (Laye 1966).

As narrator, Laye's insights, conferred by his distance from home and his experience of the pain of separation, as well as the act of recording these memories and events, imply for him, as for others, the elevation of a privileged term. We are not surprised to find that this is always the one associated with metaphor: symbol, spirituality, heart, mystery. In a sense, the presence of truth, for Laye, and for Birago Diop and Senghor as well, is given, and the term functions as immediate signifier and transcendental signified simultaneously. We are present to the forces of "masks" that speak, of statues that are "ridden," of "carriers" that transmit, not in their own name or through their own power, but through the agency of the ancestors, the dead, the gods.

However, the mysterious does not remain invisible, disembodied, or omnipotent. It must wear the "face" of another, must be given a face that is often only the temporary form it assumes. After the dance, the mask may be discarded. Indeed, according to Duerden, not only can the dead eventually die, they are made to die. Earth rules over sky, in African mythic thought, and the inscription of permanent lines is intentionally suppressed. Thus Duerden's most astonishing conclusion: "It appears . . . that the artist in nonindustrial African society, be he poet, painter or storyteller, wishes to avoid making his symbols permanent, wishes somehow to prevent them from becoming universally accepted symbols" (Duerden 1975, 11). Duerden then proceeds to "turn [Victor] Turner's and [Mary] Douglas' model [of initiates and deities] upside down" (Duerden 1975, 14) by postulating that the general African avoidance of common contact with divine forces is due to the polluting influence that would follow: "It is possible . . . to regard the infinite as polluting, the whiteness of the sky as a symbol of impurity and deity as a destructive force to be kept isolated and guarded, hidden away except when its use is absolutely necessary" (Duerden 1975, 14). This explains, too, the elaborate ritualism involved in the passage of the dead to the other realm, the second burials intended to ensure their removal and the process of distancing the living from their potentially dangerous influences. Duerden's reversal is actually a deconstruction of the entire bipolar system elaborated above, not only because it reverses the conventional privileging, but it does so by demonstrating that the dismissed term, impurity, is actually the basis for the entire structure.

The same holds for the opposition of metaphor and metonymy as applied to time. We would expect metaphor to be associated with the eternal values of symbol, and metonymy with the linear, realistic passage of time. Conventional mythological analysts—Mircea Eliade, Turner, E. R.

Leach, Wole Soyinka—would have us believe that African societies adhere to typical nonindustrial patterns of cyclical time. The cyclical/linear distinction is replicated in the narrator's atemporal frame versus the linear diegesis of the protagonist's story in *L'Enfant noir*. And this same division is repeated in the way images of atemporality and cyclical time are associated with the king in *Le Regard du roi,* and in the "mundane" time frame of events associated with Clarence. If we can not escape these divisions by inventing a new time-space frame, we can reverse the act of marginalization, just as Duerden turns Turner and Douglas upside down. As Duerden rejects the temporo-centric bipolarity in favor of a pattern of defamiliarization, he recaps the very processes by which *L'Enfant noir* establishes itself within the frame of African literature.

> African societies and African art are not trying to stand outside linear time and are not celebrating the eternity of a myth. Their time is admittedly not linear because it is the time of each group in relation to each group. . . . It is clear that time, in the societies we are concerned with, is regarded by each group as related to the actions of ancestral figures in the past. In other words, the passing of time does not just mean a renewal of the same physical events each year, the fertilising of the crops by the rain from the sky in the spring and the cutting off of the ripened heads of corn in the autumn, so that the events keep coming round on a turning circle; nor does it mean simply the alternation of generational solidarity or marriage alliances. It means instead a series of events in the past which helps to create the group in its unique character but which fits into a different series of intervals for another group so that their character was created by their own series of time intervals. (Duerden 1975, 17)

The process by which the group "creates" its character is remembering, or, to be precise, both remembering and forgetting: "Events are forgotten if they are destructive to one group, but they might be remembered by another. Each group embraces events in its memory which adds to its personality as a creation of that group" (17).

Just as the narrator of *L'Enfant noir* remembers selectively, in the reconstruction of the life of the protagonist—the father's battles successfully fought, the mother's tears over the son's departure—so, too, is the forgetting selective: the colonialists by and large absent, the Malinke words put aside. The circle of events expands outward in the novel, always excluding as much as it includes. In a sense, metaphor can not function, can not perform the gesture of comparison, without excluding the metonymical gesture involved in establishing contiguity. Turning to initiation enables Laye to work out these gestures of inclusion and exclusion, and to link them to the formation of an identity that is also, like time, both that of an individual and that of a group.

Initiation and the Problematics of Change

The images of change in Laye's first two novels are similar ones. In *L'En-fant noir* one finds the change from child to adult, that is, initiation; in *Le Regard du roi* it is the change from being asleep to being awake. Growing up, waking up. These patterns should be set against the earlier discursive models first developed by the European colonialists from the 1880s to the 1920s, and subsequently followed by the Africanist discourse beginning around the 1920s (cf. Kane 1982, 35–60; Ngaté 1988, 19–27). In the former exotic or colonial literature, Africans were portrayed as children and Africa as a continent of somnambulism. In the early African novels, such as Socé's *Karim* (1935), the confirmation or sign of acceptance and success appeared in the form of an autobiographical statement that established the emergence from the state of childhood or sleep to adulthood or wakefulness: adulthood was signified by the model of the European, by civilization; wakefulness by the European work ethic or the Christian sensibility.

In a sense Laye undermines the givens of both patterns of change, while simultaneously, and openly, borrowing their forms. He turns the paradigm to his advantage, though not to the satisfaction of all his critics, such as Mongo Beti or others who voiced revolt, such as Léon Damas or David Diop (Kane 1982, 89). *L'Enfant noir* provides us with the story of an African child's coming of age, marked by his success in overcoming the hurdles of the French school system. At the end, the ticket to Europe has been won, the child is en route to Paris, a metro map in his pocket. Additionally, the coming of age is marked by the child's sexual development. The protagonist's intellectual development is matched by the sequence of his girlfriends, a "progression" from the African to the "European," from Fanta, back in Kouroussa, to the *métisse* Marie, in Conakry. The European girlfriend will exist only in anticipation—a bit like Lucienne in *L'Aventure ambiguë* (Kane 1961), a bit like France herself, awaiting the dark child's accession to manhood. This accession was already accomplished in his African past through traditional rituals, and is prefigured by the map that will swell and harden, providing the means to penetrate the subterranean passages. As Laye leaves a sorrowful Marie for Paris, this is the image we are given: "Surely I would be coming back! I sat a long while without moving, my arms crossed, tightly crossed over my chest. . . . Later on I felt something hard under my hand: the map of the subway bulged in my pocket."*

---

* "Sûrement, je reviendrais! Je demeurai longtemps sans bouger, les bras croisés, étroite-

We recognize Laye's sentimental manner of portraying emotion, a trademark of his writing—a winsome quality, marked by restraint and by his ability to evoke feeling by suggesting its suppression. Thus we might focus our attention on the emotions being contained by the crossed arms, "étroitement croisés pour mieux comprimer ma poitrine" (190) [literally, "tightly crossed the better to compress my chest"], and easily recall the same flow of crossed-armed moments, beginning with the opening epigraphs dedicated to his distant mother: "Black woman, African woman, O, my mother, I think of you. O, Dâman, O my mother, you who wiped my tears, you who gave my heart such joy, you who patiently bore with my foolishness, how I would like to be once again close to you, to be a child close to you!" *

Our first response would naturally be to the emotion itself—heightened, refined by the sign of constraint, cherished in its mélange of the son's expression of love and the Negritudinist language. The first level of the Western response would naturally focus on the emotion and the ideology. But personal emotion is not generally expressed in public in Africa; this, we assume, is as true of Kouroussa as anywhere else. The crossed arms, which hold in the chest, are not gratuitous signs, but frames, as Derrida would put it, that belong both to the inside and the outside of the emotion. This frame, like the supplement to the emotion, in fact constitutes the essence of the gesture when considered from the point of view of the *initié*. Children who have not yet reached the age of initiation may feel freer to express emotion without the constraint of a frame. But the initiate soon comes to realize the importance of the gesture of holding in, holding back, crossing the arms.

The gesture of constraint certainly takes precedence over the sentiment as the frame shifts into focus from the adult point of view. Similarly, the child's—or the European's—focus on the academic rites of passage, graduation, his enthrallment with subjects and with teachers, tends not to be privileged in *L'Enfant noir*. School appears more as a site for various conflicts, and the moments of passage return us to the home and family.

---

ment croisés pour mieux comprimer ma poitrine. . . . Plus tard, je sentais une épaisseur sous ma main: le plan du métro gonflait ma poche" (190).

* "Femme noire, femme africaine,
ô toi ma mère je pense à toi.
[. . .]
    O toi Dâman, ma mère, toi qui essuyais mes larmes, toi qui me réjouissais le coeur, toi qui patiemment supportais mes caprices, comme j'aimerais encore être près de toi, être enfant près de toi!" (7).

We don't encounter the school, except peripherally. The scholastic successes are noted, but matter only as they lead us back to the more significant preoccupations with the personal passage to adulthood. Thus the novel could be said to be centered around the serious, menacing test of circumcision—"a truly dangerous trial this time in which the element of play is totally absent: circumcision."* The chapters that follow lead us to the anguish of publicizing secrets, in a sense the critical twist of all of Laye's work, especially with this first venture into publication for the European market. This anguish should be contrasted in its importance with the brief mention of the key school examination Laye took to gain his scholarship to France: "Finally the test arrives! It lasts three days; three days of anguish. But one must believe that the marabouts provided real help: I was first among the seven candidates who passed." †

The significance of his academic achievement should be measured against the weightier importance the narrative attaches to Laye's passage into adulthood. As we might expect, the passage is in a sense invisible. We may share in his apprehension before the knife, his pride in passing the test of not crying out, not shaming his parents, not failing himself for life, which would have been the case had he shown his emotion and pain. But the passage occurs behind those physical demonstrations that merely serve as a vehicle for an act that was already accomplished, accomplished always elsewhere. No secret can be revealed when the action is offstage, and that is why the focus of the narrative might be said to be placed on the backward glance, after the fact, and not on the event in itself. The drama of the glance, naturally enough, reenacts the event itself, but on an emotional plane in which description and feelings become possible: the frame becomes the full contents.

This is what occurs when Laye's mother visits him after the circumcision ceremony is over. The boys—now "men"—are lodged in seclusion during their time of recuperation, but discreet visits with women may now be held, although physical contact is still to be avoided. The central drama for Laye in *L'Enfant noir* is separation from his mother, and so her visit provides the opportunity both to reenact that drama and to look back upon the transformation that has invisibly taken place. The space provided for the visit is defined by the "hymen," that is, the blank wall of the "seuil" [threshold] that both separates and joins the visitor and the visited.[3] The

---

* "une épreuve vraiment menaçante cette fois et dont le jeu est totalement absent: la circumcision" (109).

† "Enfin l'examen vient! Il dure trois jours; trois jours d'angoisse. Mais il faut croire que les marabouts furent de bonne aide: je fus reçu le premier sur les sept candidats admis" (168).

frame, once more, is placed so as to contain a powerful emotion that it is permitted to express only within its circumscription: "Listen! says the young man. Listen to me first! You are going to see your mother; you are allowed to see her from the threshold of the enclosure: you cannot go beyond the enclosure!"* The visit thus takes place with both parties restrained, held, as in a prison, apart from each other's presence: "She was standing in the dusty road a few steps from the enclosure: she, too, could approach no further."† The threshold, which we have been taking as a frame that contains and a hymen, the transparent membrane that delineates both inner/outer, youth/adulthood, virginity/defloration, is what is constructed by the initiation in which the youths are "deflowered." Thus it serves as the repressive mechanism itself, through which can flow only those expressions of emotion that are socially acceptable. The stichomythia of question-answer that follows from this structure is defined by the frame and the emotion: "And all at once I felt a lump in my throat. Was it because I could go no closer, because I could not hug my mother? Was it because I had already been separated too long, because we were still to be separated a long time? I do not know."‡ For the narrator, the significant components of this visit involved first his emotion: "All I know is that I could only say, 'Mother!' and that after my joy in seeing her I suddenly felt a strange depression";** next his state and the realization that accompanied it: "Ought I to attribute this emotional instability to the transformation that had been worked in me? When I had left her I was still a child. Now.... But was I really a man now? ... I was a man! Yes, I was a man!";†† and finally the gap thus created between him and his mother: "Now there was this distance between my mother and me: a man! It was a distance infinitely greater than the few meters that separated us."‡‡

---

* "Ecoute! dit le jeune homme. Ecoute-moi d'abord! Tu vas voir ta mère, il t'est permis de la voir du seuil de l'enceinte: tu ne peux pas franchir l'enceinte!" (Laye [1953] 1973, 129).

† "Elle se tenait dans la poussière du chemin, à quelques pas de l'enceinte: elle non plus ne devait pas s'approcher davantage" (129).

‡ "Et j'eus tout à coup la gorge serrée. Etait-ce parce que je ne pouvais m'approcher plus près, parce que je ne pouvais serrer ma mère dans mes bras? Etait-ce parce que tant de jours déjà nous séparaient, parce que beaucoup de jours devaient nous séparer encore? Je ne sais pas" (130).

** "Je sais seulement que je ne pouvais que crier: 'Mère', et qu'à ma joie de la revoir, un brusque, un étrange abattement avait succédé"(130).

†† "Ou devais-je attribuer cette instabilité à la transformation qui s'était faite en moi? Quand j'avais quitté ma mère, j'étais toujours un enfant. A présent ... Mais étais-je déjà un homme? ... J'étais un homme! Oui, j'étais un homme!" (130).

‡‡ "A présent, il y avait cette distance entre ma mère et moi: l'homme! C'était une distance

This space, into which the narrator pours all of his newfound being, that of "un homme," is discovered at the moment he perceives new barriers between himself and his mother. The self now separated from his mother, that of a man, is what occupies the space between the two of them. The man then becomes the semipermeable membrane through whom emotion can be filtered and in whom it is simultaneously retained.

The figure used by Laye to represent this barrier/being/membrane is the "seuil" [threshold] and the place set off by the "seuil" is the "enceinte" [enclosure]. "Two steps and I could have joined her; I would certainly have joined her if there had not been this absurd prohibition against crossing the threshold of the enclosure."* The word "seuil" is the strange term chosen and repeated to give significance to this state of being a man, of being constrained, of keeping a distance between himself and his mother. Its strangeness derives, in this instance, from its dual function as a physical space and as a space filled in by a man—by manhood. The space itself—"le seuil"—is metonymically joined to that which is trod underfoot upon crossing the threshold, when understood in its most literal sense as a "slab or piece of wood, forming the lower part of the opening of a door."[4] It is also, figuratively, an "entrée," a "commencement" or beginning. "Entrée" and "commencement" describe the new life of the man now formed by the initiation. But, while functioning as an entrance, it also delineates a space filled by those who had already made the passage across the threshold: "On the threshold [seuil], several young men were seated; they signalled me not to go beyond it."†

The ambiguity of the condition of manhood—at once a space and a barrier—a limit and a passageway, an entrance—is furthered by the use of the term "enceinte." The condition of the men is delineated by that which separates them from the women. To be contained within an "enceinte" at the critical moment of emergent manhood, when all contact with women is forbidden, is to be defined by the space of what symbolically one is not. Thus when the young men are healing, all contact is totally forbidden: "The rule is simply intended to ward off impediments to the healing." ‡ The women who are shut off, barred from entry, "return" by the back door to fill out the space with their uniquely female qualities. Only

---

infiniment plus grande que les quelques mètres qui nous séparaient" (130).

* "En deux enjambées j'aurais pu la rejoindre: je l'eusse assurément rejointe, s'il n'y avait eu cette défense absurde de franchir le seuil de l'enceinte" (130).

† "Sur le seuil, plusieurs jeunes hommes étaient assis; ils me firent signe de ne pas aller au-delà"(129).

‡ "L'interdit tend simplement à ne pas contrecarrer la cicatrisation"(127).

women can give birth; it is a mystery to which men can not attend; and the passage out of a state of pregnant enclosure—the "enceinte," like the womb—depends upon the very term being excluded, just as the "healing," that is, the birthing, depends on the act of excluding. The excluded term returns to fill the space of manhood, and it is no surprise for us to learn that when Laye's mother departs from their interview, her comportment is informed by those selfsame masculine qualities of constraint: "She hadn't even hugged me! However I am sure that she departed holding herself very straight, with dignity; she always held herself straight, and because she held herself straight she appeared taller than she was." *

This portrait of initiation would seem to be complete, were it not for another gap, the characteristic gap of *L'Enfant noir,* between the narrator (or subject of the speech act) and the protagonist (subject of the discourse)—that is, between the one who is ostensibly speaking and the one who is subject of the discourse being spoken. There is a complicitous space, like the space of initiation, created between the narrator and the protagonist (both identified by the pronoun "I"), a space also built upon exclusion: the voice that addresses us may adhere to the illusion that it represents one who is the same person as the character he describes, but through repeated expressions of nostalgia or regret, the narrating "I" opens up that space as though the exclusion of the protagonist from the narrator's space were a natural fact of narration. But the excluded term invades the space denied it. Here the narrator attempts to erect a "seuil" that permits only legitimatized narration to pass: when we learn that the exclusion of women is intended to permit the healing process to occur, the authorizing voice of the narrator adds, "I don't think that it is necessary to search any further for explanations." †Yet in practically the same breath the identical narrator reveals his own untrustworthiness as he tells us that the teachings he has just summarized, those imparted as part of the process of initiation, are not intended for women or noninitiates: ". . . neither were we to reveal any of the secret rites of circumcision." ‡5

The excluded term—the noninitiate (in this case, woman)—not only serves to define the space from which it is set off, but also establishes the "seuil" between the narrator—the one who looks back on past events

---

* "Elle ne m'avait seulement pas serré contre sa poitrine! Pourtant je suis sûr qu'elle s'était éloignée, très droite, très digne; elle se tenait toujours très droite, et parce qu'elle se tenait si droite, elle paraissait plus grande qu'elle n'était"(131).

† "[J]e ne crois pas qu'il faille chercher des explications plus lointaines" (127).

‡ ". . . pas plus que nous ne devions rien dévoiler des rites secrets de la circoncision"(128).

through the lens of one formed by the European school—and the protagonist, his alter ego. That backward look is thus more than nostalgic, it is an act of betrayal, as it refuses to honor the "men," the space, and the membrane's function. All this is captured in Laye's well-known lament, which summarizes his sense, and his portrayal, of his condition: "Secrets . . . do we still have any secrets!" *

The "seuil" is a sullied space once this unhappy consciousness enters it. The Latin origin of the term is "solea," indicating both the "sandale" that treads and the "dalle" [plank] on which one treads. The double gesture of being provided with a threshold and of planting the "sole" (another derivation of "solea") of one's foot upon it, suggests the familiar situation of the African writer unhappily trapped, as V. Y. Mudimbe would have it in *L'Odeur du père* (1982), on an elevator that perpetually moves up and down, set to motion by another's hand, powered by another, regulated by another, its rider confined in all senses by another. That the literatures of *témoignage* should be informed by this ambiguity, as in Laye's gaze, is now recognized as their basic trait: at one extreme they entail all the self-denying qualities that accompany acculturation in African autobiographical stories of success; at the other they entail a celebration of Africanity. Subtextually echoed in all these versions, is the doubled, troubled status of the man on the elevator, the "boy" in the "enceinte," the dancer surrounded by the onlookers, including not only his or her family and friends, but the narrator who provides the *témoignage* for us.

Laye succeeds in moving literatures of *témoignage* beyond the limits of Africanist discourse on two fronts. First, he moves the narrator's consciousness into the foreground, compelling us to respond not only to Africa as a black woman, or to the oppression of Africans and the injustices they might have experienced—paths first cleared by Léopold Senghor, Léon Damas, Aimé Césaire, David Diop—but to his *particular* voice, his own personal feelings and life. Africanists concerned themselves with "Africa" and "Africans"; Negritude was concerned with essential qualities, or with social conditions, of race and culture. Laye talked about himself, about the one who was presently narrating his story, and about the one he had been. This familiar and personal approach was totally new to African literature.

Second, much less obviously, and ultimately much more significantly, he utilizes the European discourse so as to validate the Malinke and Islamic conventions of thought, not as an "objective" outsider—like

---

* "Le secret, . . . Avons-nous encore des secrets!" (108).

Griaule—would perceive or describe them, but as givens of the narrator's discourse. We see this not at the end of *L'Enfant noir,* where the act of separation, of departure for Europe, is the subject, but at the end of the penultimate chapter, the one that points significantly across *all* the rest of Laye's work and to the often-missed Islamic elements in the writing of other West Africans. Here it is not the new life that is described, but the passage to death. Kouyate and Laye see their close friend Check die, and after his death they continue to be haunted by the experience. The youth's fear of death is now set against the narrator's more mature reflections: "I no longer think about death as I thought then, it has become simpler." *

The reflections that follow have the familiar ring of the Muslim believer whose thoughts on death would be framed by his approach to God and whose destiny is given as a path, a "chemin": "I think about those days, and very simply I think that Check had preceded us on the path to God, and that we each take that path one day. . . ." † As Laye's subsequent novels were to demonstrate, this path is defined for the mystic once again by an act of exclusion or exile: "this path which is no longer more frightening than that other one . . . That other one? . . . That other one, yes: the road to life, the one we encounter on birth, and which is only the momentary road of our exile . . . ." ‡[6]

A Supplement

Derrida's reflections on the frame taunt my analysis. Despite his seeming predilection for dismantling categories that he himself establishes ("There is a frame, but the frame does not exist" [Derrida 1979b, 39]),** his comments on the frame, or *parergon,* with respect to the work, the *ergon,* bear directly on my analysis. The *ergon* is enframed by the *parergon,* which acts as a supplement, as an outer text that is "*against,* beside, and above and beyond the *ergon,* the work accomplished" (Derrida 1979b, 20). Its ambivalent status is similar to that of the supplement, which is external to the text, and yet essential to its completeness. But the *parergon* differs from the supplement because of its proximity to the work: a frame is always a border—and its problem becomes one of belonging:

★ "[J]e ne pense plus à la mort comme j'y pensais alors: je pense plus simplement" (179–180).

† "Je songe à ces jours, et très simplement je pense que Check nous a précédés sur le chemin de Dieu, et que nous prenons tous un jour ce chemin . . ." (180).

‡ "ce chemin qui n'est pas plus effrayant que l'autre . . . L'autre? . . . L'autre, oui: le chemin de la vie, celui que nous abordons en naissant, et qui n'est jamais que le chemin momentané de notre exil . . ." (180).

★★ "Il y a du cadre, mais le cadre n'existe pas" (Derrida 1978, 93).

> The *parergon* detaches itself both from the *ergon* and from the milieu; it detaches itself first as a figure against a background, but it does not set itself off in the same way as the work, which is also set off against a background. The parergonal frame detaches itself from two backgrounds, but in relation to each it backs into the other. In relation to the work, which serves as its background, it disappears into the wall and then by degrees into the general text (context). In relation to the background of the general text, it backs into the work which is set off from the general background. (Derrida 1979b, 24)

For us the problem of the threshold reflects this ambivalence. On the one hand, it would seem to belong to the house, as does the frame to the picture to which it is attached. On the other hand, it can not be subjected to the same conditions as the rest of the house, given its special status as the limit established between permissible/impermissible. This status is reflected by the presence of the young men *on* the "seuil," not before or beyond it. They not only mark the limit to which Laye, the initiate, can go, but, as those already initiated and healed themselves, they also function as those who can belong to the outer world without fear of contamination. They hold Laye's hand, conducting him up to the threshold they occupy, and they guard him against coming close to his mother. They are the frame that holds in the emotion, that gives the space of the "enceinte" the possibility of existing as a space set aside, and at the same time they are part of the world of the "enceinte," just as the crossed arms are part of the one who feels emotion. We might also evoke the dual nature of the mechanisms of repression with respect to the conscious/unconscious mind which Sartre has analyzed in his work on bad faith in *L'Etre et le néant*.

But the crossed arms are also, at the same time that they enclose, the sign of the emotion. The presence of the young men on the threshold is significant only in terms of an enclosure pregnant with a new batch of initiates and an outer world contaminated by the presence of women and noninitiates. Depending on whether the young men are seen by Laye or his mother, they would seem to fit into either the inside or the outside world.

The reader's preoccupation with the status of the men on the threshold fades as their role in the scene is eclipsed. As Derrida notes,

> Always a figure against a background, the *parergon* is nevertheless a form that has traditionally been defined not as setting itself off but as disappearing, sinking in, effacing itself, dissolving just as it expends its greatest energy. The frame is never a background as the milieu or work can be, but neither is its thickness of margin a figure, unless a self-razing figure [figure qui s'enlève d'elle-même]. (Derrida 1979b, 26)

The young men, without names or identities, sink into immediate oblivion once they have served their function of setting or framing the scene between Laye and his mother, between the inner and the outer world.

The drama of Camara Laye in *L'Enfant noir* ought to be considered in this same light. From the opening scene in the family compound to the progressively enlarged circles of family and friends, expanding from the confines of Kouroussa and Tindican to Conakry, and finally, in prospect, to Africa as a whole, we witness the episodes of Laye's childhood and youth as though they were enclosed within a protected space. Check's death might remind us that life is an exile, but that is only the view from outside the frame, of one who looks back at a later date—a view from without, of one who regains his world with the certainty of his Islamic convictions. The youth himself only knew of the nightmare and fear that the encounter with death engendered.

The enclosure and the frame are set off by an excluded term, and this time—in contrast to the earlier works of African or European authors—the consciousness that inhabits the enclosure, the frame, and the horizon, is African. The excluded term in question here, then, must be the European presence and consciousness, an absence incredulously noted by Mongo Beti (1954b). Nonetheless, as Jonathan Ngaté has noted, the excluded European presence returns in the most direct of fashions in the act of narration (Ngaté 1988, 31): Laye's mastery of French, "the classical limpidity of [his] style," his able play on French narrative verbal registers, deny the image and act of exclusion by virtue of the very language with which it is evoked. Furthermore, this return of the excluded, this insistence of the European factor to impose itself, enters the text at the most distinctively African moments, during scenes of celebration and dance.

As Laye and his young fellow initiates blithely dance immediately prior to the initiation, they are joined by the entire community in the celebration. Here there is nothing of the "outer world" with its school, its administrators, its language, or its religion. "It is . . . the festival, the great festival of circumcision. . . ."* But even this African cultural ritual can not unfold without the return of the repressed term. At first it is merely adumbrated:

> We did not celebrate without second thoughts: the ordeal that awaited us was not of the sort that whetted the appetite. . . . This thought reminded us, brusquely, of our apprehension: we applauded the donor [of gifts to

---

* "C'est . . . la fête, la très grande fête de la circoncision . . ." (114).

the family], and abruptly our thoughts returned to the ordeal that awaited us. . . . Didn't we dance to forget what we feared? *

But more than the symbol of the return of the excluded term is needed to evoke the unstated role of the European factor. Just as the narration of the secrets unfolds in a lament over the loss of secrets, just as the initiates dance to forget the anxiety of their impending circumcision, so too is the community's celebration of its soon-to-be new members marked by the sign of those outside the community. The dance is the expression of a common joy: a circle of dancers is formed, with single figures often detaching themselves briefly and dancing in the middle, then rejoining the circle. The circle resembles the family, a community whose identity is marked by such signs of closeness as are conveyed by terms like "mother," "brother," "father," even when applied to those who are not immediate relations. When a child is raised in a polygamous household, the co-wives act as co-mothers, and the children are raised as natural siblings. Thus it is significant that the actions of Laye's other "mother," his response to her actions, and his description of her intervention all indicate the force of the outside French presence, even at the height of the dance. As the narrator explains, a relative often brandished a sign of the youthful initiate's condition, such as a hoe, which would indicate a good farmer.

> This was when I saw *my father's second wife* make her appearance holding aloft an exercise book and a fountain pen. I must confess that this gave me no pleasure at all, and, rather than encouraging me, it somewhat embarrassed me, although I knew quite well that my *second mother* was merely observing an old custom, and doing so with the best will in the world, since the exercise book and the fountain pen were symbols of a profession which, in her eyes, was superior to that of a farmer or a mechanic. (Laye 1978a, 117; my stress) †

No sooner is this sign of distinction evoked than it is dismissed. Derrida's definition of the "figure qui s'enlève d'elle-même" [self-razing figure] is pertinent to the movement of the narrative, which immediately

---

* Nous ne nous en réjouissons pas sans arrière-pensée: l'épreuve qui nous attendait n'était pas de celles qui aiguisait l'appétit. . . . Cette pensée nous remenait brutalement à notre appréhension: nous acclamions le donateur [des cadeaux pour les familles], et du coup, notre pensée revenait à l'épreuve qui nous attendait. . . . Ne dansions-nous pas pour oublier ce que nous redoutions? (115).

† Il y eut ainsi un moment où je vis apparaître *la séconde épouse de mon père*, un cahier et un stylo dans la main. J'avoue que je n'y pris guère plaisir et n'en retirai aucun réconfort, mais plutôt de la confusion, bien que je compris parfaitement que *ma seconde mère* ne faisait que sacrifier à la coutume et dans la meilleure intention de la terre, puisque cahier et stylo étaient les insignes d'une occupation qui, àses yeux, passait celles du cultivateur ou de l'artisan. (115–16; my stress)

ceases to describe the customs and the indiscretion of the second mother, but returns to the correct, discreet comportment of Laye's own mother: "My mother was infinitely more discreet; she contented herself with observing me from a distance, and I even noticed that she hid herself in the crowd."* The pleasure Laye takes in the greater discretion of his mother joins his judgment to her behavior, just as his terms used to describe his "petite mère" reflect his distance from their relationship: she is his father's "second wife" or his "second" mother.

The drama of Laye's life, in this autobiographical account, is marked by the anguish of separation from his mother. But the pattern established by all the ambiguous scenes that entail setting off excluded terms— women, children, non-initiates, or, on another plane, the European presence—prepares us for the rather understated scenes that follow later in Laye's youth, in which constraint is not marked by pride and dignity, but by annoyance. We see this, for example, when Laye returns to Kouroussa from Conakry for a visit. His mother "smothers" him with her overbearing concern, going so far as to exclude the participation of some of his friends from a social gathering, at times embarrassing or making it difficult for the young people to enjoy themselves on their own.

L'Enfant noir plays these various features against each other in ways never seen in African literature before. "We were never more numerous, and I never felt more alone."† Literatures of *témoignage* move decisively onto a stage of personal narration that refuses the complacent monologism of the Africanist expertise. Yet their acts of exclusion, however nostalgically evoked, however painfully recalled, and however marked by the return of the excluded term, attest to the iterated assertion of new certainties and values that stand over and against—"against, beside, and above and beyond"—the colonial *ergon*—preparing us for the logic of the supplement, soon to be elaborated by the full blossoming of literatures of *témoignage* and literatures of revolt, in which "the marginal becomes central by virtue of its very marginality" (Culler 1982, 196).

---

* "Ma mère fut infiniment plus discrète: elle se contenta de m'observer de loin, et même je remarquai qu'elle se dissimulait dans la foule"(116).

† "Nous n'avions jamais été plus nombreux, et jamais je n'avais été si seul" (140–141).

Chapter 5

Flying Without Perching—Metaphor, Proverb, and Gendered Discourse

CHINUA ACHEBE, *Things Fall Apart*

Eneke the bird says that since men have learnt to shoot without missing, he has learnt to fly without perching.

—*Chinua Achebe, Things Fall Apart*

From Past to Present: The Action of Metaphor

African literature has always moved between the past and the present. In this regard it is like all other dynamic aspects of African society, and like all other literary movements, which also must bring the past into relation with the present.

One aspect of this relationship is confrontational: there is always a sense of dialectical movement when the forces of change encounter entrenched positions. The past becomes another convention, especially in the world of literature, and in African literature that convention, or, rather, set of conventions, has long been mistakenly associated principally with orature on the grounds that oral literature is unevolving, unchanging, and merely inherited. Yet African traditions have never shunned change per se. To the contrary, change has become institutionalized, and lies at the core of all ritual renewal. As such it constitutes the basis for all mythic, all metaphorical expression in conventional orature—riddle, proverb, tale, myth, and epic. All are based on the recognition of the need for the earth, for society, for the individual, and even for the gods to seek renewal as the condition for growth and life. Eneke the bird is the figure that stands for adaptation, for the continued need to confront the past so as to survive in the present.

For Harold Scheub, written African literature contains oral sources that also are built around change, and specifically the meeting of past and present. This is borne out by the trope that lies at the core of oral African literature, metaphor. Its function, too, is to play the role of eneke, to burst the fetters, to remove the blinders, created by the weight of the past and its way of seeing and doing: "The purpose of metaphor, at the core of the mythic process, is to harness the emotions of the members of the audience, *trapped as they are in images of past and present,* thereby divining paradoxes and resolving conflicts, and to move that audience into a new perception of reality" (Scheub 1985, 4; my stress).[1]

In fact, we know that there is nothing in metaphor that will assure new perceptions, or defamiliarization. Essentially, all that metaphoric discourse assures is, as Benjamin Hrushovski (1984) puts it, that two different frames of reference meet—or clash (Ricoeur 1979)—with the resultant effect being the transfer of one signification, one verbalized sign or perception, onto another. That transfer might function to reassure, to reinforce an existent order as well as to disrupt the perception of it. However, it might be more accurate to adduce that the various kinds of change that move literature into new areas are to be understood as shifts in vision resulting from the clash of two different frames of reference. Metaphor becomes a necessary, but not sufficient, condition for literary change to occur.

In his discussion of the heroic epic, Scheub places the notion of change and its motor force, the metaphor, at the core: "The hero's epic is the means of revealing the great shifts on a cultural level . . . for a whole people. . . . [I]t is dependent on the same metaphorical transformations as the tale" (Scheub 1985, 2). The hero is central to the epic, and, as we see in the case of Sundiata or Mwindo, he or she acts as the focal point for the change: "Heroes, whether or not they have existed in fact, become emblematic of change . . . ," a change portrayed as the renewal of leadership, the revitalization of a people, or the relocation and conquest of territory. In "intensified images [of] transitional periods in a culture's life . . . ," the past in epic, as in ritual, is both carried forward and reborn: "The epic carries with it images and experiences of the past, what the society has traditionally stood for, into the new world" (13). The moment at which the "past" is born, or reborn, always changes, just as the "past" itself is reconstituted anew with each new gaze. Reification and renewal war, leaving gaps as broad as those generated by metaphorical transfer. Epics are constituted by the attempt to ignore those gaps—to create a vision that assumes a *totality* in its account.

Ritual effects change through the act of transfiguration or sacrifice because the victim or "carrier," as Wole Soyinka calls him, is the dual inhabitant of two realms; he or she is like Esu—messenger, horseman, bridge—who moves between the human and the divine. So, too, does the hero belong to two worlds and act as the bridge from the one to the other:

> The hero is part of both realms: he would not be able to take his people with him if he were not identifiably a part of the cultural past. But he has a vision of the new world. If he dies in the process of realizing it, if his flaws are exposed, his vulnerability exploited, that is a part of the change, and the atmosphere of yearning, regret, and loss are a part of the epic tradition, because it involves leaving a familiar world, and a transition into an uncertain one. (Scheub, 1985, 13)

Both hero and epic share the qualities that flow from the fact of embracing both worlds. Change in either is reflected in the other. Thus "to make the change, the hero moves to the boundaries of his community, necessarily so; and as he escorts his society into the new world, he becomes its original insider" (13).

Likewise, the boundary that lies between the two terms of a metaphor, between the two frames of reference, pretends to a certainty that can only be acquired at the cost of ignoring the role of *différance* with respect to each of the terms. Boundaries exist between states that can guard their territory and that know where the inside and outside begin and end. Boundaries are the very signposts of presence, and the sign of their resistance to change can be seen in their resistance to being moved. Metaphor, ironically, is based on the certainty of the difference between the two terms, the two frames of reference, of there being a boundary of otherness between them, as well as on the totally unfixed space or gap created by their coming together in the trope—a space filled in anew with each reading, a space whose newness is both resisted by the weight of the terms and inevitably encouraged by their clash and transfer (Hrushovski 1984, 6–15). Soyinka gives us the play on this tension in *The Road* (1973) when Professor removes the sign that marks the border of the road—"Bend"—a bent sign transferred from its original fixed position to a junk collection of words, moved there by the sorrowful, demented figure searching for unchanging signifiers.

At the opposite end of the literary scale from the extended tale qua epic lies the riddle, which Scheub views as "the model for all oral art" (Scheub 1985, 2). It functions like the metaphor by bringing figurative images into combination, testing their contours, and forcing a new conclusion, a new insight, on the margins of the old territory. In Henry Louis Gates's terms, the riddle signifies on a set of divergent figures, breaking the mold of each and reestablishing insightful perception (Gates 1989, 44–54). Metaphor acts no differently, especially if we bear in mind Paul Ricoeur's stress on the notion that metaphor is more than a relationship between words; it is a semantic shift whose action engages two spaces, two frames of reference, with a new sense emerging along with the gaps engendered by the tension between the terms. Like nature itself, its essential quality is action. And in its play on likeness it resembles the action of mimesis, which is governed by the same principle as that which it is supposedly imitating (Ricoeur 1977, 39).[2]

The basis of all metaphor is action—an act of turning that involves the juxtaposition of two unlike figures, and that at times gives us insight by shocking us with an unusual way of seeing. It is the same with riddles. If riddles provide the model for oral literature, we can say that all literature shares this trait in relationship to its literary past. This is what defamiliarization means. The crucial question for *Things Fall Apart* would be to determine how it stands in relationship to its literary past, and how, in turn, this quintessential African literary classic has become part of our automatic response to African literature, has become the object of subsequent acts of defamiliarization. The key to these issues can be provided by examining the proverb—what it means in terms of African figuration, how it informs African discourse, and finally how it shapes the structure of the novel.

The Proverb and the Process of Change

Scheub views the proverb as an extension of metaphor, as a "metaphorical relationship, tying an old saying to a situation," thus producing "a 'valid cryptogram' for that real life experience" (Scheub 1985, 5). Past and present meet through the new "situation" confronting the "old saying." In Scheub's formulation, the past is equated with conventional wisdom, frozen into stasis: "The proverb is similar to the riddle in the sense that metaphor is intended, as *the ancient truth of the culture* touches contemporary experience" (5; my stress). "Ancient wisdom" and "the culture's sages" construct the intellectual fortress of the immutable fathers. Children have no chance to effect change in this schema, only to become initiates, follow the models, imitate the old forms, and, in contrast to Soyinka's unsuccessful carrier, Eman, in *The Strong Breed* (1973), negotiate the passage of renewal like the snake shedding old skin for new, in rigid cyclical fashion.

In this model of the proverb, the dictum is equated with art, which, curiously, is distinguished from the experience on which it is brought to bear: "In the proverb, the only way for the metaphor to be realized is by means of the instant connection between the art form and reality" (Scheub 1985, 5)—this being the equivalent situation to that of myth in which, presumably, the same conjunction is also made via the use of metaphor: "When the realm of art and reality are brought into contact and that relationship is caused by metaphor, the audience is in the presence of myth" (3). The key element in both equations lies in the process of change accompanying the use of metaphor: "metaphor implies transformation" (3).

The level at which the change takes place is generally placed by Scheub outside the literary act itself, that is, in "reality." Further, "[m]yth is not a tale, it is a process within a tale." The myth's subject matter relates to stories of the gods "because gods are creators and are thus involved in *primal transitions*" (Scheub 1985, 3; my stress). The list of changes is then extended to encompass virtually all subjects of oral forms: "The *shifts* wrought by the gods have their parallels in those brought about by culture heroes, epic heroes, even tricksters and tale characters" (3; my stress). Myth itself, always in transition, is grounded in "the dying and reborn god, the hero transforming society, [like epic]; it is the tale character shifting identities through the dramatization of a cultural rite of passage" (3). "Myth," he concludes, "is a metaphor . . ." (3).

Scheub's reliance on "ancient wisdom" as applied to "reality" rests uneasily upon a simple dichotomy between the intra- and the extramental world, and on intellectual stasis. By denying the cultural process of creating new wisdom, the viability of a constant renewal of tradition, he reifies culture. And he brings proverbs to bear on reality instead of on proverbs, thus separating Art from Nature and denying Art's self-reflexive ontology.

Just as the African novel is not the direct product of African society, but the heir of earlier texts, including novels—society functioning more as context than as cause of the novel's creation—so, too, is the proverb not a direct commentary on society but on a proverbial view of society. The "society" that is the object of a novel's discourse is, among other things, a creation of that novel. By the same token, the "reality" on which a proverb bears is that vision of the world generated by the proverb, or by the speaker of the proverb. The novel and the proverb are equally self-reflexive, and nowhere is this made more apparent than in the scene in *Things Fall Apart* in which Okonkwo's early unease over his relationship with his father is mirrored in a proverb's play on proverbial unease: "Okonkwo laughed uneasily because, as the saying goes, an old woman is always uneasy when dry bones are mentioned in a proverb" (19).*

The narrator highlights his own presence with the gratuitous aside "as the saying goes," serving to distance the reader from the action, from Okonkwo's feelings, and at the same time drawing our attention to the action of the proverb itself. It is a common feature of Achebe's style:

---

* All page references to this text are to the 1972 edition.

"*Among the Ibo* the art of conversation is regarded very highly, and proverbs are the palm-oil with which words are eaten" (6; my stress). The effect is not only to position the narrator so as to suggest that the one being addressed is a foreign narratee—this sense of a non-Ibo audience is suggested directly by the author's explanatory asides and indirectly by the use of English—but also to identify the narrator as a speaker of proverbs. It is significant for the kind of literature Achebe is creating to note that these distancing markers draw the audience closer to the teller of the tale than is the usual case with the realist novel. African conventions meet European ones on all levels of *Things Fall Apart*.

The space created by the narrator's self-reflexive markers is ostensibly outside that of the narrative—like the frame (or *parergon*). The one who presents Okonkwo's story to us, who speaks at times in English, at times in Ibo, who identifies with the tradition and its way of seeing the world, occupies a particular position from which we are invited to view the story. Okonkwo's more restricted space gives the occasion for the proverb to be voiced—his situation surrounds the frame of the proverb and directs its meaning towards him. We expect the space occupied by the proverb to be outside the "reality" occupied by both the narrator and Okonkwo. Yet if it is to comment on the situation, it must invade the frame around the space occupied by Okonkwo, and its meaning must invade the frame from which we are invited to view the events. At the moment that the meaning emerges, when Okonkwo's unease becomes a form of self-awareness and of fear of death, the old woman shifts into Okonkwo, and is invaded herself by the force of his predicament and his presence. There is no more essential, fundamental space in *Things Fall Apart* than that shifting ground occupied by the old woman in the proverb. Her existence is presented as solely intramental, and yet it is permeated by/permeates all other levels of the Real with which Achebe seeks to invest the space of the novel. Her world, like that of the novel's hero, when viewed as that of a story whose meaning bears upon the lives of the readers, is as real as the bones and death with which it is built, and as unreal as a figure of these images. They move us forward when set into juxtaposition so as to play out the action of metaphoric transfer. At that moment the space within which they and we were confined dissolves, and, instantaneously, is reconstituted in the new architecture. Okonkwo's fears hover all the more insistently, preparing us for the encounters with *agbala* that run through the text.

Proverb and Metaphor in *Things Fall Apart*

When we first encounter Okonkwo he appears as the proverbial Ibo champion wrestler/fighter. Gradually his image shifts to that of an intractable father, finally turning into that of a victim of circumstance and colonialism. Proverbs haunt his progressive demise. At the outset he is part of the folktale setting, the "art," rather than the real-life situation to which the proverb applies. The novel begins like an oral tale whose hero is appropriately presented in terms of his fame, a consequence of his great victory over Amalinze the Cat. Okonkwo himself appears larger than life:

> He was tall and huge, and his bushy eyebrows and wide nose gave him a very severe look. He breathed heavily, and it was said that, when he slept, his wives and children in their out-houses could hear him breathe. When he walked, his heels hardly touched the ground and he seemed to walk on springs, as if he was going to pounce on somebody. (4)

Hyperbole sets the stage for his great accomplishments, and accommodates us to his dimensions.

This folkloric discourse does not continue, however. Okonkwo is also the focus of a realistic story, and his personality is rapidly unveiled. No sooner do we learn of Okonkwo's parentage than we are presented with the sources of his sense of inferiority and his acts of compensation. "He had a slight stammer and whenever he was angry and could not get his words out quickly enough, he would use his fists. He had no patience with unsuccessful men. He had no patience with his father" (4). Like a shock of cold water the last line thrusts us into the world of psychological realism, shifting the tone of the discourse from the beginning of the paragraph with its colorful simile—"That was many years ago, twenty years or more, and during this time Okonkwo's fame had grown like bush-fire in the harmattan" (3)—to the quiet letdown in the straightforward description of his feelings of impatience with his father.

We view him, as we do the proverbs, as a product of the past, the time *always* presented as having gone by when he had won his laurels and had taken his enemies' heads. Now, in the present, he sits and drinks with his friends, sharing kola nuts. The great deeds of war or wrestling are memories; the restricted arena of the *obi,* marked by chalk lines, circumscribes his world and provides the setting for the more subtle exchanges between host and guest. He is the object of the proverbs, as Bernth Lindfors (1968) has shown: like the little bird *nza* he challenges his *chi* (28); he says yes to his *chi* (24); he cracks his own palm kernels even as he agrees that a "benevolent spirit" cracked them for him (24–25). Simultaneously we learn he needs to be shown the importance of humility by his elders (24), and that some people said "his good fortune had gone to his head" (28). The narrative moves him in and out of the proverbial setting, alternating its registers as in the shift from straightforward simile to more subtle metaphor.

The direct descriptions of Okonkwo place him in the center of the proverb. For an instant, he is *nza*. But then direct attributes leave no room for suggestive play. He is fixed by his reactions to his weak father. His roles as tyrannical father and husband appear determined, first, by his society, which rewards him for macho behavior (wrestling and fighting to produce a champion), and then by his own given character flaws (compensations for shame over his weak father). However, proverbs are metaphorical, not mere statements of resemblance like similes. When Okonkwo says yes to his *chi,* and four pages later becomes *nza,* the one who challenges his *chi,* there is a shift away from the rigidity of simile. The shift relies on the interplay between Okonkwo as a proverbial figure and as an actor in the situation evoked in the course of the novel, that is, the "real life" to which the proverb needs to be applied. Achebe places Okonkwo in both contexts by having him appear from the outset as both an unreal folk hero and as a "real," psychologically flawed protagonist whose weaknesses coincide with the historical demise of his society's independence. This shift echoes that of the interplay between the perspective of the subject of the enunciation and the subject of the *énoncé.*[3]

"It was and it was not" (Ricoeur 1977, 244). This preamble to a Majorcan folktale, cited by Ricoeur, has its echoes in African models.[4] For Ricoeur it sums up the split function of metaphor: addressing two references at the same time, "the double-sensed message finds correspondance in a split addressee, in a split addresser, and what is more, in a split reference" (Ricoeur 1979, 151). Okonkwo's character—his "personage"—is thoroughly monological, in Bakhtin's sense, because Achebe has conceived of this "hero" as a product of psychological and sociological forces. However, the juxtaposition of his realistic and his proverbial functions works to "split" the reference, as Ricoeur puts it, so that the frame of reference provided by the story hovers over, or echoes and reverberates throughout, the proverbial enunciations, without obliterating their shifting and suggestive nature. It is as if we are trying to pin *nza* down in the form of Okonkwo as he struggles to succeed, and then find ourselves having to challenge our *chi* in reconstructing *nza* as a rebel against his own good nature.

Okonkwo may well be undone by the very social forces that were responsible for his rise—a fitting fate for a tragic hero—but when *nza* challenges his *chi,* he is emerging into the foreground of combat with *no* psychological or sociohistorical grounds to explain his action. It is in his nature, in the structure of the words that give us this image, and is devoid of the ironic reflexiveness that characterizes tragedy. By compelling

Okonkwo to inhabit both spaces—*nza*'s and Umuofia's—Achebe doubles the echoing, and we reconstitute Okonkwo above and beyond his immediate circumstances.

This could not occur if the proverbs functioned as "dead metaphors," that is, clichéd tropes in which the original meaning of the words is lost. This is C. L. Innes's argument (1978b), and it is presented with respect to the early scene in which Okonkwo is seeking to borrow yams from Nwakibie. Just as Scheub lets fall the phrase "the ancient truth of the culture" (Scheub 1985, 5), thus betraying his attitude toward traditional African intellectual production as frozen, with proverbs reified into long-held, unchanging forms, so does Innes reveal a bias against the Ibo discourse in the novel when it emerges in the form of proverbs. In his view the language bears the burden of a fixed value—the social norm—and a fixed meaning in which the metaphorical transfer and clash have disappeared, leaving only the residual meaning, a dead metaphor. An example would be any phrase whose figurative significance is all that is left, like "red herring."

Thus, when Okonkwo uses the proverb about the lizard who praised himself in order to justify his boldness when appealing to Nwakibie for yams, Innes refers to the proverb as the "expression of the social norm" (Innes 1978b, 114). For Innes, Okonkwo uses the proverb in a contradictory fashion: although he appeals to the social norm when employing the proverb, he asserts that he is not like the other young men "these days"— he is a hard worker who will repay Nwakibie's investment of trust in him. Innes, for his part, goes on to call into question all the traditional linguistic forms with which the exchange is carried out. Okonkwo's "ritualistic" greeting, "Let the kite perch and the eagle perch too. If one says no to the other, let his wing break" (17–18), is employed without care for the immediate significance of the words since Okonkwo is anything but accommodating and flexible—he wishes to break the wings of the Christians, not sit down with them. The proverbs, Innes asserts, are used to reinforce or establish the positions already taken by Okonkwo and Nwakibie—positions for which proverbs are the vehicle. The proverb is not employed so as to open discussion but so as to state a previously decided conclusion. "Phrases or statements which reaffirm rather than extend the existing world view of a person or society are typical of Okonkwo. . . . [T]he proverbs for him have solidified into units of thought which are no longer questioned" (Innes 1978b, 114–15).

Similarly, for Innes this "tendency to cliché" in Okonkwo or Nwakibie's discourse reveals itself, *through* the language, as a freezing or hardening of thought. When Okonkwo reflects that "one cannot begin too early

[to prepare seed yams]" despite his own knowledge that Nwoye and Ikemefuna are too young, he closes off the internal debate by letting the
phrase itself make the decision. And as the phrase is a cliché, it functions
like a dead metaphor whose meaning is already provided in advance. For
Innes, this results in "a kind of hardening of the arteries of language"
(Innes 1978b, 115). Innes concludes that Okonkwo has reduced the metaphorical aspect of language to synecdoche, or, to respond more directly to
the sense of Innes's remarks, to metonymy. Thus, when Okonkwo
reflects, once again, that "yams stood for manliness" (115), and that that
justified his decision to push the boys into work on preparing the seed
yams, Innes finds that this "commonplace" reflection concerning yams
and manliness has degenerated into another frozen signifier: "For
Okonkwo the relationship between yam and manliness is no longer perceived as metaphorical, and the particular aspect of manliness signified by
that metaphor has been replaced by all the qualities of a 'very great man
indeed'" (Innes 1978b, 115).

Whatever Innes means when he says that the relationship between
yams and manliness is no longer perceived as metaphorical is certainly not
clear. The relationship has not been transformed into a literal one. No
doubt Innes wishes the conventional Ibo reading of "manliness" here to
encompass something less than "greatness," for he criticizes Okonkwo for
the inflation of the trope. However, nothing leads us to dissociate manliness from greatness in the other instances in which it occurs. It is only in
excessive manliness, manliness without womanliness, that Okonkwo's
flawed character is to be seen.

For Innes, this rigidity of character in "Okonkwo and his compan-
ions" (Innes 1978b, 114–15) accounts for their use of an ossified discourse. However even the moderate, reflective Obierika is faulted for having recourse to the dead weight of proverbial thought. Obierika raises the
question of the killing of twins, and of the expulsion of Okonkwo for his
inadvertent killing of Ezeudu's son, asking himself what crime they had
committed. He concludes that the Earth had decreed that there were
offenses and that everyone would pay for the sins of the offender ("As the
elders said, if one finger brought oil it soiled the others" [Achebe [1958]
1972, 114]), from which Innes once again deduces that the patterns of
social norms, conveyed in conventional expressions and proverbs, closed
off the inner thought process. The "language the culture has developed"
functioned "to justify what is" (Innes 1978b, 118).

Innes's "insight," as Paul de Man would have it, bears on the key
weakness signaled by the text—the rigidity of Ibo culture, its stress on
manliness, and a resultant incapacity to adapt to the new conditions posed

by colonialism. However, this insight is achieved at the price of inferring qualities about Ibo culture and language that ironically contradict Innes's own praise singing over the oral tradition: "In addition to establishing the richness and vitality of the oral tradition of that area, these interwoven proverbs and sayings provide an ironic and ominous counterpoint to the story of Okonkwo" (Innes 1978b, 114). Thus, on the one hand, the proverbs and ritual greetings function independently of circumstance and context, serve to end dialogue or reflection, are frozen, rigidified, reified, monological statements of social norms—in short, have become dead substitutes for thought, killing off their originary metaphorical function—while, on the other hand, they attest to the richness and vitality of the oral tradition!

Innes's inconsistency is not the issue. Rather, it is his conclusion, that this "hardening of the arteries" is in the language itself, especially as reflected in proverbial or clichéd language, that is important. Innes removes both addresser and addressee from the act of producing meaning when he imputes to language the hard and fast property (*propriété*) of containing meaning. The free play to which metaphor gives rise, allowing us to claim two different perspectives on Okonkwo as *nza,* is denied when the frame of reference within which metaphor or proverbs are constructed is viewed as incapable of shaping the metaphorical transfer. Innes sets himself up as the owner of the words' meanings, as the judge over their propriety, when he finds Okonkwo at fault in his use of the greeting or in his reflection on yams' manliness.

However, there is no more reason for the proverbs to have become dead metaphors for the speakers employing "palm oil," than for us to close down the proverbs' action. It is the Innesian reader who finds Obierika's thinking ossified when his reflection on the spreading of oil from one finger to the others is taken to signify "his society's inability to deal with such questions as the abandoning of twins, [etc.]" (Innes 1978b, 118). In fact, we are not compelled to accept either the judgment imposed on the patterns of social thought *or on their meaning.* To accept either is to be grounded in a very different set of presuppositions. The thought that the Earth found offense in the land because of the birth of twins, in the inadvertent killing of a clansman, signals an attitude toward motivation, community, and offense radically different from the logocentric patterns of social control developed in the West. Why should Obierika's reflections in *both* directions—his questioning as well as his ultimate acceptance—signify his or his society's inability to deal adequately with them? More significantly, they do not signify a closing down on the issue, but a tension indicative of the dialogic space generated metaphorically—an inconclusive tension since the evocation of a community identity (one finger soils the others) does nothing to settle the interplay between motive and guilt. Obierika hardly condemns Okonkwo; nor does he exonerate him. He presents us with alternate ways of dealing with his situation. Only if the inward direction of guilt and conscience, of Christian morality, provides all the answers to moral dilemmas can Obierika be said to have fallen back on the hardened arteries of language. And it is precisely that direction that Innes would have us take when he posits Obierika's reflections as torn between genuine questions and unthinking answers. "The questions of Nwoye and of the women who have lost their twins are less easily silenced by the formulas of the elders. They are searching for a new language which will close the gap between their inner feeling of what should be and the language the culture has developed to justify what is" (Innes 1978b, 118). We are not left in doubt about the Christian doctrine informing this "new language" of the inner being.

Innes's assessment of Ibo discourse may be limited by his insistence on a narrowly Christian reading, but, more significantly, it bears directly on the question of proverb and metaphor in the men's speech. If the essence of metaphor lies in action, its role being realized in the act of transformation, no one would appear less likely than Okonkwo to represent that role. Instead of embracing a traditional father whose role he would have to inherit in order to establish his own authority, he rejects his father and prevents his own son from achieving any positive identification with him. His all-encompassing demands, like totalizing figures, behave as though forcing his metaphorical function into that of a simile.[5] There is, in fact, a hermeneutic space that metaphor permits and that is shrunk by the directness of simile. Generally, the proverbs function in this novel more like metaphors than similes, and they appear in Part One, while the second and third parts are more likely to feature similes.

We see this in the following comparison: In Part One Okonkwo tries to justify his participation in the death of Ikemefuna, by telling Obierika that "the Earth cannot punish me for obeying her messenger." He then consolidates this argument by adding, "A child's fingers are not scalded by a piece of hot yam which its mother puts into its palm" (61). Obierika loses no time in entering into the spaces created by Okonkwo's argument: who appointed Okonkwo messenger? That Okonkwo, likened in a previous proverb to the king whose mouth never sucked the milk from the maternal breast, should now appeal to the figure of the mother for justification in the death of a son, appears all the more strange. It is, however, an acceptable strangeness, given the play of proverbial space.

In Part Two Okonkwo finds himself fallen from the heights of fame and power, and must return to the mother's protective homeland. Once there, the mythic past recedes even further, and simile dominates in the description of Okonkwo's hardships: He must learn "to become left-handed in old age," a figure immediate in its sense, and not particularly Ibo in expression. This is reinforced by the equally banal figure, "He had been cast out of his clan like a fish on to a dry, sandy beach, panting" (119). The addition of the adjective, "panting," gives emphasis to his unaccustomed and desperate state, but it does so with an uncharacteristic directness and flourish. It suggests embellishment more than metaphor, does not surprise or generate a resonance of unstretched meaning.

This shift in figuration is capped in the third part of the novel, in which the clan meets for the last time. There the orator Okika appeals to the sons of Umuofia. But they are not all there—"they have broken the clan and gone their several ways" (183). As Okika attempts to revive the faltering resistance of the clan, he returns to the metaphor of eneke, suggesting, despite himself, the need for change, not for a turning back to the past. However, it is not the ambivalent use of the Ibo proverb that provides the last note of his speech, but English aphorisms: "We must root out this evil. . . . We must bale this water now that it is only ankle-deep" (183). It is at this point that his speech is interrupted by the arrival of the court messengers. But in a sense he has already interrupted his own discourse, his speech is already fatally infiltrated by the foreign element; the proverb is now recalled, not as a living word but as a relic.

Similarly if Okonkwo's folkloric appearance is greatest at the outset, his psychological makeup appears largely frozen into place after the death of Ikemefuna. The tension between Okonkwo's status as great folk hero and yet realistically flawed protagonist also decreases as the crisis of the present throws the heroic stature of the past into obscurity. Okonkwo's role shifts: once clan leader and key player in the cycle of father-son relationships, now he is turned into the tragic victim of historical processes to which he can not adapt and that he seems incapable even of comprehending. Social change and decline, not mythic renewal, prevail.

Epics and Heroes in *Things Fall Apart*

The logic of Okonkwo's role becomes most apparent when viewed in terms of the epic. The hero's role in the epic, as Scheub has indicated, is to embody the society that he leads through change. But the dual nature of the heroic figure is indicated by the fact that the hero participates in two realms: he embodies his people by identifying with their cultural past; he leads them into the future by negating that past (Scheub 1985, 13).

Okonkwo incarnates a reified past, refusing the present the rights of succession. On the basis of character, Ikemefuna would normally have been the logical replacement for clan leader when he matured, but

Okonkwo's role in his death signals the rigidification of Okonkwo's position. In complementary fashion, Nwoye, the legitimate heir, is driven into rejecting the path to his father, and Ezinma, like Ikemefuna, is blocked by the social limits placed on her gender from acceding to the father's position. Thus the younger generation recapitulates Okonkwo's own failure to find in his father the necessary virtues to inspire emulation or permit succession. In the end, Okonkwo embodies only that portion of the epic hero that identifies with the traditions of society–the past.

The epic hero's function as harbinger, as the one who leads his people into change, is assumed by all that Okonkwo rejects, ultimately including his son. Father and son split the two aspects of the epic hero, removing from Okonkwo's death the quality of sacrifice: his death doesn't bring change but, rather, is a gesture denoting his failure to prevent change.

In a sense, Okonkwo's failure to attain the level of tragic scapegoat can be traced to his psychological limits, or, more precisely, to his depiction as a psychologically flawed being, rather than as a folk hero. This is established at the climactic moment in which Okonkwo surrenders to feelings of insecurity: warned not to participate in Ikemefuna's death, Okonkwo not only joins the executioners but strikes down his adopted son. He destroys the possibility of achieving the greatness of eneke and becomes merely *nza*.

In the semiobscurity of the moral dilemma posed by deciding whether an act of murder or of sacrifice was committed, we lose sight of the terrifying reality of a father killing his son: Ikemefuna turns back to Okonkwo who had "withdrawn to the rear" (55). As he is struck, the pot he is carrying falls. The choppy sentences that follow leave spaces between them: ". . . Okonkwo looked away. He heard the blow. The pot fell and broke in the sand. He heard Ikemefuna cry . . ." (55). We stand with Okonkwo, outside the act, fascinated as crime and blood are evoked, waiting after the sound of the broken pot for the next step, the youngster's cry, "My father, they have killed me!" There is a relentless march of images: Ikemefuna must rush toward Okonkwo, forcing him to participate in the act he had sought to avoid by retreating to the rear. Then they are joined in the moment of death, culminating the series of fated encounters begun earlier with the self-confident march of Okonkwo into Mbaino as the "proud and imperious emissary of war" (12).

Despite the warning not to accompany the executioners, Okonkwo joins the band without any sign of second thoughts: it is as though the march through the forest, the "deathly silence" that pervades the atmosphere, the growling, anonymous man who commands Ikemefuna to continue on his way without looking back, were all leading an abstracted

Okonkwo to his doom. "Dazed with fear" it is Okonkwo whose blow, finishing off the pathetic figure of Ikemefuna, has all the appearance of an automatic gesture. The narrator's conclusion to the episode marks Okonkwo's participation as an act of compensation: "He was afraid of being thought weak" (55). With this judgment, Okonkwo's development comes to an end: he never advances to a higher age grade, never acquires the desired titles, never initiates his sons into the *ozo* society. His nature, like his rank, is inscribed permanently in this moment, and he ceases to confront events in his life with any further potential for change.

Okonkwo's inflexibility and "fiery" nature do not appear out of sync with Ibo male society, and it is that society's collective role in the death of Ikemefuna, so often overlooked in the shock of Okonkwo's participation, that we must signal. Who are the men designated to kill Ikemefuna? Faceless and nameless they represent the collective paternal authority bent on the serious business of performing the Oracle's bidding. Together they are drawn from the nine villages of Umuofia (52), and when they come to discuss the matter with Okonkwo, it is first through the good offices of the "oldest man in this quarter of Umuofia" (51), Ezeudu.

Okonkwo appears more and more as an inevitable product of his society, not an aberration. The wrestling matches, the warlike behavior, and the social celebration of male conquest and domination, are all the substance of Part One of *Things Fall Apart*. The party of Ikemefuna's executioners accentuate this quality, even as they are set in contrast to Obierika, Nwoye, and even Ikemefuna himself. If Okonkwo appears exaggerated and isolated when beating his wives, ridiculing his opponents, belaboring his sons, here in Ikemefuna's death he fits in: "At the beginning of the journey the men of Umuofia talked and laughed about locusts, about their women, and about some effeminate men who had refused to come with them" (52–53).

The spaces in the descriptions are deliberately left open. The men's identities are never given. Where are they going? Why do some join in and others not? We fluctuate here as we do throughout Part One, especially between answers that depend on psychology and sociology, and those that depend on myth or folklore. The command of the Oracle comes from beyond the ambit of human motivation; the men who carry it out bring us back into their everyday lives. They attempt to live a ritual, place themselves on the plane of the god's commands, but can not, for all that, pass beyond the realm of their bodies, their situation, as the silence and the growling voice imply. If ritual sets them in motion, Okonkwo's fear cuts short the scene, and ends the sacrifice without any visible or invisible sign that a transcendental gesture was accomplished.

If they were mistaken about the Oracle, then they were murderers, filicides. In epics, where patricide is always implied if not carried out, the risk of such acts is always acceptable. In the realm of the proverb, one truth tends to be bounded by another, and the taciturn Okonkwo can do no more than drown his thoughts in palmwine. The definitive consequence of Ikemefuna's death, in fact, can be seen in Nwoye's reaction: "Then something had given way inside him" (56), and the father's place, as such, comes to an end.

Ironically, despite this stasis, the image Achebe employs to convey Okonkwo's character is fire. He is the embodiment of violence, of power represented in terms of brute force, strength, conquest, domination, control—ideals often associated with manliness and greatness, with titled rulers, with fighters battling in the center of the ring. "Roaring Flame" might seem best to evoke these qualities, although "Cat" or "Leopard" might be employed as well, suggesting thereby more flexible and awesome properties. Okonkwo is the "bush-fire in the harmattan" (3), the village champion in wrestling and in war. For Innes, Okonkwo's association of fire with himself and ash with Nwoye suffices to shut off further reflection on the father-son relationship: the metaphorical transfer is reduced to an act of renaming: "Okonkwo merely renamed the relationship; it remains unexplained, and his questions [about Nwoye's character] remained unanswered, although for Okonkwo the act of naming has silenced those questions" (Innes 1978b, 117). For Innes, the unanswered question has an answer: it is provided by Okonkwo's repressed thoughts about his father. The inner, psychological life is not only central and real to Innes, it provides the basis for our understanding of Okonkwo's character. Metaphorical transfer is thus subordinated to psychological analysis, and the heteroglossic force of the metaphoric signifier is subdued into an empty process of renaming.

Okonkwo's use of figuration, however, does more than simply shift the burden of thought from the unpleasantly personal to the rigid, fixed patterns of nature. It is ironically suggestive of all that is rejected and that is acceptable. Fire might seem most suited to conveying the notion of change, of self-transformation. Yet that process can only be completed by its passing into ash, as with the farmers' or herders' actions of setting the blaze so as to clear the ground either for cultivation or for new grasses to grow. It may be fierce and dangerous, like the "bush-fire in the harmattan," but it is also self-consuming. The figure of self-consumption, of destruction without change, is negative, and it implies something arrested, like a childhood state or an unresolved trauma. It evokes the two kinds of clash that give tension to the novel: the one created by the deployment of proverbial terms, like the fire begetting cold ash, as well as the clash engendered by Ibo resistance to the colonial presence. The ironic subtext is seen in the dual nature of ash: a cold, dead product without life or process, and yet a fertile source of new life for crops, of new life for resurrected souls, of new communities, new families. That fire should beget ash, so natural a process, should also suggest, to Okonkwo's chagrin, that he could have begotten a Christian son in an equally natural fashion, which demonstrates something of the ironic space that is generated when both figurative and literal readings meet.

This irony also prepares us for the final use of this trope, when Okonkwo voices his fear that Egonwanne's rhetoric will turn the wrath of the community away from action against the white man: "His sweet tongue can change fire into cold ash" (180). That Okonkwo, who has killed off change in his family, and who resists it in society, should view as a threat the notion that fire must change is logical, if ironic. Here we can anticipate that the speech to be made, like that of Okiko which actually follows, will be heavily marked by proverbial or metaphorical turns. As we have seen, the clash that is implied in these tropes generates new visions, new gaps. More specifically, Ricoeur identifies the resultant tension as arising from the need to maintain a sense of the difference in the terms while simultaneously recognizing their likeness: "To see *the like* is to see the same in spite of, and through, the different. The tension between sameness and difference characterizes the logical structure of likeness" (Ricoeur 1979, 146). Ricoeur stresses the role of imagination in this play of likeness, and we can understand Okonkwo's resistance to change, like his apprehension over Egonwanne's rhetoric, as phallocentric resistance to allowing the interplay between sameness and difference, much less allowing the new visions thus engendered to emerge.

Women's Versus Men's Narratives

Nwoye's reactions, as well as Obierika's later reflections on the traditional sanctions brought for a "female" crime—one committed unintentionally, like Okonkwo's—point out the humane, compassionate side of Ibo society, the side that questions past traditions, that suggests psychological motivations to actions, and, especially, that gives women's readings of events. The concept of Ibo society as encompassing both male and female dimensions is developed by Cathy Ramadan and Donald Weinstock, and by Solomon Iyasere, in their essays on *Things Fall Apart*. Iyasere also stresses, along with Bu-Buakei Jabbi, the aspects of harmony, accommodation, and flexibility to be found in Ibo culture, which Okonkwo attempts to deny in his rejection of all things feminine. The above critics generally argue that Okonkwo has denied the feminine aspects of life, rejecting the Ibo blend of masculine and feminine—"a compromise of which Okonkwo is incapable" (Iyasere 1978, 108).

The women's point of view emerges in their narratives. Okonkwo's struggle to define himself as a hero, to define his society as fixed by tradition, by a noble past, and most of all by immutable, divine values (a refusal of social creolization and of foreign influences) is summed up in the form of the phallocratic narrative he attempts to impose.

In *Things Fall Apart* male and female narratives are presented from the outset as being in opposition to each other.[6] Generally, critics agree that Okonkwo has rejected the balanced Ibo approach to life, though none has actually analyzed what constitutes the feminine discourse. Innes finds Okonkwo's preference for male narrative linked to the privileging of "factual and historical" discourse in opposition to the womanly poetry linked to the world of myth and to fictional tales. Thus, "poetry, myth and fiction are all associated with the spiritual, the sacred, the feminine, and, paradoxically, the inner unspoken word" (Innes 1978b, 119). In the end, this view of Okonkwo's rejection, overly grounded in Innes's Christian perspective, leads to such totalizing as to allow no space for a male discourse of any consequence.

In one sense, this struggle between gendered narratives embraces all levels of conflict. Okonkwo's rejection of his father is cast in terms of a strong male son versus his weak, effeminate father. Even Unoka's flute is presented as being in tune with his weak character, as opposed to the strong male drum of Okoye. Unoye's borrowing, fear of fighting, and love of music are all qualities that encourage his enemies to label him an *agbala* (13), a woman—the same epithet Okonkwo used to "kill a man's spirit" (24). Okonkwo's disappointment with his son is expressed in similar terms: He wants Nwoye to grow into a man, but "there is too much of his mother in him" (60), a judgment repeated in more bitter terms after Nwoye has left Okonkwo's household to join the Christians. At the gathering of his sons, Okonkwo says, "If any of you prefers to be a woman, let him follow Nwoye now while I am alive so that I can curse him" (156). Okonkwo's good fortune with respect to his daughters is repeatedly presented in the form of his regret that Ezinma was not a boy.

Okonkwo's strengths are portrayed as monolithic, that is, all-male: "Looking at a king's mouth, one would think he never sucked at his mother's breast" (24). Appropriately Okonkwo continually attempts to control the nature of the discourse around him. At the large gathering of the clans at the marketplace, Okonkwo is not numbered among the orators: he is brusque and taciturn; his tongue trips and he stammers in his anger. His fists then serve his needs for expression. Thus he is apprehensive that other speakers will prevail. Obierika senses this: "Are you afraid he could convince us not to fight?" Okonkwo's reply is characteristically gruff: "Afraid? I do not care what he does to you . . ." (181). Similar differences in discourse can be heard when Okonkwo is in exile. Uchendo meets Obierika and hears about the coming of the whites. Whereas Okonkwo sees only the need to have fought them, Uchendo, older and more appreciative of the mother lode of settled wisdom, views their presence more philosophically and relatively, seeking to understand them and to act with the aplomb of the elders: "The world has no end . . ." (127). Okonkwo's response to opposition is to gnash his teeth and strike out, a response shared by many of the men in their dealings with the new missionaries and their settlement. The men who refused to join the group of Ikemefuna's executioners, the ones who listened to the missionaries, or who adapted to change, employed a discourse that differed significantly from Okonkwo's.

That was why Okonkwo tried to raise Nwoye on an exclusive diet of male narratives. He encouraged Nwoye to "grumble about women" (48), so as to demonstrate that "he would be able to control his women-folk." Ruling women became the only sign of possessing true manhood: "No matter how prosperous a man was, if he was unable to rule his women and his children (and especially his women) he was not really a man. He was like the man in the song who had ten and one wives and not enough soup for his foo-foo" (48). Most of all, Okonkwo tried to fill his sons with stories of "the land": "masculine stories of violence and bloodshed," stories that never pleased Nwoye as his mother's tales about "tortoise and his wily ways, and of the bird *eneke-nti-oba* who challenged the whole world to a wrestling contest and was finally thrown by the cat." Though Nwoye loved this form of narrative (perhaps secretly enjoying the reversal of his father's famous victory over Amalinze the Cat), "he now knew that they were for foolish women and children, and he knew that his father wanted him to be a man. And so he feigned that he no longer cared for women's stories" (48–49). Such tales or songs did not fit into Okonkwo's narrative regimen, but stories of male pride, of Okonkwo's war successes, such as the account of how he stalked his victim, "overpowered him and obtained his first human head," were told as they sat in the darkness "waiting for the women to finish the cooking" (49).

The attempt to control the influence of the female narrative upon the boys fits in with the larger strategy of controlling or stifling all forms of female expression. The first appearance of women in the novel is placed within the context of just such a hegemonic regime: When Okonkwo brings Ikemefuna home, and his senior wife (known only through the honorific title, "Nwoye's mother") asks, "Is he staying long with us?" Okonkwo's response is to thunder at her, "When did you become one of the *ndichie* of Umuofia?" (14). She falls silent and takes the boy in.

The narrator clearly presents the story from the same male-oriented perspective. For example, when the men are drinking palmwine, it is explained that the dregs "were supposed to be good for men who were going in to their wives" (20). We never see references to the sexual act, or other forms of male-female interaction, from the women's point of view. To the contrary, when Obierika's daughter Akueke appears, the narrator's lascivious gaze travels over her "full, succulent breasts," concluding with the judgment that she was not only beautiful, but "ripe" (64).

Generally the male domination extends over speech acts, so that when a woman speaks, it is the man who conveys her words. The noble figure of Anasi, Nwakibie's first wife, is introduced when Okonkwo first comes to beg for Nwakibie's assistance. Although the gathering must await her appearance before the others could drink, her words are reported indirectly, not repeated: "She rose, called him by his name and went back to her hut" (19). The narrator, who "sits" in on the male gathering, speaks for her. Speech is inseparable from space, and both are given here, always, from a gendered point of view.

Just as women's speech is focalized through, recast, or governed by, the male discourse, or simply silenced, so, too, is the women's presence limited and controlled. When "Evil Forest," the powerful *egwugwu,* or ancestral spirit, wished to demonstrate his terrible force, he "ran a few steps in the direction of the women; they all fled in terror" (84). The act of excluding the women is portrayed in a similar vein. The *egwugwu* house is decorated by the specially chosen women, but "these women never saw the inside of the hut. No woman ever did. They scrubbed and painted the outside walls under the supervision of the men" (80). Likewise, their words remain "under the supervision of men." When Ekwefi dares to "murmur something about guns that never shot" (35), Okonkwo fetches his gun and is saved from tragedy thanks only to his poor equipment.

Though Okonkwo doesn't approve of Nwoye's preference for his mother's tales, Nwoye is not prevented from hearing the women's stories. If the women can not see into the sacred hut, and are chased away by the *egwugwu,* this doesn't stop them from "return[ing] to their places almost immediately" (84). If they had no strengths to begin with, what would be the achievement of the men in asserting control over them? Though the white men are ruled by a woman (the English queen), and though the men joke over the idea of a woman making love on top of a man, the male preoccupation with control betrays a surface tension fully expressed in Okonkwo's fears of being thought weak, that is, womanish. His stammering accentuates the repression of these fears, figured as a difference or flaw.

Deities and spirits are periodically evoked in testimony to feminine power, though in conformity with the rule that as female they stand outside the ordinary structure of social authority. Thus Ani, the earth goddess, is the ultimate judge of morality and conduct (33), and the powerful medicine that accounts for the successful market at Umuike is attributed to "an old woman with a fan" (103), just as the potent war medicine of Umuofia is called *agadi-nwayi,* "old woman." The powerful Oracle of the Hills and Caves is referred to as "he," but his name, "Agbala," means "woman" (13). Clearly there is a compensating factor in the response to male domination, and it is fully expressed in both ideological and narrative forms.

The place of proverbs in this combat of gendered narratives is crucial. It is never made clear what constitutes the masculinity of a male narrative other than its content. Women's stories would seem to be free to range over a broad spectrum of topics with total creativity. Proverbs, of course, can address any subject, and would not seem to be intrinsically male or female. That's what makes it all the more significant that no woman utters a proverb in the entire novel.

In fact, there is an apparent exception to this general rule: the Priestess of Agbala, Chielo, who is also protectress of Ezinma, is the perfect figure to break the rule. The strongest of all the women in the novel, she stands apart from society as well as her gender when exercising her priestly function. In this, she recalls those other female priestesses and incarnations who also had become foci for power while functioning as outsiders to normal society[7]. Thus, Chielo's predecessor, Chika, "was full of the power of her god, and she was greatly feared" (16). When Unoka begins to make his feeble excuses to her, she remonstrates in tones decidedly more masculine than feminine in terms of the novel's normative patterns of discourse. Accordingly, her aphoristic advice verges on the proverbial: "When a man is at peace with his gods and his ancestors, his harvest will be good or bad according to the strength of his arm" (16).

In "ordinary life" Chielo is described as kind and friendly (44). However, when exercising her priestly function, she is altogether different: "Anyone seeing Chielo in ordinary life would hardly believe she was the same person who prophesied when the spirit of Agbala was upon her" (44). The night Chielo came for Ezinma, she was no longer Chielo, but the priestess of Agbala. Accordingly her discourse changed. When Okonkwo tried to dissuade her, she responded to him in terms, like those of Chika, that echoed proverbial formulae, though here stating a warning: "Does a man speak when a god speaks?" (91). She then shifted to the direct form of warning, "Beware!" Chielo further demonstrated her extra-ordinary state by carrying Ezinma on her back for phenomenal distances. When she heard the footsteps of Ekwefi behind her, she again uttered warnings in quasi-proverbial form: "Whether you are a spirit or man, may Agbala shave your head with a blunt razor! May he twist your neck until you see your heels!" (95).

As if to give definitive distinction to the Chielo of that night, the narrator qualifies her as performing impossible tasks because "Chielo *was not a woman* that night" (97; my stress). That being the case, we can say that when she comforts Ezinma with the following proverb, "A baby on its mother's back does not know that the way is long" (92), it is not a woman who is talking.

The gender of the speaker is subject to permeation. Is Chielo a woman speaking like a man, a woman changed into a man, or a woman through whom the god, beyond human definitions of male/female binary oppositions, is speaking? If the latter explanation comforts us with its transcendental logic, we should not forget that for Iyasere the opposition of Okonkwo to the great men of his society, Ndulue, Ezeudu, and Obierika, resides in the fact that the latter have achieved "the union of the masculine and feminine attributes essential in a great man"; that Ndulue found the "balance of strength and sensitivity, of masculine and feminine principles" (Iyasere 1978, 104). This balance Iyasere finds exhibited in Ezeudu and Obierika's reservations about Okonkwo's participation in the ritual killing of Ikemefuna. "The way which both Ezeudu and Obierika espouse is the way of compromise, of blending the masculine and the feminine, but this is a compromise of which Okonkwo is incapable" (101). Iyasere's assessment, commonly shared by other critics of *Things Fall Apart,* assumes a conventional interpretation of gender roles and identities, a binary opposition not really overcome, but joined in compromise by the flexible, wise male elders. It fails to challenge the roles or the concepts of discourse, the *conditions* that make gendered discourse possible. Thus, when Chielo crosses the gender line and utters words in a male format, as a proverb, their content reflects her femininity as they deal with babies and mothers. And when the wise men counsel humane actions tempered by understanding, they maintain the stature and status of counselors whose words retain the weight of authority and of advise that bears upon significant actions—not the status of storytellers. When Uchendu wants to tell Okonkwo a story about names like Nneka, it is also not to entertain, but to cause Okonkwo to change his behavior. Even as he advises Okonkwo that

"Mother is Supreme," he, the surrogate father, transmits the message of authority through his proverbial wisdom—even to the point of constructing a role for himself in the center of that discourse: "I had six wives once. I have none now except that young girl who knows not her right from her left" (122). We are not told if "that young girl" has borne him any of his many sons and daughters, or if it is only for others that the words "Mother is Supreme" apply.

To qualify the rule on gendered discourse and proverbs, then, we may say that no woman in a conventional Ibo female role utters a single proverb in the novel; normative female discourse does not contain proverbs.

Woman's discourse is, however, clearly delineated, and it contains more than tales. Close to proverbs are figurative expressions of folk wisdom, such as the belief that a twitching eyelid portends an imminent sight of something important, as Ekwefi explains to Ezinma before the wrestling match (37). Similarly, epithets, names, like metaphors, function to designate a quality while indicating a person: Ezinma is called "Ezigbo," meaning "the good one," while Obiageli called her "salt" due to her dislike of getting wet (150). It would seem that the line between this kind of troping, and the full-blown proverb, is a fine one, as we see in the mild rebukes Akueke's mother addressed to her when she was cooking: "Remove your *jigida* first. Every day I tell you that *jigida* and fire are not friends" (65).

If neither metaphorical usages nor indirect speech are reserved for the men, it might seem odd that proverbs, the quintessentially African form used to express wisdom, are so regulated in *Things Fall Apart*. However, the larger pattern of control and power exhibited in the novel explains this feature: proverbs are expressions of wisdom that indicate the power of the speaker—the power to persuade, to control others, to justify decisions or actions. Further, it is a legitimized power, since its origins lie with the primal source of authority, the ancestors. In a phallocratic society, this power is reserved for the males, or for those females whose functions lie outside the norm and who thus confirm the ordinary divisions of power. Proverbs are apparently the palm oil with which *male words are eaten.*[8]

Thus it is clearly not enough to identify the gender of the speaker to know what kind of narrative is being created. For one thing, males are counted by Okonkwo as female if they are not aggressive enough for his taste, and his daughter Ezinma so pleases him that all he can think is that she should have been a boy. The strong male-female polarization collapses at the margins, as we have seen with Chielo and her god, *Agbala.*

Indirect discourse, like the proverbs themselves, is also "the palm-oil with which words are eaten" (6). It is the appropriate means of expressing one's maturity, humility, and discretion. Above all, social grace and spiritual common sense meet in indirect discourse. Thus, Ekwefi answers, "Is that me?" when called from outside. People "never answered yes for fear it might be an evil spirit calling" (38). In contrast, when Unoka gets old and sick, it is his "love of talk," that is his lachrymose garrulousness, that "tried Okonkwo's patience beyond words" (23). Clearly, words, in all their forms of "superfluity," threaten Okonkwo. Ironically, the white District Commissioner echoes these sentiments as he totalizes all the Africans' discourse, when he observes: "One of the most infuriating habits of these people was their love of superfluous words" (185).

In the end there is no distinction between discourse and behavior as both combine to produce the appropriate kind of narrative. The contours of male narrative are defined less by genre than by attitude: Unoka's self-pitying remarks, the women's commiseration, are both obviously seen in opposition to male jokes about fear, expressions of male forms of honor. "Correct" speech is reflected in Obierika's concern for Okonkwo's welfare, as well as in Okonkwo's expressions of gratitude, as we see in the two men's bantering exchange:

> "I do not know how to thank you," Okonkwo said.
> "I can tell you," said Obierika. "Kill one of your sons for me."
> "That will not be enough," said Okonkwo. (128–29)

Obierika's final parry typifies the male play, with its submerged friendship hiding in back of a screen of ironic catachresis: "Then kill yourself" (129). Okonkwo's rare expression of gratitude shows his pleasure in such "strong" ways to demonstrate feeling, as well as his acknowledgment of Obierika's sentiments: "'Forgive me,' said Okonkwo, smiling. 'I shall not talk about thanking you any more'" (129).

Behind the wordplay, so rare in Okonkwo's discourse, are male attitudes that tug in opposing directions. Camaraderie and closeness are expressed in indirection, playful terms, or understatement. Conversely, male fortitude implies reticence and inexpressive patterns, as though the purity of the blow or the wrestler's hold could never be matched by verbal substitutes. Ibo society would seem to encourage this pattern of inarticulation, especially in the youths, while the older generation develops the art of applying wit and traditional truths to contemporary situations. Proverbs not only make words more palatable, they are hortatory devices utilized in place of force, especially in the large meetings of clansmen as well as in smaller encounters with family or friends. The larger the gathering, the more they function as acts of persuasion; the smaller the gathering, the more they approach the griot's function of praise singing, or its converse, as when Okonkwo's use of the epithet *"agbala"* "kill[ed] a man's spirit" (24).

As it is the women who are associated with telling tales, and the men with maintaining the prestige of their positions, with convincing others, with expressing judgments as well as opinions, it appears that the emphasis on "instructive" discourse is male, while that which is "entertainment" would seem to be female. This division may be of little use in understanding other societies where male storytellers might be more common, or where women might participate more in the process of social rule, but in *Things Fall Apart* it is central to the novel and its hero: Okonkwo is flawed because of his rejection of the female discourse *within* himself. The storytelling narrator signals his distance from Okonkwo in this regard in many ways. We see it when the term of opprobrium "*agbala*" is also used to denote the powerful Oracle; and it becomes the subject of Uchendo's lesson to Okonkwo in exile, which is to understand the need for "Mother," for the female powers ultimately expressed in the name Nneka, meaning "Mother is Supreme" (121).

This fits Iyasere's judgment that Okonkwo can not see compromise, overlap, spillover in gender roles—that Okonkwo is absolute in his definitions of gender: "For Okonkwo, one is either a man or a woman, there can be no compromise, no composite. . . . This one-sided concept of what it takes to be a man determines Okonkwo's actions and attitudes" (Iyasere 1978, 104). Iyasere calls this a "monochromatic view of what people should be . . . " (104). Although he is referring to tasks, we could apply his statement here to discursive practice. If Okonkwo is the one who accomplishes this by "wrestling with his *chi*," as Iyasere puts it (105), we can only conclude that the female principle must reside with the *chi* in some way that is not too obvious.

Chi and the Last Word

We generally encounter the *chi* in *Things Fall Apart* in proverbial spaces. We have seen how Okonkwo is depicted through the two proverbs dealing with personal initiative as one who compels his *chi* to say yes ("Okonkwo said yes very strongly, so his *chi* agreed. And not only his *chi*, his clan, too" [Achebe (1958) 1972, 25]), or as one who turns his *chi* into a personal nemesis by his hubris ("[He] so far forgot himself after a heavy meal that he challenged his *chi*" [28]). As for the former, Okonkwo equivocates a number of times about whether his *chi* is saying yes or no to him (25, 119, 139, 156); *chi* here is an externalization of good or bad luck, without any space of its own. But when it is figured as the nemesis that corrects hubris, as the wrestler's other self who borrows strength from its victim, it appears more personal, more invincible, more specific. It is, in form, an ironic correction to excess. Its ironical nature is indicated by its tiny size. The perfect story about Okonkwo is really told in Achebe's *Arrow of God*

([1964] 1974), in which the wrestler who challenges all comers, who overcomes all the great men and great spirits, becoming a champion in both realms, would not "come away" from the realm of spirits until, finally, "his personal god, a little wiry spirit . . . seized him with one hand and smashed him on the stony earth" (Achebe [1964] 1974, 27).

This ironic inversion of size suggests that there is an antithesis to the strong male ideal, a countervailing principle that defeats Okonkwo, lacking as he is in the qualities of the feminine principle. However, the male-female opposition does not suffice to give us *chi*. *Chi* is essentially a spirit being, and as such is in nature the inverse of all that is human. Thus Benjamin Ray characterizes African mythic cosmology: "[T]he concept of inversion is important, for it explains the world in dialectical terms as the relation between opposing spheres: order/disorder, cosmos/chaos. Whether the original state of affairs is conceived as cosmos or chaos, it is always the opposite of the human situation—hence it is sacred or divine" (Ray 1976, 39). Its oppositional qualities, however, do not remove it so far from the human as to end any encounter between the two. It is in some way a quintessential part of the very being whose nature is radically different from it. It is, in a sense, the undefinable quality of *différance* that accompanies every well-defined being, every centered presence. It is Okonkwo's otherness, not simply his other gender. And Achebe provides us with the means to sense that quality of otherness in his discussion of the names associated with *chi.*

In addition to defining *chi* as personal spirit, Achebe offers the more interesting information that *chi* signifies a *cusp* in time, the "transitional period between day and night, or night and day" (Achebe 1975, 93). It is a liminal, in-between space: "We also have the word *mgbachi* for that most potent hour of noon that splits the day in two" (93). *Chi* is the ontological negation of oneness, of monological presence: "the central place in Igbo thought [is] the notion of duality. Wherever Something stands, Something Else will stand beside it" (94). In addition to rejecting the absolute, this affirmation of the "Something Else" gives us this key: the Other is our complementary other self—it is what completes us while being outside of us at the same time. In Derridean terms, it is our supplement.

Further, what Achebe sees in the moral of the story of the wrestler destroyed by his *chi* is that "the place where *chi* inhabits is forbidden to man" (Achebe 1975, 96). If the building for the *egwugwu* is forbidden to the women, there is the complementary custom that reserves such areas as kitchens and menstruation or female-initiation houses to the women, as well as such activities as the preparation of food, assisting in childbirth, ritual cleansing, and so forth. In discussing the names associated with *chi,* Achebe focuses on one that signifies Great God, Chukwu, thus linking *chi* to the god in the sky—a male figure whose home is like that inhabited by *chi*—a place for gods, not humans. However, the other name for this deity is Chineke, a name of uncertain etymology, but one that Achebe concludes must signify *chi na* [and] *eke. Eke,* "the mysterious second member of the duality" (Achebe 1975, 101), is linked, like the other names given to *chi,* with creation. But its most distinctive quality is its function as a double for *chi*—the two names perhaps occurring in different regions of Iboland, both conveying the notion of Supreme God. The doubling of the names for God, not unusual in the joining of two communities, comes to signify the principle of doubling that would lie at the very core of divinity itself, returning Achebe most naturally to the gendered doubling that haunts Okonkwo. This possibility, suggested to us by a casual, throwaway statement in Achebe's essay on *chi,* brings the earth (home of the female goddess Ani) and the sky into union: "From the foregoing it would appear that *chi* and *eke* are very closely related deities, perhaps the same God in a two-fold manifestation, such as male and female" (101). Though the notion of joining the genders is given in an offhand simile, it is appropriate for the God "whose role in the world is shrouded in mystery and *metaphor*" (102; my stress). It is a short step from mystery and metaphor to the implication of proverbs in the gendering of discourse.

The women who serve as Agbala's priestesses are both linked to the male sky divinity through their names—Chika and Chielo; the offenses committed by Okonkwo are all against the female goddess of the earth, Ani—as when Okonkwo breaks the week of peace, when he inadvertently kills Ezeudu's son, and, conceivably, when he kills Ikemefuna. The mysterious death of Ozoemena, as Iyasere points out, implies the same kind of joining of the genders. "The union in life and in death of Ndulue and Ozoemena is a symbolic dramatization of the masculine and feminine attributes essential in a great man" (Iyasere 1978, 104)—and in a great woman, like Chielo, we would add. The principle that divides the day, that divides the genders and their discourses, that is itself a figure of dualism, of division, and of otherness within itself, that is at once one's essential being and that which is needed to give completion to being—what is this figure of clash and tension but metaphor, and its extension into proverb. This is that same split trope that carries its meaning on the back of another, like the figure of the mother and child in which the child "does not know that the way is long" when "it is on its mother's back" (92). This proverb is the one spoken by Chielo when carrying Ezinma.

Okonkwo's attempts to impose a male-only discourse on his family, especially Nwoye, and subsequently on all of Umuofia and Ibo society in general, all meet with failure. And it is a failure, also, of the society that created him as a hero, that invested him with its dominant values, and that he, in turn, summarized in his demeanor. Yet in its larger project, the novel reinscribes the women's discourse into the narrative.

When Obierika's in-laws come to visit him, they pray for children like Okonkwo—to them he is the essence of manhood and of Ibohood. But Okonkwo also stammers. Unoka may be a failure, but he is also depicted as an artist—as one happier making music than making war. Achebe cast this image—the closest to that of the role he himself plays as writer—in ambivalent terms. If Okonkwo condemns Unoka unsparingly, his harshness can be attributed not so much to Unoka's despised nature—he is described as a peaceful soul, after all—but to a son's inability to accept an *agbala* for a father. For the narrator, however, if Unoka is idle, he also loves gentleness (13).

Nwoye, who is the first in Okonkwo's family to abandon traditional ways, and who is also the reincarnation of his grandfather, Unoka (140), behaves like the artist cum mediator. He learns English, converts to Christianity, and as the newly christened Isaac enters the new training college for teachers (165). Okonkwo feels Nwoye's conversion is a betrayal of the ancestors, and he shudders at the thought of being neglected himself as an ancestor. Nwoye, like Ezeulu's son Oduche in *Arrow of God* ([1964] 1974), looks not to the past but to the future, to the "reign of the son" ([1964] 1974, 230).

If the epic hero is "a part of the cultural past," and "typifies a cultural ethos," he becomes still more "emblematic of change. . . . He has a vision of the new world" (Scheub 1985, 13). Scheub's description of the struggle created by that vision suggests Nwoye more than Okonkwo: "The revolutionary zeal of the hero, his insistent posing on the borders of society, his vulnerability and mental struggles, his agonizing battles with the traditions of society and the teaching of the gods, have emancipated him from the submissive tale character" (13). Together the son and the father divide the figure of the epic hero in two, just as the hero, "caught between past and future," must choose to act, moving the community, and the story, forward.[9]

Past and present meet in Achebe's synthesis of these traditional elements within the framework of an historical novel, thus echoing the proverb itself, which comes from the past to be applied to the present. *Things Fall Apart* works like an African proverb whose employment is invariably a deployment, whose message is always inferred and never averred.

Achebe views his task as that of educator.[10] But the novel avoids any tone of strident didacticism. In part this is because, as with the proverb, the message is to be found less in a preconceived conclusion than in dialogic implications, in part because the women's discourse is reinscribed into the novel's larger project.

Achebe "signifies" on the older testimonies of arriviste novels like *Mr. Johnson* (Cary [1939] 1962) that prevailed in the 1950s, and turns the expert ex-pat testimony given in "The Pacification of Primitive Tribes" (187) into an indictment of colonialism. The act of proverbial signifying entails telling a story that is entertaining, which clearly places the narration within the camp of female discursive practices, while enjoining the readers to redefine their attitudes toward colonial history and African society as well as toward contemporary Africa, which is clearly a male strategy in terms of the novel's definitions. This balance is expressed perfectly in the self-conscious use of the proverb in which a point is always being made efficiently and yet elegantly. In short, *Things Fall Apart* is an extended proverb on disruption, on the need to accommodate change, and the tragic consequences of the failure to "fly without perching" when men learned to shoot.

Chapter 6

▼▼▼▼▼▼▼▼▼

Of Fathers and Sons—A Cusp in African Literature

FERDINAND OYONO,
Une Vie de boy; Chemin d'Europe; Le Vieux Nègre et la médaille

Une Vie de boy; Chemin d'Europe

Whatever happened to Toundi's parents? They are dropped from the story line of *Une Vie de boy,* their deaths only casually mentioned. The relationships are left dangling and thus are easily transposed: Toundi's father is replaced first by Father Gilbert (now "mon père," remembered for his swift kicks, albeit with some measure of gratitude for his kindness and especially for his efforts at "civilizing" Toundi).

Like the small boy in Mongo Beti's *Le Roi miraculé* (1958), the young Toundi is a kind of pet to Father Gilbert. His rapidly acquired command over French is the sign of his intelligence and the key to his success with this new father. When Father Gilbert dies, Toundi dies a "first death" (my trans.).* The declension of white fathers, from the mistrustful Father Vandermayer, who did not scruple at humiliating Africans he regarded as sinners, to the brutal Commandant, merely continues the pattern established by Toundi's own father. The young protagonist moves in protest/revolt against the brutalities of a selfish, stupid, or unjust African father into a system ruled by white men. He encounters the economic rule of Greek merchants and bus drivers; the political rule of French commanders; the religious rule of French priests; the cultural rule of French teachers; the linguistic rule of French-language speakers; and he uses all of them against his African father.

---

* "mort une première fois" (Oyono [1956a] 1970, 32). All page references to this text are to the 1970 edition. Unless otherwise indicated by reference to the 1982 translation by John Reed, all translations are my own.

The lesson of *Une Vie de boy* reverses that of *L'Enfant noir* (Laye [1953] 1972): it is that under colonialism the African child can not grow to manhood in the normal way, that is, by eventually replacing his father, ascending into his position of authority to enjoy his prerogatives. Toundi finds that his path of revolt is a false one because he is ultimately blocked by colonial strictures ("You suffer from illusions of grandeur," * Madame tells Toundi). Toundi's own death may be seen as a consequence of a determined revolt—but it is nonetheless ambivalent as such because it takes the form of a flight, and even of a final reversion to the childish weakness of gluttony: the dying Toundi smacks his lips in appreciation of the fine *arki,* failing to heed his mother's warning that gluttony would do him in one day. Like the deluded parrots trapped by village children using grains of corn, as a child he had followed the priest who distributed candy and gave Toundi his "delicious" leftovers. . . .[1] Toundi, however ambivalently regressing, does not become an eater of leftovers at the end. Having been one initially, he matures and learns the meaning of leftovers, ragged clothes, unrequited love, and feelings of exclusion; he shares the fate of colonized Africans who witness the feast being devoured by the gluttonous whites—which explains why, in *Le Vieux Nègre,* the white High Commissioner is portrayed as a sow.

When Toundi and the others gather to watch the whites at M. Janopoulos's Cercle européen, they lose their identity as "hommes-mûrs" [grown-up men], becoming both anonymous onlookers and bit players in a comic scene as the dogs are unleashed and they take to their heels or to the trees. If the dogs are a crude device to turn the gaze from whites to blacks, they are also effective symbols for the whites' nonchalant dismissal of the blacks as less than human. As Arthur Flannigan (1982) has shown, gazing on the other is the primary device in *Une Vie de boy* for establishing domination, thus forming the link between the comic technique of using dogs and the brutal beatings Toundi endures at the end, all of which are intended to force his gaze down.[2]

For Oyono colonialism is a fraud best exposed in its small deceptions and not on a grand scale or on abstract ideological terms. Madame becomes upset when her hidden prophylactics are discovered, as if a public view of the seaminess of the whites' lives, their feet of clay, would undermine the ideological basis for their claim to a superior position. Colonialism is also marked by betrayal: the promises of Christian love betrayed by the insensitive, prejudiced, degrading actions taken by the

---

* "[Tu]as la folie des grandeurs" (Oyono [1956a] 1970, 88).

priests, even by the well-intentioned Father Gilbert; the humanist ideals mocked and derided when the teacher, M. Salvain, attempts to put them into practice; the rhetoric of "la mission civilisatrice" [the civilizing mission] contradicted by the actual living conditions of the blacks and the whites. Toundi's "elevation" to a status of importance is dismissed by his own sardonic evaluation of himself as "the dog of the king and the king of the dogs."*

Colonial ideology, the indispensable factor in any analysis of Oyono's fiction, provides the key to all relationships. Without it the Commandant's poor understanding of Christian doctrine would not be relevant, and Madame's immoral behavior would not disillusion Toundi; most of all, the true African father would have had no rivals to usurp his place, nor would the white fathers be in a position then to betray the trust placed in them. Without it we would have relations of force, roles based on brute power, rule validated by the mastery of the weapons of conquest. That Meka, in *Le Vieux Nègre et la médaille* ([1956b] 1979), was obliged *somehow* to *yield* his lands, and that they were not appropriated outright testifies to its implicit force. It serves as the excuse employed by Engamba's wives to leave him as quickly as possible. Every image that plays on the laughable contrast between boorish villagers and *civilized* types or their minions recalls us to this factor in Oyono's fiction.

In *Une Vie de boy* Oyono marches us past a series of minor figures who oscillate between two poles, those who have resisted colonialism and those who were co-opted. This dualism is best exemplified by the two chiefs who come to pay tribute to the Commandant. The first, Akoma, "the King of rings,"† displays all the negative qualities associated with Oyono's father-figures, namely, control of women, abuse of positions of authority, a subservient demeanor and a lack of dignity before the whites that is shown by crude attempts at acculturation. Akoma's antithesis is Mengueme, the elder who lost two sons in the war, and who earned praises for his wisdom and his ability to hide his strengths from his enemies: "He is an old man as cunning as the tortoise in the fables. He understands and speaks French but always pretends not to. . . . Mengueme has never traveled. His wisdom doesn't require travel. He is an elder" (56–57).‡

---

* "le chien du roi [et] le roi des chiens" (32).

† "le Roi des bagues" (Oyono [1956a] 1970, 55)

‡ "[Il] est un vieillard aussi rusé que la tortue des legendes. Bien qu'il comprenne et parle le français, il fait toujours semblant de ne rien comprendre. . . . Mengueme n'a jamais voyagé. Sa sagesse n'a pas besoin de voyages. C'est un ancien."

Toundi's last moments with his father occur when his father comes to the Mission to request that Toundi return home. Toundi refuses and sticks out his tongue, enjoying the protection provided by the missionary. With Father Gilbert nearby, he could say, "I wasn't afraid of anything." *
His father returns home, a beaten man who dares not raise his eyes against the white authority. "His gaze seemed to spellbind my father who lowered his head and retreated completely, taken aback." † Toundi's revolt is completed when his mother comes the next day and gives him her blessing, approving of his departure from such an unloving father. Father Gilbert then provides Toundi with a pair of pants and a red jersey, assuming the new role of parent. However, after the death of the benevolent Father Gilbert, Toundi is passed on to the less paternal Father Vandermayer, finally becoming the "boy" of the uncircumcized Commandant. By that point we are not surprised to find his original naive acceptance of the French "father" challenged by the comparison of the ridiculed, acculturated Akoma with the self-possessed traditional figure of Mengueme. The problem of finding a father cannot be separated from the issues raised by colonialism.

The death of Toundi's parents is mentioned without any comment, whereas the death of Father Gilbert is presented as a calamity. This is the point of departure for Toundi to find himself, to define himself in a new world. It also leaves us without a solution to the son's problem of developing his relationship with a father who was not acculturated. This is precisely the issue taken up in *Chemin d'Europe* (Oyono 1960) with the series of relationships between Barnabas and his actual father, and his father's surrogates. While sharing the brutal, oppressive nature of Toundi's father, Barnabas's father is marked by the additional disfigurement of a humpback, which increases in prominence over the course of the narrative. A crude symbol of the man's graceless nature, it evokes images of the Hunchback of Notre Dame as the father scurries around the church where he works and to which he devotes his life. In a memorable scene, Barnabas enters the church and observes his father clumsily performing his tasks. As he carries out his functions, walking down the aisle, he approaches his son who views him without, himself, being seen. "And my father was coming closer, the little excrescence of flesh that was crushing his neck became more and more luminous, more and more fantastic, when conjoined with the glitter of his braid. He stopped at the level of my

---

* "je ne craignais rien" (22).

† "Son regard semblait fasciner mon père qui baissa la tête et s'éloigna tout penaud" (22).

pew and then moved away to continue his route . . ." (Oyono 1989, 41). *
The approaching father looms like a nightmare vision, and fades away
again into the obscurity of the church. His disfigurement appears grafted
onto his back, as though by an external, malefic demiurge. The son sits
frozen in fear that this laughable, pitiful disfigured creature will claim
him, or even berate him. The narrative then flashes forward to the father's
burial, with a processional leading through that same church. Barnabas is
one of the coffin bearers, and what with the roughhewn coffin and the
father's hump, the solemn act of bearing the body is turned into another
grotesque nightmare. The corpse rolls about unevenly, due to the hump,
bumping against the insides of the ill-fashioned box; the water that col-
lects in the grave keeps the coffin afloat, and it must be weighted down
with rocks and tilted on one end to get it into the ground.

It is difficult to find a more striking image of the difference between
the early works of African literature and this novel, than that conveyed
here by Oyono's description of the funeral of Barnabas's father. For
Achebe, heroic figures such as Okonkwo and Ezeulu, representatives of
the old ways, have great and admirable qualities that are undermined by
equally important flaws: if they die failures, it is with nobility. Though
they are compromised, they do not compromise the order they represent
and embody. And, at their best, the fathers, in this literature, are visionar-
ies, guides, and saviors for their sons, as in the case of Laye's father.

The model father provided by Laye in *L'Enfant noir* is close to his son,
and he laments the loss of his son to the new life brought by the Europeans. In *Dramouss* (1966), Laye completes the portrait of his father—a man
known to us, appropriately, just as "père"—as a thoroughly admirable figure. His outstanding qualities include his dignity and, as we saw in *L'Enfant noir,* his hospitality, extended to a fault; his indifference to crass materialism, resulting in relative impoverishment in *Dramouss*; his perspicacity,
both with respect to people, like his wife, and to politics; and, most strikingly, as seen at the end of *Dramouss,* his mystic powers, grounded thoroughly in Malinke traditions and especially in Muslim righteousness and
faith. In short, the father figure attains an apotheosis in Laye's oeuvre, and
is held up as an ideal.

---

* "Et mon père se rapprochait; la petite excroissance de chair lui écrasant le cou devenait de
plus en plus lumineuse, de plus en plus fantastique, sous l'éclat des galons. Il vint s'arrêter
à ma hauteur, puis s'éloigna pour continuer son itinéraire . . . " (Oyono 1960, 59). All page
references to this text are to the 1960 edition, and to the 1989 translation by Richard Bjornson.

The immediate differences between Laye's father and Barnabas's are established at the outset of *Chemin d'Europe* where Barnabas states, "No matter how devout and *mystical* he was, my father was nevertheless a brute" (18; my stress).* The image of the father as brute is carried through in much of the work of revolt. In their early works both Oyono and Mongo Beti depicted fathers as mentally and physically abusive of their wives and sons. This pattern is carried through with Yambo Ouologuem, with the portrayal of the village fathers by Gabriel Okara or Wole Soyinka (as in *The Strong Breed* [1973]). In *Chemin d'Europe* and Beti's *Mission terminée* (1957a) the father or chief is further denigrated for either direct complicity or collaboration with the colonial authorities, or for his materialistic, greedy connivance with the powers of the new dispensation. The grotesqueness of Barnabas's father suggests the maladroitness associated with the early years of acculturation; he is seen as a curious kind of clown from the perspective of the early colonial administrator (reflected in such creations as Mister Johnson or Conrad's cannibal helmsman) and from that of his own disaffected son. Thus, Barnabas's father would typically be decked out in his "uniform . . . black with silver braid and a matching two-pointed military student's hat, all in all rather solemn and sinister, but papa was barefoot, and the effect was not what it might have been . . ." (38).† The effect is more than comic. When the prostitutes assume an appropriately Western appearance, they become "traîtresses" (Oyono 1960, 108).

There is no reference in the scene of Barnabas's father in church, or elsewhere in this novel, to a pristine African tradition besmirched by this collaboration. The only possibility envisaged is to move forward in time, though the prospects are unknown. Barnabas has to learn to put on an act, to become a performer for the white man, in order to escape his condition. Instead of an act of reclaiming or recuperation, revolt literature takes the more negative route of dismissal. The paternal heritage is experienced as a shameful betrayal, in the last analysis an almost unbearable burden. This is what Oyono captures in his most striking image, that of Barnabas carrying the full weight of all that his father represents on his head: "my father's emaciated body rolled above my head and clumped ceaselessly about like a mole carrying a heavy load and stumbling across an attic floor; he was constantly off balance due to the hunchback that, undiminished by death,

---

* "Si croyant et mystique qu'il fût, mon père n'en était pas moins une brute" (9; my stress).

† "costume . . . noir, galonné d'argent, avec un bicorne de polytechnicien bien assorti, le tout sinistre et solonel en somme, mais papa étant pieds nus, l'effet n'était plus celui qu'il aurait pu être . . ." (51)

caused him to bump the thin planks of the coffin with a lugubrious frequency" (39).* For Barnabas, the remains of a father who was always "en déséquilibre" [off balance] convey the opposite of the wisdom of the "sages"; he experiences nausea at the thought of the Biblical injunction "Blessed are the poor in spirit!" (42)† and concludes by denying the tie: "the pulpous mass of someone I cannot call my father moves through the emptiness inside my head . . ." (42).‡

Further, his father's death does not end his relations with paternal figures. At the end of the novel M. Isadore Bendjanga, leads Barnabas to a night spot where M. Bendjanga is mistaken for Barnabas's father. As the evening has unpleasant consequences, Barnabas tries to avoid the fracas by asserting, "He's not my father!" (101).** Just as Laye completes the elevation of his father as sage in *Dramouss,* so, too, does Oyono complete his fall in *Chemin d'Europe.* Mocked and crudely buried, the original caricatural image of obsequiousness is dismissed in absentia for his betrayal of African traditions and values with nearly the same words used by Olunde in *Death and the King's Horseman*: "I have no father" (Soyinka 1975, 61).

The father resists the son's dismissal; the son must bury him with difficulty. Barnabas assumes the weight of the father only in the act of ridding himself of him. It is the fulfillment of their relationship, the hard condition of the cycle of repetition, of sons burying fathers, working itself out. Yet, for Oyono, it is marked by ambivalence because the sign of this Christian father's weakness, his subservient insertion into the white man's world, is at once the source of Barnabas's embarrassment (his father is referred to as "someone I cannot call my father" [42]) †† and the source of Barnabas's own success, predicated as it is on his ability to read and write French better than the others (he is "a chap who speaks French better than anyone in the neighborhood" [81]), ‡‡ which culminates in his taking the "chemin d'Europe," or road to Europe.

---

* ". . . sur mon crâne roulait, vrombissait avec un bruit de course pesante et sans répit de taupe, errant à travers un plafond, le maigre corps de mon père sans cesse en déséquilibre sur sa bosse que la mort n'avait pas diminuée et qui lui faisait heurter les minces planches du cerceuil . . ." (54–55).

† "Bien heureux les pauvres d'esprit!" (60).

‡ "dans ma tête vide remue la masse-poulpe de quelqu'un que je ne peux appeler mon père .- . ." (60).

** "ce n'est pas mon père" (186).

†† "quelqu'un que je ne peux appeler mon père" (60)

‡‡ "un gar qui parle français comme pas un au quartier" (145)

The same ambivalence obtains in Barnabas's relationship with his mother. When he leaves home, he takes his mother with him. However, she eventually finds his drinking too unpleasant to bear and decides to return to her husband. Barnabas's sense of indignation with himself comes from the realization that he was acting as his father had. In the space between these two positions, the son, a split subject, must attempt to navigate a new identity.

If the father is not "un vrai ancien," but merely a sycophant of the church, Barnabas becomes a pitiful performer for some well-meaning American missionaries in order to gain his passage to Europe. The ambiguity of his position is as basic to his being as the language with which he constructs his *récit*: a sophisticated French, with complex sentences employing deep embedding, and a vocabulary marked by terms that are often recherché.

Barnabas's and Toundi's relationships with other characters are double-edged, love/hate bonds with all that is African/European, whether those characters represent one dimension of the Janus-headed figure, or combine the two. This ambivalence is matched by the interior schism in the heart of the protagonists themselves. Doubling or splitting is the most important feature of Oyono's work, and it is most prominent in *Une Vie de boy* and *Chemin d'Europe,* which are both narrated in the first person and which are presented in the sardonic tone of mock autobiography.

Nothing in *Chemin d'Europe,* inspires us to believe that Barnabas's new life in Europe will be liberating or fulfilling. The death of Toundi, the lack of closure for *all* the youthful protagonists in Oyono's as well as Beti's early fiction testify more to profound uncertainty than to unquestioned commitment. Whatever foundation the writers of literatures of *témoignage* needed to inspire their efforts at recuperation or reclamation, it was no longer available to the angry young generation of writers that succeeded them.

Le Vieux Nègre et la médaille: Esu's Double Laughter

Both Oyono and Beti in their early novels employ naive protagonists whose perspective we initially share; we also share the narrator's apparent attitude toward the protagonist, changing our views as the protagonist experiences his successive disillusionments. From the start there are hints, sometimes blatant, sometimes more subtle, concerning the protagonist's naïveté. These hints are never given without a wink. The naïveté then appears to be a kind of sham: the characters put on a mask of naïveté at the same time they actually are naive. Glimpses behind the mask are permitted us, unsettling our initially comfortable attitudes. Indeed, *Une Vie de boy* begins with the device of an external narrator whose encounter with the moribund Toundi encourages us to distance ourselves from Toundi's unreflexive acceptance of the whites from the outset. But from the first the entry of the young Toundi into the mission is presented as an enlistment into an abusive system, ridden with cynicism and corruption. Both Toundi and Denis, Toundi's counterpart in *Le Pauvre Christ de Bomba* (Beti [1956] 1976), seem *immediately* to be aware of the corruption of the system, and to take it for granted. If they are awakened, it is not to the abuse of the women in the *sixa,* but to their mistake in thinking that their participation would privilege them in a way that the others could not share, that they would escape the fate of the other dupes. They saw themselves as being on the side of the ruling class, as having joined the whites. Nowhere in *L'Enfant noir* does Laye's pain derive from an awareness that this privileged place was merely an appearance. In more *engagé* works, there is no self-awakening for the ideologue who sees the flaws of colonialism and opposes them from the outset. There's no need to be awakened if one's purpose is to celebrate the glories of one's heritage or past: it's the illusions of *others* that are exploded in literatures of *témoignage.*

In *Le Vieux Nègre,* the reader is directly engaged by the humorous accounts of the "country bumpkins." The question is, Through whom is the humor focalized? When presented with our familiar division of the subject into three identities—the three "I"s (Todorov 1981, 39)—we expect a dominant or authoritative discourse to emerge. This competition is what is glossed over when the three "I"s merge in classic realism. The merging of the three "I"s can be read as the submersion of the distinctions between three subjects who stand in different places in terms of time and place, but whose identities converge. They are, as Catherine Belsey puts it, paraphrasing Louis Althusser, subjugated by virtue of becoming the subject of another's vision (Belsey 1981, 62). The act of subjection is one of both submersion and subjugation. For Althusser it is the acceptance of the ideological assumptions, the givens, understood to be the props of the narrator's point of view. This acceptance is accomplished when the feeling that a statement is natural or normal is transferred without resistance from the text to the reader via the reader's textual surrogates, the narrator or protagonist.

Belsey would have it that this is the project of classic realism, and one could thus argue that the "normalized" world of literatures of *témoignage* is one that reassures the reader. The subject that addresses us with such confidence as to win our assent never betrays himself or herself, never shows the wink of the con man. Between Ibrahim Dieng, the duped protagonist of Sembène Ousmane's *Le Mandat* (1965), and the knowledgeable narrator, there is no exchange of roles. The ideological assurances of the narrator are acquired through the hard lessons Ibrahim Dieng has to learn, as is generally the case with Sembène's protagonists. We are the surrogate subjects whose point of view merges with that of the narrator and that of his awakened protagonists. The subjection is made complete as the reader follows the path of Ibrahim's enlightenment. This is possible only if the propositions, the hard lessons, are made to appear convincing. This is the role of the various wise voices—that of the postman or of the public scribe in *Le Mandat,* of the tailor Mussinga in Jose Vieira's *Luuanda* (1980), or of Ngugi and Micere Mugo's Dedan in *The Trial of Dedan Kimathi* (1976). It is reinforced by the mise-en-scène, which may simply involve the juxtaposition of corrupt leadership with Mercedes Benzes and bottles of imported water.

The assent demanded by comedy is not exactly the same. Laughter is elicited when a set of premises is demonstrated in a particular set of circumstances. The premise may be the belief that villagers are naive, and the infinity of circumstances that would generate laughter would be intended to evoke that naiveté, as when a foolish villager gets lost, finds it difficult to cross a street, wears ragged or inappropriate clothes, speaks in a ridiculous manner, and so forth. Further, the premises do not necessarily have to be shared by the reader for the comic effect to be felt—one can suspend one's disagreement with the premises, reading "as if" they were shared, so as to get the joke. This suspension is the first act in the interpellation of the reader, and it is where Oyono likes to initiate his complicated relationship with the reader who naively assumes that the premises of the joke, like those so confidently assumed in literatures of *témoignage,* are the ones on which the narrative is based. In other words, the assumption is that the subject addressing us is both unified and to be trusted. Chez Oyono the subject is never one or the other.

Oyono begins *Le Vieux Nègre* with a succession of humorous images that interpellate the reader with the most forceful of stereotyped images, that of Africans as animals. At prayer Meka and Kelara kneel "like camels waiting to be loaded."* More positively, Meka suggests that Essomba, the clever one, had eaten Tortoise (a clever creature). Coarseness is repeatedly suggested, by the sight of naked buttocks in particular, but also by naked flesh exposed through worn clothing. Finally, allusions to darkness of skin are also employed to the same ends. All this gives us the slightly uneasy sense, building throughout Part One, that the mockery into whose spirit we are invited to enter, is too exaggerated to be real, that Oyono could not

---

* "comme des chameaux qu'on charge" (Oyono [1956b] 1979, 10)

possibly mean it, that these silly, weak "villageois" [villagers] could not be irrevocably condemned to *otherness*.

Oyono barrages the reader with images related to animals, nudity, physical decrepitude, and color. Sardines and sows greet Meka as he begins his day. The white chief of police is nicknamed "Gullet" (literally "bird gullet" [gosier d'oiseau]) both here and in *Une Vie de boy,* while the waking villagers open their doors to let not only themselves out, but also the domesticated animals with whom they share their habitations (Oyono 1969, 13). At thirty, Mvondo, Meka's nephew, is "bald, wrinkled, and gnarled like an ancient lizard" (Oyono 1969, 18),* and Evina the cook, not likened to an animal, is made even more grotesque: with no teeth left "his mouth had sunk in, dropping his chin down on to his neck . . ." (18).† The foolishly proud catechist wants to be thought of as a missionary: "we missionaries are like owls" (22),‡ he pontificates. The humorous story about the clever Protestant catechist centers on the image of a man who hunts monkey, kills a baboon, and, concomitantly, makes sexual advances to the chief's wife. Deeper in the countryside, the references multiply, at once in number, intensity, and degree. Strangers lap water like dogs (29); an old sponge named Mbogni is likened to a "tapeworm with a head like a bat's" (28);** Engamba is first seen eating viper, spitting over ducks, and then greeting a stranger whose nostrils are as "black and hairy as a gorilla hide" (30).†† Naked buttocks dropping to the ground, and gorilla-like figures proliferate.[3]

The ambiguity of this imagery can be seen in the way camels are employed. The association of Christian prayer with the undignified camel-like posture suggested by raised buttocks is made three times in Part One, yet Engamba refers to Meka as "the camel that will pass through the eye of the needle" (59).‡‡ Toward the end of Part One the comic image is broadened: "'Now let us pray,' said Meka, kneeling down in his usual fashion with his behind up in the air. . . . When all the behinds were up in the air he laid his hand against his forehead" (79).***

---

* "sans cheveux, ridé et rugueux comme un vieux lézard" (Oyono [1956b] 1979, 24). All page references to this text are to the 1979 edition, and to the 1969 translation by John Reed, unless otherwise indicated as my translation.

† "Sa bouche s'était affaissée en rabattant le menton sur le cou . . ." (24).

‡ "Nous autres, missionaires . . . nous sommes commes les hiboux" (29).

** "un vieux ver solitaire à la tête de chauve-souris" (35)

†† "aussi noires et velues qu'une peau de gorille" (38)

‡‡ "le chameau qui passera par le trou de l'aiguille . . ." (68)

*** "Maintenant prions, dit Meka en s'agenouillant le derrière en l'air comme il avait l'habi-

Similarly, Meka is associated with the "panther-rat." As he appears at Mammy Titi's bar, his trousers soaked, he states his preference for paths over roads. A neighbor laughs at him: "Your mother must have eaten a panther-rat when she was carrying you" (7).* The others join in the laughter now, though later the association of Meka with the panther is reinforced. Here the mockery is directed at Meka's "bush" qualities—qualities that come into play again toward the end of Part One when Meka, ridiculously attired in the latest Parisian fashion, a "zazou" suit, incurs the wrath of his wife. When Engamba tries to mollify her, she upbraids her brother: "We are not in the bush here" (75).†

References to blackness and apes would appear to be less ambivalent, but in fact occur in ways that surprise and confuse us. Generally they are applied to real villagers, those whose darkness or simianlike qualities suggest a distance from "civilization." Thus the Gabonese soldiers brought in for the 14th of July celebration are "black as the bottom of a pot, . . . their heads the same shape as a ram's scrotum and their teeth like the teeth of a saw" (33).‡ We see the same blackness on the foreskin of De Gaulle, a snotty-nosed child Engamba encounters in a village en route to Doum. The Gabonese function as stock images of dark savagery, akin to Mendim in *Une Vie de boy,* though here they are completely reified, appearing as pure scenery. They lack the reality of characters like De Gaulle, the *desired* child, whose existence has special resonance for Engamba and Amalia who are childless, or for Meka and Kelara who lost both sons to the white man's war. The blackness, then, like the ape imagery, is a stock negative stereotype, complicated by its application to less-than-negative characters. This is especially the case with the hunter of monkeys, Mfomo, a sympathetic figure who warmly embraces Engamba on his departure. Mfomo's exit is characteristic of the coarse "bush" imagery: "Like a huge ape [un énorme quadrumane], Mfomo disappeared into a thicket" (40).** Like the messenger Nkolo, whose black nostrils are compared with those of a gorilla, Mfomo is both sympathetic and, as a villager whose life is least touched by the white man and his religion (again like Nkolo who is the only polygamous man in the novel), described more than other characters by coarse animal imagery. Yet the French term "quadrumane," translated into

---

tude. . . . Quand tous les derrières furent en l'air, il posa la main sur le front" (90).

* "Ta mère a dû manger du rat-panthère quand tu étais dans son sein" (13).

† "Nous ne sommes pas en brousse ici!" (86).

‡ "noirs comme un fond de marmite, . . . une tête en forme de bourse de bélier et les dents semblables à celle d'une scie" (41)

** "Mfomo, comme un énorme quadrumane, disparut dans un fourré" (48).

English as the more banal "ape," is more elaborate than "singe" [monkey] or "gorille," and its usage suggests a subtle shift in the direction of mockery from the subject of the narrative (*l'énoncé*), Mfomo, to the subject of the discourse (*l'énonciation*), the mocking narrator.

Having established the imagery, Oyono extends the linkage between animals and humans to Doum, the last African outpost before the white man's city. There Meka's family congregates to celebrate the award Meka is to receive. The older men are described uniformly as physical wrecks. But the young nephew Essomba is a strong, positive character. Meka greets him with a standing family joke: "I have always wondered how a gorilla like you came to marry such a pretty wife" (68). * At this point we are not yet acquainted with Essomba. His nickname, "pygmy," does not endear him to us—in Cameroon pygmies are often the butt of jokes. Like the dark Gabonese, Essomba is mocked by the epithets "gorilla" and "pygmy," the metonymic external qualities. But what are we laughing at? As long as Essomba remains quiet or makes jokes, we are not too confused by the imagery. " 'This is a man here,' said Essomba thumping himself with his fist on his chest" (68).† But the uneasiness of our feelings can only increase when, on the next page, Meka's shadow, cast on the "soot blackened raffia of the roof," is described as that of "an ape [un quadrumane] sitting on its hindquarters" (69).‡ Both the darkness of the raffia and this reference to an ape and its hindquarters function to bring together the general series of images—evoking at once color, the animal world, and body parts—inserted in the heart of our African setting, Meka's "case" [hut], and attached to our protagonist himself who is not just "le vieux" but "le vieux nègre."

The situation Oyono has created here is complicated by our sense that there is one voice that expresses these humorous attacks using the stereotypes, and another voice *behind* the first one that is coyly playing games with us via the first voice. The sense of laughter across a second voice is reinforced by the play in French, and on French, as in the difference between a "gorille" and a "quadrumane," a difference involving linguistic as well as social pretentiousness. We sense the presence of this dual voice when we first encounter Engamba. He is finishing off his breakfast of serpent, hiding the delicious morsel from his neighbors, and when he finishes he belches:

---

* "Je me suis toujours demandé comment un gorille comme toi avait pu épouser une aussi jolie femme!" (78).

† "Ča, c'est un homme" dit Essomba en se frappant brutalement le poing sur la poitrine" (78).

‡ "la toiture de raphia noire de suie" . . . "un quadrumane assis sur son train de derrière"(80)

"this time scratching his belly with his little finger. *This was the sign that he had eaten well*" (27; my stress).* Whereas Achebe would have given the ethnographic detail and its explanation so as to enhance the stature of the Ibo community, Oyono lends mock authority to the narrative voice so as to open a comic space into which the double-voicedness of the text can enter. We hear a borrowed language echoing behind masks of characters, or, as Bakhtin puts it, *"another's speech in another's language,* serving to express authorial intentions but in a refracted way" (Bakhtin 1983, 324). This he also calls double-voiced discourse, and it is not only the sign of the novel's successful evocation of the world in its fullness and complexity, but it is particularly characteristic of the parody so well constructed by Oyono. Bakhtin sees this relationship of voices as a dialogue, as the play of voice with voice, and especially as voice within voice, what he describes as being "internally dialogized." And of course his favored examples are comic, ironic, or parodic discourse.

For Bakhtin the richness of this quality of prose is a consequence of the social component of language that accounts for language as being "refracted" and multidimensional. The carnival of life is evoked in language when the play of voice within voice is successfully created by the novelist, giving "the living, heteroglossia of language, and in the multi-languagedness surrounding and nourishing his own consciousness" (Bakhtin 1983, 326–27). What this exuberant vision of literature doesn't account for is the special circumstance created by the domination of one linguistic group over another, when the dominant voice speaks across the field of privilege and authority, rather than within the free exchange of multicolored voices. The double-voiced dialogue in African literature is *always* marked by that element of coercion that entered into the acquisition of the author's *written* language, containing and constraining the unvoiced echoes in Ewondo or Ibo or Wolof or Kikuyu.

Henry Louis Gates (1989) notes those peculiar qualities of force and authority, as well as the dodges employed to evade or manipulate them, with the result being a double-voiced dialogue between the white conventions of language and literature and black revisions of them. This echoing of earlier linguistic usages in *both* white and black traditions is termed "signifyin(g)": "Signifyin(g) is black double-voicedness; . . . it always entails formal revision and an intertextual relation" (Gates 1989, 51). Gates takes Susan Willis's fortunate term "mulatto" to describe the black text, because

---

* "mais cette fois en se grattant le ventre avec l'auriculaire. *C'était signe qu'il avait bien mangé*" (34; my stress).

of its "two-toned heritage" involving the enclosure of the black vernacular tradition within the standard European languages (xxiii). The pattern of repetition with difference, the appropriation of a term, a trope, a voice, with a turn, an improvisation into a newly shaped trope, is viewed by Gates as the key to the black tradition. With Oyono it seems that the broader linguistic and cultural division, the colonial context, and the decisive changes in sociopolitical relations that were taking place during the 1950s gave a radical edge to the African double-voicedness. It is more than a refraction of light into a multitude of colors; it is the subversion from within of the dominant voice itself that is being attempted. And this is all the more daring as the only overt vehicle for accomplishing this remains the standard European language. In this case French built within itself the vocabulary to construct this discourse, beginning with the word "nègre" [Negro or nigger]. Not only is it a standard term that became pejorative by the Eighteenth century when used as a noun, it is also used as a familiar, informal term within the black community, as the "correct" formal term when used as an adjective—a term whose usage is colored entirely by context and voice. Oyono's "le vieux nègre" carries these multidimensional meanings, permitting him to play on a seeming naiveté and to reach for more bitter tones toward the end of his work.

For Gates the figure that best expresses the tradition of black literature is Esu, a double-headed god who conveys ambiguity, special knowledge, and wealth. For us, Jonathan Ngaté's choice of a passage from Jean Genet's *Les Nègres* ([1958] 1960) as an epigraph for his study of the Francophone African novel is most appropriate as the figure for Oyono's double-voicedness, wherein a voice within a voice is played by a member of one race wearing the mask of another. "Let Negroes negrify themselves. Let them persist to the point of madness in what they're condemned to be, in their ebony, in their odor . . ."* (qtd. in Ngaté 1988, xvii). For Genet, as for Oyono, the black becomes the one who wears the black-faced mask— indeed, whether the actor is black or white. Unlike Achebe whose narrator *explains* things to uninformed readers, Oyono's double voice *plays* for the audience, exactly as do Genet's actors in black face (or Ouologuem's narrator, for that matter). In Belsey's terms we pass here from classic realism, which hides its constructs, to interrogative texts, which expose them.

The key issue that arises is the relationship between the two voices. Classic realism would have the authority of the text grounded in the narrative voice that explains the action or dialogue outside of itself, a voice

---

* "Que les Nègres se nègrent. Qu'ils s'obstinent jusqu'à la folie dans ce qu'on les condamne à être, dans leur ébène, dans leur odeur . . ." (Genet 1960, 76).

that directs our gaze away from itself and toward the narration. But the narration can not speak without *appearing,* without using a voice of its own, and at the moment it does so it puts a second face on the events, both obscuring as well as elucidating. This is Gates's point in indicating how black double-voicedness necessarily involves a revision or shift of an inherited white discourse, a shift necessarily qualified as obscuring by Gary Saul Morson (through whom Gates reads Bakhtin): "I find it help-ful to picture a double-voiced work as a special sort of palimpsest in which the uppermost inscription is a commentary on the one beneath it, which the reader (or audience) can know only by reading through the commen-tary that *obscures* in the very act of evaluating" (Gates 1989, 50; my stress). Again, my argument is that the obscurity in question here is not simply built into the double-voicedness as a universal quality, but is guided, in the case of Oyono, by the specific project of his humor, which is itself given meaning through an anticolonial frame. The voice that both obscures, derails, and discloses is not a disembodied Absolute Subject, but a small black figure, not unlike Achebe's ideal incarnation of spiritual force, the *chi.* I find Gates's intuitive turn to the "Signifying Monkey" an ideal model for this shadowed second voice of Oyono. For Gates, the Signifying Mon-key is the figure for black rhetoric itself, a figure not only for troping, but for a dissimulation *within* the context of social oppression—a figure for trope reversal in the spirit of a discourse that turns to language for a rever-sal of extralinguistic circumstance. Oyono's play on the ape/gorilla/man is fully captured in Gates's recuperated figure of the quick-talking monkey:

> The ironic reversal of a received racist image of the black as simianlike, the Signifying Monkey, he who dwells at the margins of discourse, ever punning, ever troping, ever embodying the ambiguities of language, is our trope for repetition and revision, indeed our trope of chiasmas, repeating and reversing simultaneously as he does in one deft discursive act. (Gates 1989, 52)

Finally, in addition to this particular twist of language, the Signifying Monkey adds the quality of self-consciousness, the "meta-figure itself" (53), which is apparent in Oyono's ploys to expose the presence of the narrative voice.

We can see the possibilities of double-voicedness played out in two examples. In the first, the African voice turns the French language into the instrument derisively dubbed "petit nègre" by the colonialists. Here the Commandant's "boy" designates the drinks being provided at the award ceremony, such as "sampagne." The seventh case is a bit different from the others: "'Not sampagne,' he said 'but the same thing.' He then went 'fchfchfchfchfchfchfch.' M. Fouconi went over the crate and read 'Vin Mousseux'" (47).* Here we see how the straight act of explaining and translating is provided with the words on the written label, while the comic routine is built into the houseboy's discourse, which is "pas tout à fait" French.

At the other end of the linguistic spectrum, where a more formal Latinate vocabulary is employed, the effect is equally "pas tout à fait." In this instance, our second example, the tailor designs a "zazou" suit for Meka, in the latest Paris style for jackets with tails. "Well, you look at the jackets the whites wear, they're a bit like the coat of a baboon that does not cover its behind. They've got their buttocks showing. Well, what I'm going to do is to make you something which will come right down to your knees. This will be called the zazou jacket" (49).† Again, as in the first example, we have the voice that explains and translates, and in both cases the act of explaining is turned on itself so as to expose its own naked buttocks. M. Fouconi's superior reading of the label is soon mocked by the revelation of his immoderate thirst for whiskey, and the elaborate, disdainful reference to baboon's clothing reveals the true nature of the elaborate disguise of words and labels themselves as coverings for naked buttocks. The zazou suit, the latest style from the fashion and cultural capital, is the modish turning that our double-voiced figure employs to give us a sense of both playing at—acting and laughing at—or revealing: it is the costume, the spiritual language, of the Signifying Monkey.

This then helps us to understand how the reference to "quadrumane" re-turns upon us when it is used to describe Meka. The description of Meka's shadow as that of a "quadrumane" is linked subsequently to the image of his upturned toes, which give him great anguish when he is wearing shoes. The total portrait contributes to a parody of villagers as not fitting easily into the mold of white civilization: "Meka's feet had not been made to go into the white man's shoes" (76).‡ However, the extreme pain Meka experiences at the mere thought of wearing shoes qualifies the laughter, attenuating the reader's distancing of him/herself from Meka.

---

* "Pas tout à fait sampagne, dit-il, mais même chose, fchfchfchfchfchfch . . . fit-il. M. Fouconi s'approcha de la caisse et lut 'Vin mousseux'" (56).

† "Eh bien! regarde les dolmans des Blancs, ça ressemble un peu à une crinière de cynocéphale qui ne cache pas son derrière. Ils ont les fesses dehors. Eh bien! moi, je vais te faire quelque chose qui te descenda jusqu'aux genoux. C'est ce qu'on appelle la veste zazou"(58).

‡ "Les pieds de Meka n'avaient pas été faits pour pénétrer dans les chaussures des Blancs" (87).

Thus, Oyono has pushed *us* to the limit: if Meka is an ape, if Africans are naked, dirty, animallike, foolishly simple creatures, there is nothing to prevent us from laughing along with the text at their naked behinds plumping down on dirt floors, or at their apelike features. Yet a queasy feeling can not be repressed because of our knowledge that behind the laughter an African is training the spotlight on the images that we are *overhearing* as an African joke. This uneasiness is present in our laughter at the remark Kelara makes to her own brother: "We are not in the bush here" (75) Did we not learn earlier that Meka had known Kelara "when she was still at the age when girls run naked" (38)?*

The situation into which the reader is cast is best captured at the outset of Meka's journey to town when the general laughter erupts at Meka's expense chez Mammy Titi. Meka is saved by Mammy Titi herself when she reprimands the general company: "Men like him . . . they don't come like that any more . . ." (7).† But her praise here is of precisely those qualities against which the humor is directed: his Africanity, so to speak, which reflects his traditional African rank and the values bred in the village culture, now callously disregarded or lost in the white man's city. The same ambiguity occurs subsequently when someone recognizes Meka as the one who gave his lands to the church. A voice in the crowd then expresses the sentiment, "Quel couillon" (14) ["what a damn fool" (my trans.)]. But even here the remark, and the reactions that follow, do not permit us to share with complete ease in the response. Meka's answer gives us room to empathize with him, as he says, "At least you're frank about it"(7).‡ While the implied silence of the others interpellates the reader, Meka answers both the spoken and the unspoken voice with the weight of a man of years, unruffled by the younger man's brashness. Despite the candor, the disparaging remark is double-edged—if others have "couillons," or "balls," of sand, like those policemen Meka challenges to fight in prison, Meka is at least associated, if even by a mockery, with what makes a man when daubed with the epithet "couillon." The next remark shifts the reader's sympathy toward Meka: "'If they'd taken it [his land] away from him, that wouldn't have surprised me,' said another" (my trans.).** We are not, however, completely prepared for this reputedly devout Christian's reply, "Well it was a

---

* "à l'âge où les filles courent encore toutes nues" (46).

† "Des hommes comme lui . . . il n'y en a plus . . ."(14).

‡ "Toi, au moins, tu dis ce que tu penses!" (14).

** "'Ca ne m'étonnerait pas qu'on la lui ait arrachée,' dit un autre" (14).

bit of that too" (8),* an absolutely crucial revelation in establishing the ambiguity of Meka's allegiance and subservience to the white man's culture and religion. It has its parallel in Engamba's "voluntary" concession to Christianity. Engamba saw the way the wind was blowing, and attempted to anticipate the inevitable by giving up his wives. Because the question of *how* Meka was forced, more or less, to cede his land is left open, we are prevented from judging him, as does his interlocutor, as a "couillon," while remaining free to laugh at his toes, his apelike shadow.

Though this is not always the case, much of the imagery in Part One succeeds in having it both ways. Of course, there is certainly no ambivalence, for example, when the Commandant's red face is likened to a chimp's bottom! But there are two sides to the coin in the case of Engamba, the second "vieux nègre," the one who has children and who lost half a dozen wives with the coming of Christianity. As Engamba leaves Zourion, his dignity is conveyed by the assegai he carries in one hand, and his generosity by the gift of the goat that he holds in the other. Tied to the goat, which unceremoniously tugs on the rope, Engamba is pulled against his will. "The first step he took loosened his cloth which had got in between his buttocks and the slit at the base of his khaki jacket revealed the huge panther tooth that he was wearing around his waist" (44).† The powerful predator is mockingly linked to the pretentious old man pulled by his goat, his only "prey," and led by his much sturdier wife. His childless state, and the loss of his inherited wives, adds to the portrait of his impotency.

Throughout Part One of *Le Vieux Nègre et la médaille* the animal imagery almost uniformly acts to reinforce in various characters such qualities as superstition, impotency, pretentiousness, poverty, naiveté, and so forth. Potent figures such as panthers are evoked in ironic circumstances to highlight the weakness of the character; baboons, chimps, gorillas are linked to coarseness or to rusticity; fish and dogs to foolish appearances; elephants and donkeys to docile servility and dumb forbearance. Even honeymoons in the "bush" are represented by antelopes. The goat, a symbol for fertility and a sign of generosity, turns on its owner, Engamba, mocking his "strength" as a hunter by dragging him ignominiously. The porcupines, antelopes, and panther-rats are all trapped; the goats, dogs, and simple domesticated creatures have no threatening traits, emphasizing

---

* "C'est un peu la verité" (14).

† "Le premier pas qu'il fit détendit le pagne qui avait pénétré entre ses fesses, tandis que la fente arrière de sa veste kaki dévoilait la grosse dent de panthère qu'il portait attaché à la taille" (52).

the Africans' helplessness or weakness. The culmination of this imagery is reached in a kind of mad crescendo at the very end of Part One when Meka and company are going to sleep: Kelara is described as curling up like an "antelope," Meka hears partridges, sees the goat and thinks of eating it, and reflects on the story of the hunter who caught the baboon, before he finally drifts off to sleep.

Lizards, pygmies, rams' scrotums, all invest an ironic universe with subhuman traits. Oyono constructs a farcical, colonial view of Africans as foolish, likable, animallike peasants. The further the setting from the city, the cruder the imagery. Thus Nkolo, the happy polygamist, with black, hairy, gorillalike nostrils, lives beyond Zourion, that is, at the farthest remove from the city and from the influences of Christianity on traditional marriages. Mfomo, the amiable hunter from Engamba's village, lives on a shrinking stock of monkeys, and is described as a "huge ape" (40). The only article of clothing described in detail in the "bush" is the fragment of a dress that fails to hide Agatha's attractive body—this in a village through which Engamba passes en route to Doum. And as we approach the city, Africans still are given tongue-in-cheek descriptions, as with Meka's "zazou" jacket, his ill-fitting shoes, his insect-infested safari helmet, and his other articles of clothing.

The shift in perspective. The second part of the novel reinforces our uneasiness by throwing into confusion the simple indices established in Part One. All of Part Two takes place in the city, as though the momentum of Engamba's journey now carries the action on to its logical end in a world that is the antithesis of that of the villages. The space into which the action enters can best be represented by the chalk circle that Meka is forced to occupy, an unforgettable image leaving Meka standing "between two worlds" (88).* The Africans remain on one side, on the edge of the field set aside for the award ceremony, the whites move about within its limits, and Meka—he who gave his lands and sons, and now is to receive a medal in compensation—is placed mercilessly beneath the broiling sun in the indeterminate no-man's-land where "[h]e was not with his own people, and he was not with the others" (85).† 4 Here Meka finds himself in great discomfort. Despite his advanced age, echoes of the key moment of an initiation ceremony are suggested by Meka's trials.

There is an obvious continuity suggested here between *Une Vie de boy* and *Le Vieux Nègre*: in both the protagonist is a figure who belongs to two

---

* "entre deux mondes" (85)

† "Lui, il ne se trouvait ni avec les siens ni avec les autres" (96).

worlds and yet is trapped in the space in between. He must suffer to establish himself firmly in the camp where he can be true to himself, as if to compensate for the initial violence done by his adhesion to the world of the whites. By belonging and not belonging, Meka becomes a supplement to both worlds without entering totally into either: he is the figure for the colonized African, the excluded term. Appropriately, his "special" condition inside the chalk circle is followed at the reception after the ceremony by his exclusion from the inner circle of whites, just as his solitude in the circle is continued in the celebration following the ceremony, where he is "the only black and khaki spot amongst the white suits of the Europeans of Doum" (96).*

Meka does not emerge from the circle any more enlightened than when he entered. For that we have to wait for him to experience the full depths of the violence the city is capable of wreaking on him. But there is a critical turning point that occurs as Meka waits in the circle, and that is in the brief moment in which Kelara overhears and responds to a chance remark made by a stranger concerning the insignificant worth of the medal compared to Meka's lands and two sons. At first, full of pride over Meka, her eyes, wet with joy, reflect her delusions: "When the whiteman shook Meka's hand she thought her heart would stop beating" (94).† Then she haphazardly overhears the voice, the "fausse note," that dampens her enthusiasm, but removes the deception. Appropriately, the subsequent emphasis is placed on her sight, on seeing Meka for what he is. The episode ends with the identification of the speaker as the Commandant's boy—another ironic intertextual reference to Toundi. Kelara breaks down and weeps, and, more important, views Meka and the entire award ceremony as if with new eyes: "She saw her husband, his head gleaming in the sun, grin foolishly at the Chief of the whitemen. Something happened inside her which she could not understand. Meka seemed to her like someone she had never seen before" (95).‡

Kelara's transformation is symbolically linked to the no-man's-land of the chalk circle. It is a place where Meka experiences intense physical discomfort. Some of this can be attributed to the exigencies of the "initiation," the trials the initiate must endure, such as bearing up under the scorching sun. However, the excruciating pain caused by Meka's shoes

---

* "le seul point noir et kaki au milieu des complets blancs des Européens de Doum" (107)

† "Quand le Blanc serra la main de Meka, elle crut que son coeur s'arrêtait" (105).

‡ "Elle vit son mari, le crâne luisant au soleil, sourire bêtement au Chef des Blancs. Elle ne sut ce qui se passa en elle. Meka lui apparut comme quelqu'un qu'elle n'avait encore jamais vu" (106).

differs from that which is caused by the sun: it is not a natural force he must resist, but one which is culturally inflicted, linked more closely to the unbecoming zazou jacket than to the powers of nature. It signals the painful inappropriateness of his attempts to conform to the demands placed on him by the new white conquerors.[5] It is this that Kelara sees.

As yet, these insights are not perceived by Meka, who is sustained by the thought of his ancestral heritage—"Was he not the son of the great Meka who held out for so long against the first white men?" (87)[*]—only to be undercut by the narratorial satire. "Suddenly his forehead wrinkled and an ominous expression crossed his face. There seemed to be a heavy weight at the bottom of his belly. From far away he could feel approaching the urge to satisfy a need" (87).[†] Meka's ordeal is reduced again to farce, the noble gesture, like the rhetoric of Chaucer's Chanticleer, done in by the eruption of basic physical needs.

At this point Oyono throws the farce itself into confusion by shifting the perspective from which the humor is launched. When Meka wishes to draw strength from his ancestors, it is the image of the former Meka resisting the whites that comes to his mind. He calls on them so he can bear up in order to receive a medal of commendation from those same whites for sacrificing his land and sons to their war efforts. His position is riddled with contradiction, and the animal imagery begins to shift in this direction. Antelopes were used in Part One to signify marriage: Nkolo was going to "break the legs of the antelope for the sixth time" (37).[‡] This usage conforms to other indices of women as victims (e.g., Amalia is associated with the donkey who patiently bears burdens), and of Africans in general as victims. We see this in the case of Engamba's wives described as "goats straining at the leash" (37)[**] to be released by the preaching of the red-faced priest. Now, for Meka the white men are described as resembling antelopes because "their faces all looked the same" (85).[††] In *Une Vie de boy* it was the whites who saw no difference between one black face and another when M. Janopoulos unleashed his dogs on the crowd of onlookers outside the European Center. The reversal is significant, setting the stage for the change in perspective.

---

[*] "N'était-il pas le fils du grand Meka qui tint longtemps tête aux premiers Blancs?" (97).

[†] "Tout à coup, un pli barra son visage qui prit une expression sinistre. Il lui sembla que son bas-ventre lui pesait. Il sentait venir de loin, de très loin, l'envie de satisfaire un petit besoin"(98).

[‡] "'briser les pattes de l'antilope' pour la sixième fois" (45)

[**] "tiraient sur la corde comme des chèvres attachées" (45)

[††] "ils avaient tous le même visage" (95).

The first animal image Meka assigns to himself is the same one he had applied to his wrinkled nephew Mvondo, that of the lizard, a sign of old age. "I am a poor old man but I have to leave my head baking in the sun like a lizard" (89).* In a world made up of the strong and the weak, predators and victims, poor old men and lizards are ostensibly placed with the weak. On the other hand, lizards exhibit powers of endurance and patience. When Meka receives the medal, his spirits soar, like those of a bird—another weak creature, one trapped by hunters. Here the image of "a bird poised for flight" (93)† suggests patterns of escape and elation—again curiously close to Toundi's final hallucinatory flight from the hospital, his head bursting like a bomb. Meka hopes, in his delusions, to acquire just one of the guns he sees being paraded before the crowd, so as to be able to hunt out the gorillas, "unclean creatures that devastated the banana groves" (94).‡

The ambivalence of these images is matched by Meka's increasing moments of disillusionment following the awarding of the medal. First, like the child Toundi, he is treated like a pet by the whites: "Every now and then a white hand passed over his head or by his ears before making a perfunctory gesture of admiration at the medal hanging on his chest" (96).** Then he finds himself excluded: "Meka did not know how he came to be standing outside the circle the Europeans had made round their Chief" (96).†† When he tries to penetrate this closed circle, he is rebuffed by an angry glance from Father Vandermayer. This surprises and humiliates Meka, and "his mouth hangs open with astonishment like a fish."‡‡ As Father Vandermayer reveals himself to be a hypocrite, like Madame in *Boy,* Meka again becomes a victim: "Meka stared down at the floor in stupid fascination as if the cement had the eyes of a snake."*** The priest's predatory nature is exposed, as he had "carelessly let his claws show"†††

---

* "Et moi, pauvre homme mûr, je suis obligé de laisser mon crâne rôtir au soleil comme un margouillat" (100).

† "un oiseau prê tà s'envoler" (102)

‡ "ces sales bêtes qui dévastaient ses champs de bananiers" (104)

** "De temps en temps, une main blanche passait sur son crâne, sur ses oreilles avant d'admirer négligemment la médaille qui pendait sur sa poitrine" (107).

†† "Meka ne sut comment il s'était retrouvé à l'extérieur du cercle que les Blancs avaient formé autour de leur grand Chef" (107).

‡‡ "[Meka], complètement abasourdi, porta sa main à son menton en ouvrant la bouche comme un poisson" (108).

*** "Il fixait le sol, bêtement fasciné comme si le ciment avait eu des yeuxde serpent" (108).

††† "sorti imprudemment ses griffes" (109)

The animal imagery evokes contradictory qualities suggesting that the lines that separate animal and human properties, like the chalk circle or M. Janopoulos's "cercle," which separates black from white, are as artificially constructed as are the subjects in a colonial society—as is the frame around any excluded term.

The deconstruction of this artifice coincides with Meka's glimpse of Father Vandermayer's briefly exposed claws or unveiled eyes. Meka responds to the discovery of Father Vandermayer's duplicity with "the first angry look he had ever given in his life" (98).* The effect of this look is to freeze the laughter on the priest's lips, momentarily reversing the two characters' positions as aggressor and prey. In the scene that follows, in the African Community Center, the imagery of predator and victim carries forward the anomalies of the chalk circle. At first we see the whites and blacks sipping their champagne "like birds at the edge of a pond" (my trans.).† Eventually the white Commandant becomes so angered by the sight of the Africans being served whiskey that his face turns red: "it looked as if something had caught fire inside his head" (104). ‡ This recalls the earlier fiery expression of the priest who had come to convert Engamba's countrymen, as well as the first association of M. Fouconi's face with a chimpanzee's bottom. The malefic colors and animalistic imagery, so invidiously associated with Africans in Part One, now are transferred to the whites. In Meka's eyes Father Vandermayer "changed into a huge black dog, waiting sagely at the door for Meka to throw him the bones. Meka's arm grew so long that he gave the animal a punch and drove it away" (105).** The qualities of "huge" and "black" echo earlier passages, like the one in which Mfomo is described as a gorilla. Here, however, the size and color do not hide the priest's essential quality as a sycophant; in fact, the imaginary joins him to the actual dog Djofar, waiting impatiently to be fed his scraps by Engamba and chased out of the circle of visitors when there is no more room for him. The transformation of Father Vandermayer occurs in Meka's drunken vision. When Meka stands up to speak, he rebuffs the missionary who turns scarlet; now it is Meka who laughs aloud at him. Even the High Commissioner comes in for a comic swipe as the narrative eye settles on the pouch ["jabot"] under his chin: it

---

* "la première oeillade courroucée de sa vie" (108)

† "comme des oiseaux au bord d'un étang" (114)

‡ "son visage était tellement rouge qu'on eût cru qu'un incendie était allumé dans son crâne" (117).

** "transformé en gros chien noir, attendait sagement près de ls porte que Meka lui jetât les os. Le bras de Meka devint si long qu'il éloigna l'animal en lui donnant un grand coup de poing" (117).

swells up and is deflated, while "his whole body seemed bowed down by the great weight of his double chin."*

Alternatively, the animal images evoke conflicting values associated with the strong and the weak. Thus, when Meka's kind neighbor passes a hand over his sleeping head, "Meka twitched his nose like a rabbit" (111).† In contrast, as he begins to snore, he is "like a young panther" (113).‡ Most telling, his sleep is what the villagers call "the death-sleep"—a state of in-betweenness through which all initiates must pass.

Up till the award ceremony Meka is seen in comic terms—he plays the role of the alazon, or dupe. Once the medal is awarded the mockery can go no further. Meka has been given all he is going to get and has experienced elation. His "urgent needs," which come in moments of stress, when he is awaiting the medal or waiting to ask the Commandant's assistant for a gun, are merely comic and reduce him in the reader's eyes. Indeed his loss of his sons and land are felt and treated as immeasurably less important than the pain in his feet and kidneys and intestines, as less significant than the animals around him and the drink and food he procures. From the outset Oyono creates comic moments based on Meka's physical reactions, usually at his expense. Thus the novel begins with "le 'bonjour du Seigneur'" (Oyono [1956b] 1979, 9) falling, absurdly, into his left nostril through the chinks in the rotten raffia roof. The contrast between the mocking tone used here and Ngugi wa Thiong'o's weightier beginning of *A Grain of Wheat* (1967), when the rotten raffia admitted drops of water that fell in Mugo's eye as he was having guilt-ridden dreams, highlights the difference between low mimetic comedy and pathos. Whereas Ngugi strives to recapture the historical moment so as to reveal political truths, Oyono engages the reader's own prejudices much more subtly by masking his purpose with comic techniques and by playing on perspectives. Oyono's universe is deliberately made to be unreal, so unreal that the spirit of the creator enters his creatures through their nostrils. We are prepared to laugh, not to engage in political thought, and thus are open to any possibility except the serious.

The return. It is a curious structural feature of the plot that we jump from Meka's story in Chapter 1 to Engamba's in much of the rest of Part One. Engamba is absent from the narrative in Part Two: Meka has center stage, except in Chapter 2, where Engamba's absence is explained by his aching feet. Again, in Part Three, he disappears when Meka appears, and

---

* "tout son corps semblait accablé par le poids du dessous de son menton" (120)

† "Meka remua son nez comme un lapin" (124).

‡ "comme une jeune panthère" (126)

vice versa, until the end. It is almost as if one actor were playing two parts, and this impression is reinforced by the mirroring of the two couples, Meka and Kelara, and Engamba and Amalia, both old and now childless, both Christian and therefore monogamous. Similar chiropodial afflictions are experienced by both men on the same important day. By a simple shift, we can view Engamba's story as an extension of Meka's, as essentially one story split into two parts. Engamba's long journey, which receives such extensive treatment, fits into Meka's experience if regarded as the outset of a typical quest tale. The quest pattern, with its special messenger, important summons, gifts, obstacles, and goal, clearly structures Engamba's story in Part One.

The medal is the ostensible goal of the quest when seen from the colonial perspective. However, in Part Two that perspective is shown to be false when another "messenger," the Commandant's boy, brings Kelara the gift of an insight she had previously lacked—for which she gives her thanks. "Thank you. The Holy Spirit spoke through your mouth" (95) .*
The gift or goal, then, is a symbol for truth itself, or some form of clear-sighted vision. In order for Meka to attain this, he must learn to discard the glittering medals that symbolize his former deception. The transition, then, is from deception to enlightenment, both for the protagonist, and, indirectly, for the reader. The project here might well be taken as social melioration, but it is not one enacted through the naive strategy of mimesis, of mirroring the process of achieving it, but by actually *effecting* it through the deliberate manipulation of the reader in his or her reactions to the text. By placing the emphasis on point of view, rather than on action, Oyono recapitulates Paul de Man's ([1971] 1983) notions of the passage from a fiction of mimesis to one of irony, in which the eventual outcome is less "authenticity" than awareness of the limitations of action.

This is why the emphasis falls on Meka's transformation, the subject of Part Three, which, in terms of the quest, might best be labeled "the Return." Meka's "death-sleep" is appropriately designated for the critical phase of his transition: he leaves in one state and returns in another. Though the change is invisible, it has its meteorological counterparts in the violent storm that occurs on the eve of Independence in *A Grain of Wheat* (Ngugi 1967), or the one that leads to Sekoni's death in *The Interpreters* (Soyinka 1965). Here Meka's reactions to the storm make clear this same extraordinary, metaphysical, symbolic dimension.

---

* "Merci, c'est le Saint-Esprit qui a parlé par ta bouche" (106).

The contrasts Oyono sets up are striking. From the broiling heat and blinding sun of Part Two we pass immediately to pitch darkness, complete with cascades of water and shivering cold; from a room packed with notables to an almost empty corrugated iron shed. In broader terms, from scenes usually crowded with participants and onlookers, to the dangerous solitude experienced by Meka. Meka's moment of glory, too, has passed: his admirers, and his medal, are gone, as well as the basis for the false admiration; now he is to be scorned, mocked, and beaten.

The storm prepares us for the changes that follow by clearing out the false rhetoric, the empty edifices of colonialism. It gives Meka the experience of complete solitude. "Man in a solitary creature" (my trans.),* he realizes, as he just manages to escape. In this state he is prepared to face what he had become, that is, a man who was conditioned by years of fidelity to the church and the state (his is always the driest cocoa, his sons give their lives, and he his lands, to the new dispensation). For his fellow Christians, "Meka was the great favorite in the Paradise stakes" (10).† Thus, the novel opens with the sunlight given the name, "le bonjour de Dieu," and with Meka's new day marked by devotional prayer. In the city, Meka deals with his solitary anguish in the circle again by praying. Now, with the violent storm Meka finds himself caught in a collapsing building, and he automatically interprets the events in Christian terms. As everything crashed about him, "[h]e wondered if perhaps this was the end of the world" (my trans.).‡ As lightning and thunder follow, he crosses himself again and again, and as he feels the teetering roof, he feels around his neck for his St. Christopher's medal. When he finds it, he becomes "quite calm. Good St. Christopher was beside him" (my trans.).** And when he realizes the award medal is gone, he crosses himself and says an Our Father and a Hail Mary. The narrative ridicules these impulses, as the next reaction he has is to suck his thumb.

The religious terminology is accentuated as Meka escapes into the storm: "He loomed up in the glare of the lightning like a corpse raised by miracle out of the waters, a vision from the apocalypse in the midst of the warring elements" (121).†† This reference to death and rebirth prepares us for the radical change that follows, though the animal imagery mocks the

---

* "L'homme est un être solitaire" (134).

† "Meka était un grand favori dans la course au Paradis" (17).

‡ "[il] se demanda si ce n'était pas la fin du monde" (131).

** "il ne s'affola plus, ce bon saint Christophe était avec lui" (133)

†† "Il surgissait à la lumière des éclairs comme un cadavre miraculeusement ressuscité des eaux. C'était une apparition d'apocalypse au milieu des éléments déchaînés" (135).

sacramental vision by confirming the portrait of Meka as weak, trapped, and finally ridiculous—as anything but one of the notables, the "princes," among whose assembly he was only just sitting. Thus, he rolls over like a "rabbit"; fears dying like a porcupine in a trap; moves as slowly as a tortoise; blows out water with a mouth shaped like a chicken's behind ["cul de poule" (134)]; and thinks longingly of the goat waiting to be shared.

Meka's experience could be described as a radical challenge to the African subject as constituted by the colonial enterprise. He is left isolated on the stage, under the spotlight, reduced to a pitiful state, and inadequately armed in the face of the darkness, death, and solitude—the circumstances having so rapidly changed from what he had been experiencing when he had gone to sleep, snuggled up like a rabbit against the comforting shoulder of his neighbor. His awakening leads to the discovery that his assurances were an illusion. How was it possible that he who took the right path all his life, and won his medal in the end, "a member of one of the largest families in Doum could be all alone in the middle of the disaster that was overwhelming him?" (my trans.).* To fortify himself Meka recalls the greatness of his father and his resistance to the whites; ironically, he has become the example of abject Christian humility. The porcupine, the rabbit, the tortoise, and the hen may all have qualities that enable them to survive, but in the end they are all harmless prey for the predators.

In all of Oyono's work the colonial realm is represented as a world of chaos: hypocrisy, abuse, abnegation, despair, and death are the fate to be expected by the African subjects who become either its victims or its servants. It is a world the meaning of which is rationalized by priests whose actions or, as Beti would put it, whose ignorance undercuts their message. In the end the Africans are left with a world based on power yet ruled by hypocritical authorities wearing the disguise of a higher idealism that is continually contradicted by the reality of daily life. The phrase "[i]n the midst of the warring elements" (121)†, used to describe Meka caught outdoors in the storm, also evokes the physical and metaphysical conditions of Africa under the whites' occupation; the storm's turbulent destructiveness reaches into the wellsprings of the hero's being, and into those of the fragile communities whose homes are turned topsy-turvy by the wind and rain witnessed by Meka on his return home.

---

* "lui, qui faisait partie de l'une des familles les plus nombreuses de Doum, pouvait-il se trouver tout seul dans ce cataclysme qui le dépassait?" (135).

† "[a]u milieu des elements déchainés" (135)

Meka's descent reaches its nadir with his arrest. He enters hell itself: the "corpse raised by miracle out of the waters" (121)* turns into a phantom. The guardians of this hell, here as in *Une Vie de boy,* are Africans who are beyond the appeal to tradition. They are cruel counterparts to the gospel-preaching missionaries, with the same innate predator instincts as those of the sadistic Father Vandermayer. Thus, the guard who arrests Meka is dubbed a "cerberus" ["cerbère"] and in response to Meka's pleas he beats him. His superior is depicted as ignorant and brutish; the brigadier sticks out his tongue "like a dog about to copulate" (my trans.)† when concentrating on writing Meka's name, and his writing hand "describes circles in the air like a bird of prey before it swooped down onto the blank page" (127).‡

Meka becomes their victim, the figure of all the helpless dumb beasts that crowd onto the landscape: the first blow of the guard lifts him in the air so that he wonders if he is in "the claws of an eagle" (122).** The guard calls him a pig, an old tortoise, an "old man" ["vieillard"], while Meka snorts "like a dog" (124) ["comme un chien"], and cries "like a terrified chimpanzee"(124) ["un cri de chimpanzée apeuré"]. He and the guard stare at each other like china dogs. He is driven in the rain "like a sheep" (126) ["comme un mouton"], and jumps like "a shooed cockerel" (128).†† In this hellish night, in a "rain for the witches" (128) ‡‡, Meka is thrown into a cell described as "creation's first darkness" (my trans.).*** He has ceased, by now, to be the butt of any humor, although the same animal images used in the earlier satirical passages continue to be employed.

In the cold, dark cell, alone with his desperate thoughts, Meka's experiences form the perfect counterpart to his painful confinement to the chalk circle earlier in the day. The oppositions of heat and cold, sunlight and darkness, crowds and solitude, are completed as Meka's passive compliance turns to resistance and battle. Even the irony gives way as Meka begins to draw upon the resources of the past, the ancestors and their

---

* "un cadavre miraculeusement ressuscité des eaux" (135.

† "comme un chien qui va s'accoupler" (142)

‡ "se mit à décrire des orbes comme un oiseau de proie avant de se poser sur la page blanche" (142)

** "les serres d'un aigle" (136)

†† "un coq qu'on éloigne"(143)

‡‡ "pluie de sorcellerie" (143)

*** "les ténèbres de la création"(143)

praise names: "'[t]he stock-unshakeable-beneath-the-storm,' the 'River-without-fear-of-the-forest,' the 'Pythons,' 'Rocks,' 'Cotton-trees,' 'Elephants,' 'Lions'" (130).* The "kapok tree" ["fromager"], the serpent-python, the elephants and lions express a nobility and strength strikingly absent earlier in the text.[6] Their titles convey conquest and implacable resistance to outside forces: "souches-immuables-sous-l'orage" [stock-unshakeable-beneath-the-storm], men who never had bowed "to another man's strength" (130).† Meka's memories take him back to the time before the coming of the whites, to the moment when he first acquired his manhood. As a wrestler, "his shoulder blades had never known the dust under the force of another man" (my trans.).‡ He casts aside the more recently acquired gestures of humility and innocence—in this world "where virtue and honesty no longer paid" (131)**—and challenges the guards as he had once learnt to do, "one knee on the ground, stretching out his right arm towards his unseen opponent . . ." (131).††

The attention given to the praise names of the former Mekas contrasts further with the mockery of the illiterate guards who bandy his name about. Meka remembers being newly circumcised and the excitement of the news that an "homme-fantôme," the first white man, had arrived—a missionary with "panther eyes" whose skull soon became a treasured prize. When Meka killed his first panther, as a reward he was given the skull of the missionary. In prison, Meka recollects the moment he threw the skull in a river, the day he was baptized: "The day I became a slave!" (137).‡‡ With his new awareness, Meka renews the old struggle, while simultaneously the animal imagery is reversed.

The changed Meka can confront the guards directly, but with the white administrator he must take a different tack. The key weapon in Oyono's arsenal in combatting colonialism is not physical force, but the mask. We noted how the Africans saw through the façades of all the whites in *Une Vie de boy,* while the Africans remained invisible and unknown. When Toundi learned his trade and like Meka had arrived at an understanding of the whites and their system, he began to dissimulate—like

---

* "les Souches-immuables-sous-l'orage, les Rivières-qui-n'ont-pas-peur-de-la-forêt, les Serpents-pythons, les Rocs, les Fromagers, les Eléphants, les Lions" (145)

† "sous la force d'un autre homme" (145)

‡ "[J]amais ses homoplates n'avaient touché la poussière sous la force d'un autre homme" (146).

** "la vertu et l'honnêteté ne payaient plus" (146).

†† "un genou en terre, tendait le bras droit à l'invisible adversaire . . ."(146)

‡‡ "Le jour où je suis devenu un esclave!"(152).

Sophie, like Kalissa, and, especially, like Mengueme. Inside the kitchen, away from the whites' view, Toundi can spit in the glass. Now in the prison the interpreter tells Meka that his case has been fixed and to act with prudence: "You can think what you like about him when you are out of here" (137).* Thus Mengueme in *Une Vie de boy* hides his knowledge of French, and Toundi feigns being beaten, simulating cries and producing false blood stains, with Mendim's help. Similarly, in *Le Vieux Nègre,* when the white Commissioner, Gullet, forces a cigarette on Meka, at the interpreter's urging Meka takes it and pushes it into his mouth, in "the gap he had made between his upper incisors" (137),† and smiles back at Gullet until his mouth stretched from ear to ear (137).‡ As Gullet offers him his hand, Meka gives an embarrassed grin: "'Poto-poto,' he said, looking at his hands ochre-coloured with dried mud and then at Gullet. 'I don't want to dirty the white man'" (138).** Using the excuse of his dirty hands, Meka refrains from shaking hands with his enemy. The scene is uncompromising in its feel for the truth about the pain and humiliation generated by an oppressive system.

The refrain that evokes the community of the "wretched of the earth" in a colonized country, used with such effect in *Une Vie de boy,* is "pauvre de nous" [poor us]. As Meka throws off the enslaving beliefs, this is his reflection on the guards' foolish laughter: "pauvre de nous." He not only commiserates over their common condition, but, most important, recognizes the fracturing of the subjective self that alienates and isolates all: "Man is all alone in the world!" (130).††

On Meka's return to Doum the disavowal of colonial ideology is completed when he rejects even the mention of the Lord's name in his presence. The animal images, too, reappear, giving a sense of proportion to the earlier, confused attributions. For instance, the comic comparisons of Meka and Mvondo to gorillas, reflected in the derogatory reference to M. Fouconi as resembling a chimp's bottom, are resolved by disavowing any relation between the powerful figure of the gorilla and his weaker simian counterpart: "The chimpanzee is no brother to the gorilla" (151).‡‡ Porcupines, whose

---

* "Tu pourra penser tout ce que tu voudras de lui loin d'ici" (152).

† "dans la fente qu'il avait taillée entre ses incisives supérieures"(152)

‡ "[il] fendit maladroitement sa bouche jusqu'aux oreilles"(153).

** "Poto-poto! dit-il en regardant tour à tour ses mains d'ocre de boue sèche et Gosier d'Oiseau. . . . Je ne veux pas salir le Blanc" (153).

†† "L'homme est seul au monde" (145).

‡‡ "Le chimpanze n'est pas le frère du gorille" (168).

tasty meat is held to be particularly desirable, are repeatedly evoked as Meka's mind is flooded with hunting images. Now the animal references generally turn on the notion of trapping: instead of resembling the rabbit/victim, Meka is bent like "the lever on a porcupine trap" (140):* he remembers the thrill of hunting them, and brings the villagers to share with him the view that "we are not porcupines" (153).† As Nti puts it, "Who will walk into the trap again, with his eyes open?" (153). ‡ With "les yeux ouverts" [his eyes open], he now sees the resemblance, hitherto hidden to him, between his sow and the great Chief of the whites: creation is turned to mock the Christian notion of the creator, and his appointed administrator over the land: "The world comes from the hand of God. No one can deny the same workman made the Chief of the whites and this pig . . ." (144).**

Baptizing the forest through which he passes "the Forest of Homecoming" (143),†† Meka tells his fellow villagers he has come from the road that leads to "fantômes." He needs only to speak the words "[t]he whites! Just the whites" (145)‡‡ to awaken the community to his *prise de conscience*. The catechist is quickly chased out, and Meka now, transvaluating the past, brings the advent of a new gospel, a new "bonne nouvelle" like the one presaged by the bird's excrement that falls on his head. Whites are exposed and rejected: "But what about all this! You talk about the whites as if they were the people in the next village. Is there anyone here with a red face and uncircumcised?" (151).*** Mvemas, in contrast to the whites, know how to avoid traps because they are great hunters, "hommes circoncis, hommes murs." With this spirit of revolt, the sense of community is reawakened on Meka's return: "what happened to the man of ripe years called Meka has happened to all of us through him. . . . All of us, all of us!" (153).††† The gentler humor, now so to speak "entre nous," does not take on the form of ambivalent mockery, but of a shared joke. The narrator's

---

* "le levier de piège à porc-épics" (157)

† "nous ne sommes pas des porc-épics" (170)

‡ "Qui donnera encore dans le piège, les yeux ouverts?" (170).

** "Le monde vient vraiment de Dieu. On ne peut pas dire que ce n'est pas le même ouvrier qui a fait le Chef des blancs et ce cochon" (160).

†† "la foret du retour (159)

‡‡ "Les Blancs! Les Blancs seulement" (162)

*** "Mais enfin quoi! Vous parlez des Blancs comme si c'étaient des gens du village voisin! Qui a un visage rouge et est incirconcis parmi vous?" (168).

††† "ce qui est arrivé à l'homme mûr appelé Meka nous est arrivé à tous par lui. . . . A nous tous. A nous tous" (170).

and the protagonist's points of view converge: Meka is no longer the feeble butt of belittling jokes but a powerful figure of righteous indignation. His "powerful palms" crush the lemon grass with which he sweetens his morning breath; his stoic glance takes in calmly the women's noisy lamentation over his fate; his generosity makes available to all the constituents of the new congregation the palmwine of commiseration. The tide of laughter has turned on the former audience—on us.

The force of the humor strikes us in full at the end of the novel, not that the jokes are funnier, but that their perspectives have been completely reversed. Initially Engamba's gluttony was humorously depicted, at his expense. The same was true of all the crude imagery and behavior associated with "country bumpkins" ["pequenots de la brousse"]. Now the masks are turned inside out. The initial line thrown to Meka haphazardly at Mammy Titi's, "Whites are easy enough to take in" (8),★ appears less gratuitous by the time Meka uses the mud on his hands as an excuse for not shaking hands with Gullet. Laughter reshapes the structure of the world inhabited by the villagers, reaching all the way to the white missionary and the white Administrator. This laughter flows from the powers of the mask, from the faces hidden behind it: "The laughter burst with the violence of seething water long held back, at last breaking out. Laughter came gushing out of the hut, spreading panic amongst the poultry peacefully chasing cockroaches, and floated across the cemetery of the Catholic Mission where Father Vandermayer, who was reading in his office, muttered an oath" (166; trans. altered by me).†

Laughter functions as the novel's ultimate strategy of revolt, reversing the previous perspectives: the initial laughter at the whites' hypocrisy and failings turns into an affirmation of a long-suppressed identity. As Engamba puts his spear away, saying "These things are useless now" (164),‡ the promise of a new kind of revolt is held out by the ribaldry. The spirit of rebellion that comes to full fruition by the end of the novel makes more ominous, more promising, Meka's words as he sends everyone out to their appointed tasks: "We can't do anything about what has happened. The whites will always be the whites . . . . Perhaps one day . . ." (167).★★

★ "les Blancs, c'est facile à avoir" (15).

† "Le rire éclata avec la violence d'une eau bouillonnante longtemps contenue qui rompt sa digue. Il jaillit de la case, sema la panique parmi la volaille qui chassait paisiblement les cancrelats et disparut au-delà du cimetière de la Mission catholique où le Père Vandermeyer, qui lisait son bréviaire, poussa un juron" (Oyono [1956b] 1979, 185).

‡ "Ces choses sont devenus inutiles" (184).

★★ "Nous ne pouvons rien sur ce qui est fait, les Blancs sont toujours les Blancs. . . . Peut-être qu'un jour . . ."(186).

The novel ends with the three elders, Nti, Engamba, and Meka, alone in the house. Nti has had his say and remains silent. Engamba now worries about what he will say when he returns to Zourion, having left so proudly. It is Meka who has the last word: "I'm just an old man now . . ." (167). * With this bitter tone that follows the laughter, a sense of the harsh realities facing the three men prevails. The optimistic signs of mediation between the white and the African cultures featured in the literatures that preceded those of revolt—the various "success" stories or those based on a positive recuperation of the past—as well as such powerful moments of revolt as the Mau Mau insurrection or the strike along the Dakar-Niger line, have been superseded by this insistently more pessimistic picture. The political hopes for imminent independence, so widespread in the late 1950s, or even its realization by the early 1960s, do little to alter this sense of a darker, even more cynical world.

What is so striking with Oyono is his presentation of this dark vision, his skillful manipulation of themes and perspectives, in ways that depart significantly from earlier works of African literature. We see this in the animal imagery in Part Three, which shifts values and foci: the panther/predator, the gorilla as opposed to the chimp, and the porcupine trap, all emerge in the Africans' eyes as strong. The comic gorilla now represents power, while the mocked panther is unequivocally associated with predation. Likewise, with the new approbation of the villagers, nude buttocks are presented as unashamedly natural—not as ridiculous, but as a kind of family joke. This transvaluation extends to the warning not to walk into porcupine traps with one's eyes open; to the new consensus rejecting Christianity; to the new sense of community; to the importance of being "hommes murs," unlike the uncircumcised whites. In the final peripeteia laughter at the whites becomes a device to demystify and to expose the gaps in colonialist ideology. It is this laughter that completes the reader's shift in perspective.

This manipulation of the reader is typical of the new turn in African literature, which uses parody and distancing devices and is more concerned with manipulating perspectives than with giving us the narrator's view of the world in a straightforward fashion. Achebe's vision of a transparent "Reality" is altered here by a deflecting medium in which the light itself becomes visible, and is visibly refracted and reflected. Esu sows confusion; the solid basis for the subject and the world crumbles. A sense of revolt remains, but the basis of assurance on which it had rested for writers of the Negritude generation is no longer there.

---

* "je ne suis plus qu'un vieil homme . . ." (187).

Chapter 7

The Ironic Limits of Revolt

YAMBO OUOLOGUEM, *Le Devoir de violence*

In fact, *Le Devoir de violence* is not one book but many. It oscillates from style to style, theme to theme, story to story, mode to mode. If there is an overriding central quality, it would be the ironic treatment to which the variety of elements is subjected. And as irony, it can be understood only in terms of a direction that the irony indicates, not in any affirmation of positive value. In this sense, it shares the spirit of revolt of Mongo Beti and Ferdinand Oyono, and at the same time, their choice of irony and parody as means of attacking oppressive institutions. Unlike the Cameroonian authors, Yambo Ouologuem makes the position of the narrator less explicit—the irony seems to turn inward in ways that undermine the narrator's point of attack, leaving some commentators perplexed.[1] Nonetheless, *Le Devoir de violence* is a key text that brings to the fore the role of ironic negation in revolt, and that brings revolt to its limit.

Parody is revolt. For Jean Genet, the Marquis de Sade, or, better, the latter's impersonation in Peter Weiss's *Marat-Sade,* to represent is to play at a role, to dress up, like the Haouka (re-presented by Jean Rouch in *Les Maîtres fous* [1953]), a religious cult, formed in colonial Gold Coast, whose adherents assumed the roles of colonial authority and power in trancelike states. As they became governor, governor's wife, general, and other colonial figures, they foamed, spoke in tongues, and in the end violently sacrificed a dog they then consumed in the raw flesh. The acting [out] could not be called a mimesis, but an exaggerated miming that, in the final analysis, was also a miming of colonial pretensions and power. In short, they behaved like Saïf, but without restraint.

Parody becomes both a loving embrace of the role—one is enraptured by the authoritarian, powerful, godlike ruler—and a continual process of dragging through the mud, through the *ordure.* As soon as the "history" begins, in *Le Devoir de violence,* so, too, begins the litany of horrors, of atrocities, which become part of the style of the account, part of the role playing of the narrator, whose use of the *griot* Koutouli as mouthpiece is immediately mocked by the un*griot*like nature of the account ("Not far from the bodies of the countless slaughtered children, seventeen fetuses were counted, expelled from the gaping entrails of mothers in death agony. Under the eyes of all, those women had been raped by their husbands, who then, overpowered by shame, had killed themselves" [Ouologuem 1977, 4])*—a narrative style that fits written, not oral accounts, and especially not the formal and stylized epic style of the *griots*. For example, we may consider the scene in the epic of Sundiata transcribed by Camara Laye, in which Sundiata first hauls himself to his feet, after having been unable to use his legs in his childhood:

> When he judged that he had climbed high enough, his knees, which for the first time he tried to brace, began trembling frantically, like a field of corn whipped by the harmattan. . . .
> The son of Sogolon paused a moment, racked with fatigue, drenched with sweat, and panting, but satisfied with himself. When he stood upright there, really upright, and cautiously began to stretch his legs, Balla Fassali, Kanko, Nana Triban and Sogolon jumped for joy.

And the chant of the *griot* Balla Fassali Kouyaté follows:

> Filth, filth, filth
> Everything is covered by filth,
> But nothing can cover you, you filth! (Laye 1981, 134–35)†

Epithets, praise singing, elliptic phrases, speech that hides the person of the declaiming voice while it proclaims the public person of the one

---

* "Non loin des corps de la horde des enfants égorgés, on comptait dix-sept foetus expulsés par les viscères béants de mères en agonie, violées, sous les regards de tous, par leurs époux, qui se donnaient ensuite, écrasés de honte, la mort" (Ouologuem 1968, 10). All page references to this text are to the 1968 edition, and to the 1977 translation by Ralph Manheim, unless otherwise indicated as my translation.

† Quand il jugea qu'il avait grimpé assez haut, ses genoux, que pour la première fois il tentait de redresser en s'arc-boutant, tremblèrent frénétiquement, tel l'harmattan fouettant le moisson. . . .
   Le fils de Sogolon s'arrêta un instant, recru de fatigue, trempé de sueur, haletant, mais satisfait de sa personne. Quand il fut debout, bien debout, et qu'il détendit nerveusement les jambes, Balla Fassali, Kanko, Nâna Tribân, et Sogolon bondirent sur leurs pieds. . . .
   Ordure, ordure, ordure
   Tout s'abrite sous l'ordure
   Et toi, ordure, rien ne te sert d'abri! (Laye 1978b, 144)

whom it praises—these, in all respects, form the antithesis of a speech act that details "the bodies of the countless slaughtered children" (Oyono 1977, 4).*

In *Devoir,* the "epic" list of glorious conquests is mocked and parodied: famous *griot* names like Kouyaté, or his subject matter, are turned, inverted, or slyly evoked. Thus history becomes "history." The empire of Mali is repeatedly suggested by textual indications of time and place, but the game of disguise is played on the names of neighboring states. Thus, the story ("la véritable histoire") of the Empire's rise begins in 1202 with the Saïfs and "the African Empire of Nakem south of Fezzan, long after the conquests of Okba ben Nafi al-Fitri" (3)† [2] Nakem is an anagram of Kanem, a medieval empire located indeed to the south of the Fezzan, and ruled by the Sefawa dynasty, which derived its name from the ruler Sef [Saïf]. Fitri is the name of a lake within Kanem (now Chad); Oqba (Okba) ben Nafi did conquer the Fezzan in the seventh century, so that the rise of the Saïfs was indeed "long after the conquests of Okba ben Nafi el Fitri." The date 1202 is important for the temporary ascendancy of the Sosso king Soumangourou who conquered Ghana at about that time, and who saw his kingdom eclipsed by the rising star of Sundiata and Mali. The city of Tillaberi-Bentia, mentioned in the novel as the capital of the fictitious empire of Nakem-Ziuko, does not evoke either Kanem or Mali, but the Sosso, as the real Tillaberi lies on the east branch of the Niger as it descends south of Gao.

The point of locating these historical markers seems to have been missed by some commentators who might have been misled by Ouologuem's stated intention to "restore an historical dimension" to African history.[3] Wole Soyinka weakly states that the novel "marks a studied repudiation of historic blinkers," that it "re-writes the chapter of Arab-Islamic colonisation of Black Africa," that it sets an "exhumed *reality*" against "accepted history" in dialectical fashion (Soyinka 1979, 100; my stress). This view is echoed and reechoed (de Leusse 1971, 88; Ohaegbu 1978, 124). However, the dates, names, play on history, serve to clothe the actors and situate their discourse, not so as to expose the actual facts of the historical record but to create a mise-en-scène for the action that follows. And here one is not disappointed in Soyinka's appraisal of that action. As one would expect from the acerbic master of Wordplay, creator of the Professor, of Brother Jero, and of the demonological purveyors of the system

---

* "des corps de la horde des enfants égorgés" (Ouologuem 1968, 10)

† "L'Empire africain de Nakem, au Sud du Fezzan, bien après les conquêtes d'Okba ben Nafi el Fitri" (Ouologuem 1968, 9).

of As, Soyinka accurately assesses Ouologuem's style : "The method is invariably iconoclastic: nothing survives in it" (Soyinka 1979, 101). "A neutral, tight-lipped humour fitfully relieves the oppression, varying from the mordant and sardonic to cosmic belly-laughs; great passages from history are set in motion by a public split in the trousers of the great" (100). Soyinka highlights the act of deflation—"The Bible, the Koran, the historic solemnity of the *griot* are reduced to the histrionics of wanton boys masquerading as humans"—and effectively captures the frenzied extravaganza that marks Ouologuem's style: "Ouologuem leaps beautifully from the cliché 'café au lait' joke to the sadistic guffaw with the lofty indifference of a ringmaster manipulating his whirl of freaks at the touch of a footpedal" (Soyinka 1979, 100–101).

As Eric Sellin (1976) points out, Ouologuem's style calls attention to itself. We can see this at the outset as the first three lines perform *at least* three ironizing gestures: "Our eyes drink the brightness of the sun and, overcome, marvel at their tears. *Maschallah! oua bismillah!* . . . To recount the bloody adventure of the niggertrash—shame to the worthless paupers!—there would be no need to go back beyond the present century . . ." (3).* The first sentence, ambivalent, directs us to the weeping eyes—eyes inviting, as Jonathan Ngaté has noted, the African reader's identification. The slightly sad, slightly ecstatic glimpse is immediately dismantled by the ironic imitation of the Muslim exclamations in the name of Allah and his Will. The third sentence shifts directly to a French-speaking voice that mocks the judgment implied in "aventure sanglante" by the stiff undercutting of the victims, the "négraille," rendered variously as "niggertrash" or "niggerscum." By the time we finish the third sentence, we have become conscious of the style. A rereading, then, of the first sentence plunges us into the abyss of which Paul de Man spoke when indicating the endless regressions occasioned by irony: the verbs border on hyperbole; the sun refuses submission to mere symbolic status; and the weeping immediately opens the path to the ironic use of the Muslim appeals to the divine, themselves precursors to the aside that follows, shame on the worthless men.

The narrative voice is too strong ever to let the reader go: "An account of the splendor of that empire . . . would offer nothing but trivial folklore" (my trans.);† our attention is immediately captured by its presence. We

---

* "Nos yeux boivent l'éclat du soleil, et, vaincus, s'étonnent de pleurer. *Maschallah! oua bismillah!* . . . Un récit de l'aventure sanglante de la négraille—honte aux hommes de rien—tiendrait aisément dans la première moitié de ce siècle . . ." (9).

† "Raconter la splendeur de cet empire . . . n'offrirait rien que du menu folklore" (9).

soon learn its parameters: no subject is sacred to it, no emotion can be imputed to it: it is the voice that ironizes, "qui ironise," as French would have it. It is the voice that concocts an embittered chronicle of violence and domination with which to frame the sequence of psychosexual episodes that punctuates the history of Nakem. The episodes, like the history, are equally concocted, equally surrounded by quotation marks;[4] less a plagiarism than a turning; less a turning than a *staging*. We seek in vain for the backstage. The narrator is not only invisible, he is absolutely nothing but an "ironizing" voice, and thus a voice that is compelled to revolt, always turning the real names, real heroes, real leaders, real empires, real colonizers, real feelings, real encounters, real historical drives, and especially real relationships (social, class, individual, or self-reflexive) into verbal gestures. The one who so manipulates discourse is thus in revolt against the object of the parody, and at the same time situated beyond the features he generates into a mask. The voice, or the presence of the voice, can then be described as free, and its only value consists in its freedom.

Thus, though Soyinka appreciates the comedy and the ironic distancing, he fails to see that there can be no dialectic between reality and common acceptations or distortions of African history—the "exhumed reality" is a parody of contested ideological versions of reality or of historical truisms, cast in the ironic form of the negative image that is then displayed so as to be mocked. Soyinka prefers to see Ouologuem's intense contemptuousness as a reflection of the alienation of the executioners from the victims, as well as a form of "self-inoculation" practiced by the author (Soyinka [1976] 1979, 101). Simultaneously, he describes the "devaluation" technique as pushing iconoclasm to its limits. However, we must distinguish between Sembène Ousmane's use of satire when attacking neocolonialism in *Xala* (1974), and Ouologuem's use of parody, which brings us so much closer to the language of the satirist. With Sembène, there is a visible bedrock of values upon which the satire stands; with Ouologuem the narrator's freedom is established. Instead of a narration with characters or descriptions that delineate normative standards, there is distance and freedom. The narration continually refuses to allow an identification with the characters by presenting the cast as if they were wearing masks, speaking parts self-consciously overwritten, thus forcing on us an awareness of the artifice ("God's curse on his kingdom"; "God refresh his couch"; "God take his soul" [my trans.]).* The language of the poseur becomes hyperaudible: the ventriloquism cries aloud. And as the puppeteer refuses to

---

* "Dieu maudisse sa royauté"; "Dieu rafraîchisse sa couche"; "Dieu ait son âme" (13)

appear, it is his freedom that becomes the ultimate statement, his distance that forces the reader to respond as if to masked players.

The irony then moves us in two directions: the first takes us to awareness and commitment, and is in response to the demystification (and here we have the principal project of early literatures of revolt); and the second is toward an awareness of the ironist—that is, from the mask back to the puppeteer. The greater the focus on the former, the greater the ideological impress; but as the latter comes increasingly into prominence, as with Ouologuem, it is the act of distancing, the freedom, that is privileged. We can call this freedom not only existential, but ironic as long as it does not imply direct action, committed action. Awareness without change, it represents a vision of the world as fixed, static, if not in a stable equilibrium.

Ouologuem's parody creates the effect of freezing the figures, utilizing at least three devices:

1. *Repetition.* The same events, patterns, or names occur. Thus Saïf ben Isaac El Héït is the namesake of Saïf Isaac El Héït, and the dynasty of the Saïfs is based on the name Saïf, which evokes the historical Sef, itself a generic term for ruler drawn from the Arabic. Kassoumi's son Raymond Spartacus becomes Kassoumi; the killers are schooled in the same sadistic tricks, their language and instruments of pain, knives, snakes, penises, all are variant means of penetration. The typing of character and action creates something close to what Erich Auerbach (1953) referred to as figural representation. Shrobenius is the figura for a generation of Marcel Griaules and Maurice Delafosses, Africanists and ethnologists.

2. *Timelessness.* All the historical markers, dates, and wars, the emplacement of empires and battles, the play of opposing forces and the deployment of their armies, are almost immediately supplanted by individuals and their personal stories, as if the wars and their consequences were merely incidental, merely settings for cycles of human dramas that endlessly repeated themselves. (Derrida's two appropriate terms, in "Living On: *Border Lines*," for this chronospace are "atopical" and "hypertopical," that is, placeless and over-placed [1979a, 105]).

3. *Reduction.* The reduction of motivation to basic drives for control, sex, food: greed and appetite not only rule, but constrain the characters' freedom to act.

Opposing forces are evoked—such as with Saïf versus Henry—but the dialectic is one without synthesis or progress. Saïf will always be there, always in struggle with Chevalier, always in dialogue with Henry. Names like events become interchangeable and recurrent. There is no stabilizing point on which emotions can center: "there is no still point in the text, no acknowledgment signaling immutable fact, only the counterpointing of competing false rationalizations" (Dunton 1989, 438). The emotional response is dissolved, catharsis, sympathetic identification, and mimesis discarded. Time itself becomes an eternal present moment of conflicting partialities. The freedom is largely reactive and negative.

Yet the dispersion generated by the ironic play is not defeatist or even ultimately pessimistic. We follow the coiling edge of ironic rebellion against abusive authority as it tackles complacency and naive complicity—the two evils Mongo Beti countered in *Le Pauvre Christ de Bomba* ([1956] 1976)—and ultimately are led down the roads first trod by Camara Laye and Medza the Conquistador. Raymond Kassoumi embodies the adventures of those predecessors, maps out the "migration" to the north, the misadventure of the exile, the return of the been-to—always bound in each one of those stages, always trapped in the tragedy of his empirical condition, the empirical condition of the African intellectual, and yet always implicated in the divided subjectivity of the narration that lies beyond. The final exchange between Henry and Saïf captures this situation; the result is less tragic than existentially absurd:

> Saïf: "Then there's no choice."
> Henry: "Oh yes there is. You become free because you have no choice."
> (180)*

Both positions are contained, and thus supplanted, by the self-conscious staging.

This is the existentialism of Genet for whom the unmasking of Authority was tantamount to the expression of his own freedom. For Genet blacks could serve this goal by mounting a self-conscious "clownerie" in which even skin color could be played at—*Les Nègres* ([1958] 1960) is subtitled "Pour jouer les nègres" [To play the role of the blacks]: being a black becomes playing a black, and, according to Genet, playing this role requires a white spectator or the mask of a white or perhaps even a mannequin of a white person in the audience. The situation Ouologuem creates is particularized by the relationship between Africa and Europe. It is therefore similar to Genet's framing of the demystification of bourgeois European culture, which he views through the gay and the outlaw perspective. But Ouologuem's text has the specificity of the African, and especially of the

---

* Saïf: "C'est qu'il n'y a pas de choix."
  Henry: "Si! Vous devenez libre parce que vous n'avez pas le choix." (206)

Malian, of the modern period, for whom Negritude and Africanist discourse have an immediate presence, and for whom the early responses of
African literary voices to the European presence took the forms of literatures of *témoignage*.

Thus we are not surprised to find the staging placed in relation to the
four configurations of *témoignage* already noted. The novel begins with history and folklore combined in "La Legende des Saïfs." Saïf Isaac El Héït
emerges into the limelight by "standing out from this portrait of horrors"
(my trans.).* Words like "splendeur," "sinistre" [disaster], "mort"
[death], "défait" [defeated/undone], "redoutable" [fearsome]—a vocabulary of power, domination, force, and extravagance mark the sketches of
the past. The drama is purple: "all in the same night they were carried
away by . . . three asps. O tempora! O mores . . ." (17).† The events flow in
a rapid succession in which the characters are reduced to silence before the
overpowering narrative voice. The sequence of atrocities blurs all distinctions. The murderous Saïf Isaac El Héït returns to life as the vicious Saïf
ben Isaac El Héït; between violent African and intriguing French sover-
eigns there is no appreciable difference. "Legend" is turned inside out. No
proverb or tale appears, as we would expect in an epic account. Instead, the
turns in the text are generated by a gamut of extreme tropes—hyperboles,
litotes, oxymorons, metaphors, comparisons by which to measure distance. The public discourse puts historical *témoignage* on display, and the
largest part of the novel rehearses the actions of historical posturing.

But the tempo of the chronicle gives way to that of the personalized
narration with the stories of Kassoumi and his son Raymond Spartacus
Kassoumi. Here the defamiliarization is effected with respect to social and
especially autobiographical *témoignage*. At first blush the scenes of flirtation
and courtship between Kassoumi and Tambira offer relief from and a contrast to those brief, flash sketches of mayhem and degeneracy and those
parodies of intimate intrigue and murder that characterize the lives of the
public figures, including the French officials, Saïf and his assassins, the
nameless notables, and, on another modulated register, Shrobenius and
his family. Eventually we realize that the moments of relief offered by the
stories of Kassoumi and Raymond are mere interludes, pauses in the
tempo of Brutality and War.

The initial scenes of violence, with Saïf's court and the French administration, present us with an unrelieved portrait of the world as governed

---

* "se détachant sur ce tableau d'horreurs" (11)

† "Ils y furent ensemble ravis en un même soir par . . . encore trois vipères aspics. O temps!
O moeurs . . ." (23).

by destructive forces of power, one in which chaos or the absence of meaning is implied rather than implicated into a larger order. The universe is monstrous—delirious with power, and not, like that of the Marquis de Sade, in rebellion against divinity. Likewise, the characters are either unstoppable agents of evil impulses and intents, or hapless victims. Clearly, we are placed within the mode of satire, not realism, not mimesis, and Ouologuem is faithful to this mode: all actions terminate in a demonstration of the helplessness of humanistic forces to resist a power that characterizes the world and that naturalizes relationships governed by force. Thus all the criticisms of Ouologuem on the ground that he has exaggerated or misrepresented are misguided: how could satire do otherwise?

Yet Ouologuem's text does not remain uniformly ensconced in mayhem: if it did, the monotony of evil would level the text and the world it portrays to the point of erasing the force of the evil itself. This may explain how the personalized scenes that begin with the "négraille," that is, with the servant family Kassoumi, function: not only do they relieve the racecourse pace of parodied history, but they highlight the violence by offering a contrasting mood and mode, one that conveys the image of a caring world in which love and tenderness restore life. The text then weaves at least two divergent threads into the "historical" chronicle: the parodies of purple prose—anagrams of melodramatic pornography set in a pseudo-Sudanese setting; and the romantic, well-ordered converse of these scenes governed by family or personal ties of tenderness, and by visions of self-sacrifice marked by traces of sublimity. Eventually the "romance" nose-dives back into the original modes associated with chaos and destruction. The text is manic-depressive both in its view of history and of individual lives or biography.

The manic-depressive view alternates between hope and despair; it is basically manichean. Pairs of opposites inform the text so thoroughly that no single individual can appear without his/her counterpart/counterfoil, eventually complementing, confronting, and finally opposing him. Thus we have the paired Wampoulo and Kratongo, like Rosenkrantz and Guildenstern—a double term that functions to highlight the underlying doubleness of the informing vision, the twinned master trope. But more deliberately it is the figure of the oxymoron, represented by the coupling of Saïf/Henry, Chevalier/Awa, Sonia/Madoubo, Raymond/Lambert, and so forth, that characterizes the relationships. Typically, the opposites invoke the familiar pairing of domination and subordination: Chevalier/Awa, Sankolo/Awa, Saïf/Chevalier, Dougouli/Tambira, [Kratongo and Wampoulo]/Tambira; conquering chiefs/conquered slaves; notables/négraille . . . a world comprising masters and slaves.

There are no relationships that escape this pattern, yet the insistence on it is not equally distributed. For example, Saïf is automatically placed within this master-slave dialectic, so that his sparring with Henry in the end, which is more equally balanced, still takes the form of maneuvering for power, and Henry's refusal to play on the same grounds, his affirmation of a different set of values, merely places the fundamental pattern of struggle and power on a higher intellectual plane. On the other hand, the sweet relations between Kassoumi and Tambira, or Raymond and Lambert, which counterbalance the basic pattern of domination/subordination, can not escape this dichotomy, with the result that either moments of domination penetrate their sexual encounters or these characters are eventually made victims of the larger forces of domination.

The resistance to this pattern can serve to highlight its presence, and to suggest Ouologuem's own subversion of the easy cynicism it entails. We can examine the resistance in closer readings of two exceptional developments that differ from the general tendencies established by the prevailing mode, that is, the episodes involving Shrobenius, and Raymond's love affair with Lambert. Both of these sequences are significant because they take us to the edge of Ouologuem's changeless universe by challenging the static elements of parody.

Nothing is more ambivalent than the kind of distance parody establishes. The parodist is free inasmuch as he or she is always situated behind a mask. The mask is a focal point of awareness; highlighting the artifice of the mask leaves one with the impression that there is no solid, undergirding foundation, but a gratuitous spirit of revolt. However as long as the parody is tied to a specific text, discourse, or ideology, it remains historically determined, completely fixed. Saïf's freedom is matched by his servants' or killers' lack of choice: the blacksmith Barou is forced by Kratongo and Wampoulo to kill Doumbouya; and on another level, Saïf and Henry are constrained to fashion arguments in defense of cynicism and of faith. The caricature of Shrobenius is a function of the name Frobenius, as the parody of Africanist ethnology, of which Frobenius is one of the principal creators, is delimited by the project of addressing an historically constructed discourse. Parody's freedom is thus relative; it is totally tied to its object, just as a being-for-others, as the existentialists would have it, exists in the gaze of the Other. We can see this clearly in the case of the ur-father of European Africanists.

Fr(Shr)obenius was a founding father of the Africanist values that inform the very literature Ouologuem is principally parodying, that is, Negritude, and more largely, literatures of *témoignage*. His appearance in the text raises the question of change in two ways: First, it signals the conventional portrayal of African history as grounded in patterns of growth, following Frobenius's well-known encomiums on the values on which African civilizations rest. Second, his views dialectically measured African against European civilization, again suggesting a pattern for change, later to be repeated in the philosophy of Negritude that Léopold Senghor proposed as moving a moribund European civilization forward.

The historical Frobenius is reified into the risible figure of Shrobenius, while the generation of Negritude authors who were inspired by him are indirectly mocked. ("Shrobenius's head teemed with ideas. Reeling off spirituality by the yard, the men paced the courtyard . . . " [87]).* The precise date that establishes Shrobenius's arrival is dropped into a timeless sequence in which there is no sense of a before or an after. He is located in the space we associate with puppet figures and animals. His wife, Hildegaard, becomes a synecdoche for mechanical ethnography: her legs, "little wader bird stilts" (my trans.),† are like tripods, and she is the camera ("Hildegaard took the photos" [my trans.])‡ while he is the recorder ("the ethnologist took down the words of the informants sent by Saïf" [my trans.]).** For Ouologuem the immediate historical setting is an occasion for theatrics: Shrobenius the ethnologist becomes an object, a photo occasion: "A large stout man, the [typical] *bel Allemand,* red side whiskers, florid complexion, blue eyes, grave and full of feeling, nascent paunch, *wèrèguè wèrèguè!*" (87; my alteration of trans.)††; and the parody proceeds: "Saïf made up stories and the interpreter translated, Madoubo repeated in French, refining on the subtleties to the delight of Shrobenius, that human crayfish afflicted with a groping mania for resuscitating an African universe—cultural autonomy, he called it—which had lost all living reality" (87).‡‡

The vilification of the Negrology that follows is accompanied by the further puppetization of Shrobenius; thus, as he evokes romanticized notions ("African life . . . was pure art, intense religious symbolism"

---

* "Les idées emplirent la cervelle de Shrobénius, et tous, vendant de la spiritualité au mètre, se promenaient . . ." (102).

† "petits échassiers en croissance" (102)

‡ "Hildegaard prenait des clichés" (102)

** "l'ethnologue transcrivit les dires d'informateurs mandés par Saïf" (102)

†† "grand, gros, bel Allemand, avec les favoris roux, la teint fleuri, l'oeil bleu, tendre et serieux, le ventre apparent déjà, *wèrèguè wèrèguè*" (102)

‡‡ "Saïf fabula et l'interprète traduit, Madoubo repéta en français, raffinant les subtilés qui faisaient le bonheur de Shrobénius, écrivisse humaine frappée de la manie tâtonnante de vouloir resusciter, sous couleur d'autonomie culturelle, un univers africain qui ne correspondait à plus rien de vivant" (102).

[87]),* while deploring "l'aridité spirituelle" that resulted from the influence of European civilization, Shrobenius simultaneously falls into "[a]
sort of somnolent stupor" (87).† [5] The parody, in fact, is aimed at the Sen-
ghorian enthusiasms of the type dismantled by Stanislas Adotevi in *Négritude et Négrologues* (1972) and Marcien Towa in *Léopold Sédar Senghor: négritude ou servitude* (1971), rather than the more radical or surrealist tones
taken by Léon Damas or especially Aimé Césaire, whose *Cahier d'un retour
au pays natal* ([1939] 1971) contains verses actually in harmony with much
of Ouologuem's more bitter vision.[6] Thus, Césaire "unleashes" a litany of
monstrosities ("je délaçais les monstres" [Césaire (1939) 1971, 29], while
simultaneously evoking the antiphrasis, the other side of disaster ("I heard
the ascent from the other side of disaster, a river of turtle doves and clover
from the savanna" [my trans.]).‡

Ouologuem completes the Shrobenius sequence by dropping the
ethnologist and following his daughter's sexual adventures, which soon
occupy center stage. The reader's voyeurism is focalized through Sankolo
whose arousal and masturbation is witnessed by his fiancée, Awa. Ouologuem transforms ethnology, in graduated sequences, from viewing to
violence and violation as he concludes the meeting of Madoubo and
Sonia, the African prince and his European belle, with Sankolo's sadistic
smothering of Awa. The regression, from the initial sexual act, witnessed
through the rearview mirror by Sankolo, back to Awa, and then back again
to the reader placed as surrogate spy in the position of safely hidden witness, is repeated by the passage of the reader from enthusiast for African
culture/literature to secret delectator of forbidden texts, a pornographo-
phile. The position of concealment and the surreptitious viewing of illicit
acts and pleasures stands in contrast to the stance of the rebel whose cause
is publicly stated, and who bears witness to injustice and pain, not to pleasure, with the goal of arousing public indignation, not private titillation.
Yet rebellion is masked by the parody: the gaze that is turned so attentively
on the violence and eroticism returns to the figure in the shadow, the one
who might next turn victim, who might be compelled to speak, who lacks
the freedom of the actors and who doesn't share their responsibility. "A
shape vanished in the tall grass: Kassoumi, on his way home from the
banana tree, had seen it all. *Alif minpitjè!* (93).**

---

* "la vie africaine était art pur, symbolisme effrayablement réligieux" (102).

† "une sorte de somnolence hébétée" (102)

‡ "j'entendais monter de l'autre côté du désastre, un fleuve de tourterelles et de trèfles de la
savane" (Césaire [1939] 1971, 29).

** "Une silhouette s'enfonça dans la savane: Kassoumi, qui revenait de sous son bananier, et
qui avait tout vu. *Alif minptjè*" (109).

Kassoumi denounces Sankolo, but must have recourse to Saïf, that is, to the ultimate source of force, and so can not escape a similarly violent end for himself, his wife, or his children. Ouologuem's universe is as tightly bound as the mode he chooses to represent it. And the only possibility he opens to freedom is in terms of existential authenticity. For this option he chooses the theme of homosexual discovery in the person of Raymond Kassoumi.

The counterpart to the parodic sexuality portrayed in the Shrobenius episode is Kassoumi's love affair with Lambert—a love with the possibilities of enabling Kassoumi to change personally, to confront his feelings and inhibitions, to allow his sentiments room to flower, to achieve a more exalted state than that offered by relationships based solely on domination. This possibility offers a challenge to the parody itself, and is therefore not only anachronistic, it calls into question the view of the world and of history established though the novel.

The constraints placed on Raymond's choices and freedom are the ironic result of his personal difficulties: he is penniless when he meets Lambert, and he is a black intellectual living in colonial France. The discourse of love that he selects is given its possibilities by these two factors. His entire voyage to Europe, placed within the context of the student generation of the 1920s, is seen as a continuation of the patterns of domination enforced by the notables back home. Like the other African intellectuals, Raymond is "maintained by the notables in a state of gilded prostitution" (136),* limited to the roles preestablished by the ruling forces: "ambiguous balancing acts in which the master turned the slave into the first of the slaves and the arrogant equal of the white master, and in which the slave thought himself master of the master, who himself had fallen to the level of the first of the slaves . . ." (136).† As V. Y. Mudimbe has pointed out, the degree of subordination passes beyond the level of the physical to that of the discourse when the colonized no longer recognizes that his very revolt is inscribed within an alien system: Raymond became "a second shadow of himself. . . . The white man had crept into him and this white presence determined even the moves that he, a child of violence, would make against it [Europe]" (137).‡

---

* "tenue par la notabilité dans une prostitution dorée" (157)

† "jeux d'équilibres ambigus, où le maître fit de l'esclave l'esclave des esclaves et l'égal impénitent du maître blanc, et où l'esclave se crut maître du maître lui-même retombé esclave des esclaves . . ." (157)

‡ "autre ombre de lui-même . . . parce que l'homme blanc s'était insinué en lui, sa présence commanda les gestes même qu'il fera contre elle [l'Europe], lui, l'enfant de la violence" (Ouologuem 1968, 158)

Raymond turns inward, a problematic gesture for the play of parody's masks. While the elements of the universe are all caught up in a game— "And such was the earth of men that the balance between air, water, and fire was no more than a game" (182)*—the text is limited to the play on words. Hence the significance of the name: now "Raymond," the baptised son of Kassoumi, his name is a partial anagram of the letters of Ouo- loguem's first name, Yambo. Like the author at one time, Raymond is a student in France. The autobiographical air is suggested by the student's rebelliousness, this time marked by phrasing that suggests the autobio- graphical act of reshaping/reforming one's own life through words. By now we are not surprised at the degree of hatred and ambivalence joined to the employment of the colonizer's language for that purpose:

> And so, taking refuge beneath the dead tree of academic complacency, a mage of knowledge without hearth or home, *living amidst the dead car- casses of words,* Raymond Kassoumi, after a period of apery in which he took on the accent of a Paris wise guy, *gave himself up to literary drivel,* turning his learning into a demagogic ventriloquism and sinking under its weight. (137; my stress)†

This remarkably self-referential passage is torn by internal stress. It plays at the novel's strategies of "singerie" [apery] and "ventriloquisme," encas- ing the basic oxymoron of life and death, taking refuge in the very word- play that enables the student-author to survive, and that sinks him back into the shadows, "sombrant," perishing in the illusion of power, the demagoguery of inscripted violence. Raymond carries the Christian name along with the African patronymic: Raymond Kassoumi. At times the "fils de Tambira," at times the silent interlocutor with Saïf, he remains thor- oughly encumbered by his past: "he could no more rid himself of Africa than a plant of its roots" (137).‡

The passage from Camara Laye's dark child to Oyono's houseboy to Ouologuem's Raymond Kassoumi has something complete about it. There was a changing of the guards for a generation of students in 1968,

---

* "Dans l'air, l'eau et le feu, aussi, la terre des hommes fit n'y avoir qu'un jeu . . ." (Ouo- loguem 1968, 208).

† Et donc, refugié sous l'arbre mort de la souffiance scolaire, mage de savoir, sans feu ni lieu, *ne vivant guère que parmi les carcasses de mots,* Raymond Kassoumi après s'être fourvoyé, avec un accent de titi parisien, dans la singerie, *cultiva la palabre littéraire,* faisant à sa culture un ventriloquisme de démogagie, et sombrant avec elle. (158; my stress)

‡ "il ne se débarrassait de l'Afrique, pas plus que la plante de ses racines" (158).

the year in which *Le Devoir de violence* appeared. Raymond's love affair is set in 1924: but the literary traces it bears were clearly left by Laye, Kane, Oyono, and Genet, not to mention André Schwarz-Bart, and they etch in the lines of Raymond's love and his hatred. Comparing himself and Lambert to the image of two birds cruelly tied together by their Chinese captors, bringing their own destruction through the illusion of flight (Ouologuem 1968, 193), Raymond sees in his affair his apotheosis and, as its illusory reflection, his own enslavement. At the height of the lyrical exultation, the language of love used to describe their relationship becomes effulgent: "they formed the apogee of the natural order of love" (my trans.).* In the description of their tender lovemaking, Raymond evokes the same organic metaphors earlier mocked in Shrobenius's rhetoric about black civilization. Thus we hear from the ethnologist: "'The plant,' Shrobenius went on, 'germinates, bears fruit, dies, and is reborn when the seed germinates' " (94).† For Raymond, the mixture of his breath with Lambert's is compared to a harvest with the taste of rose petals, one that gives life and death: "and what was born and what died, the sap that flowed, wrapped in the guilt of their two bodies, was he, Kassoumi, the son of a slave, the cornered, alienated nigger engaged in being reborn well-born" (155).‡ Ouologuem then employs the same language we encountered above: "He germinated like the earth . . ." (my trans.).** There follows a shift, made possible in the French text only through the ambiguities of gender-specific language, in which Ouologuem carries the theme of identity and self-discovery forward by suggestively sliding the masculine "il" used to refer to Kassoumi into the feminine "elle" whose antecedents, all metaphors for Raymond, happen to be feminine: "et son angoisse était une dune de sable aride qui parle à la sécheresse des vents, silencieuse, comme par rite; comme si par son silence, elle voulait affirmer sa solitude, clamer qu'elle était sereine, irrémédiablement elle-même . . ." [and his anguish was an arid sand dune speaking to the parched winds, silently as in a rite; as if by its [her] silence it [she] wished to proclaim its [her] solitude,

---

* "ils formaient l'apogée de l'ordre naturel de l'amour" (177)

† "La plante, poursuivit Shrobénius, germe, porte son fruit, meurt, se renaît quand la semence germe" (110).

‡ "et cela qui naissait, cela qui mourait, cela qui coulait en sève enrobée de la culpabilité de leurs deux corps, c'était lui, Kassoumi, le fils de l'esclave, le Nègre acculé, aliéné, occupé à bien naître" (178).

** "Il germait comme la terre . . ." (178)

to shout that it [she] was serene, irrevocably itself [herself] ...(my trans.)]. When we arrive, at the end of the sentence/breath, the female is joined with the male pronoun: "et que jamais elle n'avait eu d'autre désir que d'être sereine à la fin de cette seconde, à la fin de cette respiration en lui, à la fin de lui-même" (Ouologuem 1968, 178) ["that it [she] had never had any other desire than to be serene at the end of this second, at the end of this breath in him, at the end of himself" (155; my additions to trans.)].

The language of this passage is doubled with pain linked to ecstasy, "elle" to "lui," breath to breath, time and space to solitude. But it is in the writer's discovery of the self through his words that one can locate the autobiographical gesture: the dune of arid sand, like the poet's blank sheet of paper, is made to speak to the "sécheresse des vents" (Ouologuem 1968, 178) [dryness of the winds (my trans.)]. As in the mystery of initiation, "silencieuse, comme par rite" (178), silent and yet empowered—like Samba Diallo when he first mastered the French alphabet—Raymond's ecstasy is depicted as a self-affirmation, joining the silence of discovery with vociferous proclamation: "*clamer* qu'elle était sereine, irrémédiablement elle-même" (178; my stress) [to shout that it was serene, irrevocably itself (my trans.)].

The flood of images that Raymond recalls/creates is nothing less than the full spectrum of the novel's own imagery. The author and the text are evoked as if we were sharing with Raymond a vision of the entire novel, its strategies and multitudinous moods and roles in miniature: "And then from the depths of forgetfulness faces and symbols rose up before him; ... his misery appeared to him as a concrete familiar object followed by spinning shapes, a solemn, slow, and fecund dance, delirium, tumult, a welter of images, faces, lightnings, and cries ..." (156).* The sequence of tragic images, coming after the joyful self-discovery in the tenderness and lovemaking, culminates with the proclamation of the speaker's identity: rebel, slave, author of a new text that is liberating in its defiant gestures and its open embrace of all the hidden, soiled features—in celebration of the act of destruction from which emerges the concealed name Spartacus: "and his search was not so much for ecstasy as for the profound meaning of his

---

* "Et c'est alors que du fond de l'oubli, des visages renaissaient devant lui, des symboles aussi ... misère soudain concrétisée, devenue objet familier et reconnu, puis vertige, danse solonelle, molle et féconde, délire, clameur, avec une débauche d'images de visages d'éclairs de cris ... tout apparaissait" (178–79).

own destruction, the stain on his face suddenly splattered by his name: Spartacus!" (156).*

These themes of rebirth, identity, and freedom, especially as they are applied to the situation of the African living in France, and to that of the gay couple for whom love leads to the discovery and choice of the self, are distinctly existential. The freedom we associated with the parodist's position behind the masks that s/he creates, accords perfectly with Lukcs's view of the novel, expressed in his *Theory of the Novel,* as a quest for wholeness of self in a world that refuses that demand: "In the novel, irony is the freedom of the poet in relation to the divine . . . for it is by means of irony that, in an intuitively ambivalent vision, we can perceive divine presence in a world forsaken by the gods" (qtd. in and trans. de Man [1971] 1983, 56). As de Man puts it, following Lukcs, irony determines the organizing principle of the novel, undermining claims of mimesis (which underlie the projects of literatures of *témoignage*), and substitutes the conscious awareness "of the distance that separates an actual experience from the understanding of that experience" (de Man [1971] 1983, 56). The resulting act of mediation described by de Man fits perfectly Ouologuem's extreme shifts of mood from manic to depressive, from historical to personal, accompanied by the satirical exaggerations of the parody: "The ironic language of the novel mediates between experience and desire, and unites ideal and real within the complex paradox of form" (de Man [1971] 1983, 56). Indeed one could say that every personal story in the novel comes down to a mediation of experience and desire through the use of irony.

De Man goes on to criticize Lukács for restoring a sense of wholeness, an organic unity lost on the ironist, by Lukács's reinvestment of the element of temporality, wherein time is seen to triumph as a positive principle. Ouologuem's hopelessness and "pure negativity," of the sort which Lukács deplored in the postromantic, inward action of Novalis and Gontcharov, prevail throughout *Le Devoir de violence* because the rapid shift onto the parodic level effaces all sense of temporal continuity. In breaking with *témoignage* literatures, Ouologuem also breaks with their mimetic, pedagogic, and ameliorist tendencies. Revolt can go no further without turning on itself, without evoking its own contradictions. Ouologuem

---

* "et il a recherché non point tant le délire, que la signification profonde de sa propre déstruction, souillure de son visage qu'éclaboussa brusquement son nom: Spartacus!" (179).

holds up the image of the birds bound to each other, straining in their flight to freedom within the controlled setting of the theater, refusing to step outside the set.

De Man attributes temporality to allegory, in contrast to symbolism, as the former always reenacts a scene already played out in an anterior time to which it refers. Symbolism evokes a unity between the image and its "substance" that denies temporal movement, and that exists outside of time. At first sight it would appear that Ouologuem's construct of contemporary events merely rehearses or recapitulates its former historical incarnation, as though all Saïfs were atavistic versions of the original ancestor. But the shift to irony reduces the original model from an historical figure to a universal type, and temporality is dissolved. Instead of allegorical references to earlier signs, we have ironizing references back to the ironist. Yet symbol does not supplant allegory—the demystifying action is almost always performed. The principal objects of demystification—the rhetoric of the civilizing mission, its various religious representatives, and the secularized versions of Negritude mystification—all adhere to temporal notions of progress. For de Man, "It is a historical fact that irony becomes increasingly conscious of itself in the course of demonstrating the impossibility of our being historical" (de Man [1971] 1983, 211). This is because irony redirects the inquiry from a preoccupation with outward forms, with changes to be wrought in the social domain, to an awareness of the inner self and its encounter with the sentiment of the absurd—the absurd arising, as in the work of Albert Camus, in response to the silence of the universe before our demands for coherence or sense. The self to which the ironist then refers, or that is reflected back, is split between an "empirical self" that is "immersed in the world" (de Man [1971] 1983, 213) and a reflective self that is aware of its own division and separation. The language of irony is the language of the consciousness of this split subject. Ouologuem's divided position is thus reflected in language that insists on bursting the bubble of mystifications. It is characteristic of Ouologuem to use the parody of sadistic eroticism to effect this act. De Man's description of the relationship between language and the subject is constructed along the same existential lines that describe Ouologuem:

> The ironic, twofold self that the writer or philosopher constitutes by his language seems to be able to come into being only at the expense of his empirical self, falling (or rising) from a state of mystified adjustment into the knowledge of his mystification. The ironic language splits the subject into an empirical self that exists in a state of inauthenticity and a self that exists only in the form of a language that asserts the knowledge of this inauthenticity. (de Man [1971] 1983, 214)

The danger of the schoolboy's preoccupation with the self, with his own rebellion, is overcome by the shift onto the plane of the ironic subject whose play with language supplants the overly serious solipsism. Language becomes the weapon, the frustrated instrument of power, for the self divided against itself. Ouologuem's deployment of that weapon is manifest in his parody of all the forms of *témoignage* literature, and, as a consequence, of the mystifications arising from their flow of temporal experience. For instance, Laye's *L'Enfant noir* ([1953] 1973) presents us with the growth of a child in the successful passage to adulthood—a mimetic mystification based on the notion of the organic unity of life; his *Le Regard du roi* ([1954] 1982) presents us with Clarence's allegorical journey, along the path already traced by the beggar, to the South and to the encounter with the king—a mystification based, this time, on the notion of organic spiritual wholeness. Against both Ouologuem erects the repeated journeys of the "négraille," always in the form of flight, always leading to defeat and disintegration.

The formation of the Empire of Nakem is initially grounded in a series of scattered flights of the "négraille." Later Sankolo is drugged into a zombie state, reenacting a mock journey *south*: he echoes the refrain of "Le Sud, le Sud" (Laye [1954] 1982, 88) in *Le Regard du roi,* mocking Clarence's experience of the descent into sensuality with his own enslavement to the drug dabali and sexual dependency, and finally mocking the king/god who embraces Clarence by substituting the monstrous slave owner to whom he is "sold"—"Maybe it's just a nigger's life. Slave. Sold. Bought, sold again, [educated]" (108; my correction to trans.).★ Soyinka (1979, 102) sees a parody of Cheikh Kane's *L'Aventure ambiguë* (1961) here. Although the immediate target might appear to be Laye, the sense of the attack is the same. Similarly, Raymond's life as a student in Paris turns immediately from his studies to a series of catastrophic misadventures, about which he eventually comes to the same conclusion as Sankolo: "Bought, sold again, [educated]." De Man's description of irony as "dividing the flow of temporal experience into a past that is pure mystification and a future that remains harassed forever by a relapse within the inauthentic" (de Man [1971] 1983, 222) is thus appropriate not only in terms of the novel's own sense of temporality, but even more in terms of its relationship to its literary predecessors. Its demystification is directed not only at the mystified self, but at the mystified subject that constructs its unities and verities through the mimetic mode of representation. Both

---

★ "Peut-être est-ce un peu cela, une vie de Nègre. Esclave. Vendu. Acheté, revendu, instruit" (125).

levels of meaning evoked by Senghor or Soyinka, the mystic and the mundane, are targets for the ironist, whose task is to demystify the notion of "an organic world postulated in a symbolic mode of analogical correspondences or in a mimetic mode of representation in which fiction and reality could coincide" (de Man [1971] 1983, 222). De Man's conclusion is particularly apt for Ouologuem: "It is especially against the latter mystification [mimesis] that irony is directed" (de Man [1971] 1983, 222).

The experience of time that emerges for the ironist, for its free-floating and devastating narrative self, is reduced to the immediate moment of the perception, or, more accurately, the moment in which the linguistic barb is launched. These moments are continually reconstituted in discontinuously ordered scenes. The narrative subject's divided self is reflected in its discourse. We see this, for example, in the representation of time. When Kassoumi first consummates his love with Tambira in the small clearing in the reeds, the two lose track of time in the atemporality of their physical sensations: "Transfigured and half delirious, conscious of nothing but their possession of each other, of their profound penetration, they lay enlaced, saturated with the mingling of their bodies" (42).* Ouologuem uses his characteristic imagery of power, domination, and sadism in evoking any sexual act—here he uses the image of poison as though to freeze the climactic moment into an unchanging state: "The venom spurted; and suddenly they felt suffocated, on the point of explosion or death—an instant of intolerable joy, chaste [idéal] and wanton [charnel]—terrifying [affolant]" (43; my additions to trans.).†

The dialectic remains without motion: "idéal" and "charnel" lead only to ex-stasis, the state outside of oneself properly described as "affolant" or delirious. This is the state of being in which discontinuity comes closest to the experience of reality, and in which change as a result of a positive force of intentionality, is a mystification: "irony comes closest," in de Man's deconstructed portrayal of existence, "to the pattern of factual existence and recaptures some of the factitiousness of human existence as a succession of isolated moments lived by a divided self" (226). Yambo Ouologuem concludes with the factitiousness of the African historical

---

* "Transfigurés et comme délirants, étendus là, sans conscience de rien que de leur possession, de leur pénétration profonde, ils s'étreignaient, sursaturés de l'emmêlement de leurs corps" (56).

† "Le venin jaillit; et soudain ils sentirent qu'ils manquaient d'air, qu'ils allaient exploser ou mourir! Ce fut une seconde d'un bonheur suraigu, idéal et charnel–affolant" (56).

experience by invoking the succession of moments of rule and domination under thirty reincarnated versions of Saïf throughout an Africa still divided against itself.

Chapter 8

▼▼▼▼▼▼▼▼▼▼

Change on the Margins

BESSIE HEAD, *The Collector of Treasures*

Introduction

The subject of Bessie Head's stories is change, and specifically the threshold on which change takes place. Change has become the issue of women's writing since Independence—change and not simply rights or equality. Though there has been a continuing concern with the abuse of women, a concern voiced in such miserabilist works as Sembène Ousmane's *Voltaïque* (1962) or Buchi Emecheta's *The Joys of Motherhood* (1979), or presented in more chauvinistic terms in Cyprian Ekwensi's *Jagua Nana* (1961), it is in the novels and stories of Bessie Head, Mariama Bâ, Buchi Emecheta, and Ama Ata Aidoo that the very boundaries between men and women, between past and present roles, are called into question. Those same boundaries are set in place in the constitution of women's identities. In fact, boundaries, the forces that maintain and perpetuate them, and the forces that dissolve them could be said to be both the focus of and the key to Head's work.[1]

We find qualities that support this approach especially in Head's short stories. There we find characters who are sketched, rather than fully portrayed, and whose one or two dominant traits assume such proportions as to give the stories an allegorical aspect. The characters appear for an episode or two in which the point of their appearance is established and the question of their fate determined. The lines of their lives are reduced, brought into focus, and purified. The crossing of lines forms the quintessential action.

An ironic fatalism governs the lives of the women depicted in *The Collector of Treasures* (1977), as is seen in the gap between the narrative point of view and the points of view of the characters. Galethebege's Christian faith, in "Heaven Is Not Closed," is described as sincere and heartfelt by a narrator whose sympathies are closer to those of Galethebege's non-Christian, skeptical husband. More often the irony stems from the internal gap inherent in the position of the women themselves: caught in a network of social custom and constraint, the women in Head's stories experience moments of transition, blasphemy, violence, and death, either because of the strength of their desire, as with Galethebege, Life in "Life," or Rankwana in "The Deep River," or because of their insistence on preserving integrity and independence, as with Life, Dikeledi in "The Collector of Treasures," and Mma-Mabele in "Witchcraft." When there are conflicts, they often occur within the characters themselves, even when external constraint is brought to bear. What emerges is a pattern of struggle between powerful, repressive forces and equally adamant drives grounded in desire and refusal.

The passage across this landscape of combat does not lead to a new vision of history, nor pave a path through history, but, rather, traces magical lines and horizons that set off one time and place from another. Dawn, nightfall, cusps of existence where existential decisions are made—these are boundaries given meaning by personal choice and not historical movement. Even death takes on significance in this way, as though ultimate forces were contained in each individual fate.

However, along with this larger, allegorical vista, one finds the particular features of a present time in which the conflict over social roles has become exacerbated by historical change. The strategy of representing this conflict as one involving boundaries, with accepted frontiers of action being transgressed, or with conventional space being protected, permits the joining of allegorical and historical time. It also suggests that broader meaning is inscribed in larger divisions of power, as Fatima Mernissi has postulated in the more obvious case of Morocco:

> The institutionalized boundaries dividing the parts of society express the recognition of power in one part at the expense of the other. Any transgression of the boundaries is a danger to the social order because it is an attack on the acknowledged allocation of power. The link between boundaries and power is particularly salient in a society's sexual patterns. (Mernissi 1987, 137)

We can see this in the story "Heaven Is Not Closed," and especially in the blank spaces surrounding Ralokae's first wife.

"Heaven Is Not Closed": Ralokae's First Wife

"Ralokae had been married for nearly a year when his young wife died in childbirth. She died when the crops of the season were being harvested, and for a year Ralokae imposed on himself the traditional restraints and disciplines of boswagadi or mourning for the deceased" (Head 1977, 8).*

What is the name of Ralokae's first wife? Why is she called only "Ralokae's first wife," whereas Ralokae's brother Modise is identified by name? Twice at the outset of the narration there are references to "the old man, Modise" (7, 8). He is also the narrator, and when the narrative setting is placed within the context of Modise's story, Modise passes back into the conventional anonymity of the third-person omniscient narrator. He is empowered by his special relationship with the reader, has access to the hidden truth, and shares it with us, as with his grandchildren, who constitute his immediate audience. He is the focus of their attention—they look at him, as he addresses them. He creates the mood, and the children's reactions are orchestrated into a single response—our response: "A gust of astonished laughter shook his family out of the solemn mood of mourning that had fallen upon them and they all turned eagerly toward their grandfather, sensing that he had a story to tell." We wait with them in anticipation for the beginning of the telling. " 'As you know,' the old man said wisely, 'Ralokae was my brother . . .' " (8).

If one can speak of the power to represent things, as well as the authority of inherited literary paradigms and structures to engender a set of reader expectations and responses, then one should also be able to speak of the resistance to these forces. Within "Heaven Is Not Closed," a point of departure for resistance is provided by the unnamed first wife of Ralokae whose untold story is centered on a single clue, her death, which came "when the crops of the season were being harvested" (8).

To enter the text through the opening in the story that occurs with the reference to this young woman is to write her-story on a series of blank slates. We are not told a number of things about her that are essential to our understanding of the relationship she had with Ralokae. Who was she? Who was her family? What kind of marriage was it? Ralokae, we are told, was a man who scorned the new European/Christian way, and who adhered to the traditional customs. This did not mean he was conservative. To the contrary, he was something of a rebel. Her position is unknown. If he chose her because she, too, ignored the new Christian way, then all we can say is that her image is gained through the reflection cast by her husband, by Ralokae, whose name is clearly of significance to the storyteller.

We don't know if they had children—merely that she died in childbirth. If there were children, then the tie to their mother's family should

---

* All page references to stories in *The Collector of Treasures* are to the 1977 edition.

continue to weigh in Ralokae's life, and, more important, they would now be raised by Galethebege. Although it is her grandchildren who listen to Modise, we are not told whether those grandchildren include any off-spring of the first wife. Indeed, the listeners are also described as Modise's children and his grandchildren, although he himself never took Galethebege as wife. If the description is intended to be generic—an old man is generally called "grandfather" out of respect—the narrative does not present it in this fashion. This might appear insignificant were it not for the unique detail with which we are provided about Ralokae's first wife, the time of her death. She passed away at a time that corresponded to her coming to full fruition (a year of her marriage had passed, she was about to give birth), when the crops were being harvested. The child was to be the harvest. She died in childbirth, and left no other visible trace than her absence, her death, the time of her dying. With neither children nor a name she faced the worst of fates customarily reserved for the childless and dispossessed, oblivion. In Modise's telling of her story she is completely unobtrusive, except for the key opening her absence provides for Galethebege.

"He was young and impatient to be married again and no one could bring back the dead" (9).

Death brings irreversible change. A one-way passage across a threshold that is visible to us from only one side, it culminates the movement toward quietude—a linear movement, like thermodynamic flow, in contrast to the seasonal cycle of renewal. Like her life, Rolakae's wife's death is recorded in the dossier of Ralokae's life.

Following her death, Ralokae observed the traditional custom of mourning, a "discipline" that Head identifies as "boswagadi." There seems to be no reason to identify this custom by its Setswana name, but for the fact that Ralokae is a traditionalist and strictly observes the "traditional restraints," which one must assume include sexual continence—a detail that ironically outweighs the importance to the narrator of naming or discussing the woman whose death was the cause of his boswagadi. At the end of the period of mourning, Ralokae "take[s] note of the life of Galethebege" (9) and begins to court her. Despite their differences in belief—she is a devout Christian and he an averred traditionalist—he overcomes her reservations and convinces her to marry him. They marry, after he tells her "firmly": "I took my first wife according to the old customs. I am going to take my second wife according to the old customs too" (9).

Ralokae's firmness is set in contrast with Galethebege's "uncertainty," which marks her declaration to Ralokae about her Christian faith. She must inform the missionary of her decision to marry a man who is set in

"Setswana custom," thus engendering the story's principal conflict, the antagonism between Christianity and traditional "custom."

Ironically, it is the discipline imposed by boswagadi that causes Ralokae to take note of Galethebege: "It was the unexpectedness of the tragic event and the discipline it imposed on him, that made Ralokae take note of the life of Galethebege" (9). Her quietly ordered life, once too insignificant for him to notice, is now what attracts him. As her faith in the "will of God" is what gives her existence its special quality for him, one has to assume Rolakae's first wife was a different sort of woman, had a different set of qualities. And it is, perhaps, the appeal of difference, of contrast, that the absence and the discipline awakened in Rolakae.

The direction taken by the narration is one that moves away from these ironies. Even Ralokae fades into the background as Galethebege finds herself caught between Christian and Setswana customs, between the missionary and Ralokae. Although her husband does not insist that she give up her faith, he refuses to convert; and the missionary refuses to marry her to an "unbeliever," going so far as to announce that heaven is closed to Ralokae. Although this situation might not have been unique to the community, it is presented by Modise as though it were special, as though the conflict it engendered, always potentially there in the presence of the two antagonistic communities, were realized in the story of Galethebege, causing a considerable commotion. There is no indication that Ralokae faced this with his first wife, and every indication that an important decision was being made by Galethebege. She is thus placed between two forces which appear to be clashing for the first time.

However, the nature of the conflict is not as evident as it might appear. At first, we learn that the matter of her Christian faith and his insistence on tradition stood between them "like a fearful sword." This phallic image initially appears odd. The conventional phrasing used to describe it serves to trivialize her uncertainties and would more naturally seem to suggest the firmness of Ralokae, the unswerving male. However, the conventional phrasing, matching her nature, is immediately deconstructed by Galethebege's passion. Blood pounds in this quiet Christian woman's fingers, and when she commits herself to Ralokae, "the sword quivered like a fearful thing between them" (9). Clearly desire takes priority in this struggle, a struggle begun with the discipline of abstinence, the control of desire. The sword that stands between the lovers, like that of Tristan representing his fidelity to his monarch, soon becomes identified with the instrument of desire itself.

Between Ralokae and Galethebege desire and passion replace the discipline of boswagadi and the quietude of Christianity. For Galethebege the conflict remains, but the tension it produces is displaced onto her desire. Thus when she tells the missionary of her fiancé's Setswana custom, he conflates sexuality and traditional beliefs and condemns the two. His views reflect the distance of foreign eyes: "sexual malpractices were associated with the traditional marriage ceremony (and shudder!), they draped the stinking intestinal bag of the ox around their necks" (10).

Galethebege's interviews with the missionary were intended to bridge the gap between the two men and the two customs each represented. Instead, she finds herself trapped between the missionary's interdictions and her husband's adamancy. She had hoped, by means of the passage of love through her, to overcome the conflict between the two men—to mend the rift between their institutions with their two sets of customs. She had sought to achieve a "compromise of tenderness," but instead of providing the occasion for a flow of love, thus satisfying the people's "cry for love" engendered by the intrusion of colonialism, she becomes herself the occasion for hatred. Seeking to unite, she is excluded. The missionary's "rage and hatred were directed at Ralokae, and the only way in which he could inflict punishment was to banish Galethebege from the Church. If it hurt anyone at all, it was Galethebege" (11).

The missionary's reaction to the Setswana custom of uniting the couple under the yoke of the cow's intestines validates Mernissi's assertion that the setting of boundaries, and their transgression, reflect the distribution of power within society, and that it is especially in respect to sexual relations that this relationship between boundaries and power emerges. The act of allegiance is represented as a joining—the intestines yoke the couple under the aegis of Setswana custom, just as the choice of Christianity was to "*embrace* the Gospel" (8; my stress). In the struggle over the power to join and his hatred for a man he did not know, the missionary erected impermeable barriers, as seen in his speech about the closing of heaven to the unbeliever, his exclusion of Galethebege from the church.

As a result, Galethebege failed to serve as a mediator, as a semipermeable membrane or hymen (in Derrida's sense [1979a] as both border and *alliance*), and instead became the trembling sword of desire. Before the missionary's anger her reaction was to "tremble," and her trembling gave alarm to the missionary. Despite his fulminations and banishment of Galethebege, in the end it is he who is excluded from the story while our attention is turned to the effects of the men's struggle for power on the would-be mediator, the woman.

The ultimate irony is that Galethebege suffers the missionary's wrath because of her faith, because of the same quietness grounded in the certainty of God's will that had attracted Ralokae's approving attention. Though it is her faith that wins her Ralokae, the result leads to the missionary's harsh judgment. Her trembling, both from passion and from conflict, signals not only the impossibility of mediation as each views the other with intransigence, but the emplacement of the woman between two competing males. She becomes the boundary. Instead of permitting the flow of understanding, instead of fructifying the community, she serves as the occasion for positions to harden, forming an absolute barrier between them. Death will no more restore Ralokae's first wife than Galethebege will restore wholeness to the community. Irony condemns the mediator to the role of divider.

The unnamed woman Galethebege replaces died at harvest time. One year later, again at harvest time, Galethebege takes this woman's place in Ralokae's affections. If the role of the first wife was simply to bear harvest fruits, her successor's is to awaken desire as well as division. Condemned to a trembling quietude, Galethebege assumes the very tension implicit in her role, transforming the failure of her attempt at mediation and the need to please two incompatible orders into the form of desire. Although the vocabulary of Galethebege's acts is co-opted by another's testimony, it ironically turns on its original speaker. Modise never sees beyond the dimensions of the male conflict, and the community is set to laugh at Galethebege's continued acts of prayer and faith. But the laughter acknowledges the triumph of desire, as the prayers become, in the listeners' minds, appeals to open the doors of heaven to Ralokae—that the desire might empower Galethebege's words to achieve the act of ultimate penetration.

"Life," "Snapshsots at a Wedding," "The Collector of Treasures": The Return of the Excluded Term

"It was the first time love had come [Galethebege's] way and it made the blood pound fiercely through her whole body till she could feel its very throbbing at the tips of her fingers. It turned her thoughts from God a bit, to this new magic life was offering her" (9).

With love, Head suggests an alternative to the restrictions associated with institutions and their power, to a life confined and hedged in by the force of social convention and phallocratic rule, and debased by the latter's association with human cruelty. Her universe is that manichean, that absolute in its judgments about people, that rigorous in the demands placed on life to fulfill the need for happiness. Love frees its guest to experience life, frees its guest from the oppressive side of existence and all its petty beliefs. Love takes its guest to the limits allowed by life, where magic begins.

In "Life," the eponymous protagonist is a victim of the harsh and implacable enforcement of limits on her conduct. The time and setting for this story are more precise than in any of Head's other stories. She tells us

that in 1963 the borders were first set up between South Africa and
Botswana and that, pending the independence of Botswana in 1966, all
Botswana nationals were obliged to return home. Ironically it is the end of
colonialism in this British territory that accounts for the expulsion of the
migrants and the rigorous enforcement of borders; during the prior
period the movement of migrant laborers was unimpeded.

The return of Life, a smart "city girl," to her parents' home village was
greeted by her women neighbors with the expectation of a new brightness.
"She is going to bring us a little light" (38). Again there is irony here, since
it was Life's free and easy way of living in South Africa that sets her at odds
with the solid, respectable members of the Botswana community. The
only ones who follow in her footsteps are the beer-brewing women, "a gay
and lovable crowd who had emancipated themselves some time ago" (39).
Free to drink and have babies on their own, they elevated Life to the status
of their Queen, and enjoyed carousing in her compound where "food and
drink flowed like milk and honey" (40).

At the end of the story, "Life" has been killed by "Death." Life is
attracted to her opposite, Lesego—a straight and determined man who
refuses to compromise. She must adhere to the lines he draws around her,
or else be killed. Ironically, she sees in him the high-life excitement of the
Jo-burg gangster and he sees in her the freshness of the new spirit. But
whereas on the surface both Life and Death share a higher agenda than
that defined by social convention, their subtextual opposition is what
prevails—she is killed by him, and he is imprisoned because of her.

In a sense, they clash and destroy each other because of a misreading.
Instead of complementing one another, each attacks the other's weakness:
he attempts to end her freedom, and thus her "life"; she refuses him, a
wealthy and generous cattle man, his right to possessiveness. Each saw the
beauty in the other and was blinded to the ugliness, the potential menace
in their commitment.

Life is represented as a figure of freedom who refuses to accept the
constraints of boundaries. She is trapped in an ironic fate: her return to the
village is forced upon her by the state's imposition of national borders, and
on her return the village installs Life in her dilapidated family compound,
following the conventional social patterns. Thus her living space is
defined for her, though not in a malicious fashion. Her women neighbors
help restore the compound to a livable state, and their effort takes on the
air of a community celebration. However, the village is as much governed
by its own authorities, with their normative set of limits and confines, as
by the state. Power flows through the ruling males in public and social
institutions, conveyed through public actions, attitudes, and gestures, all

of which are condensed into the laconic command Lesego issues to Life when he first meets her in a bar: "Come here" (41).

Life's motto is to live fast and die young. "All this was said with the bold, free joy of a woman who had broken all the social taboos" (40). The brief account of her life traces the tragic consequence of repression, the demise of the unconventional spirit. It details the acts of men who conspire to stifle "life" through their desires, possessiveness, and judgments. Concupiscence is set against warmth, possessiveness against freedom, and judgment, the ultimate expression of power, against the magic whose "dizzying heights" offer the only escape from society's confinement and condemnation.

However, even within the men's circles, questions about freedom and magic persist. Lesego's friend Sianana attributes the tragedy of Lesego's incarceration to the crossing of boundaries: "Lesego, . . . why did you kill that fuck-about? You had legs to walk away. Are you trying to show us that rivers never cross here?" (46). The story ends with this question unanswered.

If magic has its positive side in love and in Life's frenzied pace, it has its dark side as well, a demonic counterpart to the impossible joy of "dizzying heights." Like magic, Witchcraft is set against the confines of Christianity and its fixed values of good and evil. In "Witchcraft," Mma-Mabele regards herself as a faithful Christian, and so possesses, as do all other believers, "some mental leverage to sort out the true from the false" (48). However, this does not protect her from the mysterious invasion of a magical, destructive force. Although she closes herself in, shutting the door and barring the window, the "hideous unknown presence . . . invade[s] her life during the night" (51). Obviously the actions of this presence know no limits or barriers. Like Life's joy, it springs from sources that lie beyond the coldly rational universe over which men have dominion. Its powers to do harm are more than physical or psychological, they suggest the root of Head's deepest apprehensions.

In all of Head's short fiction, there is one overarching concern that returns to haunt us, and that is the fear of exclusion. In general, the conventions of Setswana society are viewed with misgivings because they oppress the free or kind spirit, opposing any resistance to their narrow bounds. But this borderline rebellion of the unconventional merely masks the deeper struggle where the darker, more hideous features of total exclusion act to destroy the spirit of plenitude given the evocative name of Mother of Corn—Mma-Mabele. Exclusion is the flip side of extinction for the woman victimized by the greed and power of male relatives or chiefs.

In "The Special One," a woman is cheated out of her inheritance by her brothers. "I lost it," laments Ms. Maleboge, "because women are just dogs in this society" (81).

However, the same women can destroy men through their own dark and "dirty" powers. "Many women have killed men by sleeping with them during that time" (84), says Ms. Maleboge's friend, in reference to the period of menstruation. The great illuminating powers of awakening are more than matched by the profound, impenetrable night of despair. Head is a Manichean romantic when she gets done with the business of social criticism. The earth, the sun, the night, demonic and angelic forces, haunt the ordinary lives that people lead in the village. Always there is a margin at which exile, exclusion, and the threat of death are felt.

Correspondingly, the margin is also the key feature in the awakening consciousness, nowhere expressed more poetically than in the image of dawn in "Snapshots of a Wedding." Here the line that separates night from day expands to cosmic dimensions. "Wedding days always started at the haunting, magical hour of early dawn when there was only a pale crack of light on the horizon. For those who were awake, it took the earth hours to adjust to daylight" (76). The wedding guests emerge from the haze like disembodied spirits, and slowly we enter into a world in which a new, coarsely materialistic bride, named appropriately Neo, is contrasted to her openhanded rival Mathata. Their one-sided struggle for the hand of the well-to-do bridegroom Kegoletile is superseded by the movement of the larger forces of light and darkness, of water and earth, of life and death, all of which meet at the pale crack of dawn when the force of magic works best on the human players. "The cool and damp of the night slowly rose in shimmering waves like water and even the forms of the people who bestirred themselves at this unearthly hour were disturbed in the haze; they appeared to be dancers in slow motion, with fluid, watery forms" (76).

At Neo's wedding, her strong-willed aunt pounds the earth in her demand that her ill-bred niece, scion of the younger generation, turn to more solid ways. "Be a good wife! Be a good wife!" (80). This is the point at which the self-assertive will and the pressures exerted by society have the potential to clash. From the aunts' point of view, "Be a good wife" means remember the respect due them. To Life, it would entail submission and self-rejection, and to Dikeledi in "The Collector of Treasures" it ultimately signifies prison and isolation. "Be a good wife" thus leads us from the victory of a disrespectful and insensitive "modern" woman to the depths of exclusion for those who are vibrantly alive and sensitive.

To understand how Head treats woman as the excluded term, we turn to Birago Diop's short story "Les Mamelles," from *Les Contes d'Amadou*

Koumba (1947), where conventional marriage practice leads to exclusion and resistance. There, too, the cry of the narrative voice might well have been "Be a good wife!"

Khary is Momor's first wife, and she is a curmudgeon, not unlike the classical shrew Dame Van Winkle. The story of Khary, as undoubtedly she herself would not have told it, is one of an ill-tempered person who, as a child, failed to accept a disfiguring hump on her back. Often she fought with other children who taunted her about her "baby." As an adult, married to Momor, Khary's self-consciousness prevents her from successfully fulfilling her marital obligations. Fear of ridicule keeps her from going out to help him in the fields or bringing him a hot meal. At night her bad temper alienates him. To relieve her burdens he takes a second wife, Koumba, who has a still larger hump. Koumba is good-tempered, eager to help her husband, and even willing to assist Khary in her chores, but Khary's spitefulness is only exacerbated. When Koumba finally succeeds in ridding herself of her hump, thus becoming as beautiful in form as in spirit, Khary faints in envy.

If Khary is not a good wife, if she is the classical "bad wife," it is because of her failure to give of herself, to overcome vulnerability and pain that she venomously turns against others. Her flaws separate her from others; defensiveness turns to aggression against the very ones with whom she would be close. Excluded because of her failure to please, because of the pleasure she takes in inflicting pain on her tormenters and rivals, she becomes a victim of the pleasure enjoyed by Momor and Koumba.

At the outset we are told that in the matter of wives, two is not a good number. The proper number is one or three, and as Spite and Khary become Third Wheels, it is the couple, Momor and Koumba, who appear suited and suitable, while Khary, wedded to her disposition, acquires the further burden of Koumba's large hump as well as her own.

In the final scene of "Les Mamelles," Khary fully assumes the role of the excluded term. She flees the happy twosome and seeks to drown herself in the ocean. However, the humps refuse to be submerged and are transformed into "Les Mamelles," the marginal outposts of Africa formed into two hills lying off the west coast of Cape Verde—signposts of the extreme western limit of Africa, and, as they appear in the story, boundary markers designating the borders of black Africa.

Amadou Koumba's conventional wisdom is that the humps are signs of warning against the unsocial comportment of a "bad wife." However, they are also signs of refusal: Khary's two "mamelles" "refused" submersion, thus refusing exclusion. They return after the conventional reading condemns the bad wife, after the pleasure we share with Momor and Koumba in excluding her is turned by the recognition that this pleasure is no different from the taunts of her playmates, from the very spite that jus-tifies our own spiteful rejection of Khary. In short, we are trapped by our self-righteous appeal to a moral or ethical value when it is that same value that denies our right to take pleasure in the pain of others.

When Khary's "malveillance" [malevolence] is described, it is likened to the bitterness of tamarind juice. Ironically, it is the magic of the spirit found in the tamarind tree that helps Koumba to disburden herself of her hump, resulting in Khary's final frustration. Just as Khary's spirit of refusal can not be submerged, emerging transvaluated from the water in the end, so, too, is the very symbol of her bitter rejection ambiguously linked to the tamarind tree's spirit whose power and knowledge cure Koumba of her hump. In the end the disobliging wife is discarded, at least as far as the narrator is concerned, but her more forceful demands are recast into the indomitable boundaries of her world, signposts of the irrepressible spirit of rebellion, of the far limits to which women may be forced to go. As "mamelles" the islets conserve something of the womanist essence writ large on the landscape; but as transformations of "babies" into "breasts," they proclaim the refusal of submission to the fixed roles of ideal wife and mother embodied in Koumba who succeeds in weaning her "child" (removing the hump), only to return to her position of subordination to Momor. Above all, Khary embodies the refusal of submission to fate, to essentialized womanhood altogether. The boundary is a warning of the dangers of refusal, but also a refusal of that warning.

Head takes us to these same limits in the story of the excluded wife Dikeledi in "The Collector of Treasures." Dikeledi, too, refuses to accept her husband's insistence that she be a "good wife," that she prepare him his meals and his bath, and serve him in bed, regardless of his own con-duct and relationships with other women. Like Khary, Dikeledi pushes her refusal to the limits, and in the process attacks phallocracy at its root, sexual domination, again reminding us of Mernissi's observation that the sexual patterns of a society reflect the link between boundaries and power. Until her death, Khary fails to separate herself from her two humps, her "children," who stay on her back. Symbolically, she fails to make the tran-sition achieved by Koumba from wife as mother to wife as lover, to com-plete the act of parturition with the severance that comes at the end of the term of nursing. Thus she fails to place Momor's needs before hers or her children's. Although presented as the aggrieved party, Dikeledi does the same, and when Garesego attempts to assert his prior claims, he is killed.

Dikeledi's fate is circumscribed by the same boundary points that are found at the outset of "Snapshots of a Wedding"—the magical margins to existence at which love, resistance, or painful exclusion are located. On her way to prison, in the police van, she discovers, like all those driven to the edge, the need to awaken. Her interior landscape is projected onto the land in this powerfully evocative scene.

> At first, faintly on the horizon, the orange glow of the city lights of the new independence town of Gaberone, appeared like an astonishing phantom in the overwhelming darkness of the bush, until the truck struck tarred roads, neon lights, shops and cinemas, and made the bush a phantom amidst a blare of light. (87)

Here, at the liminal stage where bush and city exchange a ghostly reality, the harsh journey moves to its conclusion: a rude arrival and an even ruder awakening await Dikeledi, prior to her own final transformation.

> All this passed untimed, unwatched by the crumpled prisoner; she did not stir as the truck finally droned to a halt outside the prison gates. The torchlight struck the side of her face like an agonising blow. Thinking she was asleep, the policeman called out briskly: "You must awaken now. We have arrived." (87)

Though she is crumpled in despair, she is not asleep, and has indeed arrived at the destination, the ultimate outpost of male authority and power, the proper site for her ultimate refusal. In contrast to the two isolated warning signs that are erected on Khary's watery tomb, Dikeledi's last stop is to be marked by the community of like-minded women who also found the courage to fight back, and who were excluded and confined under the hegemony of the male judge and warden. There Dikeledi, a "collector of treasures," finds the place for love, caring, and giving denied her by a patriarchal society.

Exclusion, thus, is transvaluated into fulfillment. The margin turns against the center again and again, matching love and defilement, defilement and love, until a mist swirls over the lines that would distinguish them. Without the ugliness or brutality of Garesego, without his rejection of Dikeledi's legitimate demands, her own struggle would not have begun, and her own quest for the treasures of life would not have been fulfilled in prison.

At the end, transformed by the telling, she is no longer a Dikeledi, but a Mma-Banabathe—both mother of her children and killer of their father. Her story ends with pointers that indicate where that terrible combination must lead her—to exclusion and, simultaneously, self-fulfillment. As with Mariama Bâ's Ramatoulaye, in *Une si longue lettre* (1980), whose husband's death was both a tragedy and a liberation, Dikeledi and the other struggling women of Head's fiction move between two worlds in which the line of change defines/defies the ultimate borders, placing them in a predicament echoed in Ramatoulaye's drama of death, abandonment, and new life. "I listen to the words that create around me a new atmosphere in which I move, a stranger and tormented. Death, the tenuous passage between two opposite worlds, one tumultuous the other still" (Bâ 1981, 2).

Chapter 9

Literature of the Oxymoron—
The Crossed Lovers

V. Y. MUDIMBE, *Le Bel Immonde*

Literature at a Crossing

All literature is at a crossing. In *The Invention of Africa* (1988), Mudimbe cites Foucault, taking the same position as Barthes writing on the text, to the effect that the text always bears the imprint of an original mind on an already-existent discourse. For Foucault, the "origin" is not a new beginning but an individual articulation "upon the already-begun of labor, life and language." His conclusion is beautifully conceived: our sentences spring out of the uniqueness of our "precarious existence" using words that are "older than all memory" (Foucault 1973, 330).

The debate between word and sentence, like that between *parole* and *langue,* need not imply a priority, or the domination of one over the other. One need not exclude the other, nor reduce it to the margins. One need not define the other on the basis of alterity. Yet the "croisements" [crossings] inherent to literature of the oxymoron occur in the perplexing space where past and future collide, where the other and the same discard their differences in the name of a new identity, while destroying each other on the basis of received identities. Just as "tribalism" is supplanted, ethnic differences achieve a paroxysm of violence. Literature of the oxymoron, literature *as* oxymoron, not only reflects changes in "origins," but represents this crossroad as blocked by oppositions and contradiction.

This crossroad is Mudimbe's definition of the present moment in African history. The colonial past, conventionally associated with images of primitive societies, is opposed by a future in which the project of development has been realized. The terms of reference for the past and future are already provided by a Western *ratio,* which Mudimbe is at pains to describe as formed by the inherited episteme of the West and inevitably colored by an ethnocentric vision. As he views it, anthropology is unavoidably marked by the anthropologist's epistemological assumptions, by his or her construct of the world, a construct bounded by preset cultural notions. When contemporary Africa is defined as lying between an underdeveloped past and a developed future, a gap emerges for the present. That intermediate "diffused space" is characterized by "marginality" (Mudimbe 1988, 4).

Moving further and further away from conventional Western formulations, Mudimbe situates Africa's present marginality in the chaotic urban landscapes where past loyalties, forged in forsaken villages, are in the process of dissolving, and where new ties, based on class, nation, school, church, work, or other institutional entities, have not yet supplanted old ones. The basis for identity lies somewhere between the inherited adherence to "tradition," to the sacred ground on which Lords and Masters erected society, established its certainties and truths, and the new play of parodic masks that bring an end to previous notions of authority. The present becomes an age of role playing and power, with knowledge a viaduct of untruth leading to rule, grounded in force, and legitimized by material gain. The oxymoron appears in itself to be the end of the Road. Mudimbe places despair at the heart of contemporary African bad faith: "This space reveals not so much that new imperatives could achieve a jump into modernity, as the fact that despair gives this intermediate space its precarious pertinence and, simultaneously, its dangerous importance" (Mudimbe 1988, 5). Development, in this world, is illusory—in fact, is more often catastrophic than beneficial. And the past retreats, as with the Bolekaja critics or with the late works of Ayi Kwei Armah, to the fog of a mythical, romanticized, reified age.

As an archeologist of the genesis of "Africa," Mudimbe finds nothing of greater importance than origins—specifically origins of discourse that are reflected in systems of power and organized into orders of knowledge. His concern for African philosophy, traced back to missionary and colonial discourses, attests to the same demystifying impulses that marked earlier African thinkers, from Aimé Césaire to Ferdinand Oyono, when it came to dealing with Western systems of knowledge and social order. Thus it is all the more striking that in his fiction Mudimbe focuses on the marginalized present, the urbanized site of disruption, located primarily on the Congo/Zaire axis of corruption, repression, and vulgar materialism. A brash and brutal authoritarianism is matched by an unconstrained revolutionary spirit of refusal. It is not "development," as a racist like V.S. Naipaul would envision it, nor the "traditional" past, as Chinua Achebe depicted it, that figures in the glare and glitter of Kinshasa. Mudimbe's fictional world, and especially *Le Bel Immonde* (1976), is located entirely in a lost present.

The Literary Crossing of Past and Future

The novel's place as a literary "croisement" or crossroad is clear. Parodic demystification hearkens back to earlier novelists and dramatists. Corrupt power is frequently exposed as hypocritical in the writings of many Francophonic authors. Bernard Dadié adopts a satiric pose in *Monsieur Thôgô-Gnini* (1970) by demolishing the rapacity of colonialists and their flunkies. His style employs parody, verging on the absurd, and echoes the kinds of humor exhibited in the best of the Cameroonian writers—Mongo Beti and Ferdinand Oyono. What Oyono adds to the satire are elements that also marked Jean Genet's writing, including the use of masks in the service of demystification. In *Une Vie de boy* ([1956a] 1970), Toundi is not only an observer—he is a false smile, aware of the sycophancy around him, as well as in his own role playing. All of Oyono's fiction involves an awakening consciousness, along with a sense of tragic failure, as with the psychologically trapped Barnabas at the end of *Chemin d'Europe* (1960), with the death of Toundi, or with the final retreat of Meka in *Le Vieux Nègre et la médaille* (Oyono [1956] 1979). In each work the comedians' roles are placed at the center of a world of displaced certitudes, isolating them like the old man Meka, caught in his circle of delusion until the limits enclosing him collapse.

Mudimbe's fiction begins, in *Entre les eaux* (1973), with a revolutionary priest intent on constructing a new world on the basis of Catholic and Marxist beliefs. As Jonathan Ngaté has taken pains to point out (1988, 11–18), the contradiction experienced by Pierre Landu echoes that of the mentally broken Nana of Mudimbe's *L'Ecart* (1978). Both protagonists collapse under the strain of conflicting identities and discourse systems with both a Western and an African origin. The drama of *Le Bel Immonde* is different. Although situated in the chaos of a Kinshasa on the verge of political nihilism, it foregrounds the implicit concern with love that runs through the other two novels. In this regard, and in its evocation of an electric, modernist atmosphere, it points in the direction of its own defamiliarization in the postmodernist writings of Sony Labou Tansi.

Although Sony Labou Tansi signals his indebtedness to Henri Lopes and Sylvain Bemba, *La Vie et demie* (1979) is constructed around a situation, and an ethos, that refers directly back to *Le Bel Immonde*. It may well be possible to see avatars of Chaïdana and the Guide Providentiel in Lopes's President and his beautiful wife, Ma Mireille, in *Le Pleurer-rire* (1982), but the better comparison would be to Belle and her Minister in *Le Bel Immonde*. For one thing, Chaïdana's position shifts from the embrace of absolute revolution to a more ambivalently nuanced stance marked by the Guide's grotesquely expressed love and the increasing intransigence and destructiveness of the revolutionaries. The purity of an initial refusal is gainsaid by moral compromises that throw all forms of purity into doubt. Monologic expressions of truth collapse in a series of repeated postures. Butchering and brutality are multiplied incessantly; resistance and love fail to impose a serious face on the world around them. Magic realism plays with curved mirrors whose reflections insist on being seen as reflections and not, as in the case of Achebe's figure, as light that passes through invisible glass, permitting truth, pure and simple, to be seen.

What remains is the sense of exigency implicit in a moral universe and its players. Like Chaïdana, Belle is driven to revenge by the image of her disembodied father—Martial for Chaïdana, the Chief for Belle. Both fathers insist upon an ideal of justice: as patriarchs of the old order both enlist their daughters' sexuality in the struggle against the new regime. Both define the opposition in terms of village or ethnic ties now linked to revolutionary causes. Most important, both impose their patriarchal order, their moral and political values, their judgments and sense of justice on their daughters as moral obligations—conveyed by the demand for obedience to their disembodied *heads,* which float before their daughters' eyes and which command their respect and subservience. Both awaken the rebellion of the daughters before what Mudimbe, in another context, referring to another authority, called "l'odeur du père."

Furthermore, *Le Bel Immonde* is located at a crossroads between the first-person narration of *Une Vie de boy* as mock autobiography and the mock detachment of Sony Labou Tansi's narrator, whose voice is situated in the realm of magical realism. *Le Bel Immonde* has the stylishness of a first-person account rendered, as in a pop song, by the use of the second person addressing herself as "tu . . . , tu . . ." (Mudimbe 1976, 18, 20). The resultant ironic self-consciousness characterizes Belle's voice. The Minister's narrative, at times confessional or epistolary, counterpoints Belle's posing, suggesting to the reader that the standard first-person accounts, letters, and diary entries, are also poses and that the poseur quality of Belle's second-person account hides a fundamental authenticity, sincerity. The passage from Oyono to Sony Labou Tansi takes us through this introspective, individual, intensively subjective space in which Oyono's parody is defamiliarized and the way opened to the mock third-person objectivity of Sony Labou Tansi.

Thus Mudimbe stands at the crossing between the revolutionary negations of the 1950s and the postrevolutionary, cataclysmic fiction of the 1980s. Like Wole Soyinka, he sees only the end of the road, the way forward blocked. He refuses any satisfied, static position as complacent—the best of heroes are trapped in unavoidable betrayals. All sacrifices are farces, compromised, like those of Soyinka's Eman in *The Strong Breed* (Soyinka

1973) or Elesin, the King's dilatory Horseman in *Death and the King's Horseman* (1975), marred by foreign influences or inherent weaknesses. Mudimbe's *Entre les eaux* and *L'Ecart* evoke, by their titles, the lost worlds of their protagonists who go mad, commit suicide, or are betrayed by the pettiness and intransigence of ideologues. There is no exit from this world; to use Mudimbe's metaphor, no way off this elevator run by others for their own uses.

Le Bel Immonde is also closed in, but in the way that myth closes in on itself, that is, in a way that is literary, not psychological or psychorealist. There is a stratum underlying *Le Bel Immonde* that can also be seen in Mudimbe's other novels; it refers back, again, to *Une Vie de boy* and forward to *La Vie et demie*; it is the place of love. This work, in short, is a modern myth of love in a world that refuses it.

Christian Freedom and Courtly Love

Love, too, lies at a crossing whose stage is set in a smoke-filled nightclub. There the atmosphere is ripe for unlikely couples to be formed, liberated from their inhibitions by their desires. The setting is framed by a moral perspective, such as that of the religious Sisters who educated Belle, or of the lawyer who accompanied the Minister to the bar, for whom the life of sexuality, dance, smoke, drink, and prostitution constitutes vice. Opposing terms meet in the figure of the oxymoron as if in lascivious pleasure, so that prostitution appears as the site of marginality described by Mudimbe as the intermediate space between the traditional village and the Europeanized city (Mudimbe 1988, 4–5).

The African city is the home of the new woman. Belle's particular attractiveness is self-consciously adopted in this way: to fabricate the creature desired by her Minister she takes two hours, as she tells herself, "to give [her] face the look that mingles candor and perversity which he finds so appealing" (Mudimbe 1989, 118).* The "look" of candor plays to his fantasy of aristocratic rank: he sees women as slaves at his and the lawyer's feet, and dreams of this power, which he identifies as complete liberty. The perversion is defined by cultural and moral codes grounded in principles of *authority* and bound by *rules* located within the social context of a particularly Europeanized ambience. The "look" of perversion, yoked meticulously to candor, is cultivated within these constraints. As the lawyer says, not in China, and especially not in their villages, are such women,

---

* "pour donner à ton visage cet air mixte de candeur et de perversion qui l'attire" (Mudimbe 1976, 95). All page references to this text will be to the 1976 edition, and to the 1989 translation by Marjolijn de Jager, unless otherwise indicated as my translation.

so bold in their soliciting, to be found. Yet not only does the lawyer return to the club nightly, even the Minister does not shrink from the taint: "Depraved? He felt as if he were in the center of perfect harmony" (67).★

If the freedom of dreams holds the ultimate appeal for the Minister, it is a freedom based on the process of mixing itself. Belle sings along with the lyrics of a song based on the lines of the German poet Stefan Georg, or with American pop tunes, while foreign-aid workers approach her. The drinks, the smoke, and the dance unleash the powers of the liminal space where the lowest desires are reflections of the highest exaltation. It is no surprise that Tayeb Salih portrays the prostitutes' houses, on the margins of the village in *The Wedding of Zein* (1968), as echoing the mystic symbols of divine love evoked by light, song, and dance. Here the same elements of basic physical desires and frenzy are conveyed: "Possession had taken hold. It was the only real thing under this mixed canopy where madness burned, perfumes mingled and blended with perspiration of all kinds. . . . A whole world ablaze, drunk with music, raw nerves, careening down a steep slope" (my trans.).† Everything here is physical and impure. Everything is set in opposition to the juridical definitions of permissible behavior. In short, immoral libertinage is maneuvered into a metaphorical position whereby it can mirror freedom from the Law, the freedom to love, for instance.

In the novel's epigraph, Mudimbe sets up the echo of this theme with the passage from the Gospel of St. John about the adulterous woman. When Jesus asks who will cast the first stone, he does two things. He calls into question the rule of Law, justification by good deeds, obedience to sanctioned authority. This is Christian freedom, whose flip side is the total obligation to love, to surrender oneself to Love.

Le Bel Immonde is preceded by an African literary tradition and discourse that placed a priority on the obligation to serve pressing social needs. National liberation and loyalty to sociopolitical causes underlie the entire literature of revolt that spans the 1950s, 1960s, and early 1970s, spearheaded by the works of Oyono and Beti, Sembène, Ngugi, Head, Aidoo, and even Ouologuem. Individual salvation, fulfillment, angst, or introspection were viewed either as secondary, rare aberrations (as with Armah's *Fragments* [1970]), or as Western concerns. More typically African were the passages that began *Une Vie de boy* (Oyono [1956a] 1970) or

---

★ "Du vice? Il se sentait au centre d'une harmonie parfaitement achevée" (67).

† "La possession s'était établie. C'était la seule chose réelle dans cet auvent mixte des feux en folie, des parfums mélangés, en croisement avec les transpirations de toutes couleurs. . . . Un monde en feu, ivre de musique, les nerfs éclatés, roulant sur une pente abrupte" (68).

ended *Mission terminée* (Beti 1957a), indicating that the individual stories summed up the dilemmas of a generation; that, in short, the social problems of the times were best represented, and solved, in terms of these typical figures. Even with the two novels that Mudimbe wrote immediately before and after *Le Bel Immonde* we find a primary focus on the angst of a generation caught between the moral demands of liberation and the corrupting factors that undermine them. Although Mudimbe moved the action to the players' interior space in both of the novels, although he gave the dialogue a subjective orientation, an introspective bias, the themes remained within the framework of obligations and demands of a recognizably social and meliorist nature.

Now, in *Le Bel Immonde,* we again have an obvious social setting that places onstage an ambitious politician with questionable principles (he placidly pays the president a million francs for his post, contributes one and a half million to his own ethnic association along with a human sacrifice for his success, subverts honest government procedures in maintaining the regime in power . . .) and a prostitute of equally uncertain morals (she accepts the betrayal of her free life in the name of her ethnic group's revolt, betrays that betrayal in the quagmire of her feelings for her Minister-lover, and eventually betrays him, leading to his death; after he has died she betrays his memory under police questioning). Yet these features, too, are mere style, the modish covering for Mudimbe's central concern. Unlike the works of revolt, contradiction, or commitment that precede *Le Bel Immonde,* or that follow it in later Congolese/Zairean fiction, this novel ends where it begins, in a universe that poses only one essential question—not how one is to combat injustice, but how one can be free to love.

The question is framed by the conventional patriarchal order, which is why the quotation from St. John is apropos. Christian freedom, as the courtly-love tradition developed it, is the freedom of passion, of *passio,* or suffering, made complete by its association with divinity. The opposing forces that animate the struggle within this tradition could be called juridical authority and passionate love.

Just Judges

In *Le Bel Immonde* juridical authority abounds. Its usual face is patriarchal, and Mudimbe gives it a variety of visages, ranging from that of the political and religious establishment to that of the revolutionary movement. In all cases, it is easily distinguished by its rigorous authoritarianism, its demands for obedience, and its elevation of rules and regimentation. The just judges are consistent in one regard—they are opponents of freedom, or, to use the preferred existential term employed by the Minister in his encomium of the prostitute, of "disponibilité" [availability].

Although one might have expected from a writer like Mudimbe, so well versed in the historical discursive tradition of the missionaries, a standard portrayal of rigid church orthodoxies, except for the brief appearance of an Archbishop, and passing references to the religious Sisters who took charge of Belle's education, the primary model for religious juridicism is the head, or "Maître," of an unnamed ethnic association, one with all the attributes of a Central African secret society—what the Maître refers to as "notre Société" (78). The Society is governed by rules that it imposes upon its initiates. As the Minister recalls his obligations to it, he identifies the semirepressed nagging thought as "un devoir impératif" (76) [an imperative obligation]. The "devoir" made explicit takes the form of an obligation, "l'obligation du sacrifice" (77), one whose nature is appropriately defined by the voice of authority, the nameless Maître. Whereas Cheikh Hamidou Kane (1961) uses the title "Maître" to refer to a religious authority devoted to the total submission to a higher will, here the abnegation of the self is absent. The Maître appears, like the more remote ancestors, or like the members of his Society, as anonymous, almost faceless—like the father into whose eyes one must not gaze. For all his prestige, the Minister remains "le fils" [the son] to the Maître. The sacrifice, which is given an explanatory comment in the novel's postscript, is marked by a conventional prayer to the ancestors, appealing to their protection. Patriarchal order is at its purest in the appeal: "'There is nothing in the heavens,' the Maître was reciting, 'nothing in the waters, nothing on earth, nothing beneath the soil, that does not belong to You'" (105).*
Although Mudimbe does not stay away from formulations that could easily be transposed to a Catholic sentiment ("Master of Life, your death is the presence which takes on our torment" [105]),† the basic approach is juridical—a form of religious legalism: "your glory is the forgiveness for our unfaithfulness to the Law" (105).‡ The prayer seeks protection for the children, the descendants of the ancestral Patriarch under whose rule they live. Those that follow repeat the pattern: "According to the rules of the World and by the Grace of God, through which You reign" (105)** begins

---

* "'Il n'y a rien dans les cieux,' récitait le Maître, 'rien dans les eaux, il n'y a rien sur terre, rien sous le sol qui ne soit à Vous'" (85).

† "Maître de la Vie, votre mort est la présence qui assume nos tourments" (85).

‡ "votre gloire, le pardon de nos infidélités à la Loi" (85)

** "Conformément aux règles du Monde et à la grace de Dieu par lesquelles Vous regnez" (85)

the ritual formula. And when Mudimbe continues with the "authentic" prayer, "Fafa Kandi, emi bona oke Kieze . . ." (Mudimbe, 1976, 87), he insists on the continuity of the pattern by giving the translation in a footnote ("Father Kandi, my Father, I am your son Kieze; I have always lived according to your laws" (107 n.1).* Although the sacrifice and communion that follow are labeled "la farce anthropophagique" in the postscript, the liturgy is still authenticated: "The ritual litany, however, is from a Nkundo prayer" (203).† Mudimbe doesn't add all this apparatus to give "authenticité"—Zaire style—to the account, nor to place it beyond the Europeanized context of the urban landscape. Rather, he does so to suggest the continuity of the pattern of juridical authority that runs through *all* the institutional structures in society, be they statist or traditional, be they of the established government or of its revolutionary opponents.

Thus, at the same social affair where the Minister designates the sacrificial victim to the Maître, we have the transcription of the president's speech—again authenticated, in the postscript, as being a newspaper report of Kasa-Vubu's actual words—suggesting the identical set of juridical values. In addressing his ministers, and through them the nation, he appeals to the moral authority vested in law: "It is difficult to require our population to submit to the law if those who make the law are the first to trample it under their feet. . . . Is not the most pressing duty to have respect for the law" (99).‡

Finally, the rebels, who appeal to Belle for allegiance to their cause, employ the same language of obedience to a moral cause, to a code of justice grounded in a sacred mission. For them all of Belle's acts are to take on significance with respect to their cause and her allegiance to it: "Your nights and your ecstasies in beds as yet unknown would answer from this moment on to the call of a major exploit. Finally, he laid down the *rules*" (72; my stress).** Using the language of sacraments and communion, like that of the Maître and his Society, the rebel commander enlists Belle into the sanctified family of her original ethnic group, of her village, and especially of her father: "Never forget that you belong to a tribe of lords" (my

---

* "Père Kandi, Père mien, je suis votre fils Kieze; j'ai toujours vécu selon vos lois. . . ." (87 n.1).

† "La formule, par contre, est celle d'une prière Nkundo" (171).

‡ "Il est difficile d'exiger de nos populations qu'elles se soumettent à la loi si ceux-là même qui la font sont les premiers à la fouler aux pieds. . . . Et le respect de la loi [est] le plus impérieux de ses devoirs" (80).

** "Tes nuits et tes extases dans des lits encore inconnus répondraient dorénavant aux appels d'une équipée majeure. Il vous dictait enfin les *règles*" (57; my stress).

trans.);* and he defines the obedience to its rules of exclusion in terms of purification: "If you should [touch an object belonging to a European], purify yourselves according to the Law" (73).† As precepts for martyrs in a just cause, the rules provide purity and the guarantee of inclusion under the aegis of the paternal order: "In your assignment ["rôle"], never forget your people's rules" (74).‡ After the sacrifice of the young woman, the Maître voices the benediction: "The sacrifice has been offered according to the ancestral wishes and the rites" (110).** No offense against Law, against the Divinity, was committed.

Without pronouncing on the economic, political causes of the social malaise, without situating the political turbulence within the concrete historical context that made of the Congo a clearinghouse of international and internal violence, insurrection, intrigue, interventionism, and eventually brutal statist repression and corruption, Mudimbe establishes an episteme of juridical praxis and ideology that haunts both protagonists from all possible directions—revolutionary, governmental, religious, and, even at the end, judicial, in the police interrogation of Belle. "In humiliation, I felt the Inspector eyeing me contemptuously from head to toe" (195).†† It is no coincidence that every one of these institutions and orders is governed by a strong patriarchal figure whose authority is invariably vested in him by the Invisible Presence of an Original Father. The race of "Seigneurs" or Princes who constitute the members of the various orders represent Order and governance by Rules; they are accorded the power to judge guilt or innocence, and to impose these states as punishment or rewards for conduct measured in accordance with the Law.

Mixing It Up: The Language of Love

The language of purity and exclusion, along with its juridical features, is opposed by the figures of mixing and contradiction best summed up as oxymorons. They undermine the seriousness of Order and, by implication, its Rule: an altered perspective on the purity of truth reveals its staged qualities—its nature as construct rather than essence. Ultimately even the highly ranked Maître is seen as playing a role within the mise-en-scène.

---

* N'oubliez jamais que vous êtes d'un tribu de seigneurs" (58).

† "Si vous le faites [touch an object belonging to a European], purifiez-vous selon la loi" (58).

‡ "Dans votre rôle, n'oubliez jamais les règles de chez vous . . ." (59).

** "La sacrifice a été accompli selon les voeux et selon les rites" (90).

†† "Je sentais, humiliée, le regard méprisant de l'Inspecteur me toisant des pieds à la tête" (162).

We see this clearly when Belle must move into a newly appointed apartment, under orders from the Revolution to become the Minister's mistress. She sees her own actions as self-conscious constructs: "No, your new domain was just a stage set that upset you a bit. . . . Since nine o'clock last night, you were waiting for the gong that would indicate the raising of the curtain" (121).* Even there, lost in the dreams of a luxurious bed, the superego image of her father imposes itself, like that of Martial in *La Vie et demie* (Sony Labou Tansi 1979), to remind her of her duty:

> "They've killed me."
> "Why, father?"
> "Perhaps for you, my daughter. For all the young people, like yourself, who think only of themselves. . . ."
> Your eyes wide open, you were trying with great difficulty to tear from your dozing mind, word for word, the meaning of the phrases the *administrator of justice* had spoken. (122; my stress)†

The judgment of her father requires her to take revenge on his enemies, just as the choice of the Minister to sacrifice the young woman was deemed appropriate because she was an enemy. But the opposition of mixing, of impurity, the "croisement" of "alcohol fumes, cigarette and cigar smoke" (my trans.),‡ and especially of desire, spoils the purity of the original intent. A highly placed Minister and the soiled goods of a prostitute, despite their betrayals of cause, of the other's family or friends, mix like the words of the title *Le Bel Immonde* itself, beautifully and with impurity. The result could have been stylish—like fin-de-siècle decadence. Instead, it opens onto the other border of marginality where freedom is situated, and is defined by love.

Christian freedom as the freedom to love is naturally expressed by physical attraction because passion is grounded in the suffering of the flesh. The Minister's vision of Belle's "availability" ["disponibilité"] is of this sort because he views it as total, as liberating. His final postmortem

---

* "Non, ton nouveau domaine était simplement une mise en scène qui te bousculait quelque peu. . . . Et depuis hier, neuf heures du soir, tu attendait le coup de gong qui ferait lever le rideau" (98).

† "Ils m'ont tué."
   "Pourquoi, père?"
   "Peut-être pour toi, ma fille. Pour les jeunes, comme toi, qui ne pensent qu'à eux-mêmes? . . ."
   Les yeux grands ouverts, tu essayais péniblement d'arracher de ton esprit endormi, mot après mot, le sens des paroles du *justicier* (99; my stress).

‡ "relents d'alcool, la fumée des cigarettes et des cigares" (68)

letter to her underscores this: "The goodness of your life seems to person-ify an extraordinary inner freedom" (193).* She puts a similar construc-tion on her own abandonment of university studies for the call of the streets: "Scarcely one term at the University and the throbbing alarm calls of extreme freedom had conquered you" (my trans.).† Feeling trapped in the exigency of taking revenge, of assuming the father's role as "justicier" [judge], Belle identifies more with the Son, like Hamlet in rebellion against the obligations imposed on him; she evokes the words of Christ's passion for her condition: "My love, why have you abandoned me?" (my trans.).‡

Though the words in this passage are also put on self-consciously, joining revenge and love, mixing sacred text and profane prostitution, the emotion that is available only through freedom takes precedence over jus-tice. In the end, *Le Bel Immonde* is a novel about the freedom to love, a freedom and love conceived very much in courtly-love terms, validating the position enunciated by Foucault and repeated by Mudimbe (Mudimbe 1982, 12–13) that the very tools of resistance to the West turn out to be provided by the West itself.[1]

Accepting the feelings of love, Belle describes them as a total libera-tion, as if the revolutionaries' initial orders, which had been responsible for her liaison with the Minister, no longer existed. Her love confers total freedom from all obligations: "He began to talk and, at last, I felt life returning to me. The sun came out of his mouth, warmed me. I let myself go, carried away by his words. I was taken beyond all boundaries, liber-ated" (150).** It also prevents her from accepting any new obligations. Only free gestures could accommodate her feelings, and the Minister's desire to have her attend a soirée is resisted as another form of bondage. Even her lover is denied any new Authority: "He had not bothered to ask me whether I felt like going out. He had simply straddled his dream" (151).††

---

* "La bonté que tu vis me semble être à l'image d'une liberté intérieure" (161).

† "A peine un trimestre en Faculté, et les alertes frémissantes d'une liberté extrême t'avaient conquise" (99).

‡ "Mon amour, pourquoi m'as-tu abandonnée?" (100).

** "Il se mit à parler et, du coup, je sentis la vie renaître en moi. Le soleil sortait de sa bouche, me chauffait. Je me laissais faire, emportée par sa parole. J'étais hors de toute frontière, libérée" (122–23).

†† "Il ne m'avait même pas demandé si j'avais envie de sortir. Il avait simplement enfourché un rêve . . ." (123).

Courtly love poetry, the freedom from law, the freedom to love, all seek fulfillment in the eternal moment—in frozen time. One of the conventions of the literature of courtly love is that the eternal is to be found in the poetry itself. However, time is not frozen in *Le Bel Immonde*. Freedom, too, has its limits, and here they are given by irony, the point of self-consciousness at which the submersion in the other, or, as Belle puts it, in the other's dreams, halts while one's gaze turns back on one's self. If it is not judgment and guilt that turn one's look inward, it is the doubt that attends the moment of reticence. Belle gives over the revolutionary cause for her love, surrenders to him, and yet we learn, even as she shares her thoughts of love with us during her final police interrogation, that she had paid a visit to her contact, Ma Yene, which possibly resulted in her Minister's demise. Simultaneously we learn from his last letter to her that he sensed she was holding back. Ironically he suspected that concern over her family accounted for her inquiries about his political affairs, and he sought to assure her that he would attend to her family. The dream now turns somber: "So let's drive away the shadows that have come between us" (194),* and he reproaches himself for beginning to analyze himself when he is with her.

With these doubts we are now in the human realm, leaving the eternal to the dreamers. The ironic declension leads the Minister to his death, offstage, while Belle must hear of his last expression of love and uncertainty in a letter read to her by a police inspector trying to entrap her. The image Belle now fabricates in the face of this interrogation is one of strength and insouciance. Released, she rediscovers the sun and the air. "Swinging my purse with one hand, I jumped for joy, leaped up to the apartment with long strides, humming softly to myself" (195).† Faced with the silence of the universe, with a set of uncles, inspectors, and Ministers, whose deepest feelings, thoughts, and commitments are *always* communicated by physical beatings, slaps, or even murder, as in the case of her "sister," Belle discovers, like Albert Camus's Meursault, the divine "disponibilité" [availability] of the absurd—a freedom to be that does not stop with guilt or doubt. And yet, in contrast to Meursault's case, this faith in the springs of life now constitutes the limits of Belle's universe.

For a moment it seemed as though love could be the fulfillment of that freedom. But Mudimbe shuns the logic of courtly love, drawn though he obviously is to the en-*thu*siasmus of such a choice. In the end, wedged

---

* "chassons donc les fantomes qui se sont installes chez nous" (161).

† "Balançant mon sac d'une main, je sautai de soi, montai à l'appartement à grandes enjambées, en chantonnant" (163).

between the fall of a priest and the breakdown of a scholar, we find this dream of a myth, a modern myth of the return of the stranger, like Sisyphus, to a world that recognizes only the physical surface of her beauty. She calls out, like the singer in the pop song, for the joys of life to come— "Entertain me. All right? Come, let's dance . . ." (202)*—having reached briefly and absurdly across the boundaries that were located between her and her Minister for something that lay beyond them.

Epilogue

Unlike such star-crossed youths as Romeo and Juliet, Tristan and Isolde, or even that seductive, magnificent pair of over-the-hill lovers, Anthony and Cleopatra, our nameless Minister and his Belle both fail to attain, even in their words, a total commitment. They set the stage for the grandiloquent rhetoric of Sargnata Nola, Estina Bronzario, Colonel Ignazio Banda, Benoît Goldman—the whole exuberant cast of characters in the recent fiction of Sony Labou Tansi. In the realm of sentiment, Mudimbe is more comfortable with the earlier works of the existentialists, for whom subjective space provided the ground to work out the struggles over authenticity and bad faith, freedom, and the absurdity of "disponibilité." It is especially the Kierkegaardian freedom to believe in the face of contradiction that finds its echo here in the final ironies that Belle confronts. Significantly, she evokes the bringing together of ironic fact and concealed sentiment with the same term employed when the Minister waited in the bar with the lawyer, that is, "croisement" (68). "J'étais au croisement du déversement de multiples coincidences" (162) ["I was at the point where a whole series of coincidences converged" (194)] is Belle's way of putting it. The irony of her position—being taken for a lover when this role was a mask for revolutionary purposes—is not enough to prevent the outpouring of an emotion no less genuine. Cleopatra may have deceived Octavian so as to preserve her honor, but the poetry of her love is what prevails. Similarly, Belle defends the convoluted path, the winding "affluent" she dug: "And more than ever, despite my sorrow, perhaps even because of it, I felt I had just cause to defend, against everything and everyone, the tributary's bed [le lit de l'affluent] that I had dug" (194).†

The image of a river that flows, not one that divides, but that carries one along with its current, is one of life—of existential choice. For the

---

* "Amuse-moi. Tu veux? Viens danser . . ." (169).

† "Et, plus que jamais, malgré mon chagrin, peut-être même à cause de lui, je me sentais en droit de défendre contre tous, le lit de l'affluent que j'avais creusé (162).

lawyer, a life danced to the rhythm of the "Crocodile Rock," as the fast-paced music of the bar is dubbed, is one of vice. But for the Minister, it represents the freedom he associates with dreams.[2] In the end he is perhaps incapable of living at the level of those dreams. Oxymorons, after all, are figures of unresolved struggle—and the Minister can not escape the contradictions in which he is ensnared, knowing, no doubt, that his love affair began with the sacrificial murder of Belle's woman friend, which he can not bring himself to confess: "we too are dirty rivers, but we aren't strong, not strong at all" (201).*

Had he accepted that weakness, revealed to Belle his acts, given in to the current, the myth would have been Shakespearean. But Belle awaits the revelation, "une révélation importante," and in the end, "Nothing was forthcoming" (my trans.).† There we are left. An invitation to dance on the stage, "la piste," arrives; the act continues the next night, but with no further revelation in sight. Belle leaves us with the contradictions of an aesthetic pathos[3] whose perverse beauty, whose artifice grows integrally out of the desirable mixture of opposing elements: all the skillful effort, "patiently applied for two hours this morning to give [her] face the look that mingles candor and perversity which he finds so appealing" (118).‡ Both an appearance and an act, these qualities, candor and perversion, the "fleuves sales" (168) [dirty rivers] sum up the dilemma of marginality with which Mudimbe portrays the Africa of his times.

---

* "Nous autres . . . nous sommes aussi des fleuves sales, mais nous ne sommes pas forts, pas du tout forts" (168).

† "Rien n'était venu" (168).

‡ "tout de patience, deux heures durant ce matin, pour donner à ton visage cet air mixte de candeur et de perversion qui l'attire" (95)

Chapter 10

The Still Point of Transition

WOLE SOYINKA, *The Road; The Strong Breed; Death and the King's Horseman;* "Death in the Dawn"

The Road: Transition

For Wole Soyinka ritual, like tragedy and ritual theater, centers on *transition.* Transition occurs between different realms of being, or "stages," which he has described in his poetry, in *Myth, Literature, and the African World* ([1976] 1979), in his scholarly discourses at academic conferences, as well as in his fiction and theater, as the realm of the living, the dead, and the unborn (Soyinka [1976] 1979, 2, 144), as "the mystic and the mundane" (Soyinka [1976] 1979, 2), or as "Now, Gone, and Here the Future" in his poem "Alegemo" (Soyinka 1973a, 150). Between these stages lies the "fourth space, the dark continuum of transition where the inter-transmutation of essence-ideal and materiality" occurs (Soyinka [1976] 1979, 26). It is also the aboriginal chaos, the fearful whirling space into which only Ogun dared to venture, facing destruction so as to bridge the gap between gods and humans. The pattern established by Ogun not only suggests the role of sacrificial victim, but also that of tragic protagonist, and by extension, that of the artist. For Soyinka artists and poets, "the practitioners of *Ijala,* the supreme lyrical forms of Yoruba poetic art, . . . followers of Ogun . . . seek to capture the essence and relationships of growing things and the insights of man into the secrets of the universe" (Soyinka [1976] 1979, 28). Soyinka has proclaimed himself to be a follower of Ogun, though the statement appears to be more a poetic than a religious credo.

The designation "fourth stage" evokes not only a superluminary theater of ritual action and poetry, but an extraterrestrial dimension. The fourth dimension rests upon the first three, as on a scaffolding, and Ogun's nature and mythos are acted out in a concrete world of materiality, at the hard hills of Idanre, at the buttresses, boulders, rivers, and bridges haunted by Egbo in *The Interpreters* (1965). In Yoruba metaphysics, the material world, like the dead and the ancestors, encompasses more than a phenomenal reality. It is at once here and more than here, and the dead are at once gone, separate from the living, and yet present. The function of ritual is to bridge the distance between these stages.

Despite an awareness of these stages, for Soyinka

> the Yoruba does not . . . fail to distinguish between himself and the deities, between himself and the ancestors, between the unborn and his reality, or discard his awareness of the essential gulf that lies between one area of existence and another. This gulf is what must be constantly diminished by the sacrifices, the rituals, the ceremonies of appeasement to those cosmic powers which lie guardian to the gulf. (Soyinka [1976] 1979, 144)

The tragic protagonist, like Ogun, takes those daring steps in the name of the community.[1] "He prepares mentally and physically for his disintegration and re-assembly within the universal matrix of death and being" (Soyinka [1976] 1979, 30). Yet the disintegration is not complete: "The protagonist actor . . . resists, like Ogun before him, the final step towards complete annihilation. From this alone steps forward the eternal actor of the tragic rites, first as the unresisting mouthpiece of the god, uttering visions symbolic of the transitional gulf . . ." (Soyinka [1976] 1979, 143).

From another perspective, the fourth stage, the transition, the bridge in Sekoni's "dome of continuity" in *The Interpreters* (1965) is really the connecting point between two realms, each with its own mode of discourse — the mystical, corresponding to the poetical, or the mythopoeic speech, and the mundane, corresponding to prosaic speech. The relationship between the two realms of discourse is the subject of Soyinka's "difficult" plays, *A Dance of the Forests* (1973a), *The Road* (1973a), and *Madmen and Specialists* (1974). Professor in *The Interpreters* (1965), Adenebi in *A Dance of the Forests* (1973a), and in some respects Salubi in *The Road* and Lakunle in *The Interpreters* insist upon a practical, literal interpretation of the world. Oddly enough, even in the case of Professor, this occurs once in *The Road* when he makes the foolish error of mistaking a betting form for cabalistic signs. Often Soyinka's lesser characters are superbly parodied as studies in linguistic pretentiousness. After Soyinka's release from prison in 1969, his portrayals of simple ebullient fools take a sinister turn, giving us "specialists," like Dr. Bero, or even jailers, as in *The Man Died* (1972), with their brutal counterparts in *Season of Anomy* (1973b). Linguistic manipulations appear increasingly dangerous, though as early as 1965, when *Kongi's Harvest* (1974) was first performed, the playwright points to the reduction of words to debased political instruments. Even Jero turns disturbingly diabolical, leading naturally to the pompous dictators in *A Play of Giants* (1984) or to the far less picaresque charlatan, the Futurologist, in *Requiem for a Futurologist* (1985).

For Soyinka's down-to-earth protagonists, the seekers of advantage in wealth or prestige, words are never nuanced so as to suggest various levels of meaning. Samson, in *The Road,* is a step above the pompous types Soyinka so loves to deflate, but the repeated roadblocks in his communication with Professor are really markers of the material track he insists on following—and of the gulf between their worlds. Virtually all dialogue between the two characters—indeed between Professor and any of the others—brings us to a standstill, as the two discourses are continually at odds with each other. For instance, when Samson begins his consultation with Professor, they appear to be on the same wavelength:

> Professor: "I would say your problem is straightforward. You are in some kind of difficulty."
> Samson: "You have stated it exactly, sir."

But this appearance of communication soon breaks down as they go their separate ways:

> Professor: "In fact, one might almost say that you are about to pass through a crisis of decisions."
> Samson: "Ah, I don't know that one Professor." (Soyinka 1973a, 180)*

Their language is based on divergent patterns: Professor inflates his rhetoric with "might almost say," and infuses it with pseudoprofessional lingo, "a crisis of decisions." Samson not only fails to catch this slightly varied restatement of Professor's earlier, empty words, he falls back on his own proletarian speech patterns, "Ah, I don't know that one Professor." "That one" here may be viewed as a linguistic bridge between pidgin and standard colloquial English. The two trains of thought continue to move further apart as Professor pursues his own logic, increasingly indifferent to the effect of his words: "How could you? You are illiterate. It is lucky for you that I watch over you, over all of you." The effect of this line is not only to thwart Samson's efforts at reaching out to Professor or at recruiting his aid, it stops the action cold, forcing Samson to recall Professor to his original purpose: "Yes sir, Er, about our problem sir . . ." (180).

The movement is continually interrupted, stopped, and forced to recommence—very much like a vaudeville routine in which each bit ends with a neat punch line, only to resume with the recollection of the previous thread. In the present case of the dialogue between Samson and Professor, the slapstick is built on the device of a "misunderstanding."

> Samson: "Professor, what I mean is, how can a man cut off part of himself like that. Just look at him. He is not complete without a motor lorry."

---

* All page references to this play are to the 1973 edition.

Professor: "He is not? [turns to stare at Kotonu.] What sort of animal is he?"
Samson: "Animal? I mean to say, Professor ! . . . Look Professor, the road won't be the same without him."
Professor: "He was a road mender too?"
Samson: "Sir? But I told you he is a driver." (180–81)

The routine drives on, with Professor somewhat uncharacteristically playing the straight man; but it ends abruptly with Professor's return to grandiloquence, signaling his preoccupation with the spiritual sphere. Samson waxes desperate, agitated: "You see Professor. Now Murano has become his evensong." At this, Professor turns completely into his own world: "[looks at the church window]: 'It is not yet the hour of sacrament'" (181). Thus he abruptly ends all communication between them.

The mental "level" at which Professor moves is always keyed by his obscure, semimystical, at times mystifying, discourse. He never engages in a real dialogue: the above example demonstrates how he may participate in a "bit," a routine, without entering into a direct discussion. More typically, he is off in his own world, holding forth with himself; not just refusing to attend to his interlocutor's discourse, but not even seeming to hear or to be capable of responding on any plane but his own. His initial stage appearance is significant in keying us to his peculiar idiosyncratic idiom.

Professor [he enters in a high state of excitement, *muttering to himself*]: Almost a miracle . . . dawn provides the greatest miracles but . . . in this dawn has exceeded its promise. In the strangest of places . . . God God God but there is mystery in everything. (157)

Professor's speeches are monologues, at once solitary and interior. This is particularly the case with his preoccupation with the "Word" (as with the Old Man's references to "As," which so infuriate and mystify Bero in *Madmen and Specialists*). The references to the Gospel provide the framework to his "signifying"; but from the outset, Professor insists on a more personal reading. Carrying a road sign bearing the word "BEND," he expostulates, "For there was no doubt about it, this word was growing, it was growing from earth until I plucked it" (157). And though these reflections, indeed *all* his reflections, fail to call forth any corresponding response from any of the characters, he persists in voicing them, even when hiding behind a mask of subterfuge that he himself seems incapable of removing. Thus Samson's mockery of Professor's discourse is matched, unbeknownst to Samson, by an equally mocking reply, as we later learn— so that even when they play at communication, it is playing at speaking at cross-purposes with each other.

Samson: "Perhaps you missed your way."

Professor: "You think I did? Indeed anything is possible when I pursue the Word. But . . . and mind you tell the truth . . . you are not here to take the Word from me?" (157)

The irony opens onto an unending series of reflections: Samson is playing along with what he and we at this point take to be a mad, confused Professor. Later we learn Professor was feigning madness and confusion by assuming his customary mode of discourse. But when the mask is removed, the face beneath resembles the mask exactly—the language doesn't change.

The road sign as "sign" never loses it higher, indecipherable significance to Professor, just as it never acquires that significance for the others. They see two different worlds with each impervious to the other:

Professor: "[O]f all the windows of that church, only that is kept shut. . . ."
Samson [looking]: "But Professor, all the windows are open. . . ."
Professor [cautioning with a wagging finger]: "Be careful. They weave a strong spell over human eyes."
Samson: "Oh no. I can see all right. The window is wide open. . . ."
Professor: "Have you sold your soul for money? You lie like a prophet."
Samson: "But it is the truth Professor."
Professor: "Truth? Truth? Truth, my friend, is scum risen on the froth of wine."
Samson: "All right all right. Have it your own way." [Continues to cast glances at the window.] (206–7)

The two worlds would seem to be irreconcilably divided—a window, after all, may be either open or shut. Alternatively, the audience, judging the relative truth of the two positions, will observe the window having been thrown open earlier when the organist began to play, will side with the normal perspective of Samson and assume Professor suffers from delusions. And what kind of Professor, the more literate-minded may ask, would be running a business whose sign is as illiterate as "AKSIDENT STORE—ALL PART AVAILEBUL" (151)? Others might respond more sympathetically to Professor's allusive language when he tells Samson, "If you could see through that sealed church window you will see the lectern bearing the Word on bronze. . . . Oh yes, I stood then on the other side of that window—then it was always open, not barred and bolted as it now is, from fear . . ." (205–6). The comedy never lets Reality, Truth, rest in the illusion of certitude: "[Samson blinks hard, rubs his eyes] Professor: 'Through that window, my sight led straight on to this spot'" (207).

Between the True Faith and the Truth that rises on the froth of wine—sacramental veritas or Ogun's libation brought by Murano every night—the choice might be less obvious than the question of whether a casement is open or shut. When Samson steels himself to put "the question" to Professor, Professor assumes he will be asked whether he is crazy. Instead Samson asks him if he stole the church funds.

Similarly, at the end of Act 1, Professor reveals to Murano that he had only pretended to have lost his way in the morning. He calls our attention to his role by assuming the parodied speech of the pompous, foolish, mad Professor. His high, erratic, speechifying rhetoric is laced with Christian imagery, reflecting the lay reader, the Sunday-school teacher. His words and gestures are stagy and unreal, provoking mock responses and more playacting from the other actors, except in general from the more serious types, like Kotonu or Murano who address him barely or not at all. Professor is the least natural of all, and if he is more interesting than merely a typical alazon, or obsessed character, it is because we are confronted with a play that rehearses the relationship between mask and being, recalling for us the truism that onstage there is no difference between the two except by convention, which in itself is also a kind of mask.

The other characters generally adhere to the conventions of everyday speech, and see things, mostly, as obeying commonsense logic. Perhaps it is this confidence game of ordinary language, played upon so brilliantly by Soyinka's multiple voices, that wins us over to their worldview. Yet they deceive us, or rather, their masks deceive us, and as each scene, or each segment of a scene, is brought to a close, their link to the realm of higher consciousness, joined by the unnatural accents of poetic diction, is established.

Despite Soyinka's mystical formulations in *Myth, Literature, and the African World,* despite disclaimers in the preface to *Death and the King's Horseman* (1975), the idea of transition is often tied to an encounter between two opposed discourses, the one frequently Westernized (e.g., those of Eman in *The Strong Breed* [1973a], Simon Pilkings and Olunde in *Death and the King's Horseman,* Igwezu in *The Swamp Dwellers* [1973a], Professor in *The Road,* Bero in *Madmen and Specialists* [1974], Lakunle in *The Lion and the Jewel* [1974], etc.), espousing a superficial philosophy of European materialism; and the other adhering to traditional African customs, usually associated with the older generation. Often the dialogue between the two is at cross-purposes: the spokesperson for one position is blind to the other side; both are one-sided or stock figures of parody. When they are not, as in the case of the protagonists in *The Interpreters* (1965), they seem to understand both positions, but are nonetheless caught in a paradox, a trap of inaction, aware of their weaknesses but seeing no virtues to illuminate a clear path for themselves. They know, but can't believe. Whatever complexities of character and situation Soyinka constructs for this confrontation, its essence still lies in the moment created by two opposing, mutually incomprehensible voices, embodied in roles typically linked to such opposites as father/son, sensitive/insensitive, clever/dense, Westernized/traditional, educated/uneducated, and so forth. The clash is not simply between cultures or values, but between two worlds that seem incapable of hearing what the other has to say, of understanding or accepting the other's point of view.

Bero is willing to strangle his father to get an answer to his question, and yet when the Old Man replies, nothing seems to have penetrated. Professor's words, or the rhetoric of those who assume Professor's manner, drive the action to a standstill; and no one seems to understand, to comprehend, anyone else in *The Strong Breed,* where almost every bit of dialogue eventually leads to statements expressing this lack of comprehension. The metatrope for this rhetoric is clearly the oxymoron.

The characters act as participants in what Soyinka calls a masquerade in *The Strong Breed*—actors in a ritual drama whose essence lies in the evocation of a struggle that can find its raison d'être only in the matrix of "a chaotic void," an "immensity of darkness and infinitude" that responds to our deepest callings. If by irony we understand a mode in which the world is represented as lacking in order or coherence, then the oxymoron goes even further in the direction of a world represented as caught in irreconcilable conflict. The space between the two terms of the figure, terms bridged in metaphor, here remain separated, as if by a dark gulf. "Transition" reflects Soyinka's preoccupation with the struggles for the creation of being and of identity, with the new roles being shaped in contemporary African society as the products of opposing, mutually deaf elements that must nevertheless interact. The writer records that interaction in terms of two different discourses, at times bordering on or actually entailing two different languages.[2]

Transition occurs in situations where dialogue comes to a halt, where opposing discourses exhaust the possibilities of reaching across the gulf. The tragic hero is defined by Soyinka as the one whose will saves him in the midst of the swirling maelstrom of chaos, of transition, thus redeeming the community. In his own works, the final thrust of Sekoni, of Eman, of Olunde, into the gulf brings the dramatic action to a halt, without achieving a sense that the bridge between human and god, or old and new, or Now, Gone, and Future, has been forged. On the contrary, the figure of the victim, the god-man Eman, Murano, or Lazarus, either sinks slowly in an ambivalent death, or fails to complete the ritual gesture.

The final notes are not pessimistic, however. There is a sense of dramatic completeness in all the works, including *The Interpreters,* whose ending most lacks closure. But the resolution of Ogun's struggle never comes; nor does the full achievement of the peace that accompanies Obatala's sense of fulfillment or serenity. The movement stops in midair, in full transition, as in the cinematographically frozen ending of *Madmen and Specialists* in which the departing Earth Mothers are held in suspension looking back at the house going up in smoke. Appropriately, the character who best embodies the moment of transition, the still point of the frozen ritual, neither here nor there, neither before nor after, undefined by any category of being, time, or space, can not speak. This is the mute Murano. He expresses himself only in gestures, not in words, and he conveys the threat of death in Act 1, carrying out the threat in Act 2. In the deaths of Eman, Professor, Sekoni, Olunde, and in Murano's ritual death, as in those of Sergeant Burma and a host of other sacrificial victims in Soyinka's oeuvre, one does not find a passage successfully negotiated between two realms. Either the protagonist takes the leap into the abyss, leaving us uncertain as to the full meaning, motivation, and value of the act, as in the death of Elesin, or he participates in a mock passage, as with the Futurologist. At best, like "the interpreter," Egbo, or like Lazarus, he seems to have had a taste of the gulf without, as a consequence, finding a sense of fullness. Agemo remains a mystery.

The adventure is ambiguous, as we see in Soyinka's description of the "undented vastness," "chthonic space," "the abyss," "the seething cauldron of the dark world-will," where Ogun enters, only to be "literally torn asunder in cosmic winds . . . [on the] precarious edge of total dissolution" (Soyinka [1976] 1979, 30–31). That this stage is called "transition" instead of destruction or death is revealing in what it tells us about Soyinka's vision. "Transition" implies the passage, the successful change from one state to another—it is not a resting place, a point of final resolution, but a staging ground. It is a time out of time where two diachronic events are joined, and, appropriately enough, it is in itself synchronic, or out of time. However, Soyinka doesn't distinguish between the "chthonic realm" where the gods reside, along with the ancestors, the unborn—all that our intuition senses in a world of the mystical—and the "chthonic realm" through which Ogun led the gods in the first rite of passage (27–28). The unseen, whether "transition" or "stages" to which the transition leads, is described in similar terms of destruction and chaos.

The transition is never completed in Soyinka's work. This is because it represents the area of mutual incomprehensibility, and is represented as *uncompleted* ritual in a dramatic form that takes ritual as the source and structure of meaning itself. The passage is an indeterminate one—the road leads to death, not to the new world.

In Catherine Belsey's terms, the drama of transition lacks closure. The transition of the social system, of the mode of production, as she sees it, is reflected in the erosion of confidence in the ideology of subjectivity (Belsey 1981, 86). As a result, the assurance of a world order, of a subject who can reflect the sense of completeness, is also weakened. Instead of mimetic illusion, we have Brechtian distanciation; instead of closure and order, questions, self-conscious awareness and aporia; instead of clarity or the disclosure of truth, ambiguity and the projection of a tension between conflicting perspectives extending beyond the frame; instead of the dominance of a natural discourse, the still point of incomplete ritual. The interpellation of the reader, or audience, leads to a process of questioning and replaces the subjugation to ideology. In short, transition is open-ended.[3]

To understand the relationship of transition to the dynamics of closure, we must turn to the most pertinent statements Soyinka made concerning the individual undergoing transition. Using the model of gods experiencing alienation from humans as a source for their sense of incompleteness, he concludes that

> man is grieved by a consciousness of the loss of eternal essence *of his being,* and must indulge in symbolic transactions to recover his totality of being.
>   Tragedy, in Yoruba traditional drama, is the anguish of this severance, the fragmentation of *essence from self.* (Soyinka [1976] 1979, 144–45; my stress)

Further, he reemphasizes, "The weightiest burden of severance is that of each from self, not of godhead from mankind" (Soyinka [1976] 1979, 153).

When viewed as an individual, subjective phenomenon, symbolically projected onto the liminal periods occurring between life and death and rebirth, old and new (year, position, rank), and the various stages of growth, transition is presented as alienation, as a confused medley of internal dialogues, a double-voicedness in disarray. This was to be expected, given that Soyinka's generation of writers often found the maternal and paternal patterns of speech, the language of the home or one's first attachments and primary values replaced, often with great anticipation and yet also great anguish, by the acquired "official" language of school, the key to social success, and the instrument of their artistic creation.[4]

Soyinka's response to the intersection of the two languages/cultures is transition as blockage, the still moment representing the chaos within the protagonist. The image he uses for this is the interrupted ritual, the incomprehensible ritual, the ironic ritual. Sekoni's death gives us something of both, while the Bale is somewhat ironically treated, and Elesin's passing is ambiguous. The Western models give us Orpheus, who destroys the one he loves, and Prometheus, who destroys himself. Neither completes the myth by passing over, as in a transition, from one stage to another. Soyinka's choice is the figure of Dionysus, a human-god whose death is not an end, and Eman whose death brings us closer to the myths of Esu than to those of Ogun.

The Strong Breed: The Incomplete Ritual

The Strong Breed (1973a) provides us with Soyinka's dramatic paradigm of transition as turning on the question of what blocks ritual and prevents it from reaching completion. The most obvious ritual transformation involves the passage from the old year to the new, one in which a "carrier" must be sacrificed. The problem presented by the play is that of obtaining a carrier, which thus creates the link to a second ritual transformation, that of an ordinary mortal into a sacrificial scapegoat. In this case it is a question of Eman's assumption of the role of carrier, and more specifically, the role of his father. We can identify both a community component to the issue of transition, and a personal or individual one. The problems presented on one level relate to those of the other.

Both levels of the ritual involve change, bringing renewal to the community and to the year. Additionally, the rituals are bounded by borders marking off the old and the new, youth and age, life and death, parent and child, and even single and married. Between each of these stages, according to Soyinka, lies the "fourth stage," that of transition. As the home of the strong breed, this stage in some sense calls on the various carriers as if it were their natural abode, although logically serving only as the passageway to another stage. Soyinka represents it through images of virility and fertility, like the "great coil" between womb and life where the seed's role is performed; alternatively, he evokes the road through rail lines, meandering paths or byways, avenues often filled with danger and death. This stage is the dwelling place of the unborn, the gods, and the ancestors.

The ritual player, like Ogun, is only a guide to the others. All must pass through death, or to death. It is not at all clear whether death, ostensibly a means of passage, does not become in some sense itself the end of passage. This is because Soyinka always stops at the point of death, from his earliest works on, as if stymied by the question of what lies on the other side. In *Death and the King's Horseman* (1975), the praise-singer sings that even the babalawo quails before the Not-I bird, the harbinger of death. Only the one he claims as his own, Elesin, welcomes him to build a nest on his roof. Elesin, like the Old Man, the carrier in *The Strong Breed,* bears his burden of life to the waters of death. Every person has his or her own particular fate in life. Only the "strong breed" has the fate of death, what Elesin calls the death of death, and to which, as he thinks he is fulfilling that fate, he dances: "It takes an Elesin to die the death of death. . . . / Only Elesin . . . dies the unknowable death of death . . ." (Soyinka 1975, 43).

The drama begins when the dance is interrupted, when the ritual fails. The interruptions in the action provide clues to the failure of the ritual in *The Strong Breed.* Three times the chase after Eman is dramatically broken by a flashback scene. The flashbacks operate on one level as commentaries on the principal action, the diegesis, giving us information about Eman's past, his motivation, and the meaning of his ultimate fate. But as the chase is prolonged into a repeated series of increasingly intensified actions, the flashbacks grow in importance and length, taking on a kind of life of their own.

In the first, Eman's father urges him to assume the traditional role of carrier he himself is in the process of completing with his last "voyage." Eman's knowledge of his role, in the past as in the present, is partial. The ideal model of the role of carrier reflects negatively on the attempts to carry out the ritual in the present time. The flashback, then, functions to highlight the process of enlightenment as, on one level, we acquire information about Eman and the proper role of carrier, while, on another level, Eman is educated about his own role.

The critical moment in this process occurs when Eman explains that he is no longer fit for the task. "I changed much," he explains. "There are other tasks in life father. This one is not for me" (Soyinka 1973a, 134).[*] Indeed, nothing in Eman's explanation, or in his present life, suggests that his new, "modern" self is a mistake. The "mission" he sets for himself, the books on the table, the clinic, the role of "teacher," are external settings for a new self. Perhaps he might be faulted for wishing to remain a stranger. But none of the obvious weaknesses of a Lakunle would seem to function here as a fatal flaw. We are led to conclude that it is simply the duality between his new, untraditional "mission" existence, and the call of his blood, as his father puts it, that is the explanation for the tragedy.

The second flashback is richer. Omae enters the scene, enticing the initiate Eman, the newly forged man-child, from his womb-hut. The corrupt tutor intrudes and is chased off. Eman leaves Omae, the initiation uncompleted, setting off to forge a new life for himself. Here it is Eman's

---

[*] All page references to this play are to the 1973 edition.

relationship to Omae that becomes a consideration. Just as his father appeared an ideal carrier, so is Omae the picture of faithfulness. Eman eventually learns from her example, but only when, in giving birth, she loses her life, while providing him with a son and with the new role of father.

With the third flashback, her role becomes critical in leading to the confrontation with the old tutor. The father figure now appears Oedipally split into good and bad halves. In rejecting the bad half, the tutor, Eman must forgo not only his own initiation, but also a life together with his own father. Omae thus directs him to a path that leads away from that expected for the carrier. She stays in his place at home, as he instructs her to, thus furthering the notion that there will be a new form of carrier to which allusion was made in the first flashback: "There are greater things you know nothing of" (134). Thus the interrupted initiation appears to contain the potential for its own sublimation into higher forms. Eman's refusal to enter into more than a stranger's relationship with the new village, or with Sumna, might suggest his failure to fulfill the promise of this new role.

The burden for Eman's failure to assume the role of carrier would seem to fall on his shoulders, given the information we received in the first flashback. But the second suggests that the corruption of the tutor was more at fault. On the other hand, Eman's rejection of the tutor extends to his entire initiation procedure, and would presumably not have occurred with earlier generations whose members would have been more deferential to their tutors and their father's wishes, and who would not have had the option of running away to cities when it was convenient to do so. This ambivalence is echoed in the dualism of good/bad elders seen in Oroge and Jaguna. On the one hand, the oppressive hand of the sexually dominant master, the hunter-father, Jaguna, is seen exercising total power, condemning Sumna as a "viper," as the tutor tried to blackmail Omae into sexual submission, and to impose his will arbitrarily on his youthful charges. On the other, we see the positive model ignored as the son rejects its authority and the grounds for keeping faith with the past. On balance, the virtues of the past would seem to prevail, despite the tutor: initiation was modeled on age-old patterns that faithfully carried youth into the roles of their elders; elders, like the Old Man (appropriately named as a model for the older dispensation), faithfully carried the burdens of the community; and women, like Omae, faithfully kept family obligations and love across the years. In all cases, the present seems to have degenerated in comparison to the past.

The third flashback completes the picture. Omae's faithfulness is realized as her role as lover/daughter passes into that of mother/sacrificial victim. She pays the price for the survival of the strong breed. The quest on which Eman set out is completed in his rediscovery of her virtues. With typical irony, Soyinka portrays this discovery as occurring simultaneously with her loss. The sense of unfulfillment persists on every level, bringing the present more sharply into focus. Sumna's conflicts with Jaguna contrast with the warm feelings between Omae and the Old Man; Sumna's rejection of Ifada contrasts with Omae's ultimate sacrifice when she died in childbirth; and Omae's faithfulness contrasts with the girl's gratuitous betrayal of Eman. Most important, the scene at the grave, and Eman's decision to leave home as a result of Omae's death, highlights his incapacity to bear the burdens of grief and to accept the sacrifices she made. The presence of his grieving father is the last impediment to his transition. Eman can revolt against the tutor; he can not do the same against his father. Unlike Ogun he does not forge a new path, but seeks relief in flight.

Eman looks to his new role as a teacher, his table piled high with books, yet he is doomed to die for the community. Despite the dramatic apparatus of sacrifice, he makes a strange Christ figure. Halfway through the chase, he decides he has done enough, and attempts to flee from the obligation. But the hunters corner him, leading to the final confrontation with his father. Here, no longer flashing back to the past, but out of real time into the fourth stage, he is led to his role.

Ogun never appeared reluctant, and the carrier, according to Eman's own judgment, never could succeed if he were not willing. The elders of the present generation, Jaguna and Oroge, think to make even the idiot children "willing," but they have lost control over the events and in the end are only witnesses to the failure of the community to accept false sacrifices.

Eman dies unfulfilled. The village is not purified; the daughter is cursed by the father; the carrier dies, but like a trapped animal; and the redemption for such acts remains as uncertain as the motivation of the actors. Eman's death is ironic. Thinking to follow his father out of his difficulties, thinking to flee, he refuses to accept the directions that would have saved him. He dies in ignorance. Most of all, he ignores the father's words that sacrifice must entail transition. Lacking Ogun's will to face dissolution, he yields to thirst, and fails to respond to the father's warning that "we cannot give the two of us" (145).

Eman's story was simply that of the failure of the son to replace the father. The interruptions to his story were linked to the role of the woman, her failure or success in keeping faith or in assuming the position of the mother; the incomplete knowledge of the carrier, too confident in his new books to heed the words of the past teachers; the relationship of the son to the father, which never reached completion; and the intrusion of the new, Western model of sacrifice, with its emphasis on the individual's interior feelings and motives, but with its indifference to the times and place in which sacrifice must be generated. In *The Strong Breed* Eman could be said to have failed to live up to the role of the fathers because his new "mission" self was not strong, was not appropriate for the demands of the African spirit. But the tutor could also be blamed for his charge's failure to complete the initiation, thus laying the framework for a judgment against the current generation of elders, Jaguna and Oroge. The new day fails to achieve renewal, even and especially as the elders attempt to force the old patterns on the unwilling youths. The youths fail to live up to the fathers; the fathers refuse the sons the means to succeed them. The women cannot drive the Oedipal cycle to completion.

Death comes in *The Strong Breed* at the ironic moment when Eman disobeys his father by trying to catch up with him. It comes after the pitiful words "Wait for me father" (145). The postscript that follows is intended to reinforce the point that the ritual failed. The people for whom it was performed were witness to a crime: "One and all they looked up at the man and words died in their throats" (145). No doubt they saw something of themselves reflected in that unspeakable image of Eman, everyman, like the victim in the poem "Death in the Dawn" in whose immolated features the passerby saw something of himself.

Ten years after publishing *The Strong Breed* Soyinka was to come back to the same themes, attempting to give them some sort of closure, in *Death and the King's Horseman* (1975). As Soyinka puts it, the "confrontation" that is the subject of the play "is contained in the human vehicle which is Elesin and the universe of the Yoruba mind—the world of the living, the dead and the unborn, and the numinous passage which links all: transition" (Soyinka 1975, author's note).*

Of course Soyinka's warning not to regard the play as a "clash of cultures," but as contained entirely within the drama of the father, has not been entirely heeded by the critics. Indeed, that would be to ignore most of the play's action involving the story of the son, Olunde. Like *The Strong Breed, Death and the King's Horseman* revolves around the transition that leads to renewal. As Elesin envisions his passage to the home of the ancestors, he proposes one last union with the world of the flesh, as if, Iyaloja concludes, "the timelessness of the ancestor world and the unborn have joined spirits to wring an issue of the elusive being of passage" (22). But

---

* All page references to this play are to the 1975 edition.

though Elesin is able to join flesh with flesh, he fails at the critical moment to enter into the "numinous passage" and fulfill his appointment with death.

As with Eman, his failure is hedged with ambivalence. The world had changed, the white man had come and conquered, and though he never says it, Elesin's mission is to accompany the passage of a conquered ruler. Though he and the king had lived like strutting cockerels in the past, though they were the masters in the market, another dispensation dictated the terms of their rule. Thus, despite his assurances to the market women that the world would not be wrenched from its course, when confronted with the figure of colonial authority he casts the blame for his fall on them: "Who would have known that the white skin covered our future, preventing us from seeing the death our enemies had prepared for us. The world is set adrift and its inhabitants are lost" (63).

However, when his new wife appears, he is more prepared to accept the blame himself, though he couches the accusation in ambiguous language: "First I blamed the white man, then I blamed the gods for deserting me. Now I feel I want to blame you for the mystery of the sapping of my will. But blame is a strange peace offering for a man to bring a world he has deeply wronged, and to its innocent dwellers" (65). Elesin confesses how he felt more than a normal attraction to her: "I needed you as the abyss across which my body must be drawn. . . . Perhaps your warmth and youth brought new insights of this world to me and turned my feet leaden on this side of the abyss" (65). But the final reckoning fails to resolve the issue: "For I confess to you, daughter, my weakness came not merely from the abomination of the white man who came violently into my fading presence, there was also a weight of longing on my earth-held limbs. I would have shaken it off, already my foot had begun to lift but then, the white ghost entered and all was defiled" (65).

For a third time Elesin is made to explain himself when Iyaloja confronts him in his cell. There his words focus on Ogun's crucial trait, his will. His own was polluted from without and within:

> It is when the alien hand pollutes the source of will, when a stranger force of violence shatters the mind's calm resolution, this is when a man is made to commit the awful treachery of relief, commit in his thought the unspeakable blasphemy of seeing the hand of the gods in this alien rupture of the world. I know it was this thought that killed me, sapped my powers and turned me into an infant in the hands of unnameable strangers. . . . My will was squelched in the spittle of an alien race, and all because I had committed this blasphemy of thought—that there might be the hand of the gods in a stranger's intervention. (69)

The undecidability that infuses Elesin's moral responsibility is etched on the landscape, not so as to absolve him but to extend the scope of the disruption.

The suggestive, allusive quality of blame in *The Strong Breed* is replaced by new certainties and new ambivalences in *Death and the King's Horseman.* Where Eman's encounter with the greater world has changed him, so that he comes to operate a clinic and takes the title of teacher, in *Death and the King's Horseman* the new ways are represented by a British colonial officer. Where Eman's espousal of implied Christian values and the unstated Christian symbolism are set in contrast to the ugly aspects of traditionalism embraced by Jaguna and the tutor, here Pilkings and Jane are the naive instruments of destruction and pollution whose only excuse, unacceptable to their own culture, would be that it was the gods themselves whose will they were serving. That, of course, would be merely an ironic inversion of the ideology of the colonial mission. Where in the earlier play the ritual is completed in questionable terms, now it is interrupted with equal uncertainty. Both end in death, but without the assurance of its meaning.

The father shows the way to the son, in *The Strong Breed,* but the son has changed and fails to follow. It is not, however, change itself that is called into question as much as the village elders' failure to accept change. In *Death and the King's Horseman* the son shows the father the way, and it is the son who refuses to let the more obvious aspects of Anglicized education, language and dress, prevent him from assuming his father's role. Nonetheless, *Death and the King's Horseman* concludes with a definite statement about the reversal of roles that occurred, and how it carried with it cosmological implications. Iyaloja asks, "Whose trunk withers to give sap to the other? The parent shoot or the younger?" (70). Enigmatically, she evokes his failure, "Slow as it is, Elesin, it has long overtaken you. It rides ahead of your laggard will" (71), only to sound the final crushing note: "The son has proven the father, Elesin, and there is nothing left in your mouth to gnash but infant gums" (75). The praise-singer completes the liturgy of catastrophe: "This young shoot has poured its sap into the parent stalk, and we know this is not the way of life. Our world is tumbling in the void of strangers, Elesin" (75).

In *The Strong Breed,* Eman passes from ignorance to knowledge, with respect, first, to the ritual, then to his role in it, and, finally, to his role in life. That passage is left incomplete, and the ritual fails. In *Death and the King's Horseman* Elesin undergoes a similar process of enlightenment, but though he completes the ritual, it is understood to be too late. In both cases the ritual is interrupted because of the need for knowledge, as if the interrupted initiation had to be finished. However, *Death and the King's Horseman* does not leave our attention focused solely on Elesin. Olunde also acquires a Western education; he also has to learn the role of the horseman; and he also must assume the role of his father, whom he last addressed calling him an "eater of left-overs" (61).

Both plays place the one to be sacrificed in a critical relationship to women, as if the question of the interrupted ritual could not be answered without resolving this relationship. Elesin portrayed it as one of temptation and fertility; Eman saw it in terms of faithfulness and the sacrifice of the mother for her child. For both men, the path to transition required they distance themselves from women. For Olunde that distance is provided not by an act of the will nor by espousal of a higher purpose, nor even by fleeing the past, but by colonialism. The attraction between Jane and Olunde is muted by circumstance; their "natural" roles (as Soyinka would have it) are reversed as in the corrupted new cultural sphere the woman becomes dominant: not only does Jane dominate Simon, and hold Olunde against his will, but even Iyaloja eventually berates and mystifies Elesin with her elusive references to Olunde's corpse.

The causes of the blocked ritual, linked as they are to the acquisition of knowledge, to the relationship to women, and to the son's succession to the role of the father, all crystallize in *Death and the King's Horseman* around the intrusion of the British, with what Elesin calls the "spittle of the alien race." The shock waves of Olunde being called an "impudent nigger" (55) by the aide-de-camp are echoed and reechoed in each subsequent scene between the Pilkings and the other Africans. Yet in the end, Soyinka is right to insist that this play does more than rehearse once again the ill effects of colonialism.

Transition remains the ultimate mystery. Whatever comfort is supplied by the call of the ancestors, the return of the unborn, or the visitations of the gods, nothing prepares us to unravel its secret: "Coiled / To the navel of the world is that / Endless cord that links us all to the great origin" (18). But though Elesin confidently proclaims, "[I]f I lose my way / The trailing cord will bring me to the roots" [18], in the same breath he recognizes, "No man beholds his mother's womb" (18).

The Road, The Strong Breed, and *Death and the King's Horseman* all stop at the threshold of death. Over and over Soyinka would have us gaze at death's face, recognize our own in its impassive, silent form, and see in the shadow "cast by all the doomed," as he writes in *The Road,* the mysterious features of transition about which no more can be said than Professor's last words as he prepares to enter into it, "be even like the road itself . . ." (229). If the words are uncertain, no less so is the speaker and his final act.

The Still Point of Transition

Driving to Lagos one morning a white cockerel flew out of the dusk and smashed itself against my windscreen. A mile further I came across a motor accident and a freshly dead man in the smash.

Traveller, you must set out
At dawn. And wipe your feet upon
The dog-nose wetness of earth.

Let sunrise quench your lamps, and watch
Faint brush prickings in the sky light
Cottoned feet to break the early earthworm
On the hoe. Now shadows stretch with sap
Not twilight's death and sad prostration

This soft kindling, soft receding breeds
Racing joys and apprehensions for
A naked day, burdened hulks retract,
Stoop to the mist in faceless throng
To wake the silent markets—swift, mute
Processions on grey byways. . . .

           On this
Counterpane, it was—
Sudden winter at the death
Of dawn's lone trumpeter, cascades
Of white feather-flakes, but it proved
A futile rite. Propitiation sped
Grimly on, before.

       The right foot for joy, the left, dread
       And the mother prayed, Child
       May you never walk
       When the road waits, famished.

Traveller you must set forth
At dawn
I promise marvels of the holy hour
Presages as the white cock's flapped
Perverse impalement—as who would dare
The wrathful wings of man's Progression. . . .

But such another Wraith! Brother,
Silenced in the startled hug of
Your invention—is this mocked grimace
This closed contortion—I?

—Wole Soyinka, "Death in the Dawn"

Perhaps more than any other major African author, Wole Soyinka reminds us that the literary transition represented by his work refers back to European texts as well as to African ones. It is not simply that he has adapted Euripides and Brecht while also having translated Fagunwa, but that both traditions are in some central way implicated in the problems of language, subject, and world that converge in his point of view and in the style and form of his work. If there is a sympathetic resonance to his theater, it must be seen as Brechtian; just as it is also true that Yoruba mythology is revived in his thought and imagery.

Primarily a playwright and poet, he works in the present tense. He is immediately freed from the presumption of the classic realist narrator whose account of past events implies a detached knowledge, and with it all the baggage of a unified subject and a completed, unproblematic account of the world and his or her relationship to it. Soyinka's texts are obviously closer to what Catherine Belsey refers to as the interrogative text, and for our study the key question is not only what characterizes his texts, but how they represent and enact the shift or change from their predecessors—how they create a passage.

Soyinka has made change a metaphysical and a mystical concept by locating transition in the Yoruba belief system. We can consider the character of transition as being the way a text refers to itself as a point—a still point—on a discursive continuum, just as Soyinka depicts the space of transition as the "still point." In the poem "Around Us Dawning" (Soyinka 1967, 12),* from his collection titled *Idanre and Other Poems,* he re-creates the experience of flight inside a jet airplane. He is at once outside, describing it from a safe distance—"This beast was fashioned well; it prowls / The rare selective heights"—and inside, held within it as if in a container, while the poet views himself from outside:

> Red haloes through the ports wreathe us
> Passive martyrs, bound to a will of rotors.

For Elesin, the failure to complete the passage, to find the courage to die, was due to an "alien" presence that "polluted" his will. His own will is what enabled Ogun to survive transition, as Soyinka is fond of reminding us. Thus, the yielding of will is significant in denoting how the ritual subject relates to the technical, mechanical will of Western invention:

---

* All references to the poem are to page 12 of the 1967 edition.

> Yielding ours,
> To the alien mote
> The hidden ache. . . .

evokes the surrender and the pain.

This setting provides the meeting ground at which inevitably the question of death, passage, and transition appears and takes the form of suspension, of the still point:

> . . . I am light honed
> To a still point in the incandescent
> Onrush, . . .

The still point might suggest the suspension of normal time and space; here it is clear that Soyinka means the entry into the passageway that comes with Death—"Death makes a swift descent." However, although stillness might denote calmness and certitude, quiescence, purity, and mystical transcendence, this is not compatible with the Soyinkan power urge. I see the still point more as the Nietzschean tension conveyed in the oxymoron by the opposing pull of contradictory terms. In this special case of metaphor the normal transfer and shift that results in new insight does not occur. Rather, the terms come to a standstill in quivering, almost ecstatic sexual immobility, maintaining the opposition without moving toward a way out of the impasse. This fits Belsey's argument, based on Althusser, that the interrogative text includes "an internal distance" from the ideology in which it is held, permitting the reader "to construct from within a critique of this ideology. In other words, the interrogative text refuses a single point of view, however complex and comprehensive, but *brings points of view into unresolved collision or contradiction*" (Belsey 1981, 92; my stress). The authority of an unstated, governing voice is absent, and so, too, is the "single position which is the place of coherence and meaning" (92). No wonder Soyinka won the disapprobation of the "single position" Bolekaja critics.

Soyinka's verse would seem to owe much to the modernists like Eliot and his counterparts, but the point of reference is always insistantly Yoruba. One can clearly see in "Around Us Dawning" a movement away from the unified subject of the classic autobiographies of the earlier *témoignage* literature. The "linear flare of dawn" he refers to in this poem is Soyinka's preferred moment to represent transition. It provides us with a setting in which to represent the subject as "process" rather than as "fixity," in Belsey's terms.

The point of view taken by the subject is exceptionally complex in "Death in the Dawn." We begin with the voice of the poet reaching out to us in a prose statement that precedes the poem. He recounts the now-familiar circumstances in which he first experienced the smashing of a white cock against his windshield as he set out on a trip to Lagos one morning, only to come across an accident, a mile further on, with the body of a man just killed in the crash.

We normally want to locate the voice providing the "real" details by identifying it with the one addressing us at the outset: "Traveller, you must set out / At dawn" (Soyinka 1967, 10).* But as the poet who gave the prefatory account was the traveler, it is immediately the case that he stands, in a sense, outside himself the moment the poem itself begins. The line or frame, then, that surrounds the poem is not just the page, the setting, title, text, cover, and physical apparatus of the presentation, but the unseen locus across which entry into another form of presentation of self becomes possible. "Traveller, you must set out / At dawn" at once addresses and directs (commands) us, while at the same time distancing us (we know the traveler is the poet—is he talking to himself?) and inviting us to pose the question, why set out at dawn?

The first three paragraphs continue with the exhortation ("Let sunrise quench your lamps"; "wipe your feet"), and at the same time provide explanations for why this would be the preferred time to set out by describing something of the magic of this key moment of transition. The imagery is infused, as usual, with subdued sexuality ("Now shadows stretch with sap"; "This soft kindling, soft receding breeds / Racing joys and apprehensions for / A naked day . . ."). The impression left is thoroughly ambivalent. Why does the "soft kindling" lead to its opposite, "racing joys"? And if this is the desired moment, in contrast to "twilight's death and sad prostration," why are the processions of market women, part of the "faceless throng," swift and mute? Why are the byways "grey," if the waking day is filled with the fresh light of dawn, of new life? The adjective "swift" jars against the motion of "burdened hulks," which retract.

The poem resists providing us with a center from which these questions might be answered. Our observations of light and activity at dawn are shunted about here between the oxymorons of "retract" and "swift," of "racing" and "receding." We move uncertainly forward through images of fertile gestures that strike and break—"break the early earthworm / On the hoe." The movement leads us down the road, along this stretch of flat space, channeling our motion in directions already provided; we enter

---

* All references to the poem are to page 10 of the 1967 edition, reproduced above on page 242.

onto the stage where ordinary life encounters the mystical. There is no line or frame that one has crossed to indicate that one is there. The suddenness of the passage is all that one can feel, and, indeed, the one who feels this suddenness is no less undetermined. We are on another plane all at once: "On this / Counterpane." From mundane lines that give us presence on a road we pass to an ambiguous place, a painted, contained, and framed set, a "counterpane."

The term suggests a still-life scene, as is usually produced by the counterpoint of embroidery. It is a "counter" pane of glass for the bird; and it is, strangely, a blanket more appropriate for cold weather than for what one would expect at an African dawn in southern Nigeria, on the road to Lagos. But death is an oppositional figure, and so the counterpane is the place where that figure of transition is to be depicted. The entry into this quilt is abrupt and without a visible crossing: "it was— / Sudden winter at the death / Of dawn's lone trumpeter, . . ."

On this level, the oppositions are now entrenched in the fixity of proverbial wisdom, with one foot leading to joy and the other to dread. Whereas one has the choice of placing one foot first, the other must immediately follow, leaving the mother helpless in determining the fate of her child. Her only prayer would seem to be a futile one: "Child / May you never walk / When the road waits, famished." Not only is this condition of the road unknowable, it would seem that Ogun is insatiable. The sacrifice of the white cockerel was "futile," the desire for more "propitiation" continuing to speed on. Choice and fate clash, just as, in traditional Yoruba belief, the initial choice of one's fate is made by/for one's spirit in the space outside time before birth.

The poem moves us forward from the art of the counterpane to the real life of the traveler who receives assurances of this other voice, the poet's, promising "marvels of the holy hour." We are present at the alienation of the subject, the poet addressing himself, and us, as traveler, at the moment that he experienced the ironic inversion of his expectations following the interpretation *he* provided of the bird's death as a sacrifice. Death—figured in the bird, in the natural cycles of day and night, and in twilight itself—is both prefigured in art, on the counterpane, and is real as it occurs in the experience of the traveler turned narrator, turning us back to the prefatory setting. The poet encounters real death on a real road, but it is within the frame of the poem, contained by its lines and words, like the points of embroidery that must succeed each other for the image to emerge stiffly and unnaturally.

"But such another Wraith!" We have a suspended, unconventional voice that flows along, following the one who addressed the traveler:

where are we to place its presence, and whom are we to locate in the encounter with death that follows? The corpse is "silenced," but the voice describing it continues to speak after the silence of the encounter, and to transform itself into the silent sharer of both the corpse and of the reader as traveler also caught in death. We stand with the corpse as fellow traveler, with the one who comes across the corpse, and, as ourselves, outside of them all, joined only by the verse. We need to make some sense of this death. Was it propitiation? Joy or dread? Sacrifice to the famished road, or senseless, like art, outside of real life?

The answer, of course, is a question. And it is not only a question, but *the* question, that of the subject's identity. Instead of being settled, the issue of the poet's, the traveler's, and the reader's identity is totally unsettled by the poem's postulation of a new position, impossible for the subject to occupy—the image of one's self in death.

> Brother,
> Silenced in the startled hug of
> Your invention—is this mocked grimace
> This closed contortion—I?

The recognition of the self is possible only in language, through one's use of words. Discourse creates the subject. The silence and the mocked grimace are read not by the speaker, but by the witness, the reader who can only float from "Brother" to "your invention" to a closed corpse, reflected out in the interrogative, the only space left for "I," a voice followed now by a blank space, despite its earlier presence as one who promised things.

This still point is the emptied place for the quintessential dramatic moment for Soyinka. It is his dramatization of death that provides us with the indications of where to locate change in the literature of stillness and of the oxymoron itself.

For Belsey one of the traits of the interrogative text is the absence of a unified subject of enunciation with whom the reader can easily identify (Belsey 1981, 91). Barring the unusual use of a narrator, as in Arthur Miller's *A View from the Bridge* (1955), it is the norm in theater not to have a protagonist serving directly as the subject of the enunciation because no one character can say "I" exclusively. On the other hand, audience identification with various characters is natural, and eventually even a hero or a villain can be treated in a more or a less sympathetic fashion, thus inviting more or less of the audience's sympathy. If it is difficult to see Iago rendered as a kind wit, MacBeth or Shylock still present a range of interpretations. Soyinka has followed Brecht's lead by joining rascality to moral looseness in the humorous Jero figures. After the massacres of 1967 and Soyinka's incarceration, the playwright's light tone darkened somewhat— the villains were dismissed as intellectually nil, but, though laughable, they were now also murderous. The larger social concerns have fluctuated, as the "giants" developed from the obstreperous Kongi into the murderous Idi Amin and company. But though the topics addressed in his plays have become joined to greater political outrage, a similar dramatic approach is generally employed. At once interrogative and imperative, the texts pose questions and demand answers, thus fulfilling this definition: "Even if the interrogative text does not precisely, in Benveniste's terms, seek to obtain some information from the reader, it does literally invite the reader to produce answers to the questions it implicitly or explicitly raises" (Belsey 1981, 91). Belsey goes on to quote Althusser on Brecht: "[H]e wanted to make the spectator into an actor who would complete the unfinished play" (Belsey 1981, 92). To accomplish this Brecht created situations in which the easy choice was not available, and created the alienation effect—the latter not only distancing the spectator from the action, but, in a real sense, distancing the literature of interrogation, or, in our case, literature of the oxymoron, from its more absolute and self-satisfied predecessors. Soyinka is not only influenced by the European modernist tradition, he points to the new interpreters of African literature.

Change/Transition According to Soyinka's Models

Soyinka's splitting of the subject is central to the issue of change. The illusion of a unified subject, as in Laye's conventional treatment of the three "I"s, is built on an illusion of stability provided by narrative authority. By eliminating the space between the subject of the *énonciation* and the subject of the *énoncé,* the text eliminates the space in which change could occur. The possibility for change is based on resistance, on a refusal to accept the terms of a discourse that totalizes experience and subordinates the subject to an order already established within the discourse. In terms already used in reference to earlier African texts, the issue is one of a smooth succession to the father's place as opposed to a challenge to the assumptions on which the father's place rests. When Oyono carried the challenge to colonialism, he posed it in terms of a refusal of the surrogate fathers; Soyinka carries the challenge further by highlighting the contradictions of the son's position while still rejecting that of the father. The problem of succession seems to be a particularly male issue in the literature. For women, bonding, sympathy, and struggle are often set against the oppressive relationships that men impose on them.

Belsey's formulation of Lacan's approach to the subject conveys the essence of Soyinka's pattern for us, except for the absence of the specific African context, and particularly the literary context. She writes,

> It is this contradiction in the subject—between the conscious self, which is conscious in so far as it is able to feature in discourse, and the self which is only partially represented there—which constitutes the source of possible change. The child's submission to the discursive practices of society is challenged by the existence of another self which is not synonymous with the subject of the discourse. (Belsey 1981, 85)

The "source of possible change" in Soyinka's work is tied to the form of the interrogative text and its representation of the splitting of the subject, mirroring the changes occurring in African literature more generally at the same time.

"The child's submission to the discursive practices of society" becomes a new issue by the time colonialism came to an end. Soyinka moves from a vague, timeless frame in his earliest work (e.g., *The Swamp Dwellers* [1973a], first published in 1964), to the concrete time and place of *Death and the King's Horseman* (1975). But one finds throughout his oeuvre not only father-son conflict and struggle over succession, but the intrusion of the European discourse as an alternate practice, one that could be wielded as a weapon by the son. He might have first appeared as a defenseless blind beggar from another land to take the place of the proper heir. But eventually an Olunde emerges, having learned to initiate action, despite his sojourn in Europe, and to restore honor to the ancestral tradition. Olunde moves from an initial position of alienation and exclusion, as in the treatment he receives at the British Residency when trying to reach Pilkings, to occupy the central place when he chooses to die. In a sense, it is not his death that matters. He provides the harsh lesson of the times in which fathers now must draw sustenance from their sons who give the sap, "unnaturally," to their progenitors. At the same time Elesin's death ultimately strikes us not as an obligation finally fulfilled in all its transcendence, but as a questionable act, not worthy of praise. Like the death of Eman, this gesture of entering the role of carrier is not numinous, but ironic. It attests to the division within Elesin—the questionable "pollution" of the "alien will." And we are left at the end without the closure of certainty. As the praisesinger states, "Our world is tumbling in the void of strangers, Elesin" (75).

When one compares Elesin's death with that of Okonkwo or Toundi, it is apparent that the assurance of the martyr's cause is no longer available. Instead, change has moved to the interior of the figure of resistance, now weakened or split by the internalization of both the foreign and the indigenous. Iyaloja attempts to maintain the purity and oneness associated with the traditions, but on the death of Elesin can only cry aloud for the loss of the boundaries between self and other. Thus, as Pilkings moves to close Elesin's eyes, she screams at him, "Since when have strangers donned clothes of indigo before the bereaved cries out his loss?" (76). As for the Bride, Iyaloja can only suggest that she turn her mind to the future, having lost both the present and the past. Even the one whose death showed his father the path, first appeared "dressed in a sober Western suit" (49). There is no further exclusion of the stranger without concomitant exclusion of the self.

Where the line that gave shape to the circle, as it included and excluded, was once clearly demarcated, it is now totally obscured, difference having been internalized. Between Olunde and Jane the conditions of possibility for an actual relationship have been established. In contrast, the most Toundi would have expected would have been the usual degraded affair with "Madame."

In *The Strong Breed* the key to Eman's change/transition was tied to the relationship he developed with the women in his life because the father-son theme of succession can not be resolved without encompassing the relationship with women. But by the time we come to *Death and the King's Horseman* (1975), the role reversal of the father and son and the more specific function of the alien Western culture have relegated the Oedipal rivalry to the background. The role of women now shifts as they become dominant, on the one hand, acquiring power in *Death and the King's Horseman,* while they have at the same time, curiously, disappeared completely in *The Road* (1973a) and are almost entirely absent from *A Play of Giants* (1984) and *Requiem for a Futurologist* (1985). Women are the silent nonpresence. An intriguing parallel to them among the male characters in *The Road* is Murano whose roles are both male (a palm-wine tapper) and female (the one who serves, who is silent and deferential). Professor is still something of the father in control of the woman, but the revolt against him is completed by the "son," Say Tokyo, who combines Western traits in his speech and occupation, and, as a disciple of Ogun, African ones. Esu, the double god with double gender, god of the Word and communication, acts as a mediator, bringing change and transmitting continuity of the tradition through the fixed messages of Ifa. Murano, who plays the same role, caught between two worlds (limping, one foot in each realm, and serving the celestial brew), is now past the point of bringing back meaningful messages, of transmitting words. He can bring the sacrament/drunkenness, salvation/death, ritual/illusion. His silence is the point of entry into transition, and into *The Road.*

Transition's Supplementary Signifyin(g)

African literature *is The Road,* a literature originally empowered by the fathers and yet driven by the need to reject and to transcend them. The struggle for the mother, the mother/lover, or for the young village belles (Sidis), for their loyalty (*The Strong Breed*), for their affection (*The Lion and the Jewel* [Soyinka 1974]), is joined to the larger pattern of succession as a ritual passage, one from which the women are barred (Sumna and Omae in *The Strong Breed*), and yet to which they are essential. In the prefatory poem to *The Road,* "Alagemo," we understand that Murano, the ritual *agemo* figure, embodies the passage denoted by death. Yet death and night are edges to the structure of change, given here as a *she-twin* who is "snatched" into Dawn:

> Let the rivers woo
> The thinning, thinning Here and
> Vanished Leap that was the Night
> And the split that snatched the heavy-lidded
> She-twin into Dawn. (150)

Like the *ibeji,* the albino, the batlike creature of *métissage,* as Lopes later depicts it, the figure of transition—the Man-Eman, Elesin, Murano—the Soyinkan subject is the locus of radical divisions of self, gender, and discourse.

The moment of transition, of death, is depicted not as bringing sublime fulfillment or transcendence, nor even union, but as providing the occasion for the radical division of the subject to be magnified, projected and mirrored in the fate and the words of the protagonist. The final ambivalent words of Professor, "be even like the road itself . . .,"—that is, like death, like Ogun, god of anger and war—convey in broken phrasing the doubling of the subject's identity, the same splitting of the point of view we found in "Death in the Dawn." Thus the ritual act of sharing, "Dip in the same basin as the man that makes his last journey and stir with one finger," results in the partition into two: "wobbling reflections of two hands, two hands, but one face only" (228). The moments of linkage, joining the self with the transcendental, as when the traveler meets death in the face of the sun, reflects a self characterized by an internal split: "Spread a broad sheet for death with the length and the time of the sun *between* you . . ." (228). There is no "and" after the word "you." The person designated as "you" is not divided; its place with respect to the traveler, the one advised to be the road, to Professor, to Murano, is shifted beyond any grammatical stability, immediately dissolving into another multitudinous subject: "until the one face multiplies," reconstituting itself beyond material substance, "and the one shadow is cast by all the doomed" (229).

Murano and Professor sink together into darkness. There is no clear moment at which death seizes them.

The double-voiced discourse that Oyono employs to demystify the false notes of a colonialist rhetoric is here summoned to new purpose, one in which the emphasis has shifted. The failures of the dominant ideology seem now to have been replaced by subjective failures to integrate opposing discursive voices within the subject. The irony and distancing continually point to two voices that fail to connect, and ultimately to the impossibility of attaining the levels demanded by the older tradition, the latter having already been compromised before the arrival of the new generation. The key to a resolution, the faith and loyalty of the women, has disappeared along with the presence of the women, or with their transformation into outsiders, to marginal ambassadors, who are no longer the prizes in the men's struggle.

That Murano is the *agemo,* the one between, the agent of transmission and transition, and the servant, serves to remind us of Esu's role as double-figured, double-gendered messenger, coyly disguised trickster. S/he is the perfect figure for the split subject. If Soyinka prefers Ogun, it is as an impossible ideal that the god of iron is evoked. Ogun's voice doesn't ever reach out or prevail. On the other hand, the father of mysteries, the babalawo, must communicate through the ambivalent and coded figurative messages conveyed by Esu. The figurative inevitably meets the hard-nosed communication of the touts, drivers, and thugs who demand an ordinary speech for the immediacy of their lives. Esu is the god whose language is spoken at the juxtaposition of the figurative and the literal, providing Henry Louis Gates with the model for signifying: "the literal and the figurative are locked in a Signifyin(g) relation, the myths and the figurative Signified upon by the real and literal, just as the vernacular tradition Signifies upon the tradition of letters, and as figures of writing and inscription are registered, paradoxically, in an oral literature" (Gates [1988] 1989, 22).

What better figure to convey that meeting than Professor, with his obscure collection of words and forms whose significance is suggestive of the Christian Word as well as of the betting form. In Soyinka the two worlds that inform discourse arise, like Esu's discourses, from opposing domains, and yet, like Esu, are internally joined. Those worlds almost always seem to come out in characters whose loyalties to speech, manners, clothes, and values point either in a Yoruba/traditional direction or a European one. The meeting ground of the two literary ancestors is a dominant feature of Soyinka's work, and the tension that perpetually results is that of an unresolved ritual, an uncompleted dance, a collision of word/worlds— an oxymoron, limping, with one leg in this world and one in the other.

Esu, Doubling on the Threshold

The primal god of the Fon is a Janus figure; one side of the body is female and is called Mawu, while the other side is male and is called Lisa. Mawu's eyes form the moon; Lisa's eyes form the sun. Accordingly, Lisa rules the day and Mawu rules the night. The seventh son of Mawu-Lisa is Legba [Esu]. Legba is the wild card of Fon metaphysics, the wandering signifier.

Legba governs the indeterminacy of meaning.

Each Odu is comprised of "roads," or "pathways," or "courses."
—Henry Louis Gates, Jr., *The Signifying Monkey*

Esu: "One who defies boundaries and limitations with gay abandon."
—J. Westcott, "The Sculpture and Myths
of Eshu-Elegba, the Yoruba Trickster"

In his fine discussion of Legba/Esu, Gates makes it apparent that the god most in tune with Soyinka's work is the trickster. When Soyinka is being serious and reaches for the tragic, the beyond, when the terrible and terrifying power of boulders, iron, and war is being evoked, then the shadow of Ogun may be glimpsed. But from Jero to the Futurologist, even to the cartel of buffoon dictators, it is phoniness, playacting, and especially bluffing that are most typical of his work. Even Professor puts on the fool's mask. Soyinka is theatrical more than somber, avoiding the dark silence of mysterious ritual. Ritual for him is a noisy dance, a masquerade that often ends in death; not in closure, but in open-ended mystery.

Soyinka's works always end in death, in one form or another, and death presents itself not as an avenue leading to salvation but as the end of our visible exchange with the forces that govern this world. Salvation is a joke; faith is a con racket; power and majesty are passé, or are worn to hide the naked face of brutal politics. Esu skips across the stage, penis fully erect, laughing at all those pretentious minigiants whose penises pop up and down like playthings, while he asserts his divine rights. This is why the women, and their surrogates like Murano, are the key catalysts in the encounter of opposing worlds, opposing generations, cultures, ages, classes, words. Esu is the god of the threshold. For Gates he is the one who governs discourse; for our study it is appropriate to see him/her as the figure of change. He would pass, like his myths of power and trickery, from one side of the Möbius strip to the other, from gender to gender, from continent to continent, without ceasing to be what he is. In other words, he is the force that penetrates, the topos for transition.

Esu, like Legba, shares this characteristic [of being hugely oversexed] and frequently is selected to be "intermediary between this world and the next" at the end of myths that recount his sexual prowess. . . . Legba's sexuality is a sign of liminality, but also the penetration of thresholds, the exchange between discursive universes. (Melville Herskovits, quoted in Gates [1988] 1989, 27)

Hidden under the cowrie shells, Esu's sexuality is revealed to be male and female, like his Janus head, while still distinctively indicative of both genders. He is bisexual and indeterminate (29), but also recognizably oversexed and lascivious. The combination does not cancel out his sexual identity, but rather cancels the line between the sexes, "render[ing] his enormous sexuality ambiguous, contrary, genderless" (Ayolede Ogundipe, qtd. in Gates [1988] 1989, 29). If this is the god who rules over the mysterious words that guide human destiny, who renders truth in riddles and has power over the riddles themselves, then we can say that, like his sexuality, which is the meeting place for powerful, definite signs of gender identity and which becomes "Möbiusized" by the encounter between the two sexes, so, too, is it his divine role to embody the verbal encounter—figurative/literal, oral/written—that is marked by the oxymoron. In the final analysis, Soyinka is right to see *Death and the King's Horseman* as entailing more than a cultural conflict. The figure of Esu dwarfs that specific issue. But his nature is not one that would cancel out the strife between Elesin and Pilkings, or eliminate the electric lines between Olunde and Jane. Rather he assumes their strife without sublimation or reconciliation.

Soyinka inevitably brings us to this point: Eman, the Man and the carrier; Professor, the lay reader and roadmaster for Ogun's rituals; Olunde, the carrier/horseman who arrives on the scene wearing dark Western dress and departs in the robes of his fathers. Soyinka's text, like these doubled figures, refers us back to the words of Euripides and Shakespeare, Brecht and Beckett, as well as to Fagunwa, Orunmila, to *ese,* the courses laid out in Ifa, now tarred over and carrying the puns and prayers half transformed by an "alien" will.

Keeping in mind Belsey's view of the interrogative text as *process,* and not as closure, we can say that Soyinka's joining of two worlds, as in the figure of Esu, results not in resolution or determinate presence, but in a vision of transformation/transition itself. Robert Pelton, cited by Gates, characterizes this situation of having two features present to each other as providing wholeness, but still he can not freeze this wholeness. It transmutes itself into permanent change, process. Thus Esu both joins and ceaselessly exchanges the features of his being. For Pelton, the sign of Esu's being, his doubleness, is not so much rooted in the coincidence of opposites or in the mere passage between structure or antistructure as it is in a perception of life as a rounded wholeness whose faces both mask and disclose each other. These faces are simultaneously present, but this is a simultaneity of process, a turning by which one face not only succeeds but is transformed into the other. (Gates [1988] 1989, 30)

Here is the god's praise song:

> Eshu, confuser of men. . . .
>
> Eshu slept in the house—
> But the house was too small for him.
> Eshu slept on the veranda—
> But the veranda was too small for him.
> Eshu slept in a nut—
> At last he could stretch himself. . . .
>
> Having thrown a stone yesterday—he kills a bird today.
> Lying down, his head hits the roof.
> Standing up he cannot look into the cooking pot.
> Eshu turns right into wrong, wrong into right.
> (Gbadamosi and Beier 1959, 15)

"Death in the Dawn" attempts to seize the moment of transformation of one face into another. In the larger sense, just as Murano and Professor die, so, too, is Soyinka's work given to a form of passing over, of transition, that never ends, hiding its finality, disclosing life's foolish pretensions, giving us change in its most ambitious and most frustrated form, change at the still point.

Soyinka's emphasis differs from that associated with the anthropologists' descriptions of the classical Esu figure. For while Esu's double nature is recognized by Pelton, Ogundipe, Mercier, and Herskovits, they see the resultant coming together of the two sides as providing "harmony" (Gates [1988] 1989, 30), a "hidden wholeness" (Pelton, qtd. in Gates [1988] 1989, 30), or a "kind of reconciliation of opposites of discourse" (Pelton, qtd. in Gates [1988] 1989, 29). Gates gives the more ambivalent characterization of Esu as "the third principle—neither male nor female, neither this nor that, but both, a compound morphology" (Gates [1988] 1989, 29). Perhaps most commonly he is described as passing or circulating between alternate sides/discourses/languages/genders. Paul Mercier's description of his incarnation in the Fon king provides the typical mystical rendition: not dual, but "two in one" (Mercier, qtd. in Gates [1988] 1989, 29). For Ogundipe he represents both "flux and mutability" (Ogundipe, qtd. in Gates [1988] 1989, 30), and in his complementary relationship with Ifa, embodies, for Gates, the "dialectical principle."

The wholeness, complementarity, the two-in-oneness, are familiar mystical properties totally to be expected in a divine figure. As one who reconciles these opposing forces, Esu attaches a linguistic transcendence to his metaphysical state, permitting passage from one realm to another. This is the successful linguistic operation that occurs when metaphor is employed. Soyinka stops before that transfer is effected. He stops at the gate of transcendence, never daring like Cheikh Hamidou Kane at the end of *L'Aventure ambiguë* (1961) to enter into the space of transition. The opposition remains more of a permanent condition for Soyinka. Unlike metaphor, which provides us with a sense of *new* meaning achieved by the successful graft of one image onto another, the oxymoron insists on the permanence of both the irreconcilability of the two terms and of their inevitable confrontation with each other. This is Esu's new double mask as worn in Soyinka's masquerade. The borrowed robes of Brecht, Euripides, and Shakespeare are changed into Yoruba dress; behind the mask appear glimpses or shadows of the horseman who stands in for the elusive double figure of Esu who can not provide the comfort of reconciliation while crossing the boards of Soyinka's stage.

Chapter 11

▼▼▼▼▼▼▼▼▼▼

Crossing the Bridge of Change

Ahmadou Kourouma, *Les Soleils des indépendances; Monnè, outrages et défis*

For Aristotle, change implies the passage from one stage to another. Between the stages there must exist a threshold that has to be crossed in order for us to be able to say that a change has occurred. We can mark three areas in which one can locate a passage across a threshold: three *littératures* (those of *témoignage,* revolt, and the oxymoron), each with its own subject, its own "language." Simultaneously we can turn the threshold back on itself, forming a Möbius strip, and thus problematize each passage, each work. It might appear that every work that marks the tradition of African literature, that establishes a corpus rather than repeating previous gestures, is one that problematizes the passage across the threshold, and thus can be seen as being on one side of the strip as well as on the other. This is the case with many writers: Ouologuem, Oyono, Dadié, Soyinka, Ngugi. It is true of Ahmadou Kourouma as well.

Outside the strip one world exists, within there is another, and the line between them is infinitely twisted and decentered. On the outside is a notion of an external reality, on the inside a subject, and the communication across the strip is shaped by words and discourses. Thus the portrayal of "reality" might be thought of as both revealing and concealing or masking at the same time. The act of representing conveys the reality of the subject of the *énoncé* (or narrative) as well as of the subject of the *énonciation* (or speech act)—the world as well as the creative, shaping mind are represented, and both sides within the context of a discourse that is being uttered and being received.

With this in mind, we can regard each of the three African *littératures* as revealing a particular kind of external world, as reflecting a particular situation of the subject, as expressing this condition with a particular kind of representation. The image of external reality has been formulated, in general, in three successive stages.

1. We have the "reality" of everyday life presented in the literature of *témoignage.* At its extreme this literature demonstrates a life of hardship. Often its plot turns on the struggle of youth to succeed.
2. The literature of revolt offers us the "reality" of oppressive colonial times and of their consequences. This is a literature of injustice, exploitation, or even, when the tone is lighter (as in *Mission terminée* [Beti 1957]), a portrayal of the realization of one's oppressed state, bringing "consciencization" or the coming to awareness of the truth.
3. Then there is the most recent, most complex, most convoluted "reality," that of the literature of the oxymoron and contradiction, which depicts a post-Independence Africa in a state of turmoil. Social problems and corrupt officials appear on one level, while on another are found the troubled psyches of those living in a world that offers no haven of ease, no insight into truth.

Each of these "realities" can be taken as the projection of a subject, a subjective reality, a perspective that is lost when analysis focuses solely on the external representation. The image of the subject is tied to the process of change, and may be represented, following our three literatures, in three ways. Change here is understood as a process of individuation or self-realization, involving the passage from one state to another, a transformation, an initiation, an attempt to bring completion of the self.

1. Initially, as in the literature of *témoignage,* the subject presents the terms under which fulfillment can be achieved, demonstrates the obstacles and the means of surmounting them, and has success in following the right path. As the passage in this type of literature entails the crossing of a threshold, the successful maneuvering through difficulties is ultimately celebrated. Tragic defeats are no less part of this pattern than successes, as they imply a moral or spiritual triumph of a higher order, as may be seen in the concluding pages of *L'Aventure ambiguë* (Kane 1961).
2. With the younger, rebellious generation of writers who created the literature of revolt, the passage is now blocked, and states of frustration, contestation, anger, and rebellion are created. The path to follow is still indicated; the subject still seeks to complete the passage, but the conditions of life, especially within an unjust society, block the way.
3. Eventually the pattern of following a path, and its underlying assumptions (explored best in the theoretical excavations of Mudimbe), is itself

called into question. The concept of change as a given must be challenged with all the other givens, the other obvious truths that formed part of a problematic heritage. With a step back, with the gaze not just from a distance, but from the outside, the project of the passage itself ceases to be taken for granted. A metaconsciousness now emerges and returns the focus to itself. Awareness no longer can be limited to political consciousness, but is turned toward a subject ill at ease with the inherited patterns of searching.

The subject then, in the quest for the passage, undergoes change in the way it represents itself.

1. The initial quest is undertaken by a subject that either is unified or attempts to represent itself as such: individuation is not only portrayed, it is unproblematically evoked, even if the manner of its evocation reveals an underlying contradiction.
2. The contradictions implicit in the first stage ultimately move to the surface, the subject now displays its own cleavage as the blockage to the passage corresponds to the subject's own internal state.
3. The fracturing of reality is finally located within the subject whose expression is itself the representation of its own condition. The calling into question of the conditions of possibility for subjective wholeness turns the subject against its own means of representing, leaving us with the state of ironic consciousness described by Paul de Man. Revolt finds its limits in irony, and irony its limits in itself.

Inevitably the Möbius strip of passage must turn in both directions, inward and outward. The representation of reality passes from being initially unproblematic, to problematic, to self-consciously divided. At the key point in the change of these patterns of representation one finds the fiction of Ouologuem and Kourouma for whom the issue of representation becomes central. With Ouologuem reality appears over and over again as a staged, constructed artifice. The artifice takes precedent over the concrete. For Kourouma it is not "reality" that is problematized, but the discourse itself—the words that are used to represent reality. Over the course of his two novels, this concern passes from unstated to explicit, from being an aspect of a work of revolt to being the central issue.

Kourouma provides us with the contours and images of change, initially employing a discourse reminiscent of Oyono's and Dadié's literature of revolt, irony, and protest. However, his novels lack the staged quality of Ouologuem's fiction, and thus do not turn us back on the narrator and our relationship to him. Ouologuem takes us to the limit of self-consciousness within the strictures of revolt. Kourouma, on the other hand, takes us to the limits of the word, within the strictures of revolt.

Words belong to their owners. Kourouma uses French, but is the owner of Malinke. The pattern established by a Francophonic Malinke writer is created in *Les Soleils des indépendances* ([1968] 1970), it animates the novel's discourse, although the ostensible subject of the novel is the fallen world of post-Independence Africa. On the other hand, with *Monnè, outrages et défis* (1990) words become the subject of a novel whose discourse is animated by the very themes and images adumbrated in *Les Soleils des indépendances*. *Monnè, outrages et défis* is more than a sequel—it is the realization of *Les Soleils des indépendances,* the surveyor's mark permitting change to be detected: it is the counter-side of the Möbius strip first drawn twenty-two years earlier.

As there is no single point of entry into a Möbius strip, we might have recourse to the opening, or breach, that appears most visible, the one created by numerical groupings, often given as variations or riffs on "*mensonges*" (literally lies—what Tennessee Williams called mendacity, or what might be rendered better as "crap"). Lies, or their variants, rarely appear alone. Kourouma repeatedly employs certain numerical patterns, such as groups of eighty, to represent a large quantity (Kourouma 1990, 167), or, more commonly, patterns of three to emphasize an attribute. Thus the following examples of the ironic consciousness from *Soleils* give expression to forms of mendacity: "What solemnity! What dignity! What religiosity!" (my trans.),* for the celebrations on Fama's return to Togobala; "blood is prodigious, loud, inebriating" (my trans.),† for the sacrifices on the same occasion. Fama's cousin, Lancina, made sacrifice on sacrifice, and then "plotted, lied, and lowered himself" (my trans.)‡ so as to succeed to Fama's rightful position as ruler, only to find himself "dismissed, shamed, and diminished" (my trans.)** when the new authorities, under Independence, stripped him of his power. "A changing, terrible, incomprehensible world" (my trans.)††—this is Fama's impression of the impoverished,

---

* "Quelle solennité! quelle dignité! quelle religiosité!" (Kourouma [1968] 1970, 146). All page references to this text are to the 1970 edition, and to the 1981 translation by Adrian Adams, unless otherwise indicated as my own. Translations given in brackets, without quotation marks or page numbers, are my own.

† "le sang est prodigieux, criard et enivrant" (147)

‡ "intrigua, mentit, et se rabaissa" (22)

** "destitué, honni et réduit" (22)

†† "Monde changeant, térrible, incompréhensible" (103)

parched lands to which he was returning. Finally, the terrible judgment given at Salimata's excision, presents us with "the clitoris considered as impurity, confusion, imperfection" (my trans.).* The landscape is prepared to receive an old and tired ruler, himself stripped down, confused, imperfect—like Salimata's clitoris, ready for the knife.[1]

The lists generally contain invectives, not positive terms, which are mere parenthetical insertions on the few occasions when they are found: "(sun, honor, and gold)" (my trans.),† all of which have been lacking since Fama's childhood. Kourouma focuses and actualizes the pattern with the self-reflexive explanation given in *Monnè*: "In this world, a woman's lot has *three names, all with the same meaning*: resignation, silence, and submission" (my trans. and my stress).‡

With the title of his second novel, Kourouma crowns the tripling with his trademark signs: "Monnè," "outrages," and "défis." "Monnè" is translated by the two terms that follow, and so Kourouma is able to impart both the sense of the whole series as well as the signification of the act of translation/interpretation itself: an act of doubling contained by a triad of terms. Further, the title points to the impossibility of its own task: we learn immediately upon opening the book that the term "monnè" can not be translated into French, but merely approximated by an ever larger series of terms. But even within the immediate coupling of "outrages" and "défis" we are drawn along the curved strip—within the novel "monnè" is used most often to convey "insult" or "dishonor"; "outrage" passes from the aggressive act of the other to the subject's response to the act, while "défi" is even more nuanced, on the cusp between the positive notion of a challenge and the negative notion of defiance. Both novels might be classified as political fiction, but while *Les Soleils des indépendances* is primarily focused on the patterns of decline and degradation that invaded postcolonial African society, *Monnè, outrages et défis* returns us to the discourse used to narrate the history of Africa's decline—and specifically the decline of Malinke greatness from the time of the French conquest until the end of the colonial period ("the suns [or season] of politics").** In brief, we proceed from rupture to the ruptured subject.

---

* "le clitoris considéré comme l'impureté, la confusion, l'imperfection" (34)

† "(le soleil, l'honneur, et l'or)" (19)

‡ "Dans ce monde, les lots de la femme ont trois noms qui ont la même signification: résignation, silence, soumission" (135).

** "les soleils de la politique" (22)

Les Soleils des indépendances

Les Soleils des indépendances continually returns us to the impossibility of effecting passage across a threshold, both by its linguistic properties—semantic, syntactical—and by image and theme. The repetition of "mensonges" [lies] and "bâtardise" [bastardness] continually expresses the feeling of frustration: in both expression and action Kourouma seeks to demystify, a goal consistently embraced throughout his career. His reading of African history reflects this.[2] "Mensonges," "hypocrisie" are the curses of the suns of Independence. They form the horizon for the events and they define the blockage faced by the characters. *Les Soleils des indépendances* begins on this note, showing how demystification reduces the scale of the events. The solemn note of death that is sounded at the beginning is immediately undercut: "Il n'avait pas soutenu un petit rhume . . ." (7) [He had been done in by a small cold]. Not only does the use of a phrase in dialect render the event picturesque, the cause of death and the trivial resistance of Ibrahima Koné are also mocked. The dead man's shadow, or spirit, is immediately launched on a long voyage home, only to return subsequently to the ignominy of burial in the capital. The bridge over which Fama must pass, noisy, crowded, encumbered with "véhicules multicolores," is likewise diminished: lies and hypocrisy attend the life of the panther Fama, the Malinke prince, as he disputes with hyenas and vultures over the leftovers. His passage over the bridge that carries him to this degree of ignobility is "immensely disgraceful and shameful" (my trans.).* The panther is transformed by his haste: "What was he now? A scavenger . . . A hyena in a hurry" (5).†

The water of the lagoon over which Fama passes reflects the fracturing of Fama's stature: "the laguna was blinding, with its multiple mirrors that broke and reassembled" (my trans.).‡ The implicit values of wholeness, transparency, and truth are set against the seasons of corruption, debasement, and emptiness, seasons caught between two ends of the bridge, locked in an uncertain, indeterminate, and ultimately bastardized mélange: "Bastards! disorienting, disgusting, these in-between seasons mingling sunshine and rains" (my trans.).** Caught in this uncomfortable state, between epochs, cultures, languages, between former hopes of greatness and empty illusions for the future, rendered derisory by religious

---

* "les immenses déchéance et honte" (10)

† "Qu'était-il devenu? Un charognard . . . C'était une hyène qui se pressait" (10).

‡ "la lagune aveuglait de multiples miroirs qui se cassaient et s'assemblaient" (10)

** "Bâtardes! déroutantes, degoûtantes, les entre-saisons de ce pays mélangeant soleils et pluies" (11).

habits—"mensonges," "hypocrisie"—Fama lives out his existence as a sterile failure. His only recourse is to vituperate, curse, vent his spleen.

What is this state of "bâtardise"? Ostensibly the conditions that prevail during newly independent times—free from foreign rule, from oppressive domination and exploitation, and yet all the more horrible due to the dashed hopes of freedom and justice. Armah (1968) and Ngugi (1967) lost little time in laying the foundation for a literature of outrage and disillusionment. Kourouma's dismantlement of the outer garments of appearance is no less mordant: Salimata's hopes for a fertilized belly are dashed, and the image of an underlying, debased, relentlessly material existence reflects the absolute reduction effected by the language of demystification: "Salimata stroked her abdomen. A meager belly, covering only entrails and excrement" (19).*

In the dream, the hoped-for child would build anew in an unexplored, unknown, undefined future, and the suns of independence would lead to a new social life. Instead, the life in which Fama is trapped lies along a finite stretch between the two ends of the bridge. Not only is it impossible to complete the passage across that bridge, but the possibility of retreat is also denied. The resultant imagery of life "à mi-chemin" conveys a state from which there is no means of egress. This is change blocked at the point of transition, ritual caught after the departure, en route, in the liminal state, as Benjamin Ray would have it (1976), or in the fourth stage in Soyinka's terms (1976). This is the moment of the greatest vulnerability, the physical realm no longer exercising its strong hold over existence, and the invoked spiritual forces operating and effectuating the desired change. Outside of time, it is when children pass into adulthood or when fertilization is realized, the old discarded, and the new initiated. For Kourouma this moment lies on the cusp of a Möbius strip: his works portray the impossibility of crossing.

In *Soleils* we find Fama, getting older, empty, impotent, unable to resist the forbidden carrion, falling in a long cry of rage, echoed earlier across the hills by Salimata's wailing at the time of her excision and rape: "Rape! Amidst the blood and pain of excision, something had [bitten into] her like fiery pepper, like red-hot iron. She had screamed, howled" (20).†
For Fama life, like his long, drawn-out day, resembles a dying, immobilized sun, a midday sun hanging motionless and emasculated in the watery

---

* "Salimata caressa son abdomen. Un ventre sans épaisseur, ne couvrant qu'entrailles et excréments" (31).

† "Le viol. Dans le sang et les douleurs de l'excision, elle a été mordue par les feux du fer chauffé au rouge et du piment. Et elle a crié, hurlé" (31).

sky: a life that dies, consumed in "poverty and barrenness. Independence and the one-party system! Was not that life like a dead and darkened sun, extinguished in mid-course?" (18).*

"Hypocrisie" becomes another term for lying "mi-chemin" between night and day, truth and lies. If purity consists in being a Malinke, speaking Malinke, living Malinke, then in its essence as in its origins, that which is Malinke seems to lack a clear path by which to cut through the mixing. Mixing becomes existence in all its various facets. Thus Malinke are both Muslims and "fetishistes," and since the former excludes the latter, they become simultaneously both, and neither one nor the other. Malinke falsehood, "la fausseté malinké," comes out in black and white: "deep down inside they are blacker than their skin, while the words they speak are whiter than their teeth" (72).† Neither one nor the other, "neither lizard nor swallow" (72).‡ Good and evil themselves lose distinction in the creolized universe where "nothing is good or evil in itself" (72).**

At the origin of the great Doumbouya lineage, before the fall into the present low state, the mythic progenitor of the dynasty, Souleymane, entered Togobala from the north. For Fama to save himself, to know himself, he must recall and reinterpret his ancestral past. Souleymane and his disciples arrived at the city of Toukoro where he was greeted as a great marabout. Then he was offered lands and a home—the power of the whole province would follow wherever he resided. But as a great Malinke harvest festival was about to begin, he was asked to wait on lands that bordered Toukoro. However, though he agreed, he and his entourage didn't return: "Ils ne retournèrent plus" (100) [They never returned]. Their new residence and lands lay between two kingdoms, "entre deux terres," and the neighboring ruler opposed their return so that the power would not fall into just one camp.

The original version of Doumbouya beginnings, then, insists upon the cusp at the outset, on the failure to be able to opt for one side, on the mythical emplacement between two opposing forces. All of the history of Doumbouya becomes a history of deferred commitment. "The history of Souleymane is the history of the Doumbouya dynasty" (my trans.).††

---

* "la pauvreté, la stérilité, l'Indépendance et le parti unique! Cette vie-là n'était-elle pas un soleil éteint et assombri dans le haut de sa course?" (29).

† "ils ont l'intérieur plus noir que leur peau et les dires plus blancs que leurs dents" (108).

‡ "ni margouillat, ni hirondelle!" (108)

** "rien en soi n'est bon, rien en soi n'est mauvais" (109).

†† "L'histoire de Souleymane est l'histoire de la dynastie Doumbouya" (100).

The second version of this history demystifies the first—creating, at the same time, its own mystifications in harmony with the ironic narrative stance and mode of the novel. This time Souleymane's arrival and greeting are postponed due to the drunken state of the Toukoro ruler: "Let me sleep!" (my trans.),* he mumbles. By the time the chief comes to, Souleymane has settled on the margins of Toukoro territory, and once again, "Souleymane could no longer turn back, he was halfway [à mi-chemin] between two territories" (67).†

Fama looks back on a past that ironically reflects back to him his own features, his own fears: "Fama was afraid of the night, of the journey, of the funeral, of Togobala, of Salimata, of Mariam and of himself. Afraid of his fear" (68).‡ Continuing the tradition of his family line, Souleymane's descendant Bakary assumes power after misreading the divine warnings about the eventual demise of the lineage. Bakary's failure to provide for the future, or, in terms that parallel the second version of the Souleymane story, his greed for power, condemns Fama to a sterile existence. "Mensonges," "hypocrisie." Although the Malinke were conquered and dispossessed, their self-dispossession was there at the outset. Fama's failure to change, Togobala's commensurate incapacity to adapt, the dead-end suns of Independence, all hearken back to the broken narratives of Doumbouya history that fracture the surface of time, like the moiré surface of the lagoon.

Fama's attempt to turn back, to return, "retourner" or "se retourner," is linked to the passage blocked midstream. Returning is not only a delusion, it is a betrayal, a sign of falling away from Malinke courage, a lack of faith in divine support; it is cowardice, lies, and hypocrisy. His flight at the end, returning home to die, is a mock Hegira. Leaving a city of corruption, the site of his former successes, he seeks to cross over time and new borders, back into past glory. Yet, though he fails, it is, ironically, not without some redemption. Seeking power he is mocked by circumstance, attacked by the very crocodiles sacred to his lineage. Still, he finds the courage to face his fears and overcome his own lies by sacrificing himself for Salimata. His death is no less ironic, but he dies as one who is greater than the ruler of Togobala or the prince of Doumbouya: he is now "the husband of Salimata" (my trans.).**

---

* "Qu'on me laisse dormir!" (100).

† "Souleymane ne pouvait plus retourner, il était à mi-chemin entre deux terres" (100).

‡ "Fama eut peur de la nuit, du voyage, des funérailles, de Togobala, de Salimata, de Mariam, et de lui-même. Peur de sa peur" (102).

** "le mari de Salimata" (199)

The moment of Fama's death comes as he tries to cross the last bridge back to Horodougou. His return, an attempt to reclaim what was lost in his first undignified rush across the lagoon bridge of the city, underlines the ironic distance between his own perception of reality and the narrator's wry account. Thus, the noble prince who had descended to the level of the hyena, now proudly marches onto the no-man's-land as "a true panther totem" (my trans.).* His steps onto the bridge, through the gate and past the barbed wire, carry him onto the liminal "stage of transition." His *griot* absent, his sorcerer dead, now he must sing his own praisesong, create his own courage so as to reclaim what time had taken, his virility: "Fama, the One and only! The great! The strong! The virile! Sole possessor of strength and stiffness between the thighs!" (135).† Unwittingly mocking his own demise, he nonetheless succeeds in becoming more than his Doumbouya ancestors; ironically, through his wife his virility is restored—not by Balla's magic or by prayers to Allah, nor by the tradition that hands him a young wife, or by a corrupt single-party leader who hands him a wad of bills. He finds the strength of a "fou" in finally giving the gift of his departure to Salimata, enabling her to start a new fulfilling life, and he claims for himself a new identity defined in terms of his oppressed, subservient, all too generous wife: "Look at Fama! Look at Salimata's husband!" (132).‡

For the guards Fama is crazy—"Don't shoot! He's crazy! Crazy!" (my trans.).** On his initial crossing of the lagoon bridge, when he is surrounded by cacaphonous, chaotic elements, the left-hand railings, appropriately called "gardes-fous" in French††, keep this turbulence in check. Then, before him, Fama thought his goal was close. "God be praised! Luckily Fama hadn't much further to walk now; he could see the end of the harbour" (5).‡‡ Now, at the end of his journey, he runs. In his final attempt to cross over the bridge between the republics of Côte d'Ebène and Nikinai, he finds his way blocked by barbed wire and guards. Not even a fist can pass through the barrier. The ease of Fama's access to the bridge is matched by his difficulty in leaving it. He is trapped as guards at

---

* "un vrai totem panthère" (199)

† "Fama, l'Unique! Le grand! Le fort! Le viril! Le seul possédant du rigide entre les jambes!" (204).

‡ "Regardez Fama! Regardez le mari de Salimata!" (199).

** "Ne tirez pas! Il est fou! fou!" (199).

†† "[d]es garde-fous gauches du pont" (10) [the left hand-railing of the bridge]

‡‡ "[Q]u'Allah en soit loué! Fama n'avait plus long à marcher, l'on apercevait la fin du port" (10).

both ends pursue him. Desperate, Fama takes the steps that will be echoed in the wording of Kourouma's second novel written twenty-two years later: he *turns.* "Désespéré, Fama *se retourna*" (199–200; my stress) [Desperately, Fama looked back/turned around]. The guard pursues, and, trapped, Fama turns again: "Fama se retourna encore" (200). Like his ancestor, halfway between two hostile camps, Fama fails to face either one. Yet he can not remain still on the bridge, despite his own praise singing. Unlike the bridge he crossed earlier, this border crossing has no guard rails on its left side: the one who has turned and turned, finds that life has left him no more space. He advances to the left side of the bridge and hoists himself over, into the crocodile-infested waters: "The big sacred crocodiles of Horodugu would never dare attack the last descendant of the Dumbuya" (133).*

Fama performs the one action appropriate to the liminal space: the sacrifice. And as all the chickens, sheep, cows (or later, in *Monnè, outrages et défis,* the albinos and dwarfs as well) have shed their blood, so does Fama complete the gesture begun by his gift to Salimata of his departure. His cry is the expression of the sacrifice, the cry of a definitive transformation, which is signaled in the communication of liminality to all that surrounds him: the wild animals depart from their own proper place, become crazy, and reverse roles. "They showed it by behaving strangely. . . . [T]he wild beasts charged towards the village compounds, the crocodiles rushed from the water and fled into the forest, while men and dogs, amid infernal shouting and barking, scattered and fled into the bush" (133).†

Suspended in the still point of the storm, Fama lies in his blood while the crocodile that bit him agonizes from the bullet received from a guard's rifle. The Doumbouya dynasty "finishes," as Kourouma would have it, in the futility of an ignoble era. But the epic grandeur of the end is deflated: virility disappears, along with the dignity and stature of the prince. The turning and returning continue in Fama's final act of dying, even in his own imagination: "Mais Fama se retourne. Son escorte s'est évanouie" (204) [But Fama looks back/turns around. His escort has disappeared.]. The turning of a Möbius strip appears endless because any point of departure is provisional, any exit gratuitous. For the prince lost in illusions, the

---

* "Les caïmans sacrés du Horodougou n'oseront s'attaquer au dernier descendant des Doumbouya" (200).

† "Ils le montrèrent en se comportant bizarrement . . . les fauves en hurlant foncèrent sur les cases des villages, les crocodiles sortirent de l'eau et s'enfuirent dans la forêt, pendant que les hommes et les chiens, dans des cris et des aboiements infernaux, se débandèrent et s'enfuirent dans la brosse" (201).

loss of markers is overwhelming—the white "corsair" on which he rides in his final delusions brings him to an edge without end: "and the charger rears up at the edge of an abyss" (136).*

The mysteries of death, which were the occasion for Camara Laye's faith, are here the final borders of demystification. Kourouma must turn back on his language itself in order to give revolt a greater reason to exist.

Monnè, outrages et défis

Kourouma poses the question of language at the beginning of *Monnè, outrages et défis* by hypothesizing a scene in which Djigui, the centenarian Malinke monarch, learns of the impossibility of translating "monnè" into French. The issue of language is presented simultaneously with that of translation. This is because Kourouma wants to highlight the need for and the impossibility of expressing oneself as an African in a European tongue—especially French. To accomplish this he needs a vocabulary, an interpreter, and a reason to interpret. Further, he needs to deal not only with interpreting, but with translating and repeating, and with the question of faithfulness, of truth and lies, and of the power they entail. All the concerns of *Les Soleils des indépendances* are found here in their quintessential form.

Even the issue of change appears in this novel in a form that recalls *Les Soleils des indépendances.* The ur-Malinke dynasty is now Keita, not Doumbouya, and its capital is situated at Soba, ostensibly in the northwest corner of the Ivory Coast. Again the ruler is concerned with the problem of the continuation of his line, his "pérennité." Where excessive sacrifices fail, extensive prayers to Allah succeed in overturning the fate of a truncated lineage. But if Djigui's personal concerns resemble those of Fama, Kourouma quickly moves in his later novel to expand the scope of the action to include the wider historical frame. Samory is fleeing from the invading French and he calls for all the Malinke, Dioula, Senufo, and others to join in what was to become his last stand. The urgency of the issue of change now confronting Djigui and his kingdom is underscored by the legendary version given here of Soba society as closed, static, and complete in the face of irresistible forces of change intruding from without:

> For centuries, the people of Soba and their kings lived in a closed world, sheltered from all new ideas and beliefs. Protected by mountains, they had succeeded, for better or for worse, in preserving their independence. It was a frozen society. The sorcerers, marabouts, *griots,* wise men, and all

---

* "et le corsair se cabre au bord du gouffre" (204).

the intellectuals believed and asserted that the world had been completed for once and for all. (My trans.)*

Change takes the form of penetration into this closed universe. Djigui dreams of the arrival of a messenger. When the first one comes, he fulfills the twelfth-century prediction that a cavalier dressed in red would arrive, signaling the end of the Keita line and of Soba's independence. The messenger, riding a chestnut-colored horse with a red saddle and wearing a red scabbard, red fez, and red boots, confirmed the prediction, bringing news of "Fadarba" [Faidherbe] whose troops were sweeping Samory's forces before them. His message conveys the news of the change to come. "For eight days and nights I traveled to come here to tell you that the whites of 'Fadarba' are coming south. . . . All the Malinke country will become a land of heresy."†

In a sense, this is merely news of the fall, the long fall from pristine innocence in which the Malinke kingdom had been maintained. The message also succinctly summarizes what was to follow—conquest and colonization. Above all, it is a message that requires translation, for its words can not be understood on their own. The long change that was to come could be said to resemble the announcement of its coming—a change whose meaning was incomprehensible on its own. If the novel reconstitutes the legend of the conquest and colonization of Soba, it is even more concerned with the translation and interpretation of those events.

Almost all of the messenger's communication consists of definitions:

> The master griot plucked the strings of his kora and began to sing, interrupting himself and explaining that "Fadarba" and his men were French, white, Christian Toubabs; Christians, Nazareens, "Nazaras," avowed enemies of Islam. They were impure. Contact with them, as with pork or dogmeat, brought the loss of ritual purity, "*tâhara.*" After having shaken their hands, one must perform the necessary ablutions again to purify oneself before beginning to pray.‡

---

* "Depuis des siècles, les gens de Soba et leurs rois vivaient dans un monde clos à l'abri de toute idée et croyance nouvelles. Protégés par des montagnes, ils avaient réussi, tant bien que mal, à préserver leur indépendance. C'était une société arrêtée. Les sorciers, les marabouts, les griots, les sages, tous les intellectuels croyaient que le monde était définitivement achevé et ils le disaient" (20). All page references to this text are to the 1990 edition, and all translations are my own.

† "Pendant huit soleils et soirs j'ai voyagé pour venir vous annoncer que les Toubabs de 'Fadarba' descendent vers le sud. . . . Tous les pays Mandingue deviendront des terres de l'hérésie" (19).

‡ "Le maître griot pinça les cordes de sa cora et commença par chanter, s'interrompit et expliqua que 'Fadarba' et ses hommes étaient des Français, des Toubabs blancs chrétiens;

The message and the messenger point in several directions at once. "Fadarba" must be explained, and when the messenger first mentions his name, there is an "authorized" explanation placed in parentheses after his name is given: "(By 'Fadarba' he meant Faidherbe, the French general who governed Senegal)."* Here the messenger and his audience are bypassed, and the general reader, who is assumed to be ignorant of Faidherbe, is directly provided with a pithy definition. As the messenger conveys his message, in character, we observe a strange mix of both assumed and unassumed knowledge. Thus, though it is assumed that "Faidherbe" requires explanation, the terms *"griot"* and "cora" are not. The *griot* explains to Djigui and his entourage the meaning of "Français" as "Toubabs blancs chrétiens." But as "Toubab" means "white," and generally by inference also Christian, we can take the words "blancs" and "chrétiens" in the original sentence to be intended as defining Toubab.[3] It is unclear whether it is Djigui or the implied reader who is thought to require this act of translation. Further, "chrétien" itself must next be interpreted, explicitly identifying Djigui as the one in need of the translation. From "nazaréens" the *griot* next switches back to the same creolized vocabulary first used to designate Faidherbe—"Fadarba." And he thus renders "nazaréens" as "Nazaras." This complicated series of moves does not end here, as the explanations, or definitions, of "Nazaras" are then given in terms of local Islamic understanding and practice, including a shift from the Malinke universe to the Arabic, with the term *"tâhara,"* a term presumably unfamiliar to the implied reader, but one that ought to be familiar to the *griot* and his audience.

In short, it appears that as Kourouma is constructing a scene in which the isolated Malinke world is penetrated by outside knowledge, by new words, he is also explaining the world of Islam and of the Malinke to the French, or at least, to French-speaking non-Malinke readers. We might well tax Kourouma for his failure to distinguish between these two tasks, as the need for translating in one direction ought not to be the same as in the other. However, clarity of distinctions on the level of narrators and narratees—intended audiences for ostensible narrations—would seem to matter less than the larger issue of bringing words into a previously closed realm. And this point Kourouma makes explicit when he completes his definition of the closed world of Soba as one whose inhabitants believed

---

les chrétiens, des nazaréens, des 'Nazaras.' Les 'Nazaras' s'avouaient les ennemis de l'Islam; c'étaient des impurs. Leur contact, comme celui du porc et du chien, faisait perdre la pureté rituelle, la *tâhara*. L'orant, après leur avoir serré les mains, doit refaire ses ablutions, se purifier avant d'entrer en prière" (19).

* "(Par 'Fadarba,' il fallait entendre Faidherbe, le général français qui conduit le Sénégal)" (19).

themselves to be masters of words, masters through words: "Certainly it did not mean happiness for everyone, but it seemed clear for each, and thus logical. Everyone believed that they understood, that they knew how to assign a name to each object; believed, thus, that they possessed the world and had mastered it."*

As Djigui receives an entire series of messengers, eight in all, the initial prediction and its power give way to comic repetition, just as Djigui's frantic movements, prayers, and sacrifices reveal the collapse of resistance to Samori and Djigui's realization of his own weakness. This pattern of disenchantment is again presented through the focus on words themselves. As a Muslim, Djigui believes in the divine reality of the holy words, the Koran and prayer. Thus, throughout his life he extolled "the virtue of prayer, and never stopped repeating it. He felt all the unusual words of the Book, and pronounced them with such force and fervor that the king attained the All-Powerful Himself. . ."† However, despite his conviction that he had moved the divine presence by the power of his prayers—"disturbing Him in his Splendor and obliging him to budge"‡—conjuring up the Almighty presence through force of will and word, an eighth messenger arrives to break the illusion. As for Djigui's conviction that Allah would always be at his sides, "It was false; Djigui knew it when he left the mosque"** The pattern of idealization followed by demystification is thus established at the outset.

Lacking any intermediary between himself and the divine, Djigui, like Fama, gives himself up to lengthy prayer, as if there were no gap between the expression of his words and their reception in the divine ear. Similarly, Djigui becomes expert at reading telltale signs himself, as if no other interpreter were required, and as if he himself were the most capable: "The king gave the order to gaze at the sky; no one had read in the clouds the signs of imminent danger that Djigui himself was able to distinguish. He had commanded them to listen; Djigui had been the only one to hear the cries that carried the echoes of the winds blowing in from the mountains."††

---

* "Certes, ce n'était pas le bonheur pour tout le monde, mais cela semblait transparent pour chacun, donc logique; chacun croyait comprendre, savait attribuer un nom à chaque chose, croyait donc posséder le monde, le maîtriser" (20).

† "la vertu de la prière et ne cessa de le dire. Il éprouva tous les mots inusités du Livre, les prononça avec une force et une ferveur telle que le roi atteignit le Tout-Puissant Lui-même . . ." (24).

‡ ". . . Le perturba dans Sa Splendeur et L'obligea à se débusquer" (24)

** "C'était faux; Djigui le sut en sortant de la mosquée" (24).

†† "Le roi avait ordonné de regarder le ciel; aucun n'avait lu dans les nuages les signes de danger imminent que Djigui distinguait. Il leur avait commandés d'écouter; Djigui avait été seul à entendre les cris qu'apportaient les échos des vents soufflant des montagnes"

The ambiguity of the role of interpreter also appertained to Djigui. The barrier between words, between expression in one language and comprehension in another, could be overcome only by an interpreter, a translator. Similarly, the bridge between the divine and the human, the reading of signs and the sending of prayers, could only be crossed by completing the communication across the threshold of understanding. The bridges and lagoons that separated rich from poor, African from European, different nations such as Nikinai from the Côte d'Ebène in *Les Soleils des indépendances,* are now reduced to their most fundamental aspect, the barrier between words, between the signifier, and its systems of signification, and the signified. It is precisely at this level that Roman Jakobson places the essence of the experience of literary change, of defamiliarization: "It is a question, in poetic language, of an essential change in the relationship between the signifier and the signified, as well as between the sign and the concept."*

In the absence of competing spiritual leaders or marabouts, sheltered from the conquest of either European or Muslim proselytizers, and as the ruler of his people, Djigui assumes the role of master of the word, the multiple and ineffable word as Bakhtin would have it, whose properties extend to their owner: "All the Malinke spoke of him, and, because they repeated it, he became ineffable and multiple."† Ironically, Djigui's powers place him beyond the pale of ordinary speakers—he is not only able to attain the ineffable word, he becomes ineffable; he is placed within the discourse of legend. *"Legend would have it* that five times, as they crossed the work site, Diabaté, Samory's messenger, stopped our king" (my stress).‡

The quality of being legendary and ineffable does not bring communication to an end: it imposes a status on and a framework for discourse that implies that what is spoken must be taken as a departure from reality. It implies an elevated or heightened discourse commensurate with the heightened status for the speaker. This is conveyed by the use of the *griot* whose role is to give the king's words a mouth, an opening to speech in which both meaning and prominence are conveyed, in which what is said

---

(16).

* "[I]l s'agit dans le langage poétique d'un changement essentiel du rapport entre le signifiant et le signifié, ainsi qu'entre le signe et le concept" (Jakobson, qtd. in Todorov 1965, 10–11).

† "Tout le Mandingue parla de lui et, à force de le dire, il devient ineffable et multiple" (17).

‡ "La légende prétend que cinq fois le long du chantier, Diabaté, le messager de Samory, arrêta notre roi" (33).

re-presents, that is, both transmits and repeats. "While telling his beads, Djigui spoke just as one recites a prayer, and the *griot,* charged with repeating and transmitting the words of the king, repeated them one after another, like drops of water falling from a boulder in the distant bush."* Between legend and history, as between sacred text and textbook, lies a gap in discourses. The drops of water, with their life-giving properties and heavenly origins, are conveyed by repetition and transmission to the passive waiting earth. Between the silence of the distant bush—"la brousse lointaine"—and the *griot*'s voice repeating the words of the king lies the gap established by power and its authority to speak. It is the gap between truth and lies that is formed when two different discourses are pronounced.

Djigui's sacrifices, including the immolation of three albinos from the distant reaches of his kingdom, saturated the land with blood, and were performed so as to ensure the perpetuity of the Keita line. These were the first of a continuous, never-ending series of exactions, raids, thefts, and deaths that decimated the population. The signs in the sky, the divine inscription that the king read for his own message, were obscenely mixed signals of death and finitude. The first line of the novel gives us this double reading: "Already, in the farthest reaches of the sky, the vultures were sketching out arabesque patterns."† The shock of divine pretensions conveyed by the most earthly of creatures, the scavengers, provides the foundation for lies, laying the groundwork for a second reading following the disasters. Thus, the news of Samory's defeat is characterized as "an uncomfortable truth as well as an awkward position!"‡, while the divine messages received/repeated by the king pass from truth to lies:

> [I]n the morning, the birds, too, have begun to sing the verses that they usually sing at night. As for myself, in my long prayers I felt that I was accomplishing nothing of any coherence. . . . When everything was getting ready to disintegrate, to dissolve, when the truths to which we hold betray us on passing through our lips, betray us by becoming lies, then, by necessity, a messenger arrives.**

---

* "Djigui, tout en égrenant son chapelet, parlait comme on récite une prière, et le griot chargé de redire et de transmettre les paroles du roi les répétait, une après une, comme tombent les gouttes d'eau du rocher dans le silence de la lointaine brousse" (29).

† "Déjà, dans le profond du ciel de Soba, les charognards dessinaient des arabesques" (13).

‡ "Inconfortables vérité et position à la fois!" (29).

** "les oiseaux eux aussi ont commencé à chanter le matin les versets qui habituellement se disent la nuit. Moi-même dans mes longues prières, j'ai senti que je n'atteignait rien de cohérent. . . . Quand tout se prépare à se dissoudre, à s'effriter, quand les vérités que nous tenons, en sortant de notre bouche, nous trahissent pour devenir des mensonges, alors,

The messenger arrives because truth has turned to lies, because the king's construction of truth, of a discourse on reality read from the arabesques of the vultures, becomes too costly—royal control over the people's lives is threatened and the citadel of frozen, permanent, perfect meaning is undone. The messenger's words, another repetition of earlier signs and texts, are like the messenger himself, an iteration of the Muslim text sent as pealing bells to interpellate old truths, and to reveal new ones.[4]

Djigui's reaction is not to retreat, but to build yet higher castle walls: the last messenger announces that he is Kindia Mory Diabaté, the Djéliba, the greatest *griot* since Sundiata and the closest confidant of Samory. His message, whose importance and patent, he claims, is due to his presence, signifies Djigui's demise. He tells Djigui that Samory is rallying all—"tous nos peuples" [all our people]—for a last stand against the French. To make his stand effective, Samory has put a scorched-earth policy into practice, thus requiring Djigui to fall back with Samory at Djimini, and burn Soba. But as the fall of the Keita dynasty is predicted to occur when the city is destroyed, Djigui finds himself trapped—no longer ineffable, merely speechless: "Djigui ceased to tell his beads and for a moment remained tongue-tied."[*] Thus he decides to construct a *tata* "with fire and blood."[†] He mobilizes an army of slave labor: "they began to build the most gigantic *tata* in Malinkeland."[‡] The *tata* surrounds the town on three sides, while the hill behind the town on its fourth side is protected by sorcery. Intended to protect Soba, to ensure its independence, its isolation purports to keep the external world outside—a wall of supreme autarky, a Maginot line not only of defense, but of infinite dimensions: a *tata* "whose crest would be lost in the clouds, whose base would extend from Soba to the sea, a *tata* of infinite height and depth. The most titanic construction in the lands of the Blacks!"[**]

The contradictions between the "pronunciamentos" of the politicians during the suns of Independence and the miserable conditions of people's lives inspired Fama to curse the "mensonges," the "bâtarde de bâtardise." Djigui's wall was no less ephemeral in its base: exactions, forced labor, slave labor, sacrifices ("including even a dwarf and an albino"[††]), which

---

forcément, arrive un messager" (30).

[*] "Djigui cessa d'égrener le chapelet et resta un instant interdit" (31).

[†] "par le feu et le sang" (31)

[‡] "ils commencèrent à bâtir le plus gigantesque *tata* du Mandingue" (31).

[**] "dont la crête devait se perdre dans les nuages, l'empattement aller de Soba à la mer, un *tata* en hauteur et profondeur, infini. La plus titanesque construction de la Négritie!" (33).

[††] "même un nain et un albinos" (32)

denoted effort and power in the legendary account, now faced another measure, the more pedestrian, historical judgment given by Samory's *griot*, Diabaté: "Your *tata* will not be the truth."* Though Djigui is willing to stop at no effort to construct his *tata,* he is not willing to leave Soba. He is tied to his power, and in his human apprehensions over the conquering French can be easily swayed to supply even more forced labor, more slave labor, to exact more goods and arms from his people, till they are bled dry—just as he does later in collaboration with the French authorities so that he might be given a train whose tracks would reach Soba. This is the finite and humble side of humanity that Diabaté attempts to reveal to him: "Stop! We are limited and will never accomplish infinite works."†

The irony of the narrative demolishes the wall: the French troops come over the bewitched hill and take the town without a fight. The *tata,* work of infinite pretensions and exorbitant costs, no doubt recalling the great cathedral of Yamoussoukru constructed by Houphouët-Boigny, finds its echoes in monuments to earthly power. The term "*tata*" is never explained: no glossary or parenthetical definition is given to the reader, who is left to infer its meaning. Gradually other terms acquire degrees of meaning: thus we learn that "*diéli*" is the name for the caste of *griots* and that it signifies "blood." The script employed by the French in Francophone Africa imposes a *j* sound on Di: Diéli thus corresponds to Djéli, and the *ba* that ends the noun is its definite article. Similarly, we learn that "Djigui" also has a significance, that of the rogue male chased from the herd by a younger usurper (161). The sense we give to "*tata,*" "Djéliba," and "Djigui" is shaped by their usage and context: we incorporate these terms in their original untranslated form into a narrative discourse that insists on giving both their frozen, original signification and the demystified form, the more banal meanings acquired through the narrator's "historical" perception. Thus the nobility of Djéliba and Djigui—linked by the blood tie of brotherhood, the legendary origins, and the aristocratic society they governed—is continually subjected to ironic disenchantment, so that we are finally able to pronounce the words without prostrating ourselves in the process. This is the depth of the change imposed upon the Malinke: a change in the foundation of words and of worlds. Djéliba seeks to return to his home in order to come to terms with this change:

> I am rejoining my Konia . . . to learn these new truths. Infinity, which belongs to the sky, has changed its words: Malinkeland will nevermore

---

* "Votre *tata* ne sera pas la vérité" (31).

† "Arrêtez! Nous sommes limités et n'achevons jamais les oeuvres infinies" (33).

be the land of men of prowess. I am a griot, thus a man of the Word. Each time that words change meaning and things their symbols, I return to my land of birth to begin anew: to relearn history and the new names of humans, animals, and things.*

Djéliba's return home, like Fama's, risks bringing him nothing more than a knowledge of the end, and not of a beginning. As Djigui stays at Soba, the news must be brought to him, and he lives a conquered ruler under the administration of the French commandant. Foreign occupation and rule, however, are nothing more than the catalyst: the forces of change that will represent the battle for Soba are centered around two new figures who arrive in Soba: the interpreter and the marabout.

Interpreter and Marabout

The most important figure at this turning point in African history—the inception of colonialism—is neither the new ruler nor the old conquered one, but their mediator, the interpreter. The *griot* Djéliba is wrong when he thinks that the new epoch of subservience will bring only "silence, regret, and nostalgia."† He is articulating only the *griot*'s point of view. In contrast, the interpreter insists that talk of honor, challenges, magic, and royal authority is not only finished, it is "bluster" ["(des) rodomonta-des"], not worth translating into the "language of the birds," which was how French sounded to the Malinke. As a Soumaré, the interpreter has a joking relationship with the ruling Keitas, so that the serious, elevated speech of the king and his *griot* is replaced by the language of the world of experience, the language of insult and jest made legitimate, the language of demystification: "Like all Keita you are an unrealistic braggart. I haven't translated a single word of your treacherous bluster."‡ Appropriately, the interpreter's intervention proves felicitous, judicious: had he translated Keita Djigui's challenges, the king would have been shot. Instead, Djigui learned to swallow his defeat, to acquire new words.

Thus, in the course of his first appearance, the interpreter not only saves the king, he replaces Djigui's and the *griot*'s discourse with his own wisdom, his own realistic words. The interpreter becomes the key figure

---

* Je rejoins mon Konia . . . apprendre les nouvelles vérités. L'infini qui est au ciel a changé de paroles; le Mandingue ne sera plus la terre des preux. Je suis un griot, donc un homme de la parole. Chaque fois que les mots changent de sens et les choses de symboles, je retourne à la terre qui m'a vu naître pour tout recommencer: réapprendre l'histoire et les nouveaux noms des hommes, des animaux et des choses (41).

† "le silence, le regret, la nostalgie" (43)

‡ "Comme tous les Keita tu es un fanfaron irréaliste. Je n'ai pas traduit un traître mot de tes rodomontades" (36).

in the new age, suggesting that the real battle to be fought for the future is not between the French and the Malinke, not between Faidherbe and Samory, but within the Malinke community. Specifically, it will be between the ironizing interpreter and the adherents of the competing Islamic order, represented by the Hamallist marabout from the north, a second interloper in the Soba community. The rise of the marabout and his influence corresponds to the gradual marginalization of the *griot*. It represents less an authentic conversion than a futile diversion from the harsh realities introduced into African history by the successors of "Fadarba." Between the spiritual world of the marabout and the realpolitik of the interpreter, once again we encounter the familiar concept of the word and its attendant truths/lies, which forms the central issue.

With the coming of the new era the interpreter silences Djigui, teaching him that the new order and power now control the word. This new era begins with the interpreter listening attentively to the white captain, and then turning and laughing in Djigui's face like a hyena. He explains what defeat means to Djigui Keita: When two caimans fight, the winner becomes the master totem animal, the crocodile, and the loser becomes a poor grey lizard ("magouillat"): "Glory and joy to the victors! Unhappiness to the vanquished!"* As Djigui prepares to respond, he is silenced by Soumaré, the interpreter, who teaches him the new protocol: "When a Toubab speaks, we Blacks shut up, remove our hats and our shoes, and listen."† The interpreter explains, and by his explanation establishes the rules of power that put in place new values: "the times that are coming will be ruled by money."‡ Taxes, forced labor, servitude—"outrages, défis, mépris, injures, humiliations, colère rageuse" (9) [outrage, defiance, scorn, insults, humiliation, furious anger]—all inadequate translations of the experience of "monnè," a word known only to the vanquished.

The lessons of power require a new vocabulary. With the installation of the white authorities comes the need for manual labor. As slavery was now abolished, a new way of designating the same obligation had to be invented: forced labor was instituted under the title of "prestation" [service], and those who were requisitioned to fulfill the new obligation were "prestataires" [forced laborers]. The problem of interpreting becomes one of simultaneously communicating power and disguising its nature.

---

* "Gloire et joie aux vainqueurs! Malheurs aux vaincus!" (53).

† "Quand un Toubab s'exprime, nous, Nègres, on se tait, se décoiffe, se déchausse et écoute" (54).

‡ "l'ère qui commence sera celle de l'argent" (57).

This leads to a new language delivered in corrupt form. Lacking the correspondent word in Malinke, the interpreter essentially transcribes the French, initiating both a diglossia and its transformation: "the interpreter employed the word 'prestataire' in our language, which the *griot* could scarcely pronounce and changed into *pratati*."* No sooner does the new language insert itself than the new ratios of power and control over speech are asserted: "The king would have liked knowing what *pratati* were, but the interpreter signaled him to wait and began to converse with the lieutenant. Suddenly he gave the command to listen to him (we were already all ears). . . ."†

The interpreter proceeds to announce that the whites are good, that they abolished slavery, that the requisitioned labor was to be only temporary. Subsequently the selected women are marched off to serve the victorious troops, while the men are taught to build the new administrative buildings and housing. The dramatic toil of forced labor, to be accelerated horrifically with the colonial administration's railroad project, followed by the severe demands for labor and production accompanying the two World Wars, was to be the price of the new regime that now brought with it civilization, a word for which no equivalent existed in Malinke. The interpreter renders it "to become Toubab."‡ The two "laws" of the Toubabs, the law of taxes and of comfort, ushered in the new era of money, which depended on both for its definition of value. Taxes could come through labor, gold, or human bodies—everything, down to the loincloth ["cache-sex"], could be subject to appropriation as payment for the taxes. And to ensure that the chiefs met their obligation, "fire" and "pepper" would be used. Kourouma had already written that literature could not be produced as long as one was walking on burning embers.[5] In *Monnè, outrages et défis* colonization is depicted as one long march over hot coals.

The gaps between languages come out in two ways: on the level of semantics and on the level of discourse. If *monnè* on the one side and *pratati* on the other, could only cross the gap in twisted or partial form, the more subtle significations of political value in each culture remained inaccessible to the other. Thus, there are Malinke or Arabic words that are not

---

* "l'interprète utilisa dans notre langue le mot 'prestataires' que le griot eut de la peine à articuler et à changer en *pratati*" (55).

† "Le roi eût aimé savoir ce qu'étaient des *pratati*, mais l'interprète lui fit signe d'attendre et se mit à converser avec le lieutenant. Brusquement il commanda qu'on l'écoutât (nous étions déjà, tous, tout oreilles) . . ." (55).

‡ "devenir toubab" (57)

translated into French ("lougan," "racket," etc.) either because the context makes them clear enough, because their sense is assumed to be accessible to the reader (an inconsistency as some are translated and others are not), or because they can not be translated. Most generally we can say that all words in the text, Malinke or French, are at once translated and untranslatable. The model is established at the beginning when one finds the word *monnè* presented in the opening epigraph. The Centenarian reacts to the notion that this word, whose meaning is explained, still can not be translated into French: "Because their language did not have the word, the Centenary concluded that the French did not know [the experience of] *monnew*" (epigraph).*

By the same token, toward the end of the novel the Centenarian is presented with a French word for which no Malinke equivalent can be found—a word that may be thought of as the supplement to a translatable vocabulary. The condition of possibility for the existence of such a supplement is the generally untranslatable nature of the experiences of the two cultures. Thus extensive attention is paid to the gap this opens up: "The old man twisted his lips in different directions without succeeding in pronouncing the word, which was untranslatable."† This word, "réaction," is then added to the stock of political words that could not be understood, and that thus become "sigui ya son." But "sigui ya son" is not only lost on the non-Malinke reader, it can be recovered only in approximate form: it signified more or less—before and after, and not directly on: ". . . that which *could* be translated as 'be seated while waiting' or *hiriasson,* which, *without having a precise meaning,* suggested a passing ill because of the final consonance *son*" (my stress).‡

As the two languages lend themselves to approximations of each other, absorbing and twisting the sounds (*sons*) and meaning (*sens*) of the other, the result is less a creolized tongue than a *charabia.* A *charabia* is, in its origins, the language of the Other—or, as the language of the Other is never one's own (if we can conceive of "one's own language" as being a language that we understand), then *charabia* is, in fact, the form of linguistic communication that, because it is the other's, is precisely *not* a language. Thus *charabia*

---

* "Parce que leur langue ne possédait pas le mot, le Centenaire en conclut que les Français ne connaissaient pas les *monnew*" (9).

† "Le vieillard tordait les lèvres dans différents sens, sans parvenir à prononcer le mot qui était intraduisible" (270).

‡ ". . . ce qui *pouvait* se traduire par 'assoie-toi en attendant' ou *hiriasson,* ce qui, *sans avoir un sens précis,* renvoyait à un malheur passager à cause de la consonance terminale *son*" (270; my stress).

is the Arabic word for the language of those other Arabic speakers from the Maghreb, the Berbers, whose speech rendered Arabic *barbar*-ous, broken, incomprehensible . . . In *Monnè, outrages et défis,* all language that lies in the space between the two cultures, between the master and the slave, is *charabia.* It is *charabia* when appropriated as one's own, and *charabia* when received across the gap: "the Blacks are born liars," the narrator-cum-Toubab intones. "It is impossible to write a true history of the Malinke."* He then goes on to explain that, according to the African chronicles, the Spanish flu epidemic of 1919 led to such ravages that the spirits of the dead had to dig their own graves, set their own affairs in order, and bury themselves, while the vultures sang mock suras from the Koran. The conclusion: "What firm inferences can be drawn from such extravagances?"†

On the other side of the chasm of incomprehension lay the French version of reality, which, when appropriated by the African soldiers, produced its own form of incomprehension. "They spoke French (it was later that we learned that it was some gibberish [charabia] of their own, which the native French didn't understand)." The narrator concludes with the ironic dismissal: "Their speech bristled with elogies, lies, and marvels. They acted as though they had forgotten our dialects and savage manners in two years."‡

Multiple versions of events emerged on both sides of the gap, with the *charabia* produced across the bridge, continuing to frame the narration of events. Djigui's wife Moussokoro prsented one version of her life, but the narrator concludes, "What truth was there in this account of the events? Certain co-wives, including the first wife, the official favorite, responded: 'Not a grain. . . . Only one, lies, fantasies.'"**

All of the long chronicle of Djigui, of the Malinke people, of the history of colonization, is thus made available only across an untranslatable chasm at the edges of which the translator and the marabout stand, uttering one truth into the ears of those on one side and another on the other. In between, to both camps, is fabulation, *mensonges, charabia,* truth not so

---

* "Les Noirs naissent mensongers. Il est impossible d'écrire une histoire vraie des Mandingues" (85).

† "Que tirer de solide de telles extravagances?" (85).

‡ "Ils parlèrent français (c'est plus tard que nous saurions que c'était là un charabia à eux, que les natifs de France n'entendaient pas). Leurs dires étaient hérissés d'éloges, de mensonges et de merveilles. Ils prétendaient avoir en deux ans oublié nos dialectes et nos manières sauvages" (86).

** "Qu'y avait-il de vrai dans cette relation des événements? Certaines coépouses dont la première femme, la préférée officielle, répondaient: 'Pas un grain. . . . Un seul, des menteries, des fabulations'" (142).

desperate for its vision of failures, as for its embracing of the necessity for survival at a time when words were always used as the ultimate form of mystification.

Final Turning: The Second Law of the Toubab

For the few who collaborated and profited, comfort was possible, bringing mirrors, umbrellas, needles, handkerchiefs. In the Caribbean a scarf received from the master was "Tanky-massa." The "Wabenzi," the wealthy class of Mercedes Benz owners of the suns of independence, had their beginnings with the trading counter and the tanky-massas. As for Djigui, whose honor and position embodied the ideal of Malinke values, the price of his tanky-massa was a bit higher, but the principle identical. The commandant's promise of a train sufficed to convince Djigui to impose on his people all the requisitions, the "pratati," needed by the new regime. The train, the road, its labor, and civilization all communicated the same values: as Soumaré explained, the road was "the lace of the sack containing the feet and the eyes of civilization."*

If colonization served to crystallize the issues of value at the heart of Malinke society, it was the interpreter who raised the essential questions, beginning with the relationship between force and value, which he put in ironic terms: "Chief Keita, you yourself were born into power and you know that all this is clear, legal, and human; force is the truth that is above truths."† By referring to Djigui's inherited position of power, Soumaré explains that the relationship between force and value was not introduced by the colonialists, but represents a continuation of the mystification of power. This power would seem to constitute an answer to the religious, specifically Muslim mystifications of *Les Soleils des indépendances* in which the radical relativism of "nothing is good or evil in itself" (72)‡ is answered by, "It is the word that transforms a deed into what is good or turns it to evil."** Transfiguration, elevation, sublimation, the changing of mere figure, or deed, into value, into abstract goodness, is set against the pedestrian act of turning into evil—"tourne[r] en mal"—which echoes the betrayal and cowardice of one who turns back ("retourner"), as Fama does on the bridge, and as Djigui is to do as well. We see this several times in *Monnè, outrages et défis*. After rising from his prayer, after having made new

---

* "le cordon du sac contenant les pieds et les yeux de la civilisation" (69).

† "Chef Keita, vous êtes vous-même né dans le pouvoir et vous savez que tout cela est clair, licite et humain; la force est la vérité qui est au-dessus des vérités" (68).

‡ "rien en soi n'est bon, rien en soi n'est mauvais" (109).

** "C'est la parole qui transfigure un fait en bien ou le tourne en mal" (109).

sacrifices so that his train might arrive, Djigui heads forthrightly toward the commandant's residence: "without ever looking back ["se retourner"] (it is evildoers, those who hesitate, who believe in neither their own spirit or in the All-Powerful, who look behind themselves)."*

The notion of turning or looking back, both expressed by the French "se retourner," is thus introduced as defining the mystification of Power—both in its royal and its religious form. By linking Djigui's reign to the train, to the rivers of sacrificial blood, to his delusions of honor and rule, and by presenting it within the context of his actual state of subjugation and manipulation, Kourouma exposes the lowly instinctual basis underlying the high-sounding tones assigned to ruling values. This theme is echoed throughout. When Djigui is driven from his villages in the countryside by the *revenants* or restless spirits of all the victims of forced requisitions, he is forced to return to Soba, defeated by the wretched conditions of his subjects: "Djigui was undone! had been repudiated by his subjects. *He did not look back,* it would have been cowardly" (my stress).†
After the ideal of the courage not to turn, not to turn back (not to turn again, or to re-turn), the irony inevitably follows.

On Djigui's return to Soba, there was a long night of prayers dubbed the "nuit de retournement" (127) [night of the return], after which Djigui decided to forsake the project of obtaining a train, to return to the past, and so to end the forced labor, the conscriptions, requisitions, and *pratati.* Only then did he learn that he had been deposed by the administration and replaced by his son Béma. The ironic turn of events, embodied and magnified by the interpreter, mocked his illusions:

> Djigui calculated and calculated until he came to believe in the return of the old days when he was the sole ruler of Soba. These illusions and dreams led the interpreter to guffaw so noisily that he unleashed a thousand more mocking laughs, a veritable racket, which astounded the king. Djigui didn't *turn back* to see where the hullaballoo came from and who organized it.‡ (my stress)

The laughter provoked by Djigui's impotent attempt to turn back the clock was the echo of a world to which change had long since come. The change of regimes, authority, vocabulary, and leadership was a laughable

---

* "sans jamais se retourner (ce sont les méfiants, les hésitants, ceux qui ne croient ni à leur aura ni au Tout-Puissant qui regardent après eux)" (98).

† "Djigui était défait! avait été congédié par ses sujets. *Il ne se retourna pas,* c'eût été lâche" (125; my stress).

‡ Djigui supputa, supputa jusqu'à croire au retour des temps anciens où il était seul maître de Soba. Ces illusions et rêves firent rire l'interprète aux éclats. D'une façon bruyante qui déclencha milles autres rires moqueurs, un véritable vacarme qui abasourdit le roi. Djigui *ne se retourna pas* pour rechercher d'où provenait le chahut et qui l'organisait" (128; my stress).

change since it was only apparent. The change of power from father to son was equally illusory: patriarchal force was still the base of values, with domination and expropriation their principal forms. Where the change was perhaps most marvelous and least obvious was in the mask and features of reality to which only an alteration in narrative form and style could attest—altering the relationship between signifier and signified.

At the beginning there is a struggle between two narrative forms: the high-sounding effusions of the *griot*, and the ironic tones of the interpreter. Djigui was the great ruler, the embodiment of honor and strength as long as the former could hold forth, as long as the memory of the narrator could evoke legend. But colonialism was not the stuff of legends, and its incomprehensible words could not be appropriated and incorporated into traditional forms of discourse. To represent the past demanded a master of the word—and Djéliba explained that he would have to return home to acquire the new names for things. That return voyage was never made, as the king's presents of women, horses, and goods sufficed to persuade the *griot* to give up his plan to return home.

The path forward, for the Malinke, was also blocked: when the white man spoke, the black man was silent and listened to the Toubab's new, untranslatable words. Yet the change in regime was indeed real; the son indeed swallowed power; and Djigui himself knew the "nuit de retournement" [night of the return] without appreciating its significance. The narrative representation of the key moment of change, like the dramatic shift in narrative voice from the third to the first person, from the Malinke people to Djigui himself, occurs as if by magic, and the figure of Djigui that emerges is clothed in the new terms of magical realism. No longer the overthrown leader, the pathetic figure of the African past, he extends the past through his unbelievable longevity and is transfigured into an immortal, the "Centenarian" whose unreality can be matched only by the ironist's disbelief:

> Because of the winds that he brought when he came and went, the lights that illuminated him constantly, the flood of words that praised him, and especially the force and power that he held, we the people of Soba, his subjects, stopped for an instant and turned around to look at him mount his horse, and we were surprised to see that our chief had changed, had changed a lot.
>
> Yes, he had changed. The vultures avoided flying over him, the suns did not set for him; he had to approach a woman only once to cause her to be with child. He rapidly reached the age of one hundred and twenty-five.*

---

* "A cause des vents qu'il remuait dans ses déplacements, des lumières qui sans cesse l'éclai-

Immediately after this statement delineating the new magical features of the king comes the interpreter's rendition: "The Blacks of Soba don't know how to calculate their age."* Practicing an itinerant form of planting, he explained, they calculate age by the number of times the fields are left to lie fallow after the birth of an individual. As a field is customarily left to lie fallow every five years, the number of fallow periods occurring during an individual's lifetime is multiplied by five to provide his or her age. The white doctor completed the scornful revisions of the interpreter, affirming that "the Blacks are liars." Djigui could not be more than seventy-five years old, which is already a considerable age; because of the "lack of hygiene," he asserted, "the Blacks rarely reach the age of fifty."†

The figure of one hundred twenty-five was neither scientifically correct nor incorrect: it represented the newly acquired magical face of the ruler, his changed position. His age was as much a marvel as the figure of Djigui himself, representing a threshold for humans: "One hundred twenty-five, the fatal, maximal age that none of us ought to surpass."‡ To attribute to someone more than one hundred twenty-five years was to cast an evil spell on that person, so the people of Soba learned to define Djigui's age as "approaching" one hundred twenty-five. No longer a political ruler, he now had the attributes of a special spiritual being, attributes manifest through his words: "His words kept the crickets away, rendered sterile women fertile, ruined and impoverished the haughty and the impudent."** Converted into master sorcerer and healer, he performed miracles and healings with the same distance and detachment as when he had performed sacrifices or warded off offended spirits. He embodied the mystery of nobility, and his magical apparatus was represented with as much unreality as were the sadistic actions of his counterpart, Saïf, in *Le Devoir de violence* (Ouologuem 1968). Indeed, like Saïf, or more especially, like the

---

raient, des flots de paroles qui le célébraient et surtout de la force et du pouvoir qu'il tenait, nous, ceux de Soba, ses sujets, nous sommes un instant arrêtés et retournés pour le regarder monter à cheval et avons été surpris de constater que notre chef avait changé, beaucoup changé. . . .

   "Oui, il avait changé. Les vautours évitaient de le survoler, les soleils ne se couchaient pas pour lui; il n'approchait pas une femme plus d'une fois pour lui appliquer un enfant. Il a rapidement atteint cent vingt-cinq ans" (99).

* "Les Nègres de Soba ne savent pas calculer leur âge" (99).

† "Les Nègres sont des menteurs. . . . par manque d'hygiène, les Noirs atteignent rarement la cinquantaine" (100).

‡ "Cent vingt-cinq, âge fatidique, maximal qu'aucun humain de chez nous doit dépasser" (100).

** "Ses paroles éloignaient les criquets, rendaient fécondes les femmes stériles, ruinaient et appauvrissaient les orgueilleux et les impudents" (100).

sempiternal patriarchal figure of the dictator in Garcia Marquez's fiction, he lives the suns of Samory's wars, of French conquest and colonialism, and the suns of politics, before succumbing on the eve of Independence.

His departure could only be expressed in terms of the figure of returning, of the final crossing along the infinitely turning surface of the Möbius strip—a turning backward that would lead out of the endless coil. This is the regress to which irony leads, a self-consciousness that can only express awareness of its inability to arrive at the final resolution, an awareness of the completeness and harmony from which it is alienated. This is the irony of the ruler's powerlessness: usurped by his son Béma and by the French, he sees his honor called into question as Béma falsely claims his father's support in the political campaign for control of the country on the eve of Independence. His own weapon is to return to Toukoro, the city where the initial power of the arriving Keita was established, signifying his abdication and the end of the Keita dynastic rule. The only power left him lies in ironic negation, a negation that returns us to the original act of resistance against the French organized by Samory: "Djigui let fly Samory's famous dictum: 'When a man refuses, he says no.' "* However, even the power to say no was beyond him alone: without his *griot*, he could not speak or act. "He realized that the Keita, after so many years of rule, were departing without the words, the fitting praises of a great *griot*. It was inconceivable. . ."†

With Djéliba gone, a "maître de la parole de l'évènement" (276) [master of the word for the occasion] had to be found. Djélicini, a raggedy replacement, without even "an iota of reason,"‡ plays Sancho Panza to Djigui's last stand, even down to his mount. Lacking a proper courser of his own, he is reduced to borrowing a peasant's ridiculous nag described mockingly as "goussaut, pinçard, bouleux"—farfetched attributes indicating the clumsy and crude proportions and gait of the beast. Correspondingly, the foolish praise singer cries out, "Your griot, my Lord, is ready,"** so that, for the second time on his final, defiant journey, Djigui turns around—"[il] se retourna." The verb, so carefully prepared from the beginning, providing the limit of honorable action, sets the stage for the ancient patriarch's last scene. The act of turning back or around invades the language itself, as if the tropes of speech controlled the speaker and his

---

* "Djigui lança la fameuse parole samorienne: 'Quand un homme refuse, il dit non'" (275).

† "il s'avisa que les Keita, après tant de siècles de règne, partaient sans les mots, les louanges idoines d'un grand griot. C'était inconcevable . . ." (275–76).

‡ "un bout de raison" (276)

** "Votre griot, Seigneur, est prêt" (276)

acts. Thus, as Djigui declared his readiness to go forward, he "returned" through his action, through his symbolic assumption of former accents, and through his oxymoronic pronouncement—a statement best described as unintentionally ironic: "The Centenary turned around and declaimed, always speaking with a Samorian accent, 'The departure has arrived.' " *
The narration mimics the same inverted speech patterns, describing the beginning as an ending, a return: "the convoy started off and began the Keita's return to their original Toukoro, a return that the Senufo, the Malinke . . . had thought impossible. The start was without fanfare as if it were not a question of Djigui's end, as well as that of the Keita and thus of all the Malinke."†

The ironic gap between Djigui's illusions of nobility and a pathetic reality continues to be evoked as the convoy proceeds and as the *griot*'s chant of praise breaks out. By the time Djélicini reaches the fourth praise song, the *griot*, whose "folie" didn't detract from his talent, has fallen so far behind that Djigui no longer hears him. But reality had long since dropped out of Djigui's sight, and he now lives in the memory of Djéliba's great praise names that echo in his head by the thousands: the man nursed by the sea cow, the black buffalo with horns loaded with nests and haunted by clouds of swallows, and so forth.

Djigui's praise names bring back his memories—his past, his *tata,* the French, the wars of Samory, and Allama, the founder of the Keita dynasty. Djigui has become the sum of his memories—each attribute, each praise name reconstructing an ancestor recalled from the past. As the product of these words, of the *griot*'s memory, and of his past, he seeks to complete himself through the word, and specifically through the name—as if its repetition does not constitute an interaction as much as an evocation.

In his refutation of Husserl, Derrida challenges the ground of pure being, pure truth, pure essence, on the basis of the repetition, the iteration of signs. Intuitive truth, the goal of Hegel's transcendental consciousness, can be expressed only through signification. It relies on a concept of presence as self-identical and self-sufficient, what Michael Ryan calls "a ground of absolute truth" (Ryan 1984, 26). Like its ground, the sign of this truth is itself characterized by undivided unicity and immediacy. However, "a sign can

---

* "Le Centenaire se retourna, toujours avec l'accent samorien, déclama: 'Le départ est arrivé'" (276).

† "Le convoi démarra et commença ce retour des Keita dans leur Toukoro originel, retour que Sénoufos, Malinkés . . . avaient cru irréalisable. Le début fut sans éclat comme s'il ne s'agissait pas de la fin de Djigui, des Keita et donc de tout le Mandingue" (277).

function only by repeating something prior to it—the code that allows one to recognize it as a sign—and by being repeatable beyond the point of its utterance" (26), a fact especially obvious in the act of reception. The sign is thus inevitably split internally "by the structure of repetition which makes it possible and simultaneously renders its self-identity impossible" (26–27). What Djigui sought in the name was precisely the opposite of this Derridean sign: not an internally split function but an absolute, self-identical essence. Not one in which the reception of its signification depended on the codes of sender and receiver, but one that stood beyond the particularity of subject. He sought, in fact, the divine essence. And this was precisely what is mocked through the interpreter, with his broken signs, his incomprehensible vocabulary, words twisted into misspoken efforts at disguised acts of signification—such as "civilization" for "becoming Toubab," and "*pratati.*" The disappearance of the interpreter marked the discrepancy between Djigui's adherence to an impossible communication system and the new twists of the language of the colonial power.

But the old system of power, no less ridden with euphemistic expressions for exploitation and oppression, could not provide the perfect model for naming either. It required another presence at the Bolloda, a new arrival after the old ruler's fall from power, to provide the model of naming, and that was the Hamallist marabout from the north, Yacouba. With Yacouba the search for the All Powerful took a more vigorous turn, and it was centered on the utterance of the divine names—a task as complete, and as endless, as the list of names themselves:

> We ceaselessly searched for the All Powerful who is never far for the one who sincerely desires Him. Old age reminded us with each step that the road was not now long; with each step we looked far ahead and behind to make our repentance: He is also merciful. His possibilities like his names are innumerable and we all wished to repeat them in the brief time that was still allotted us.*

The passage over the bridge, our figure for change, is situated within a time frame in which the future and the past have reality while the present disappears from view. This might be thought of as the opposite of the time frame of the interpreter, for whom the immediacy of the spoken word in the present is, as for Husserl, the full source of reality. For Yacouba it is the

---

* "Nous étions sans cesse en quête du Tout Puissant qui ne se perd jamais pour qui le désire sincèrement. La vieillesse nous rappelait à chaque pas que le chemin n'était plus long, à chaque pas, nous regardions loin devant et derrière pour nous repentir: Il est aussi miséricorde. Ses possibilités comme ses surnoms sont innombrables et nous voulions les dire tous dans le court délai qui nous était encore imparti" (165).

region beyond, the other side of the bridge, that is real; for the juggler and tightrope walker, as Nietzsche would have it, it is the slip in the present that counts. Djigui lives in both worlds: the prayers at Bolloda form a mystical reality consistently denied by the dusty, sunlit world outside the walls of the mosque and the palace. Yacouba's presence is denied by that of the interpreter: they each must constitute their presence in circles apart from each other.

Thus the hierarchies of the Malinke world continue to coexist: in the first circle, the sacred tree with the "boa totem" and the "oiseaux gendarmes" [percher birds], and at the foot of the tree the Centenarian ruler. On the periphery, the ironic negation of power and glory, the beggars, the blind and the lepers. The second circle is made of Yacouba and his disciples, while beyond their realm of spirituality lie the savannah and the burning reality of the sun. Finally on the highest level, "incommensurable" in the sky, is Allah, the object of everyone's attention at Bolloda. From the world of those under the tree to the realm beyond the sky a path is formed by the repetition of God's innumerable names ["surnoms innombrables"]. We can easily pass from a temporality in which the present is absent to an act of naming what can not be named—not only because the names are infinite, but because they are never the actual sound of the divine presence, but an approximative signification, a "surnom" linked to a series that is "innombrable," and, thus, in a sense equally distant from our grasp as that which is also unnameable ["innommable"].

Yacouba is the intermediary between this unnameable reality and the people gathered around the tree, just as the interpreter is the intercessor between the two realms of the French and the Malinke. "Yacouba was the mediator between HIM and us."* His prayers at night, the suras murmured by his disciples naming the Unnameable, stretched through the hours till dawn, when the sun dissipated the mist and dew, exposing the Koranic school "in all its nakedness: an impoverished, dusty worthless entity, with a man waving a long whip in the midst of starving children in rags, covered with ashes and sores, tortured into singing out loud."† In the light of day, Yacouba disappeared.

All this is echoed in Djigui's final path: the *griot*'s calling out of his names, his recollection of past glories and defeats and of the innumerable

---

* "Yacouba était le médiateur entre LUI et nous" (165).

† "dans sa nudité: un rien pauvre et poussiéreux, avec un homme agitant son long fouet, au milieu d'enfants familiques, en guenilles, couverts de cendre et de gerçures qu'on torturait pour qu'ils s'égossillent" (166).

praises Djéliba had sung for him; the repetitions that echo not only ancestors but the model of repetitive naming elevated as worship of the divine,
in which the speaker continually seeks to deny the present, the presence of
immediate reality: the word identified by what lies beyond it and by a
wholeness and presence it lacks in itself. Yet the lack can not be denied:
Djigui can not remember his origins, his past, his efforts to construct the
infinite, the *tata,* without also recalling the failure, the ruin of the wall, the
rebellion and dishonor cast on him by his son. And as he is brought back
to the present, for the last time, he turns around, "il se retourne," seeking
to find his son, to find a reason that would permit him not to go forward.
Here the final irony turns on the weakness and dishonor of the king, his
human side, the accommodations to shame and *monnè*. And in the magnif-
icence of delusion, a patchwork *griot* on a borrowed nag sings the ultimate
words of encouragement to Djigui so that he might not return—words
that echoed El Hadj Omar and Samory Touré in their resistance:

> The hippopotamus [Djigui's totem] sinks in too deeply
> to turn back on its steps;
> The word of the noble is a mountain
> it is not taken up repeatedly;
> Death is a virtue when life is *monnè*.*

The final irony can not be denied, for even the project of resistance
and the act of naming are reduced by demystification. As Djigui spurs his
steed, the horse refuses to go forward, and as the Centenarian then stands
in his stirrups, so as to immolate himself on his spear, his heart fails him
and he falls—"the body came unhooked [from the horse's mane] and
hung there."†

The nostalgia for Djigui, the love of words, honor, glory, even the
sublime, can not be denied the believer: "for us believers the quivering
and blessed call of the muezzin ... always caught at a corner of our
hearts."‡ But for the beggars and cripples, on the periphery of the circle of
those who pray, the harsher reality of the endless sun exposes another
world: a future not filled with a divine presence, but with "mensonges,"
disguised and debased: the hard road. "Les indépendances politiques"

---

* "L'hippopotame [Djigui's totem] s'envase trop profondément
  pour revenir sur ses pas;
  La parole du noble est une montagne
  elle ne se reprend pas;
  La mort est vertu quand la vie est *monnè*" (278).

† "le corps se décrocha et pendit" (279).

‡ "l'appel chevrotant et béni du muezzin ... toujours nous tord, à nous croyants, quelque
  chose dans le bout du coeur" (160).

engendered charismatic leaders, single parties, derisory pronouncements, revolution, "and other myths,"* and an endless litany of godless slogans, "a hodgepodge of slogans" ["salmigondis de slogans"], whose vapid substance it is the perpetual task of the ironic narrator to expose.

---

* "puis les autres mythes" (287)

Chapter 12

▼▼▼▼▼▼▼▼▼▼

The Dance of the Creole

Henri Lopes, *Le Chercheur d'Afriques*

> *Blackness—*
> *the Black of it,*
> *the rust-red of it,*
> *the milk and cream of it,*
> *the tan and yellow-tan of it,*
> *the deep-brown middle-brown high-brown of it,*
> *the "olive" and ochre of it—*
> *Blackness*
> *marches on.*

—Gwendolyn Brooks, "Primer for Blacks"

For Ahmadou Kourouma, the act of crossing over entails passage over a bridge. For Henri Lopes, the crossing occurs between two different people. The central issue in Lopes's work is *métissage* [crossing/crossbreeding], as much a condition as a passage.

Where Kourouma emphasizes the act of interpretation and the importance of language, Lopes focuses on the act of love, treating it as the source and the solution of the problems essential to his characters. Kourouma enumerates series of triads that characterize each separate universe in his work. Lopes's world is decidedly dual—two beings face each other, love each other, seek each other. Two worlds, black and white, Africa and Europe, are joined, leaving a confused child torn between conflicting loyalties, in search of himself, confronted with the uncertain paths of Negritude on the one hand and of creolization on the other.

The lineage of the *métis*, the child bred of two different races, is first presented as the source of the problem. André Leclerc is the son of a French commandant/doctor and a Congolese woman. His father is known to him in his youth as a figure of power—the title "Commandant" is used whenever he is mentioned or addressed. He is his son's protector, though a certain distance is maintained between them. To the Bangangulu his name is difficult to pronounce, and he becomes Suzanne LeClerc. This act of renaming is part of the process of reappropriation and domestication, the transformation of the foreign into the familiar. In this case there is the added irony that, when the pronunciation is adapted to Kigangulu phonemes, the gender of the Commandant's name is altered—a mixing that refigures the entire issue of *métissage.*

André's mother's name is Ngalaha, and her identity is largely forged by her relationship with men—especially the three who are her "husbands" and the one who is her son. Her first husband is the French Commandant. Though André doesn't recall any conversation between them, their attachment to each other is presented as emotionally strong, and both are deeply moved when the Commandant is replaced and returns to Europe, leaving his African family in the Congo. At one point in the course of the novel we learn that Ngalaha has a Christian name, Marie. Although neither Ngalaha nor the Commandant demonstrate any particular religious or spiritual qualities, the structure of the family's names suggests a Christian paternity, as we see in the name of Ngalaha's African *métis* husband Joseph, whom she eventually marries after the departure and long absence of her first husband. On one side, then, we have a holy family in which the son, André, undertakes the quest in Europe for his long-lost father. The symbolism is Christian, the focus is on the European father, Commandant-cum-Deus, remembered for his strength and protectiveness by his lost son. Consequently, André follows the approved path, searches to win acceptance and fulfillment by achieving high scores on his school exams, getting scholarships to study in Europe, and finally obtaining his father's approval by becoming a high-school teacher of Latin and French literature.

On the surface there is the Christian story of the search for wholeness, salvation, to be won by finding and following the path to the Father. This is one side of a perfect story that can be told and repeated for those whose own stories are located within the same circle of mysteries. André, however, is *métis,* and is therefore continually thrust outside the center of the circle by the inquisitive, disapproving glances of others. He is a brother in his African family until there are disputes, and then he becomes Moundélé, a white. And when he is in Mpoto—Europe—he is lumped together with all the others who are labeled "bougnoul," "Sidi Cacahuète," "FLN," "fellagha," "sale bicot" (all terms signifying "dirty Arab"), and finally, with his own assent, "nègre."* When his last lover asks if he is Jewish, he assumes all the

---

* "Nègre" means Negro, black, or nigger, depending on the context.

identities of otherness by answering, "In fact, you're right, I am Jewish. I am Palestinian, Gypsy, Chicano."* When he is asked where he comes from, in the end there is only one answer, and that is Africa.

Although he was bred by the Commandant, André wasn't raised by him. Instead, he was abandoned. His mother eventually married, but her husband Joseph entered André's life too late to replace the missing father. However, as in much of the middle Congo region where he was from, another father is provided by the tradition, and that is his maternal uncle-father, Ngantsiala, an elder who assumes his rightful place and who is responsible for the child's upbringing.

As the European *r* sound poses difficulties for Kigangulu speakers, "André" is transformed into "Andélé," while the patronymic Leclerc is replaced by Okana when André and his mother go into hiding from the new Commandant who is intent on sending André alone back to Europe. André Leclerc becomes an African Babangulu child, raised first in the village, then in hiding on an island upriver, and finally back in the city where his mother chooses to live and marry. There he attends school and like the others of his generation finds that success is defined by the passage to Europe, an itinerary not modeled after the Christian myth of the quest, but driven by an historical exigency that saw a generation of Africans seek completion of their education abroad.

Le Chercheur d'Afriques sets André between two worlds, and the passage between them is continually evoked in his internal states, gestures, and thoughts, as well as in his external situation. Change, then, is a passage of figures, masks, selves, from European to African, from African to European. The passage is continually problematized and left unresolved, because the only closure to be obtained comes from an external world, from those around him who insist on seeing him as either an inferior being, or as a superbeing—the views of either racists or Negritudinists. Yet all of his frames of reference, experiences, horizons are mixed, reformulated, creolized. While he finds himself drawn into the easy path of Negritude doctrines that exalt race, he can not escape a preoccupation with the fact of being mixed, the fact of *métissage,* which is ultimately the nature of the identity he is seeking.

Métissage is presented under two faces: as enchantment and theft; and as enhancement and transfiguration. Love and alienation inform the first face.

---

* "D'ailleurs, tu as raison, je suis juif. Je suis palestinien, gitan, chicano" (Lopes 1990, 281). All page references to this text are to the 1990 edition; all translations are my own.

For the *métis,* exile and alienation begin with eyes and skin. Green eyes; light and dark skin; light green hues; brown, not black, features; tan tones; straight hair that is red, blond, or even blue; fine, aquiline noses; thin lips—every physical feature, and especially color, is treated with hypersensitivity: "Kani . . . asks herself whether I'm not an extraterrestial lost amongst the blacks."* This preoccupation with difference is translated immediately into concern with sources, origins, homeland: the *métis* has origins that are always elsewhere: he is eternally the exile seeking his home. Europe, France, Nantes, Chartres, are the first line of foreign ports. But so is the mysterious riverine island to which André and Ngalaha are exiled; so, too, is Kinshasa where André is a foreigner to the other children; and, so, too, in the most distant reaches of the past, is his first home on the Commandant's veranda—"home" being merely a temporary residence that the relatives would visit when they came from the village. And even the village itself could not provide the security of home, could not offer immunity from the depredations of the new Commandant. When André returns "home" to Africa at the end, and speaks Lingala with the taxi driver, he is told that he doesn't speak badly for a Martinican. After that "the conversation continued in French."† As this is the last image of the novel, we are left with the understanding that the fact of change and mixing, has become the ontological base of André's identity, has left him in a state of being permanently abroad.

The mixing penetrates the language itself: for André the smooth tonalities conjured up for him by the Modern Jazz Quartet evoke European as well as African associations, hopscotch ["la marelle"] and a "dzango." When Satchmo sings, André is thrown back to "téké or mbochi singers,"‡ while Joseph, his stepfather, indicates his preference for the smooth nightingale tones of Rina Keti, Tino, Patrice, or Mario (43). The tones of speech itself are domesticated when adapted to the African tongue: "A woman's voice, reminiscent of young mulatresses you can catch sight of in Brazzaville near the Jovourey boarding school—cooing as they soften the *r*'s and round off all the hard edges of the French language."** At times the softening of foreign terms is stretched to the limits of sense: "for a long time I struggled to repeat that Holy Mary was

---

* "Kani . . . se demande si je ne suis pas un extra-terreste égaré chez les nègres" (20).

† "La conversation s'est poursuivie en français" (302).

‡ "des chanteurs tékés ou mbochis" (43)

** "Une voix de femme, à qui je prêtais les traits des jeunes mulâtresses aperçues à Brazzaville, du côté du pensionnat Jovourey, roucoulait en adoucissant les r et en arrondissant toutes les arêtes de la langue française" (30).

full of *grease.*"* Lopes then echoes the mocking tones of Oyono and Kour-ouma for whom linguistic *métissage* was often no more than an irrational mimicry. "The students, lined up by their teacher, intoned a song whose words I could not identify as being Lingala, Kigangulu or French."†

The risk of loss is the immediate consequence of the mixing. The child's early hurt in reaching for alluring fruits, his pain at the Comman-dant's departure, with all the deception and separation that followed, cul-minate in the deepset apprehensions over change that are recorded in his and his mates' childish fears and fabulations. Books and bottled water, like foreign words, are converted into magical talismans and potions capable of engendering and transforming:

"And if you read their books, you can become the Commandant."

"Even with our skin?"

"Even . . . Seems that the books can change it . . ."

"Nope, the skin doesn't change. Look at Eboué . . . It's the soul that . . ." ‡

And the children continue with the new myth of power, affirming that drinking the water of Mpoto [Europe] enables one to slap any black. Finally, they evoke the ultimate power of magical transformation, the alchemist's power over color itself, as if in color lay the hidden essence of being: "If you yourself drink the water in that flask, will your skin change color? Will it change color? Will it change like his (a small index finger indicated me) . . . ? Will your hair straighten out like corn silk? Will your eyes become the color of cat's eyes?"**

The power to command is figured in the chameleon's ability to trans-form itself. Change and power are equated. As the elders confer and the interpreter translates for the Commandant under the palaver tree, the chil-dren continue the lesson as a sort of mock initiation, a parody of the knowledge and its transmission, echoing the unheard palaver being car-ried on by the adults. Power and knowledge are seen as the property of the

---

* "longtemps je me suis évertué à répéter que sainte Marie était pleine de *graisse*" (34).

† "Les élèves, alignés par leur maître, entonnèrent une chanson dont je n'arrivais pas à déte-rminer si les paroles étaient en lingala, en kigangoulou ou en français" (65).

‡ "Et si tu lis leurs livres, tu peux devenir commandant."
"Même avec notre peau?"
"Même . . . Paraît que les livres peuvent la changer . . ."
"Non, la peau ne change pas. Regardez Eboué . . . C'est l'âme qui . . ." (84)

** "Si tu bois, pour toi, l'eau de la dame-jeanne-là, est-ce que ta peau change de couleur? Est-ce qu'elle change de couleur? Est-ce qu'elle change comme la sienne (un petit index me pointait) . . . ? Est-ce que les cheveux se déroulent comme la barbe de maïs? Est-ce que les yeux prennent la couleur du chat?" (85).

ruler—the lesson of subordination translates into racial superiority: "if you become cunning, so cunning that force and evil tremble through your body, hey, it's clear that you couldn't become black again."*

The possibility of creolization is not yet posed: Negritude must first be affirmed, the values of both races and cultures stated before their combined offspring can be recognized. The child who values his own culture more than the power of the Commandant makes the simple statement that was echoed in earlier Negritude verse where Léopold Senghor sang of masks and Birago Diop of the dead: "Yes, I love the ancestors!"† The myth of transformation doesn't end at an impasse: acculturation may entail "death," but death is only a preliminary stage for the initiate. Its function in the rite of passage is to bring about the loss of self. Once one has embarked upon the path, the process can not be reversed. "When you take on the color of the whites, you can't drink any more samba, molengé, or boganda. If your lips touch one of the blacks' drinks, you will fall. . . ."‡ Transgression means death, destruction: "you'll die and Dongolo Miso will devour your soul."**

Normally, a myth of self-transformation should conclude with the final stage of the ritual, the return of the initiate back to the community, enriched by the experience, empowered to assume the dangerous knowledge of the elders. However, the conventional paths of transformation, purification, and communication were not designed to accommodate the new demands of *métissage*. The initiate's full return is possible only through purification, here understood as a realignment with race and tradition. The language of the birds (which French sounded like to Bagangulu ears), the blood and skin and insane practices of the new conquerors, constitute the impurities of the middle road of passage, and need to be discarded. "To save your soul, you have to reach the sacred forest."†† There the initiate must experience the final stage alone, without the Europeans' servants or militia, "sans boy, sans mboulou-mboulou." There the spiritual forces can be brought to bear once again: the Luba woman's song can be heard; the hunter's arrow, dipped in the blood of a bird, can pierce the candidate's flesh, and so the return to one's self and home can be completed: "Then you will

---

* "si tu deviens malin, malin, jusqu'à ce que la force et la méchanceté tremblent dans ton corps, clair que tu peux plus être nègre encore, ho" (85).

† "Si j'aime les ancêtres!" (85).

‡ "Quand tu prends la couleur du Blanc, tu peux plus boire, ni n'samba, ni molengué, ni boganda. Si tes lèvres touchent une boisson nègre, tu tombes . . ." (86).

** "tu meurs et Dongolo Miso dévore ton âme" (86).

†† "Pour sauver ton âme, il faut atteindre la forêt sacrée" (86).

recover the color that God gave you at your birth. Only then will madness leave you; you will rediscover your mother tongue, and, like the invisible waves whose rhythm repeats the seasonal comings and goings of the beasts, a star, the night, will lead you back to the family village."*

As for the knowledge and power of the whites, the child's final counsel to his mates is to forget them. Just as the two realms of the sacred and the human must maintain their separate integrity, so, too, is social *métissage* denied. The parallel is complete when we see that madness, death, and most of all, a loss of soul are the consequences of embarking on the white man's way without completing the final passage home.

The child's incidental loss experienced en route to acculturation, that of the mother tongue, is close to the core psychological experience for the adult. Where the child's attention is focused on the external traits of change and difference, skin color, hair, and eyes, Ngantsiala warns against the loss of the soul, and alienation from the fatherland as well as from the mother tongue, from one's own people, who know each other best through their common tongue. Thus when Mourougon, later to be renamed Vouragan, comes to André's family, announcing his presence and their common parentage, it is his foreign accent that sets him apart. Later, when he welcomes his brother, as an adult, to his home in Nantes, André is forced to speak Lingala in order to make the contact. Where Kourouma uses notions of turning and returning, and looking back, all derived from the French "se retourner," to indicate compromise and weakness, Lopes chooses the phrase "finding oneself" ["se retrouver"] to signify a positive change. And it is through language, first, that one finds oneself.

The agents for change—the Luba woman, the hunter's arrow—combine sexual attraction with language. Desire can bring the loss of self, or, conversely, can lead to self-acceptance and self-overcoming. Ngantsiala paints the risk of loss in terms of absorption—fear of being swallowed, drowned, lost within the other. Instead of a *métissage* ideally representing a successful crossbreeding of cultures, acculturation is viewed as total loss, and change as a kind of death without any rebirth. The fear of such a loss is represented in terms of language: the loss of one's mother tongue becomes the loss of the ability to use one's own words, ending all ties with one's own and forcing one to be another. Thus, when André's stepfather, Joseph, is taken to the missions by the white authorities, and is raised there

---

* "Alors tu reprends la couleur que Dieu t'avait donnée à ta naissance. Alors seulement la folie t'abandonne, tu retrouves la langue maternelle, et, comme les ondes invisibles qui rhythment les va-et-vient saissoniers des bêtes, une étoile, la nuit, te ramène au village de la famille" (86).

by the Europeans, the relatives can not recover the child. When his relatives come for him, Joseph does not recognize them: "'Listen to us, son,' they begged in vain, using the village language, 'listen!'"* The child, however, fails to recognize the tongue and runs away, afraid. For the people from the village, the child is lost. "The people of the tribe returned, reporting that their child had been bewitched; that they had stolen his soul, like those of drugged or hypnotized slaves whom some sects sold in the forests around Bolobo. His memory had been ravished by the priests and a European soul put in place of the original."† The loss was so complete they couldn't even communicate to him the fact that his mother was dead. The child couldn't listen. A new language had taken the place of the old. Change, thus, meant total loss when viewed by the people from the village. Later, Vouragan laughs at the dark skin of the Africans in a parade at Nantes, calling them Zulus. Without further reflection he assumes a French discourse.

The magical force of change, however, does not so much spring from the acquired language in itself as it is reflected in the loss of language. The powerful force of seduction must precede one's desire to assume a new language, to turn from the close embrace of the mother and find a new infectious love. The mystery of change is embodied in the seductive figures of women: the Virgin Mary full of "*graisse*" [grease/grace], the redheaded women, the blonds, and especially the mysterious foreigner, the Luba woman, whose siren song suffices to lead all men to their destruction.

Even one word from the Luba woman's lips, like a fatal kiss, suffices. Her powers can restore the African soul: "To save your soul . . . it is necessary to listen to the song of the Luba woman."‡ Yet her labia can also devour the hardiest soul, as she embodies the fatal attraction of commerce with the world of spirits, including an evil "génie" who borrows her form: "A sort of giant elephant with the head and paws of a tiger . . . , to catch its prey, borrows the traits of a Luba girl—those women from the other side of the river. . . ."** Their long and beautiful muscles awaken male desire; "they say that the lips of their vulva are larger than those of your

---

* "'Ecoute-nous, fils,' avaient-ils beau supplier dans la langue du village, 'écoute!'" (178).

† "Les gens de la tribu rentraient en rapportant que leur enfant avait été ensorcelé; qu'on lui avait volé son âme comme à ces esclaves hypnotisés ou drogués que les sectes allaient vendre dans les forêts du côté de Bolobo. Les prêtres lui avaient ravi sa mémoire et introduit une âme roupéenne à la place de l'originelle" (178).

‡ "Pour sauver ton âme . . . [i]l faut y écouter le chant de la femme louba" (86).

** "Une espèce d'éléphant géant à tête et pattes de tigre qui, pour attirer sa proie empruntait les traits d'une jeune fille louba, ces femmes de l'autre rive du fleuve . . ." (92)

mouth."* These are the sirens of the foreign shores, across the river on the dreaded plain of Ossio, where armed men would not dare to venture in groups of less than seven. Alone, all men would succumb: "there is no man, what you might call a real man ["homme-homme"], who can remain indifferent to them. The warrior with the greatest mastery over himself is undone in their arms."†

The appeal of what Denise Paulme (1976) calls the devouring mother is experienced by André in all its forms. He experiences first the warmth of the maternal embrace and succor, and then the accompanying risk of suffocation, with the failure to sever the umbilical ties. There follows the encounter with the awakened feminine sexual desires in which man can be submerged or drowned, the call of the forbidden with the danger of transgression, and, ultimately, the appeal of what bewitches—an appeal inevitably associated, for the *métis,* with the foreigner and the extreme risks of change, transformation and loss of identity.

The Luba woman incarnates this desire and its danger, the appeal of the foreign, and the possibility of losing oneself in the foreign culture. This is the desire for and fear of acculturation, of the Other, and it is portrayed both in terms of libido and of language. The mere mention of the Luba woman's name functions to trigger the powers of sexual desire, threatening all ordinary mortal men.

> But when the spirits interrupt a man's sleep and inflame his spirit by whispering nothing more than the name of the Luba woman, then the adolescent, the adolescent . . . , the father of the family, . . . even the old man feels the groaning and stirring of juvenile blood within. Which philosopher, which God even could resist the call of pleasure. . . ?"‡

For Ngantsiala, the relationship between blood and the heart explains the appeal. The spirit of the ancestors, the laws of the people, the culture of the village constitute the domain of the uncle-father Ngantsiala, who teaches and embodies the doctrines of pureness enshrined under the rubric of Negritude. Blood and the heart respond to desire as do the feet to the beat of the drum. Blackness reaches out irresistibly and naturally to its children, around whom the maternal arms instinctively close.

---

* "on dit que les lèvres de leur sexe sont plus larges que celles de ta bouche" (92).

† "il n'est pas d'homme, ce qu'on peux appeler homme-homme, pour leur demeurer insensible. Le guerrier le plus maître de lui-méme défaille dans leurs bras" (92).

‡ "Mais quand les génies interrompent le sommeil de l'homme et font lever des flammes dans leur esprit en susurrant seulement le nom de la femme louba, alors l'adolescent, l'adolescent . . . , le père de la famille, . . . [m]ême le vieillard sent se réveiller en lui les grondements du sang juvénile. Quel philosophe, quel Dieu même pourrait résister à l'appel du plaisir.. . ?" (93).

The others across the river, over the ocean, will always speak a foreign tongue, and the risk of encountering them will always lead to the danger of being swallowed, the threat of the Luba woman. For Ngantsiala, the new doctrine of one country, one people can not transcend this appeal of the blood and the heart, and the capacity of the latter to endure is perpetuated by mutual acts of exclusion: "They will never pardon us for having seduced the most beautiful women of their lands."* Furthermore, to make the risk of what is foreign more explicit, we learn through Ngantsiala, André's "père côté femme" (117) [father on the mother's side], of the boasts of the viril Bagangulu men who had led home female slaves every season, choosing the best women as their booty. "These women, after having tasted us, forgot their dialect."†

The original African myth of the devouring mother, as explicated by Denise Paulme, spoke of a calabash that consumed all—all the children, all the villagers, all the world, except for the one child or one woman who resisted. Enclosed within the calabash, originally an innocuous, round-bellied fruit, were its seeds and all the other fruits of reproduction that it refused to let go. In various ways, it was made to release them: a hunter would cut it open, the divine ram would smash it open with its horns. The male phallic instrument would assert its authority,while simultaneously the beneficent mother-provider would demonstrate control over her appetite, submission and self-control often being the conduct inculcated through initiatory teaching. If order and fertility are associated with phallocracy, or with simple patriarchy, there still remains an implicit recognition, fear, and attraction to that which both creates and destroys—the calabash and its feminine mysteries, the magic of the Luba woman, the laws of blood and the heart.

Those mysteries begin, in *Le Chercheur d'Afriques,* with Ngalaha, the original foreign woman, from the Commandant's point of view. As Marie, or black Virgin, she bears a child with special marks—light skin, lightly curled hair, green eyes—that speak of his distant, his mythic, sacred origins. Ngalaha doesn't come from the first home known to André, that is, the Commandant's residence. Rather, like her relative, Olouomo, she comes from elsewhere: "She comes from the village."‡ Like all women for whom marriage means departure and estrangement, she finds herself a stranger in a foreign place. Later André comes to fear that he is "incapable

---

* "Ils ne nous pardonneront jamais d'avoir séduit les femmes les plus belles de leur terre" (93).

† "Et celles-ci, après nous avoir goûté, oubliaient leur patois" (115).

‡ "Elle vient du village" (11).

of finding his way in a foreign land."* Marked by difference, André has foreign origins and is destined for a land beyond. Uncle Ngantsiala's explanation is that the lion creator was André's father. Ngantsiala "rather tends to believe it was from the sky that the lion creator had sent him," and that André's eventual destination is to be "in countries scattered all over."† Difference, thus, is not a source of negation, a mark of inferiority, but of specialness, of sacredness. "The details that distinguished me from the other kids of the village aren't signs of a curse, but a holy mark."‡

Both Christian and Gangulu myth meet in the person of the special child, the fruit of a divine father and a loving mother. For the males, in both versions, the Commandant, the lion, the "prince" of the savannah, is the source of the child's specialness—of his sacred marks. But in order to acknowledge those signs, to consecrate his difference, André would have to pay a price, and that would be to establish his distance from his mother. Like Camara Laye, the dark child was faced with a choice practically from the outset in which adherence to his father's ways entailed separation from his mother.

Denise Paulme's *La Mère dévorante* (1976) explains the source of this separation as the male response to the threat of being engulfed by the all-encompassing demands, appetites, and powers of the female principle. In its purest form, that is, acting in an uncontrolled manner, female creation turns into its exact opposite. "Not only does [the devouring mother] ignore the essential feminine function—transmitting life—she acts in the opposite fashion, swallowing people and domesticated animals, all the witnesses who have a creative presence that she finds on her way. The mother no longer gives birth, she wolfs things down."** The image of the threatening inverse side of maternal love and creation has its counterpart in the menacing, destructive side of female sexuality. In both cases, the endangered figure is the male child, and the powerful force that asserts its ultimate control is, like the lion-Commandant, the male ruling god-warrior whose origins lie "au-delà"—somewhere "beyond."

---

* "incapable de se retrouver dans un pays étranger" (15)

† "a plutôt tendance à penser que c'est du ciel d'où l'aurait envoyé le lion créateur . . . dans des pays par-delà, au-delà" (109)

‡ "Les détails qui me différenciaient des autres gamins du village ne sont pas des signes de malédiction, mais la marque du sacré" (109).

** "[La mère dévorante] non seulement ignore la fonction féminine essentielle—transmettre la vie—elle agit à l'inverse, avalant, avec les humains et les animaux domestiques, tous les témoignages qu'elle trouve sur son chemin d'une présence créatrice. La mère ne donne plus le jour, elle engloutit" (Paulme 1976, 286). All translations from this text are my own.

It is easy to see this devouring mother in *Chercheur*. Some years after the departure of the Commandant from the Congo, and after the return of André and Ngalaha to the village, a new Commandant arrives with the intention of sending André back to his father. As Commandant Leclerc had apparently remarried in France, there is no question of Ngalaha accompanying her son. For André the price of separation from his mother, and of her pain at losing him, is too high. Fleeing together, mother and son take refuge on an island where the white man would never find them. André's name becomes Okana.

The choice between Europe and Africa is a choice between father (and patriarchy) and mother. When André first hears the news that he has been sent for, he still does not know that his mother will not accompany him. Thus he passes from excessive enthusiasm—"Was Mpoto [Europe] really near the sky? Would we take advantage of this to meet the Good Lord?"—to bitter disillusionment on learning that his mother is not to go: "Me, I'm not going to Mpoto. . . . The Commandant is a liar."* André's tenderness for his mother, the closeness between them, Ngalaha's refusal to accept other marriage offers up till then, are all expressed in the scenes of umbilical tying, perpetuating the child's dependency as well as the mother's. André replaces his father by insisting on this dependency. "I hugged my mother in my little arms and murmured to her than I would lead her there myself. . . . She smiled at me again and asked me to go to sleep. When I stretched out on the mat, she crouched down next to me and began to stroke my head." Their exchange of words highlights the mothering gestures:

"Andélé éhé."

"Mama."

"Will you give me your hair?"

André then pulls out an invisible lock and puts it on his mother's head. "[S]he squeezed me tight. She hummed a lullaby."†

Like the biblical Mother and Child fleeing into Egypt, André and Ngalaha are forced into flight from the new Commandant, driving them into still-closer dependency. But the child's dreams and his questions

---

* "Mpoto [Europe] était-il vraiment près du ciel? En profiterions-nous pour rencontrer le Bon Dieu?" "Moi, je n'irai pas à Mpoto." "Le Commandant est un menteur" (127).

† "J'ai serré ma mère dans mes petits bras et lui ai murmuré que je l'emmènerais, moi. . . . Elle m'a souri encore et m'a demandé de dormir. Quand je me suis étendu sur la natte, elle s'est accroupie à côté de moi et s'est mise à me caresser la tête.
   'Andélé éhé.'
   'Mama.'
   'Tu me donne tes cheveux?'
   . . . elle m'a serré fortement contre elle. Elle a fredonné une berceuse" (127–28).

reveal persistent ties to his father, along with a growing need for independence. As he is carried, asleep, into clandestine flight, he dreams of being suffocated—of oppressive forests and infinite numbers of reptilian vines that "awaited a naive prey bumping into them, *to encircle and stifle it*" (my stress).* In his dream, the stifling world ["ce monde étouffant"] closes in on the child. He forces himself to cry out so as to save himself, to wake up, but a hand is immediately clapped over his mouth to keep him still. Apprehensive over being kidnapped, enslaved, sold to a people who will steal his soul and replace it with another, he bites the hand. "I bite the hand that gags me and hear my mother cry out."† He and Ngalaha repeat the earlier call and answer: "Mama?" "Andélé!" She repeats the same gesture of touching his hair and singing lullabies, but he now asks if they are going to "Mpoto." She puts off his question and as they continue on their way he feels suffocated again by the odor of the man who is carrying him. We have passed from the anguish of separation chronicled in *L'Enfant noir* (Laye [1953] 1973) to the threat of suffocation that marks Clarence's itinerary south through the cloying forest in *Le Regard du roi* (Laye [1954] 1982), or Sankolo's zombie march south in *Devoir de violence* (Ouologuem 1968).

As in *L'Enfant noir,* we recognize the familiar pattern of maternal solicitude, concern, closeness, and dependency, as well as the youthful struggle against maternal ties and against the condition of childhood. However, the paternal counterbalance to the mother-son relationship is absent, and the mechanism for establishing the child's independence—initiation—is not evoked. Indeed, when André's French lover, Fleur, asks about the circumstances of his circumcision—a question whose very articulation already indicates a distancing from the traditional conventions that separate male and female discourses—we learn that he was circumcised at the hospital, and not by the initiation master. He lies to Fleur about this but confides to the reader that "Ngalaha would never have permitted the son of the Commandant to be treated in the native manner and circumcized with a machete."‡

In *L'Enfant noir,* the moments of Laye's break with his mother are clearly marked—first by the ritual separation and the explicit reorientation of his male identity that is brought about by the initiation, and then by the repeated choices to continue schooling away from home. When Laye

---

* "s'attend[aient] qu'une proie naïve s'accroche à elles pour l'*enserrer* et l'*étouffer*" (144; my stress)

† "Je mords dans la main qui me bâillonne et j'entends le cri de ma mère" (145).

‡ "Ngalaha n'aurait au demeurant jamais permis que le fils du Commandant fût traité à l'indigène et circoncis à la machette" (282).

returns from Conakry to visit home during his school break, we are made aware of his need for independence: now he sleeps in his own house instead of with his mother; he invites friends to a party and is burdened by his mother's close scrutiny of their socializing. In short, the passage to manhood for Laye, however much complicated by the conflicts caused by European cultural domination, is clearly laid out with respect to his own family and society.

In *Chercheur* the break is never proclaimed or made to appear normal. Rather, we are presented at the beginning of the novel with an adult André searching for his father, seeking to come to terms with his African identity. His past closeness to his mother and his present love affairs are evoked as if no line between them, between past and present, had been drawn. In every one of his relationships, the issue of mixing or creolization is raised. Clearly, then, the problem of the devouring mother is projected by André onto his relations with others so that every relation becomes either an affirmation of the unique values of one's own culture or people—Negritude, in this case—or of assimilation and mixing with the culture of the other—creolization.

André seems to hesitate between the two options: On the one hand, as an African, a black man in Europe, he finds it necessary to establish a love life, renew ties of brotherhood and friendship, and maintain a public stance consistent with the values of Negritude. Thus his lecture, which picks up on themes from Cheikh Anta Diop; his daily acts of celebration of black culture, often linked with dancing; his recollections of Uncle Ngantsiala and the latter's praise of blood and the heart; and finally the memories salvaged from his past all function to reinforce his racial identification. On the other hand, he learns to accept the reality of the fact that not only is his "blood" mixed, but that his education and vocation have made him both a white man and a black one, both French and Congolese. The Creole in him is real; his language, dress, and thoughts convey the central preoccupation of the narrator: the need to come to grips with the reality of Creole, as well as to affirm that, in fact, among the black and white communities alike there is no one who is not Creole in some way. André's own brother, Vouragan, a "pure" African, is, in fact, the product of a domestic and foreign union. And on the white side, Fleur, André's white half-sister, not only exhibits affinities to blackness, she is herself the product of the union of a French Christian father and a Jewish mother. André recognizes the universality of creolization when he responds to Fleur's question whether he is Jewish at first with incredulity, and then with a grinning recognition not only that his white parent might have been Jewish, but also that he might as well have been a Palestinian, a Gypsy, a

Chicano and so on—that Creole, the excluded term from all cultures, in fact, is what gives definition to a race or culture, lies at the origin of its existence, provides for its presence as a special case of the larger condition of mixing. In Derrida's terms, the supplement, in this case creolization, the mixing of languages and cultures, deconstructs the *presence* of Negritude through the revision imposed by an archicreolization, giving the concept of mixing per se priority over the special case of purity. Mixing supplants the conflict engendered by two competing terms.[1]

The two alternatives, exclusion versus mixing, are linked to the two versions of the mother that appear in the African folktale: the devouring, consuming, oppressive figure versus the beneficent, nurturing, giving provider. If harmony is to prevail, it is only after the separation that usually ends, in the various mythic versions of the devouring mother, with the mastery, destruction, and ultimate domestication of the voracious female, what Paulme identifies as control over the female sexual force, and with the final triumph of a vision of order with patriarchal attributes. Laye's final separation from his mother may be painful in *L'Enfant noir,* but it is also portrayed as being in the natural order of things, and it validates an ethic of separation painted in characteristic terms here by Paulme:

> Separated from their mother, at the time of their initiation, the boys died in order to be reborn as adults; on the return to the village they no longer knew their mother and had to relearn how to walk and talk. . . . The victory would remain the Spirit's, the one who incarnated socialized virility, or paternity. . . . The evil expressly identified as such at the outset of the tale would be female sexuality, wild and devouring, which man must conquer and tame at all costs.[*]

The result of this "combat douloureux" [sad struggle] is not only a society of initiation and masks, but of gender occlusions, where "the small child shares in the femininity to the extent that he or she can not do without maternal care."[†] In daily life, male and female activities are defined and maintained as separate, "never mistaken one for the other during the day."[‡] Paulme concludes with the image of a society that represents not only of traditional village life, but city life as well:

---

[*] "Séparés de leur mère, les garçons, lors de leur initiation, meurent pour renaître adultes, de retour au village ils ne connaissent plus leur mère, doivent apprendre à nouveau à marcher, parler. . . . La victoire restera au Génie qui incarne la virilité, ou la paternité, socialisée. . . . Le mal expressément dénommé au début du conte sera la sexualité féminine sauvage, dévorante, que l'homme doit à tout prix maîtriser et domestiquer" (Paulme 1976, 300).

[†] "le petit enfant participe à la nature féminine dans la mesure où il ne peut se passer des soins maternels" (300).

[‡] "jamais confondues dans la journée" (300).

[E]ven during all-night vigils in the public square men and women form two distinct groups, and it is only after the initiation, which corresponds to a definitive weaning, that the boys, at the cost of a separation that is no less definitive from the feminine world, will be authorized to rejoin the men. (301)*

The articulation of this gendered pattern is represented by the refusal to cross or mix: one is either "mammifère" [mammal] or "oiseau" [bird], and there are no bats when it comes to people. "There are Whites, there are Blacks, there are Yellows, there were Reds . . . That's all. Mulatto is not a color, it exists only in the heads of certain people. . . . One is a mammal or a bird. Not a bat" (Lopes 1990, 257).† Ironically, it is Vouragan who proclaims this doctrine to André—the same Vouragan who passes the week of the Nantes festival confined to the hotel room and bed of his sexually voracious, wealthy white godmother who classically embodies the threat of the devouring mother, and yet who also endows Vouragan with a flashy car and, in the end, asks him to father her child. For if separation, Negritude, initiation, patriarchal order, all make up the response to the devouring mother, there still remains the problem that the very trait that makes the devouring mother a threat, her all-consuming love, is the same one that makes the beneficent mother a blessing. In short, the line between the two apparent opposites is, mutatis mutandis, our familiar Möbius strip, which twists back on itself—a variant of André's own description of the *métis* in the village: "In the villages the mulatto children were an embarrassment: at one and the same time animals with wings and mammals, dissonant marks on the scenery, bats that blurred the line of demarcation."‡

The joining of parents from two racial groups, as well as the joining of the good and bad mother, results in an individual who is a combination of two within one person. The two-in-one figure is the twin. For Wole Soyinka the albino and the bat represent the special spiritual force of those who are different from others. At times such figures are also given as *abiku,* another favorite of Soyinka's, and also of Chinua Achebe's—the one who

---

* "[M]ême au cours des veillés sur la place publique, hommes et femmes forment deux groupes distincts, et ce n'est qu'après l'initiation, qui correspond à un sevrage cette fois définitif, que les garçons, au prix d'une séparation non moins définitive du monde féminin, seront autorisés à rejoindre le côté des hommes" (300).

† "Il y a les Blancs, il y a les Noirs, il y a les Jaunes, il y eut les Rouges . . . C'est tout. Métis, ce n'est pas une couleur. Ça n'existe que dans la tête de certaines personnes. . . . On est mammifère ou oiseau. Pas de chauve-souris" (257).

‡ "Dans les villages les enfants métis gênaient. A la fois bêtes à ailes et mammifères, tâches discordantes sur le décor, ces chauves-souris brouillent la ligne de démarcation" (178).

will not stay, the child who dies and is repeatedly reborn only to die again. Laye introduces us to the specialness of twins in his discussion of his twin uncles, and of his mother's birth, which came after the twins' and therefore gave her a special spiritual status. Paulme indicates the special nature of twins in terms of the mystical combination of two into one: "We know the importance of the idea of twinning for African thought. The presence of two in one single individual characterizes a multiplicity of relationships where equality is, in principle, absolute, and where one of the two partners can at any moment substitute for the other."* The power of twins can be feared or welcomed—but always its uniqueness is recognized.

Twins bring us to the space occupied by Creoles—a threatened space with "precarious pertinence" and "dangerous importance," as V. Y. Mudimbe (1988, 5) puts it, in reference to the contemporary mixed urban cultures of Africa—which may explain why twins are sometimes killed. But they also occupy a beneficial space, which explains why they are pampered, or, as with the Yoruba figures of Esu, or the Ogboni, venerated.[2] The creolized space, where two meet and become one, can be blessed or cursed. When the two who meet are deemed too close, the union is ill-fated, and is called incestuous. When André wishes to refuse his Creole status and rejects his white father in favor of a black one from his Bagangulu tradition, his "père côté mère," Ngantsiala, he is rewarded with the hardest slap of his life. "At this I received the most memorable slap of my childhood. Ngalaha had never been Ngantsiala's wife. Does one marry one's brother among the Gangulu people? Evoking incest, even in one's thoughts, is to call down curses on oneself."† Nonetheless, Vouragan "crosses over" from one mother, Egon, to another, Ngalaha; André has a white and a black father, as well as an uncle-father, all of whom cross over between Gangulu and French culture and language. And most significantly, André joins, incestuously, continuously, shamelessly, the twinned features of his African past and his European present. For example, when he is attracted to Kani he recalls the fragrance of the European "frangipani" and the African "d'lang-ylang," and if the two designations of flowers didn't suffice, even the winds that appease their caresses are creolized—"les alizes" [trade winds] and "la fièvre d'harmattan" ["the

---

* "On sait l'importance pour la pensée africaine de la notion de gémellité: présence des deux en un seul individu, elle intervient pour qualifier de multiples relations où l'égalité est en principe absolue et où l'un des deux partenaires peut à tout moment se substituer à l'autre" (Paulme 1976, 295n.).

† "A ce point j'ai reçu la plus mémorable des gifles de mon enfance. Ngalaha n'avait jamais été la femme de Ngantsiala. Est-ce qu'on épouse son frère, dans la race gangoulou? Evoquer l'inceste, même en pensée, c'est appeler la malédiction sur soi" (239).

fever of the harmattan"] (100–101). When he proceeds to make love to Kani, he is aroused and made drunk by these combinations: "Mixed in with the atmosphere's pollens, she was more fetching than a marriage of wines."* It is thus all the more significant that her figure is described in terms that evoke an incestuous relationship: "the *sister* with the small of a child's back" (my stress).†

In Vouragan's coy language another kind of incest is evoked: his wealthy lover is his "godmother" and he the "godson." But Vouragan is a mock advocate of Negritude, and he rejects the doublings that characterize André-Okana's own life. The culmination of André's twinning is presented in the act of sexual union in which two women meet beneath a mask in the single figura of the mysterious lover. The first such figure, the Judex, is, of course, his double—a redheaded *métisse* whose skin, like her name, betrays the impurity of her origins. Her arms "took on the color of pale guava sherbet,"‡ and as the beneficent female she doesn't swallow him up but feeds his thirsty lips: "When you parted your lips, as if to sigh, I thought of those of mulatresses, and without asking I drank the sugary cream, wildly, by the spoonful, from your mouth. . . ."** Their dialogue becomes a guessing game in which she fails to divine his origins. When he finally states that he is African their lovemaking recommences with an image that is thoroughly creolized: "None will have seen the purified ballet where the progression of snow dances, the profound mystery of Hindu rhythms, and the irresistable fire of r'gwakas are all melded together, without jolting, as the drums, seized with epilepsy, beat."†† The mixing penetrates his dreams, and in the sequence that follows André evokes a "désordre" like that which culminates his lovemaking with Kani (102), reaching across culture and language into the depths of the psyche. "African landscapes were mixed with French, and I spoke a gibberish ["un charabia"] made up of Gangulu, European, Lingala, and Latin sentences."‡‡ It is

---

* "Mêlée à celle des pollens dans l'atmosphère, elle était plus prisante qu'un mariage de vins" (100).

† "la soeur aux reins d'enfant" (102).

‡ "avaient la couleur d'un sorbet de gouyave pâle" (225)

** "Quand vous avez entrouvert les lèvres, comme pour un soupir, j'ai pensé à celles des mulâtresses, et, sans le demander, j'ai bu, sauvage, à la cuillère de votre bouche, une pâte de sucre . . . " (225).

†† "Nul n'aura vu le ballet épuré où se fondaient, sans secousses, les enchaînements des danses de neiges, le mystère profond des rhythmes hindous, et le feu irrésistible des r'gwakas, quand battent les tam-tams saisis d'épilepsie" (227).

‡‡ "Les paysages d'Afrique se mêlaient à ceux de France, et je parlais un charabia composé de phrases gangoulous, roupéennes, lingalas et latines" (228).

inevitable that *charabia,* Oyono's and Kourouma's sign of naive acculturation and of the rejection born of colonization, should here be turned once
again back on its origins, to signal the rebirth of the *abiku* into a new identity.

The emergence of incest, as the culmination of creolization, has been
prepared throughout the novel as a response to the acts of exclusion performed by the devouring mother. Fleur's doubling of the mysterious Judex
woman, her family resemblances to André, her physical traits—red hair,
black blood, green eyes—the rendezvous at the carnival in which the social
exclusions based on race, class, and sex dissolve, all evoke a universe in
which incest, *charabia,* transsexuality, and the monumental figures for twinness preside. Thus the unknown lover, called Judex this second time, is
both male and female: "Quand Judex m'a vu tâter le mur pour y chercher
l'interrupteur, il (mais je savais que c'était *elle*) a dégainé et, me tenant à
distance, a pointé l'épée sur ma gorge" (270). [When Judex saw me feeling
along the wall for the switch, he (but I knew that it was *she*) unsheathed his
sword and, holding me at a distance, pointed the sword at my throat.] Not
only is the phallic control passed over to Judex, but the gender identification
is reversed as well. The doubled or split identity, without a mooring, is like
a boat out of control—"a dugout abandonned on the river when a paddle-
boat or some wild fishing smack passes alongside."* The way in which
gender is designated in French permits Lopes to evoke a gender reversal in
which his Judex, a masculine "il," attacks André, now *"la* proie," the [fem-
inine] prey: "Ne laissant aucune chance à sa proie, il avait droit fondu sur
elle" (271) [Giving no chance to his prey, he fell upon it]. When we consider that the "il" is a sister, and that the "elle" is her brother, we can appreciate the extent to which their union is incestuous. "Charivari"
[Hullabaloo] and "charabia" [gibberish] are the least of the many terms
used to evoke the space and sound of incest.

At the moment of climax, at the union that signifies twinness, mixing,
creolizing, the sacred character of the act is evoked. The divine madness of
love becomes the act of a mystery, like that performed in the sacred wood,
not in order to exclude but to unite two worlds, sacred and human, in a
time and space outside of the ordinary. The suffocation of cloying love is
turned, transvaluated, into a transcendent act.

> [S]uffocating, filled with a pagan grace, I kneeled in my turn, because it
> was too much, O Lord, much too much . . . Because I, too, wanted to
> adore her.

---

* "une pirogue abandonnée sur le fleuve quand passe alentour un bateau à roue ou quelque
pinasse folle" (271)

... Holding my hands, she prayed at the same time that I would carry her away, away, ceaselessly, and liberate her because it was beyond believing, Virgin Mary.... *

Figures of hermaphrodism, representing the passage from one world to another (274), soon follow these burning phrases. André sees himself through Fleur's eyes as "Palestinian, Gypsy, Chicano."† Empowered by this moment of sacred union, André comes to the end of his quest—not in the anticlimactic meeting with his father, who is no longer the clue to his identity, but in the celebration of the union itself. The song he sings could be called the song of the Creole, a song of acceptance of his multiple origins. "On prose's plains I vocalize nasal and guttural sounds. The notes of the guitar call forth those of the sansa. The magic of their union creates openings in the sands of our dreams and tinges with color the fresh fires of the matinal azur."‡ Lopes evokes the divided heritage not only through African and European instruments, the guitar and the sansa, brought together in the culture of the diaspora, but in the split inherent in the Congo/Zaire river, in the two adjacent countries where differences are never made explicit in *Le Chercheur d'Afriques,* as though the Negritude base, viewed from Europe, could be sustained.

In *Le Chercheur d'Afriques,* the principle of creolization is defined largely in terms of races and continents, not in smaller cultural or ethnic divisions. Previously we saw in both the title and the theme of V. Y. Mudimbe's first novel, *Entre les eaux,* the issue of the oxymoronic division that splits Pierre/Landu. However, the alienation of the earlier periods, the existential angst in Cheikh Hamidou Kane or Mudimbe, now yield to a postmodern celebration of the very fact of doubling. "Born between the tides ["entre les eaux"], I am a man of symmetry."** The cry of surprise, of greeting, the twinned repetition *"Yéhé héhé, yéhé héhé"* (296), expresses the mood of affirmation at the crossing where André is located: at one end is Ray Charles, whose appearance he adopts when meeting his father, and whose singing now comes back to him; at the other, a canoeist, traveling

---

* "[S]uffocant, rempli d'une grâce païenne, je m'agenouille à mon tour, parce que c'était trop, Seigneur, trop, trop, trop ... Parce que je voulus, moi aussi, l'adorer.
   ... Tendant les mains, elle me priait tout à la fois de l'emporter encore, encore, sans cesse et de la délivrer parce que ce n'était plus, Vièrge Marie, possible" (272).

† "palestinien, gitan, chicano" (281)

‡ "Sur la plaine de la prose, je vocalise les tons du nez et de la gorge. Les notes de la guitare appellent celle du sanza. La musique de leur union ouvre des percées sur les sables de nos rêves et colore les feux frais de l'azur matinael" (296).

** "Né entre les eaux, je suis l'homme de symétrie" (296).

against the current at dawn on the edge of the Nkéni river, echoing Ray Charles's song, "*Yéhé héhé, yéhé héhé.*" The edge of day and night, the meeting point across time—the frontier *is* the fearful symmetry. In Nantes, as André enthusiastically intones his chant, an approaching pedestrian becomes apprehensive and crosses to the other side of the street. The singing continues, bringing life and motion to the meeting, setting the Möbius strip in motion, like the rippling, speckled sprung rhythms of a Hopkins poem. "Right-handed, left-footed, I disrupt the rhythms of the seasons. But I want to hear with my two ears, see with my two eyes, and love with only one heart. *Yéhé, héhé, yéhé, héhé, yé. . . .*"*

The points of references that follow in the ecstatic chant of the Creole bring together images of an Africa split between the highlands and the valleys. Though charged with religious symbolism, the union of these two topographies is actually linked to the concrete history of the Congo, and especially to the forced labor of the early part of the century that brought workers from one region to the other to work on projects like the railroad, often leading to their deaths. "At the summit of the peaks I didn't shiver, though I came from the valley."† Lopes evokes the sacred union between Fleur and André, suggesting a Christian Kerygma in African dress. "I even kneeled and I sang hosanna! chanting my love of the snow."‡ The message that emerges is a Congolese consecration: "As soon as the angels raised the trumpets of gold to their lips, I heard the sound of the balafon."**

The path André forges continues the celebration of the crossing, especially as a bringing home of the miraculous, as a domestication that has the exuberance of a homecoming made at long last, along with the acknowledgment of the rapture of the salvatory mythos. The way was never forsaken. "Thank God! I had bothered to sow my way with gravel."†† The road to Damascus is now transformed into the one leading to the dangerous, mysterious land of the thorn trees, the "rôniers," a track originally taken by the Commandant to show his fearless nature. The "saveur" [flavor] of the way is domesticated in African terms. "In the midst of the *harmattan,* I

---

* "Droitier de la main, gaucher du pied, je dérègle le rhythme des saisons. Mais je veux entendre de mes deux oreilles, voir de mes deux yeux, n'aimer que d'un coeur. *Yéhé, héhé, yéhé, héhé, yé . . .* " (296).

† "Au sommet des pics, je n'ai pas frissonné, moi qui venait de la vallée" (296).

‡ "Je me suis même agenouillé et j'ai chanté hosanna! psalmodiant mon amour de la neige" (296).

** "[D]ès que les anges embouchèrent les trompettes d'or, j'entendais le son du balafon" (296–97).

†† "C'est que j'avais, Dieu merci! pris soin de semer mes graviers" (297).

rediscovered without difficulty the way to the *thorn-tree* lane. He who has known the bewitching silence of the tea-colored river will never lose its flavor" (my stress).* Losing himself in the water, in the rhythms of his chant, like the apostle Peter he finds himself on the new foundation, the "rocs du Djoué" (297).

On his return to Africa André experiences a final generatrix vision of the river as the meeting place of those whose origins lie elsewhere, whose presence signals a new beauty—a flower like Fleur whose act of love brought André to full acceptance of himself. "Tomorrow, my first visit will be to the river. I never tire of contemplating the water hyacinths, uprooted islands that the current leads toward the falls at Djoué. They did not exist when we were children."† Their origin is clouded in mystery— "nimbée de mystère." But the mystery itself is like André; it is the key to his sources, his identity. "In fact, none of all that is really solid. A little bit like me."‡

Postscript

The devouring mother must meet the beneficent mother, and there must be a reconciliation at the end of any mythic representation of their drama. On the immediate surface level of the myth it is the crushing of the rebel force of the calabash, the act of reining in, of controlling, and the simultaneous creation of a system of authority, that gives the myth completeness and presence. Yet we know that this completeness and presence are purchased at the price of ignoring the upriver mysteries where sources arise and are not to be known. In order to arrive at a position of dominance, man must adopt the forbidden, incestuous, oppositional role of the woman, deconstructing his own phallogocentrism. He must open his veins, must let the waters flow—or he must pound the millet, hatch the egg, so as to bring the monstrous calabash under control. "Man, in the absence of the beneficial mother, has no choice and for a moment adopts feminine gestures, crushing the bad seed between two stones, grinding it into flour, and cooking it."**

---

* "Au milieu de l'harmattan, j'ai retrouvé sans peine le chemin de l'allée des rôniers. Qui a connu le silence envoûtant du fleuve couleur de thé n'en sait perdre la saveur" (297).

† "Demain, ma première visite sera pour le fleuve. Je ne me lasse jamais d'y contempler les jacinthes d'eau, îles déracinées que le courant mène vers les chutes du Djoué. Elles n'existaient pas au temps de notre enfance" (301).

‡ "En fait, rien de tout cela n'est bien solide. Un peu comme moi" (302).

** "[L]'homme, en l'absence de la mère bénéfique, n'a pas le choix, adopte un moment les gestes féminines, broie la mauvaise graine entre deux pierres, la moud en farine, la fait cuire" (Paulme 1976, 313).

The figure of the twin in whom the doubling occurs, the essential pattern of change as creolization, has its complete mythic form suggested by this encounter between man and the two sides of the mother.

> The opposition death/life, which repeats that of devouring mother and beneficial mother, reflects others, to no one's surprise: raw/cooked; meat/vegetative; wild, sterile plants/agriculture and cooking. Can one go still further and see, in the actions that bring man closer to woman, two sides, beneficial or harmful, according to the feminine image that is employed? From this point of view, the dream woman would be the good housewife, the domesticated spouse who cares for the well-being of her partner night and day . . . ; while the bad woman, whose sexuality could not be conquered, dreams only of sating herself, and pursues her pleasures in intimate relationships until her partner ["l'autre"] is exhausted.*

Here "l'autre" [the other] is always the stranger, always the African in Europe who excites the eccentric gaze of the natives, whose difference is implanted in his very being as a black man. Yet difference can never be eliminated: even at home new plants are continually being fashioned upstream and sent off to float on the waters. . . . The drama of the searcher lies in his acts of domestication. The woman's difference, her appetite, is represented as a threat, so that it must be domesticated, its nature transformed, and the transcendental act of union recuperated, contained, deflated. But the meeting of a voracious demand and a questing cavalier can have more than one outcome. For Lopes the essential is to maintain the validity of the act of crossing itself as the creative conjunction—to celebrate not only difference, but the *métissage* that only difference can engender.

---

* "L'opposition mort/vie qui double celle entre mère dévorante et mère bénéfique en reflète d'autres, qui n'ont rien que d'attendu: cru/cuit, viande/végétaux, plantes sauvages stériles/ agriculture et cuisine. Peut-on aller plus loin et voir, dans l'acte qui rapproche l'homme de la femme un double aspect, bénéfique ou maléfique selon l'image féminine retenue? Dans cette optique, la femme rêvée sera la bonne ménagère, l'épouse domestiquée qui veille au bien-être de son partenaire, la nuit comme le jour . . . ; alors que la mauvaise femme, dont la sexualité n'a pu être domptée, ne songe qu'à se gaver et poursuivit son plaisir dans les rapports intimes jusqu'à l'épuisement de l'autre" (Paulme 1976, 313).

Chapter 13

▼▼▼▼▼▼▼▼▼▼▼

Wordplay at the Water's Edge

Sony Labou Tansi,
La Vie et demie; Les Sept solitudes de Lorsa Lopez; Les Yeux du volcan

Lines of defamiliarization would seem to lead from Camara Laye to Ferdinand Oyono to Sony Labou Tansi as surely as those traced by Paul de Man ([1971] 1983) lead away from a literature anchored in realism, *témoignage,* and the unity of the subject. With African literature we have become accustomed to a subject defined by circles of identity inscribed in family, clan, class, or nation. At the provisional end of this literary itinerary, perhaps the first cycle of an emergent literary tradition, we now find a literature that turns upside down, inside out every boundary of the self. The subject, in this literature, is created by a language of revolt and affirmation, and yet, because the paths of identity are imbricated, co-opted, entrapped in the labyrinth of post-Independence states of shame, damnation, and "bâtardise," as Ahmadou Kourouma, Yambo Ouologuem, Bessie Head, Ama Ata Aidoo, Henri Lopes, and Sony Labou Tansi would have it, the former certainties unfold only to be recast in new discourses.

Sony Labou Tansi may be seen as both the heir to a generation of struggle and the forerunner of a new, powerful school of Congolese or Central African writers whose works respond to a set of oppressive political and social circumstances. The contradiction that lies at the base of his work, and that joins him to Wole Soyinka, and, to a certain extent, V. Y. Mudimbe and Sylvain Bemba, is that he has repeatedly affirmed his intention to write a literature of combat while at the same time choosing a literary style that is not easily accessible, that denies the techniques of realism. We can say that his protest is anchored in a reality whose image he refuses to recast in realist terms. This choice not only follows the logic of the literary development in African literature from the 1950s on, it gives Sony Labou Tansi access to a discourse whose multifaceted features lend his

315
▼

protest far greater force than would be the case had his work remained circumscribed by the narrow bounds of realism, such as we see in Chinua Achebe's *Anthills of the Savannah* (1987).

Sony Labou Tansi has said that he wants to give his writings the anguish and compulsion of a cry. His writing belongs to a new genre, "écriture-folie" [writing-madness]. Beginning with the obsessions of Dadou in *L'Anté-peuple* (1983), who was fed up with everything "moche," signifying the full gamut from the ugly and banal to the corrupt and cruel—everything that detracted from the fullness of life and especially love—Sony Labou Tansi has produced increasingly allegorical works that bend the parameters of mimesis, refusing to accept the inherited boundaries of African literature.

As with Birago Diop, Sony Labou Tansi's dead are not dead, except that now it is their mad refusal to accept death that arms their protest. Few images in all the literature of Africa have conveyed the force of refusal as that of Martial in *La Vie et demie* (1979). Martial, the "loque-père" [rag of a father], is killed by the dictator, the "Guide Providentiel," who sinks the knife he was using to cut the meat for his dinner into Martial's throat. As the rag-father remains standing, the Guide Providentiel proceeds to open Martial's innards with the knife, and as this does not bring an end to the defiant stares or hard breathing, the brutality continues with the stabbing of both eyes. Martial responds with words of refusal, "I don't want to die this death" (my trans.),* words that reecho throughout the work of Sony Labou Tansi. Despite being cut into pieces, Martial remains upright and continues to intone his refusal.

Martial's family is completely trussed up and forced to witness the brutality, after which they are compelled to eat the rest of Martial's body. Their reactions and the dictator's barbarity are recorded in their tears and his cynicism. There seems to be no limit to either as pity and cruelty dance together. Realistic details delineate the phantasmic nightmare. The meat and drink consumed by the Guide Providentiel are provided specially by Quatre Saisons, a French supermarket chain that recalls the ubiquitous Printemps found in Francophone Africa. Recorded in minute details, this portrait of reality bears witness to an absurdly unrealistic representation. The conjunction of the two is what gives Sony Labou Tansi's work its particular quality, and its strength, which Eileen Julien (1989) is right in describing as lying at the heart of a particular tension.

---

* "Je ne veux pas mourir cette mort" (Sony Labou Tansi 1979, 13). All page references to this text are to the 1979 edition; all translations are my own.

> *La Vie et demie* juxtaposes logic and illogic, measure and the immeasurable, seriousness and folly. This alternation is manifested verbally in the text's absolute precision, on the one hand, and its repetition *ad nauseam,* on the other. The text obeys both these apparently opposing impulses, and yet, for the purpose of Sony Labou Tansi's fable, they are complementary, for the first suggests a matter-of-fact, ordinary reality, while the second gives the narrative its dimension of the fantastic. Indeed, the presence of both suggests the tension between a narrative as (empirical) chronicle and as (ideal) fable. . . . The tension between verbal empiricism and extravagance is sublimely comic and absurd. (Julien 1989, 379)

She goes on to add that "[t]he humor . . . lies in the tension between exaggeration and precise measurement (363 rapists), and in the simultaneous suggestion of the fantastic and the routine" (380).Finally, she quotes Sony Labou Tansi, whose own view of his discourse, his "parole," reinforces the notion that words are charged with the force of change. Just as Michel Foucault would link the penitentiary and the mental asylum with the discourse of power, so, too, does Sony Labou Tansi, as he states in an interview in 1986, link the subversion of that power with an attack upon accepted uses of the word: "Our word is special because it forces the world to 'change its logic'" (my trans.).*

   In an earlier interview he is more categorical in his rejection of the coldly rational, Cartesian view of existence. Life isn't always rational, he states, "it seemed to me stunning" (my trans.).† Life is charged with energy. It refuses death, or restructures it, by the force of the word—not the sacred word, but the charged word that can be wielded like a battering ram against the walls of rigidity—"Sartre used to say that he saw his words as swords. I think I make the same error."‡ More characteristically, however, Sony Labou Tansi doesn't adopt the tone of the militant revolutionary, and even less that of the self-assured ideologue. Rather, he evokes celebration and dance, or carnival. The act of living, he insists, begins with the first trace of ourselves upon the world, and that is accomplished by the inscription of our words upon the landscape around us. Sony Labou Tansi calls this the act of naming—"nommer." It is our "graph" or line that marks, delineates, defines, and creates, at once establishing a border and giving a contour to the real, to "Reality." The marvel that surges out of

---

* "Notre parole est spéciale parce qu'elle oblige le monde à 'changer de logique'" (Sony Labou Tansi 1986, 34).

† "elle me paraît foudroyante" (Mangier 1985, 6). All translations from this interview are my own.

‡ "Sartre disait qu'il prenait ses mots pour des épées. Je crois que je commets la même erreur" (Mangier 1985, 7).

Sony Labou Tansi's world is provided with a name, and thereby enlarges the scope of change itself. "You can't change things until you have named them, until you have called them by name."* At the same time, one's own life, one's own death, one's shame or honor are also given form and substance through naming: "The dimensions of the named thing tell you something about your own size."† Sony Labou Tansi sees his task as naming—not as accusing or condemning, though that can be seen to follow the act of naming, and not as delimiting or limiting: he refuses to trace a line that would separate and compartmentalize things, as that reduces their stature: "I have never had the desire to draw a real border between the real and the magical."‡ Yet the power of his discourse arises from the meeting and, as Julien noted, the tension that lies along the line between the real and the fantastic.

If that tension gives Sony Labou Tansi's writing its specific quality, it is nonetheless not one that is easy to define. For Julien it is a question of subverting totalitarian discourse, and she rightly associates its project of demystification with a tradition that extends from Aimé Césaire, Ferdinand Oyono, and Sembène Ousmane—a literature of revolt to which we might also wish to add the heritage of Negritude and anticolonial writing. The obvious differences between Sony Labou Tansi and the school of Congolese-Zairean writers to which he belongs, and previous writers of protest literature, is that now the object of the protest is the oppressive *African* regime under which they live, and that, further, Sony Labou Tansi refuses to embrace a transparent ideological line. Thus both he and Henri Lopes have felt compelled to "explain" their positions in various public statements. For Sony Labou Tansi there is a further dimension added to his writing, which he describes as his mouth-to-mouth love affair with life (Mangier 1985, 6). Each of these aspects of his work bears the stretch marks of his discourse, which is where one must search for the specific qualities of his style.

La Vie et demie

In *La Vie et demie* (1979) Sony Labou Tansi denies the idea of respecting established borders. While studiously ignoring specific ethnic cultural traits (which inform so much of the immediacy of *témoignage* literature), he nonetheless establishes a regional identity defined by various differences,

---

* "On ne change pas les choses tant qu'on ne les a pas nommées, tant qu'on ne les a pas appelées par leur nom" (Mangier 1985, 6).

† "Les dimensions de la chose nommée vous dictent en quelque sorte votre propre taille" (Mangier 1985, 7).

‡ "[J]e n'ai jamais eu le désir de tracer une vraie frontière entre le réel et le magique" (Mangier 1985, 7).

even oppositions. Thus, in *La Vie et demie* the boundaries between three fictive states are evoked, only to be mocked, while simultaneously the distinction between the forest—and the forest people—and the city is set carefully in place. The borders he rejects must exist in some form in order to be denied while the new differences he evokes are grounded in an alternate set of values.

The pattern of generating new borders while denying old ones rests upon distinctions, often rendered as oppositions, that inform all of Sony Labou Tansi's oeuvre. His elevation of this pattern into a credo could be seen in the statement cited above, "I have never had the desire to draw a real border between the real and the magical." The magical may be seen in a series of acts whose name can not be fitted to words in any ordinary sense. While escaping over the first border of meaning, it erects a new semantic system that is extended by Sony Labou Tansi's surreal images and context. Martial's refusal to die the death of a tyrant's victim in *La Vie et demie* also contains a denial of realist signifying, while simultaneously it insists on the perennial cause of social justice, following the notion that a just cause encompasses more than the individual and his or her protest. Sony Labou Tansi personalizes Martial's stance, complicating his return to the living with stormy scenes of conflict with his daughter Chaïdana, whose own manner of carrying on the protest flies in the face of Martial's interdictions. Martial remains too much of a male, a father, an individual, to be a mere symbol; he carries at least the weight of what Erich Auerbach (1953) describes as a figural identity—at once personal, historical, and symbolic. But more than this, he belongs to an allegorical universe whose points of reference are anchored in the ugly political and social circumstances of life in the region of the Congo where the weight of long-standing dictatorship and corruption already seem to have endured for generations under the unhappy direction of the authentic Guide-Providentiel.

The boundary between reality and unreality is located within the realms of both the magical and the real. Martial refuses the givens of the real, including the final irreducible given of life, that is, its last boundary line, death. He refuses what seems impossible to refuse—and if his refusal is only a play on words, it is a play that is equally serious in its rejection of the first human reality encountered *in* the world, and that is the priority of force or power. The Guide-Providentiel defines the power to administer death as his ultimate authority. *La Vie et demie* begins with the refusal of that authority and of its concomitant power to define words, to name reality and thereby to control it.

Once the verbal power over life and death is in place, all the rest follows. For example, the power over space is exercised by assigning borders and defining what actions can be taken within them. Constant checks, controls, the need for papers, and finally the reliance on those who can provide the papers, who can order the controls, all infuse the power over space, inscribing the marks of a graph upon the lives of the people.

If there is one archetypal figure that has both defined and been denied as the border, it is the river, the river between—the river with two names. In *L'Anté-peuple* (1983) Dadou crosses the river and undergoes the transformation from a school director to a revolutionary. The crossing is significant not only because of the weighty changes that are indicated as if by a rite of passage, but also because it links him to the people whose lives are dependent on the river, and whose denial of it as a frontier is grounded in the same values defined by Sony Labou Tansi as a cult of life: "My cult of life forces me to live mouth to mouth with lucidity."* Along the river the fishermen carry the passengers, transferring them from one bank to the other, living at risk and at times profiting from the risk of denying the integrity of the border. Despite their human flaws, they earn rich terms of approbation in *La Vie et demie*: "Fishermen will always be known, in all the countries of the world, for having more humanity than other men."† Though Dadou is also beaten and abandoned by these same fishermen, it is nonetheless among them that he is nourished and, in a sense, saved; and it is ultimately their spirit of refusal that is aligned with the protest against all that makes life "moche" [ugly].

In *La Vie et demie* borderlines are treated with derision. The distinction is not between the concrete conditions of the fishermen's lot and the gratuitous nature of political oppression. It is between the naive, uncorrupted view of the world provided by the forest people, and that of the worldly citizens of Katamalamasia. The two opposing views meet when Chaïdana's daughter, also named Chaïdana, escapes to the forest and eventually becomes the companion of a Pygmy, Kapahacheu. For the latter, the world is encompassed by the forest, and Chaïdana's evocation of other worlds is totally mystifying. The reader is treated to a classic case of defamiliarization, as in Viktor Shklovsky's example of Tolstoy's use of a horse to describe an opera.[1] Chaïdana first tries to define the world from which she has fled as hell:

"Hell?"

"It's something that gobbles you up. That eats you up in big bites."

"A leopard?"

---

* "Mon culte de la vie ne me laisse pas une autre vie que celle du bouche à bouche avec la lucidité" (Mangier 1985, 6).

† "Les pêcheurs auront toujours, dans tous les pays du monde, la réputation d'avoir plus d'humanité que le reste des hommes" (74).

"No."

"Lion, crocodile, tiger?"

"No! It only eats you if you're breathing—dead, it drops you."

"I don't get it!"*

Chaïdana's overly figurative descriptions fail to cross the barrier of incomprehension that persists between her and her companion, and the humor that results from this discordance touches on the sanctimonious seriousness of those who insist upon imposing their definitions.

"How many feet?"

"What do you mean, how many feet?"

"Hell."

"Oh! As many feet as they are over there. Multitudes."

The burlesque evokes Beckett at his most seriocomic:

"It's big."

"Big as a country. Big as a forest."†

The notion of "pays" [country] itself is incommensurate with that of the forest when viewed with the eyes of an outsider. For Chaïdana, the world outside the forest is "là-bas" [over there/beyond]—for Kapahacheu it is the land of the dead who are buried. For her, the space of the forest is divided among three countries: in the forest, for the pygmies, their borders disappear:

"I don't give a damn if we're in Katamalanasia, in Pamarachi, or in Chambarachi."

"What's that?"

"Countries, lands."

"The land has no name but Forest."

"Here, yes. But over there, they've drawn borders right up to people's legs."

"Borders?"

---

* "L'enfer?"

"C'est quelque chose qui vous bouffe. Qui vous mange à coups fermés."

"Léopard?"

"Non."

"Lion, crocodile, tigre?"

"Non! Ça vous mange tant que vous respirez—mort, ça vous laisse tomber."

"Vois pas!" (95).

† "Combien de pattes?"

"Quoi, combien de pattes?"

"L'enfer."

"Ah! Autant de pattes qu'ils sont là-bas. Des multitudes."

"C'est grand?"

"Grand comme un pays. Grand comme la forêt" (96).

And the answer that comes "mouth to mouth with lucidity" expresses succinctly Sony Labou Tansi's cult of life, and his refusal to accept what reduces, silences, or constrains: "Limits. To separate. You have to separate, understand?"*

And "limit," as Camus reminds us in *L'Homme révolté* (1952), is a word of Roman origin, denoting the walls—*limes*—placed by the Romans on the borders of their empire. Alternatively, it can be traced to *limen,* the root of both "limb" and "threshold."

Les Sept Solitudes, Les Yeux du volcan

With *Les Sept Solitudes de Lorsa Lopez* (1985) and *Les Yeux du volcan* (1988), Sony Labou Tansi pushes further back the rational margins of his narrative, increasing his association with the magic realism of Latin American authors. The quasi-romantic vision of the naive Pygmy as offering an uncorrupted view of a corrupt world disappears, and the allegorical dimensions of the narrative are heightened. The various borders between opposing elements, worlds, people, however, remain integral elements, constantly demanding to be deconstructed.

Like the frame, the river serves as a boundary whose own border or edge can not be delineated, at least not by itself. Where the riverbank begins and ends, whether it belongs to the river or to that which is set off by the river, can become a question of life and death (as was the case in 1989–1990 in the conflict between Senegal and Mauritania, or the earlier battles along the Congo/Zaire river following Independence). If the word "river" denotes the water that flows past the bank, then its distinction from what is not the river must be as problematic as the fluidity that constitutes its own nature. The river is the quintessential border that refuses to be fixed. If it does not turn back on itself, like the Möbius strip, it overflows whatever limits it; it dries up, turning a water course into a dry bed. Like life it moves and ceases, in the long or short term; it follows a periodicity within vaguely defined parameters; it carries and contains, is killed by what people cast off, is restored to its life as a container, and eventually is dammed up. It can be explosive and dangerous, or languorous. Water, earth, and fire meet in *Les Sept Solitudes* in a space of time that surpasses

---

* "Ça m'est foutrement égal qu'on soit en Katamalanasie, en Pamarachi ou au Chambara-chi."
  "C'est quoi?"
  "Des pays, des terres."
  "La terre n'a autre nom que forêt."
  "Ici, oui. Mais là-bas, ils ont mis des frontières jusqu'aux jambes des gens."
  "Frontières?"
  "Limites. Pour séparer. Il faut séparer, tu comprends?" (96–97).

limits, that can be known and delineated only through the force of words. The river is the discourse of *Les Sept Solitudes.*

"La Côte" [the coast] is both a definite location in *Les Sept Solitudes* and the edge or border between the land and the sea. The water is constantly evoked through markers that set it off, like the "île de Solitude" or the lighthouse, or that it sets off or swallows up, like Nsanga-Norda. The water is always linked to life or death, is indeed defined by what it joins or that from which it is parted. And yet it continually overflows or refuses any margins. If the river itself does not limit or separate, the conceptions that permit us to evoke it can not be expressed by distinctions, by demarcating it, separating it from what it is not. It is not too much to see this floating signifier as conveying the same nonspace evoked in the term *différance.* The final immersion of distinctions can not be offered within the narrative—it occurs at another place that lies beyond the discourse, only to set it off in a futile attempt at containment.

The water of life is evoked as the source of human life through its association with the vagina. Ambiguously, it also meets its opposing qualities there, as it is linked to choices and actions where water is seen as corrupt or as enhancing. In fact, Sony Labou Tansi would have us divinize the properties of water when they are seen at their most beneficent. Thus, when Sarngata Nola or Estina Bronzario sets crassness against purity or nobility, it is by recasting the aquatic terms through which the vagina is defined. In this instance it is Sarngata Nola who is speaking so as to defend his attitude toward the group of women who accompany him: "The vagina is not a flood rag ["essuie-flotte"], it's not a flyswatter, it's not a liquor; it's the will of God in flesh and water" ["en chair et en eau"].* Later Père Bona quotes Estina Bronzario to the same effect: "the vagina is the word of God in flesh and water."†

Wordplay with antithetical values is suggested by such terms as "flotte" [water, flood] and the unreified "os" [bones] transmuted into the homonym "eau" [water]. The word "os" is both received and re-formed by the people of the Coast whose refusal of the original bone ("os"), whose recasting of the water ("eau"), is commensurate with their demands, led by Estina Bronzario, for a newly sanctified view of women.

The term "flotte" and a variety of images linked to liquids are employed to evoke women seen as forced to accept men's demands. As a

---

* "[L]e vagin n'est pas un essuie-flotte, ce n'est pas une chasse-mouches, ce n'est pas un alcool; c'est la volonté de Dieu en chair et en eau" (Sony Labou Tansi 1985, 68; my trans.). All page references to this text are to the 1985 edition; all translations are my own.

† [L]e vagin c'est la parole du Seigneur en chair et en eau" (77).

synecdoche for woman the vagina, devalued as a "passkey to graft" ["un passe-magouille"] (77), is rendered as a container of variuos sorts: a "water bagpipe" ["une cornemuse à flotte"] (77) , even "a can of Coca-Cola" ["une boîte de Coca-Cola"] (68). When the water turns strong, its powers over life are augmented: "eau-de-vie," brandy (literally "water of life"), is modified into the more evocative "eau-de-fer" (117), or "water of iron" (again a play on words, as *eau-de-feu* means firewater). At their most extreme, the drink "jus-de-bronze," or "juice of bronze," is offered by Manuel Yeba as a cure for Fartamio Andra do Nguélo Ndalo, while the deadly combinations of *sowasilosuka, mtaka-ntambi,* and *koutou-mechang* are responsible for the deaths of those adventuresome enough to enter drinking contests. (In what is possibly its ugliest image in Sony Labou Tansi's corpus, we encounter "l'eau à sortir des sangs" in *La Vie et demie* [73] [water that comes from blood], a phrase Amedandio uses to describe the male fluids of sexuality poured into Chaïdana by the 363 soldiers who rape her.) But as life can be described as "nothingness that pisses in the street," * so is it also housed in the vaginal "temple," for Gracia, the source of marvels; conversely it is the container of the "merveille indicible" (81) [unutterable marvel] fished from the sea by the fishermen. The strength of water appears in Estina Bronzario's powerful curses, in which the word-magic is carried by saliva. But in its most magical appearance, it carries life and death beyond any petty or limited scope and accompanies the transformations of love. Water passes from the beneficial to the completely miraculous, until it finally attains the ultimate force of creation/ destruction.

These life-enhancing qualities may be seen when Estina Bronzario decides to bathe in the bayou. She comes into untainted contact there with the life contained within the water, changing the soiled nature of the "flotte" into something positive:

> She knew how to lay her heart on the greenish limpidity of the water, on its odor of lime and its brackish taste, savoring the delicious contact with the sand, the coolness of skin, the brown run of dace and, on the other bank, the opaque flight of storks. She loved, too, the sensuous lapping, the clucking of the water that suffocates with peace, sighs, tremors, that speaks its voice of flood.†

---

* "néant qui pisse dans les rues" (Sony Labou Tansi 1985, 148).

† "Elle savait poser son coeur sur la limpidité verdâtre de cette eau, sur son odeur de calcaire et son goût saumâtre, le contact délicieux qu'elle avait avec le sable, cette fraîcheur de chair, la course brune des chevaines et, sur l'autre rive, le vol opaque des jabirus. Elle aimait aussi ce clapotement sensuel, ce gloussement de l'eau qui suffoque de paix, soupire, gémis, parle

Her adversarial role with Sarngata Nola, clearly the male force of life, is dissipated as he sees her swimming, and as she emerges from the water with her long catfish body ["corps de silure"] (99). When Estina Bronzario and Sarngata Nola return to Valancia hand in hand, it inspires a providential panic in Fartamio Andra, signaling the transcendental quality of the event.

Henceforth the "Côte" is identified with the brown water ["la flotte brune"], now transformed into a life force (130). Sony Labou Tansi's cult of life is no less a cult of love, and when Gracia Bronzario, who narrates the novel in the first person, speaks of her love, it, too, is put in terms of its miraculous liquid powers. As for her power to love, she affirms, "I had it in my belly, disguised as viscera, the smell of love, the water and juice of dreams, a small lake of peace the color of a full moon."* At the moment of their greatest strength, the images of water and juice become blood, joined to Sony Labou Tansi's preferred symbol for passion, fire. Physical passion is not a stepping stone for him, but the very substance of the ultimate, in which the power of words, love, and the elements can meet. Passion is the great, infinite poem of blood, as he calls it, a poem that celebrates in the blood, "the blood that beats its fire against the walls of one's entire being."† Later, when disappointed in love, Gracia returns to the image of love's folly, and evokes its connection with water: "God! What heart is not an insanity? I listen again to our madnesses beneath the hubhub of the waves. All the winds are marked. Water remains our best portion of the world."‡

By the end, the force of water is brought to bear upon the hateful opposition that separates the noble people of the Coast from their shameful northern counterparts and the "authorities" at Nsanga-Norda. When Estina Bronzario emerges from her swim in the bayou, she recalls the time when the Coast and Nsanga-Norda weren't separated, when they were "a single land, a single soul, a single sigh."** The references to a divided Congo, or a divided Africa—built on the image of a divided subject—couldn't be more clear. The cathartic or purgative forces of water are evoked in the resolution of hateful divisions, as the sea sweeps up to Nsanga-Norda and submerges it in an apocalyptic flood. As Gracia leaves Valancia for Nsanga-Norda, she learns of "the hour when Nsanga-Norda

---

sa voix de flotte" (98).

* "Je l'avais dans mon ventre en guise de viscères, odeur d'amour, eau et jus de rêve, petit lac de paix couleur de pleine lune" (134).

† "fête dans le sang, le sang qui cogne son feu sur le paroi de l'être tout entier" (134)

‡ "Dieu! quel coeur n'est pas une insanité? Je réécoute nos folies sous le brouhaha des vagues. Tous les vents sont marqués. L'eau reste notre meilleure part du monde" (179).

** "une seule terre, une seule âme, un seul soupir" (98)

was eaten by the waters."* The allegorical language used to describe this event heightens its symbolism, giving the action a degree of polyvalency: the ultimate power of the water, like that of the word, is to effect change, obscuring borders while creating signposts, like islands, by which the presence and absence of reality can be known. An incredible thing occurred, Gracia says, "the sea came and took everything. We're nothing more than an island."† A Christ head, stolen by the Portuguese centuries earlier, is now returned by the waters, which clearly become both the agents and the fountainhead of a divine force: "The water gave / The water can take back."‡

As a canal, the water-trace forms a border. As an ocean, it undergoes a Möbius transformation, and what was the border trace, the water, becomes itself what is contained, delineated by the coastline. But in its final, ultimate gesture, the border-traces of space and time are effaced, washed away by a flood that restores the original unity of Valancia and Nsanga-Norda, and that destroys the effects of "decapitalization" in which Valancia's goods and wealth, and the material inscription of Valancia on the landscape of the coast—its walls, bridges, municipal gardens, public squares, its pools and train stations, its artificial lake, its drawbridges, 39 mausoleums, 15 arches of triumph, 9 towers of Babel, 16 traffic circles, 12 mosques, its boulevards, the bones of its interred, its streetlights in gold, its 79,000 artificial trees ("septante-neuf mille," in Belgian French), its 7,000 modillions, 915 monoliths, obelisks, and ogives, and its head of Christ—all awash in the flood, are returned not so much to an original owner but to an original wholeness. The effects that float about in the flood carry the imprint of the past, especially past monuments of worship, time, and glory. The water is described as "sated with ogives, with menhirs, with minarets whose bones are of hard iron, with arches of triumph, with modillions, and with the sempiternal ventriloquy of muezzins."** The hard stone and bone are set in motion no less than the symbols, synecdoches, and metaphors of permanence and primacy; the water is moved to a new song, transforming everything while under the watch of the Southern Cross; and the wild hubbub of life is danced on and on by the people of the Coast: "The water on which the Southern Cross will cast an appalled look, tonight, while in its stomach scuttle cod and

---

* "l'heure où Nsanga-Norda a été mangé par les eaux" (186)

† "La mer est venue tout prendre. Nous ne sommes plus qu'une île" (186).

‡ "L'eau a donné / L'eau peut reprendre" (187).

** "L'eau repue d'ogives, de menhirs, de minarets aux os de fer dur, d'arcs de triomphe, de modillons et de la sempiternelle ventriloquie des muezzins" (195).

piranhas, dancing the endless hubbub of this other dimension of things. We are the wounded: torn from the sky, from the water, from the hard stones that think gray."*

Thus is set in motion again, again is brought to life, the time of the apocalypse of which numerous predictions spoke. Nogmédé alludes to the time that follows the death of Estina Bronzario as the day when the earth and the waters "se recoudront" (76) [will stitch themselves together]. And all the others forecast as well, after the death of that symbol of feminine beauty, a time when the separate elements will be brought together. "When the seventh decapitalization is complete, and the bronze woman has spit upon the fisherman of rainbows, the earth and the sky will stitch themselves together again."† Like the dance of love between Gracia and Paolo Cerbante—"love being nothing but fire, it's better on the level of water. My sun! My moon!"‡—male/female, sun/moon, earth/water, fire/water, mountains/coast, join in the fusion of the terms of the oxymoron on the day of the parakeet, the day when the sky and the earth "se coudront" [will be stitched together] (174).

In the end only the tip of Nsanga-Norda stands out of the water like an island, like the isle of Solitude whose name evokes the reiterated sign of the human condition: that of a being who stands alone in a universe whose contours are given in terms that are entirely physical. For Sony Labou Tansi, love is a fire that sets solitary islands of being in motion, that brings together the opposites—the man from Norda-Nsanga and the women of the "Côte" (such as Elmunto Louma, the policeman from Nsanga-Norda, and Elma Zora Dehondora, the epileptic elder daughter of Elmano Zola). Above all, when Sarngata Nola descends from the north with his troops, the most powerful opposition of Sony Labou Tansi's universe is set into play: the gynocracy of Estina Bronzario on the coast versus the phallocracy of Sarngata Nola, with his harem of fifty women and numerous eunuchs, from Nsanga-Norda.

Perhaps one might speak of three social worlds in the writing of Sony Labou Tansi:

---

* "L'eau sur laquelle ce soir, la croix du Sud jettera un regard atterré, tandis que dans son ventre craberont lotes et piranhas, dansant le chahut sans fin de cette autre dimension des choses. Nous sommes des blessés: arrachés au ciel, à l'eau, aux pierres dures qui pensent gris" (195–96).

† "Quand la septième décapitalisation sera faite, et que la femme de bronze aura craché sur la pêcheur d'arcs-en-ciel, la terre et la mer se recoudront . . . " (120).

‡ "l'amour n'étant que feu, il vaut mieux le vivre au pied de l'eau. Mon soleil! Ma lune!" (136).

1. The *authorities* are always imposing their presence on the lives of all the inhabitants of his world. In the first three novels, they are represented, generally, under two aspects. On the face of it, the authorities are fig- ures of evil. In a universe without an institutionalized faith, with faith in life and "viande," or human flesh, evil inheres in forces of destruc- tion, oppression, and exploitation. All of the worst human impulses, the corruption of human values associated with the massacring of the spirit and the body by the tyrants of the past two and a half decades— tyrants evoking especially, though not exclusively, Mobuto—are fig- ured in the various mayors, Guides-Providentiels, presidents, and so forth that appear in Sony Labou Tansi's fiction. No visage of authority can hold out as a positive force—even the defensive and rebellious regime of Delantia, in *La Vie et demie,* can not escape being caught up in the murderous cycles of war and destruction.

2. Authorities generate *resistance,* and the second social world consists of the more pacific, honorable people who insist on integrity. Without promoting revolution or revolutionaries—indeed their recourse to force is often dictated by less-than-noble impulses, and their cause is never justified by Sony Labou Tansi on ideological grounds, or given self-righteous vindications—we can say that the protagonists or antag- onists of all Sony Labou Tansi's novels are either heroic or villainous. And when they are heroes, or, as in the case of *Les Sept Solitudes,* hero- ines, they are marked by strength of character and conviction. In the first two novels, especially *L'Anté-peuple* (written first, but published third, after *L'Etat honteux* [1981]), the figures of resistance are never exalted or ennobled to the point where a cult of personality could be constructed. Sony Labou Tansi avoids the pitfalls of Ngugi's or Beti's later works of fiction by insisting on the aleatoric, sensual, physical aspect of life embodied in those who permit love to become a reality. But these characters can be miserable, depressed, or uncontrollable: Chaïdana refuses the orders of her revolutionary father, Martial, and insists on taking revenge on the authorities, on mounting her revolt through actions that include sleeping with members of the ruling party, and even bearing their children.

3. Life's full measure demands Rabelaisian belly laughter—intrinsic to the third sort of world, one whose inhabitants are not unlike Soyinka's dev- otees of Ogun, or Dionysus. This group—let's call them the *dancers*—is the craziest of the three, their lives filled with the most brilliant jousting, with completely gratuitous, irrational wordplay and actionplay. "Mots" [words] become "maux" [evils], "eau-de-vie" [brandy—literally life- water] has its "eau-de-feu" [fire water]—and the list of invented terms,

of phantasmagoric characters, of worlds that abound in the ancient Greek, in the Medieval, in the African, and in the postmodern architecture of the imagination, all join in the construction of an alternate reality to that run by the "authorities" and their shameful state.

This is a world in which conventional ideas of good and evil are not relevant, in which positive and negative values are defined by the perceiver. We learn to disregard the degrading, weak actions of Dodou in *L'Anté-peuple,* while we share in the view of his positive, ennobling qualities, as reflected in the gaze of the prison administrator or of Yealdra. Offering up opposing discourses, Sony Labou Tansi proposes opposing views of reality, and then seeks a vision that goes beyond opposition. For example, if we lend credence to the "logorrhea" of Martillimi Lopez in *L'Etat honteux,* then we are to believe he is an exceptionally humane and yet down-to-earth ruler who repeatedly tries to leave office, but whose people can not stand having him resign. The antithetical vision of the dictator is glimpsed in the cracks of his discourse, in his irrational responses of murderous brutality. Yet beyond all these oppositions, and all other valuations, we find a dynamic affirmation.

Life reechoes with the generous spirit of an endless discourse, ministering to the solitudes of existence without love—a theme we noted in Bessie Head's writings, but treated here with far greater exhuberance. All of Sony Labou Tansi's work is devoted to the creation of figures who give themselves fully to life's force—Sarngata Nola in *Les Sept Solitudes,* or the colossus in *Les Yeux du volcan* (1988)—who come from a foreign world to infuse our own with new vitality.

Their goal is to use the force of revolt, including especially that found in words, so as to mobilize honor, love, and life against all that would immobilize the human spirit. Thus, when Sarngata Nola sees Estina Bronzario emerge naked from her swim, his impulse is to join hands with her in her effort to construct "the man-true-site-of-honor and dignity."[*] For Estina Bronzario this is the place where a new conception of life, a new beginning occurs: "We are the children of transcendence: we want to build the hope of dreaming another dream."[†] And this dream takes a definitive feminist turn in *Les Sept Solitudes,* as Estina Bronzario leads the women into a Lysistratean strike in revolt against the men when Lorsa Lopez kills his wife, Estina Benta, in a fit of jealousy.

---

[*] "l'homme-lieu-exact-d'honneur et de la dignité" (97)

[†] "Nous sommes les enfants de la transcendance: nous voulons construire l'espoir de rêver un autre rêve" (97).

However, the "dream of another dream" goes beyond the readjustment of the ratio of power between men and women. Sarngata Nola enters onto the stage as though trumpeting in another reality: he sets Valancia in motion:

> All of Valancia learned of the new tauntings of the actor Sarngata Nola and trembled for him. We knew that with his pride and his buffooneries he was going to present us with another occasion for the police to come [i.e., he would be killed, thus fostering a police investigation]. We loved the actor with a global love, a mob's love, blindly enough.... When he wasn't, as on that day, in battle dress, he just wore his buskins and his purple velvet cape, which made him look like a Nubian colossus.... The women nicknamed Sarngata Nola the Prompter, because he danced the 93 hubbubs [chahuts] of the Coast perfectly. He was the male as our Fathers intended him: full of health, voracious, inexhaustible, a fine manager of dream and of reality.*

Voracious and inexhaustible, a Nietzschean definition of life itself.

Whereas Sony Labou Tansi's fiction begins, in *L'Anté-peuple,* with the clash between the two worlds and the two rhetorics of authority and revolt, it is the third group, the dancers and their discourse, who eventually prevail in his subsequent work. The stage for revolutionary struggle is constructed with a realistic set, with recognizable references to actual places, situations, and historical figures. But with Sony Labou Tansi the signposts themselves are rarely direct—Mobuto or Sassou-Nguesso's names do not appear, the river Congo may occasionally be mentioned, its other name (Zaire) is not. More typically reference is made to "the country" or "the river"—the city goes unnamed. The first step of distanciation is taken when the specifics of time and place are simultaneously rendered in both microscopic detail and anonymous generality, leaving one with a sense of urgency about a situation in which communication must assume a certain element of disguise. One is left with the impression that the particularities of time and place can not fully account for the situation being described, that the allegorizing evokes a more widespread phenomenon whose references extend to other similar situations, whose reach across

---

* "Tout Valancia apprit les nouvelles brocarderies du comédien Sarngata Nola et tremble pour ses pauvres jours. Nous savions qu'avec son orgueil et ses loufoqueries il allait bientôt nous donner une nouvelle occasion d'attendre la police. Nous aimions le comédien d'un amour global, un amour de foule, assez aveugle....

"Quand il n'était pas, comme ce jour-là, en tenue d'offense, il mettait simplement ses cothurnes et sa houppelande de velours pourpre, ce qui lui donnait l'allure d'un colosse nubien.... Les femmes avaient surnommé Sarngata Nola le Souffleur, parce qu'il dansait les quatre-vingt-treize chahuts de la Côte avec un art sans reproche. C'était le mâle ainsi que l'entendaient nos Pères: plein de santé, vorace, inépuisable, bon gérant du rêve et de la réalité..." (68–69).

time is enlarged by the frame already set in place by historical precedent, and whose significance goes beyond the immediate appeal to mimetic art. In other words, the scope and depth of his world reach beyond phenomenological description. The seeds of allegory, with its multilayered dimensions, already appear in the first works.

With each succeeding novel Sony Labou Tansi has emphasized the supra-realistic aspects of his work. At the beginning of *La Vie et demie* we are in the presence of a world in which the boundary between "réalité" and "rêve" [dream] is rendered problematic, in which the horrors of political abuse arch into a nightmare of refusal. Eventually even the oppositional forces must submit to the melding of life and death. The force of naming, of defining honor and shame, must contend with a life force that refuses to accept the death of figures of repression or revolt, and that above all refuses the possibility of assigning a fixed name to a fixed character whose life span is of limited duration. In other words, the allegorizing tendency that effaces the clarity of difference between reality and dream prevails over the unstated assumptions of realism, rejects the boundaries and distinctions upon which a fiction of realism is erected, and creates in its place dialogic discourses of postrevolt magical realism.

L'Etat honteux takes a marvelous step in this direction in the meticulously controlled performance of Martillimi Lopez's stream-of-consciousness discourse. But the implied narrator's underlying indignation and scorn, and the mockery of dictatorship itself, controls the free-flowing voices of unreality. With *Les Sept Solitudes* and *Les Yeux du volcan* we move into a fully developed expansion of the new mode. Sony Labou Tansi's individual oeuvre recapitulates the pattern of changes of African literature itself over the past thirty-five years from witness and commitment through revolt and contradiction to the ultimate supra-artistic affirmations of postmodernist writing.

We can see this in the way in which conventional boundaries are increasingly altered or effaced in the last two novels. For example, we expect characters to be named and defined, and to meet a recognizable set of expectations. The fish with the death's head captured in *Les Sept Solitudes* confounds these expectations. It can not be named and defined, and most of all it can not be reliably placed within the boundaries set by our words. Not even the most fundamental difference between life and death can be reliably assigned: "We can't say if we're dealing with a snake or a fish."* Its name, the fish with the death's head, came from "some sort of

---

* "Nous ne pouvions dire si nous avions affaire à un serpent ou bien à un poisson" (103).

black worms that covered entirely the face of the animal, with an arrangement of crossed tibias, high on the forehead, which gave off a delectable glow."* Half modern monster, half ancient progenitor—"Years later, the sages of the anthropological laboratory of Queen City would establish the fact that the fish with the death's head was the indisputable ancestor of Man."†

This is the third option regarding humankind's descendance, following after the belief advanced by the people of Nsanga-Norda that the primeval ancestor of humankind was a monkey, and that of Valancia where it was held that it was a dinosaur. The time of the discovery of the fish, the present, is undefined, the future knowledge concerning it, the very identity of Queen-City, is equally fantastic, and finally the beast's own state of existence is cast into an ultimate state of indeterminacy: "No one was ever able to say categorically that the animal was alive or dead."‡ All that can be stated with certainty is that its properties are magical as its nature is unknown: "the rumor went around that the meat of the animal had the property of keeping eternally young whoever ate it cooked in oil from Nsanga-Norda."** While evocative of fabulous figures of mythology (possessing "the allure of a Dogon funerary mask"),†† it is defined within the narrow limits of knowledge established by "the sages of the anthropological laboratory"‡‡ whose only definitive statement is the most fantastic, namely, that it is the primeval ancestor of humankind. It is enshrined in a fortress to be preserved, and takes its place alongside Sarngata Nola and Estina Bronzario in the minds of the people whose preoccupation with life and death joined all three figures in an unreal stratosphere. "'It's a question of making it unkillable,' preached Fartamio Andra."*** In a sense, though Estina Bronzario is dismembered and Sarngata Nola immures himself in his citadel, they are both also rendered "unkillable"—both beyond the ordinary strictures of life and death. This is the source of

---

* "des espèces de verres noirs qui couvraient toute la face de la bête, avec, au haut du front, une manière de tibias croisés qui émettaient un rayon délicieux" (103).

† "Des années plus tard, les savants du laboratoire d'anthropologie de Queen-City allaient établir que le poisson à la tête de mort était l'ancêtre indiscutable de l'homme" (104).

‡ "[P]ersonne ne put jamais dire de manière catégorique si la bête était morte ou vivante . . . " (104).

** "le bruit courut que la chair de la bête avait les vertus de garder éternellement jeune quiconque l'aurait mangée cuite à l'huile de Nsanga-Norda" (104).

†† "l'allure d'un masque mortuaire dogon" (104)

‡‡ "les savants du laboratoire d'anthropologie" (104)

*** "'Il s'agit de la rendre intuable,' prêchait Fartamio Andra" (105).

Estina Bronzario's strength, a metaphorical view of identity as conviction that can not be physically destroyed.

Estina Bronzario gives voice to honor and to the place of honor for women. She is a counterfoil to Sarngata Nola, who counts life and not principle as the highest priority. Estina Bronzario is, above all, ennobled and enshrined by her steadfast integrity. Her identity is in metal, not flesh; her defense of women is not attached to the sexual-generative force associated with the vagina, but to an enduring sense of justice. She gives voice to an intransigent resistance that Sony Labou Tansi would seem both to honor and, still, to desire to transcend. Her attitude toward death is typical: the crimes of others are to be defined and resisted, the fear of death as the ultimate threat of change is to be overcome: "There's murder everywhere," she explains to Anna Maria, who expresses the fear that Estina Bronzario will be killed. "They think they'll solve the problems of the Coast if they kill me; they're wrong. I'm tougher dead than alive. They'll very soon understand: living I'm negotiable, dead I'll be God."*

However, in the universe of the Seven Solitudes, the state of death is the least certain of all. Death repeatedly fails to triumph in the works of Sony Labou Tansi, just as it repeatedly returns as the ultimate threat. In *L'Anté-peuple,* Dadou is virtually beaten to death, but is "resurrected" as a beggar, and eventually as a revolutionary who has nothing to lose. His identity, like his name, is tenuously maintained, as the threat of death would mean nothing if there were not an identifiable existence to be threatened. But the fluidity with which his roles shift displaces the realistic danger of death as the absolute extinction of self—a displacement that becomes the central metaphor for resistance in *La Vie et demie.* If Estina Bronzario's statement can be read as a credo for revolution or for feminist principle, that is, as a metaphor for the endurance of principled resistance, it can not entirely account for the manner in which death or change is treated; much less does it account for the universe, the stage setting for existence, that contextualizes its menace.

Sony Labou Tansi invariably concocts a double or triple or pluridimensional reality. "Solitudes" become thematized as the name of the street of prostitutes who are "saved" by Sarngata Nola. But the term is also the expression of life, of those who live by love and not just principle, as well as the signpost of life, which, as the islands of solitude, marks off the sea and gives it definition. "Solitude" reappears under the moon as the

---

* "On est partout chez le meurtre. Ils croient résoudre les problèmes de la Côte en me tuant; ils se trompent. Je suis plus dure morte que vivante. Ils vont très vite s'en rendre compte: vivante on me négocie, mais morte je serai Dieu" (102).

purist symbol for life: it is also the site at which life is dishonored and shamed. "In the sky, the moon danced the silvery hubbub that it had always danced above the isle of Solitudes."* Under such a moon, bayed at by the dogs, either death walked the streets, as the people of Nsanga-Norda believed, or dishonor visited Sacayo Sambo for eating salamander meat, as the people of Valancia believed. As the narrative voice presents honor as a supreme value, we accept the second view as Sacayo Sambo tries in vain to erase the shame by throwing himself in the ocean and drowning. Sixteen times he tries and fails, the sea refusing to kill him. When he finally does succeed in submitting his body to a consuming fire, his voice continues to address us: "Isn't there anyone to kill me? Death runs from me."†

The text places such events beyond legend, fable, and reality. Historicity is not denied, it is rendered richer, more suggestive and complex, and the conception of life that emerges is all the more forceful. The fabulous opens us to infinite possibilities, but we can still recognize familiar patterns of the Sony Labou Tansi universe. For example, after Sacayo Sambo's attempted suicides, the setting for an apocalyptic event is forecast. The "glyptographic Mohammedan" Baktiar Ben Sari reads the portion of the cathedral on which the monster Yongo had scratched a series of signs/messages before his disappearance, and then gives an interpretation. "When Estina Bronzario has been killed, the fire will come."‡ The prophecy was accepted, indeed taken as a confirmation of already-accepted knowledge: "Since her childhood she [Fartamio Andra] had known that Estina Bronzario would be killed. It couldn't be otherwise. Estina Bronzario had to be assassinated, we knew how and where. . . ."** The parti-colored fabric of events, the delight in anecdote, in a supra-reality, in characters whose names are barely recorded before their departure, and especially in the apocalyptic forebodings, all mark Sony Labou Tansi's narrative technique. Prognostication informs the substance of the novel—instead of *magic* realism we might style this *prophetic* realism.

We are given many predictions, including those concerning the death of Sarngata Nola and the fall of Valancia, neither of which events occurs

---

* "Au ciel, la lune dansait le chahut argenté qu'elle avait toujours dansé au-dessus de l'île des Solitudes" (90).

† "N'y a-t-il personne pour me tuer? La mort me fuit" (92).

‡ "Quand on aura tué Estina Bronzario, le feu viendra" (91).

** "C'est depuis l'enfance qu'elle savait qu'on allait tuer Estina Bronzario. Il ne pouvait en être autrement. Estina Bronzario devait être assassinée, nous savions où et comment . . ." (91).

within the scope of the novel. Though the novel is continually peppered with apocalyptic warnings, partially fulfilled with the final flood, it is also marked by inconsistencies, by resistance to its own pose of absolute knowledge and certainty. In the end, confident assertions about the future are counter-balanced by the community's refusal to resign itself to a policy of wait and see, to an uncertainty that would grow with the reiteration of the same prophetic visions. Even the universally admired tower of resistance, the colossus in *Les Yeux du volcan,* is killed by the "fou" [madman] for his failure to take action, for his submission to a passivity and millenarianism that become a form of tergiversation. These shifting positions mark the transformation of an initial moral stance, an apparently admirable resistance, into rigid moralism, and finally into inaction. Sony Labou Tansi's unease lies with two absolutes: the absolute evil of tyranny; and the absolute rigidity and purism of its opponents—those for whom principle has the power to erect definitions and boundaries that separate good from evil, the Coast from Nsanga-Norda, fish eaters from meat eaters . . . At the end of *La Vie et demie,* the heart of resistance, Darmellia, is incinerated by its own weapons after its original defiant courage and integrity give way to intransigence and a murderous series of ripostes. Estina Bronzario, Chaïdana, the colossus, all the towers of resistance are toppled, martyrs not so much to an indomitable foe as to their own resistance to the noise and dance, the hubbub, the foolishness of life.

The need for truth is given as a basic presupposition; the figures of truth, from Dadou to the colossus, march in, and, failing to negotiate with life, are destroyed in the end: "Reality and dream are negotiable. Truth never . . ."*

The Unnameable

The space beyond boundaries is never quite attained, but it is always implied. It is unnameable, and therefore defies the project of naming the actions and actors, of naming honor and shame. It is in the dreams of transcendence of Estina Bronzario and her predecessors, the two Chaïdanas, Yealdara and Yavelda. It is in the solitude of love—"what love is not a solitude?" (79)†—and it is the locus of love, which gives life its raison d'être: "love remains the absolute bond of life;"‡ "love is the precise meaning of all existence."** Like the joining of heaven and earth, the final act of the

---

* "La réalité et le rêve peuvent se négocier. La vérité jamais . . . " (37).

† "quel amour n'est pas une solitude?"(Sony Labou Tansi 1985, 79).

‡ "l'amour reste le lien absolu de la vie" (172)

** "l'amour est le sens exact des existences" (171)

flood, the unnameable topos beyond the scope of words is evoked by oxymorons—"Every sleep has its waking"*—in which the trope's conundrum, its condition of impossibility, is the condition of possibility for expression. "This world is an enormous *corpse* that fights to *live* by any means" (my stress).†

The impossible is evoked in love, in its place in life, because Sony Labou Tansi understands life as a scandal whose inevitable shame and loss must nevertheless be overcome. He cries out against those who "name" their loss and shame. This is the writer's credo, the honor of naming. But the only means of not naming one's loss and shame is to evoke their opposites, love and honor—and love is a solitude, honor another boundary set to exclude the actions of loss and shame. If dreams are the seeds of reality, then their fruition, the narrative text of honor and love, is to be realized only in the flight of dream. This is Sony Labou Tansi's contradiction—he can not name the only thing that gives value to existence without reducing the dream to hedges, boundaries, limits and words, the trivia and foolishness of words, "jaquemarts"—mechanical figures that strike the hours. As mechanical as the seriousness of classical realism, they denote triviality, "niaiserie." Lorsa Lopez evokes the time before the present era, when men were "tree-men," when the week had five days; when people had invented vessels constructed with magnetized light that "brought them to the moon and beyond a star now gone from the sky: the moon of padimontaure."‡ The magic moon of padimontaure is the place for words that are foolish and unreal, but that alone suffice to describe the impossible.

This site of impossibility is located in the image of the fisherman's catch that comes from the sea, and can not be named, confined, defined, or known: it is the one whose original unknowable reality can only be suggested through the traces it leaves, through what it is not. It is called the unspeakable marvel, and stands, like the cry of the cliff, the distant points of transcendence, as a magic beyond human ken. "That morning, the perch fishers returned with an unspeakable marvel."** The unnameable marvel is, like every child, given a nickname—"the eel of Motossé," itself an unreal name. It appears to be endless, and is finally chopped up and stuffed in the depression in the earth caused by the cry of the cliff. As this cry is unintelligible, the people do not realize they are stifling the warning of the apocalypse that will accompany the flood. The apocalyptic readings

---

* "Chaque sommeil a son reveil" (175).

† "Ce monde est un *cadavre* immense qui se bat à *vivre* par tous les moyens" (193).

‡ "les amenaient sur la lune et au-delà d'un astre aujourd'hui disparu: la lune de padimontaure" (81).

** "Ce matin-là, les pêcheurs de perches rentrèrent avec une merveille indicible" (81).

and warnings themselves are incomplete and indefinite. Warnings are scratched, recorded, cried out in mysterious, incomprehensible fashion; interpreted or divined by fools or strangers, and then taken as literal truths—some of which paralyze the people. These patterns are matched by the ludicrousness of the authorities—the mayor, the unnamed rulers—who have intimidated the people and yet whose function is to give exaggerated comic relief rather than to exercise rational powers. In the end, it is the human, and not the unnameable drama that matters.

In his last two novels, *Les Sept Solitudes de Lorsa Lopez* and *Les Yeux du volcan,* Sony Labou Tansi has reduced the size of the threat from the authorities who are diminished, burlesqued, emasculated, even made to appear pitiable and hilarious, almost aesthetes, as we see in the spectacle of the mayor adding elements of his own paraphernalia to the constructed scene of the murder of Estina Bronzario. The gap between the insignificant authorities and their opponents is exaggerated: Sarngata Nola is two meters ten; the unnamed figure of opposition in *Les Yeux* is a "colossus"; and the mayor, normally of average height, loses centimeters each time he tries to act out the role of petty tyrant: "He was sweating with anger—an anger that had reduced the one meter seventy he usually measured to a miserable one meter forty-six." The narrator adds, to give emphasis to the metaphor of height, that "anger, [has] among its other virtues, that of rendering small in stature the already-small in spirit" (my trans.).* But the strength of the figural, the dream or fabulous side of existence, pushes the narrative far past the limits of metaphorical statements. The trope overreaches itself, to evoke a fuller, larger life. The terms of this vibrant portrait of existence are reworked by the enlargement of those who resist, who insist on the impossible in the face of silence. "Art is the strength to force reality to say what it would voluntarily pass over in silence".† In *Les Sept Solitudes* what Sony Labou Tansi tries to do is to restore stature and voice to the silenced, especially to women.

New definitions of the self and human stature emerge, while simultaneously the subject's boundaries commence to dissolve. In *Les Sept Solitudes,* those boundaries are subjected to the reorientation of the lines between men and women. For instance, in Valancia the revolution of the

---

* "Il suait de colère—une colère qui avait réduit le mètre soixante-dix qu'il mesurait à un pauvre mètre quarante-six,la colère ayant, entre autres vertus, celle de rendre petits de taille les déjà-petits d'esprit" (Sony Labou Tansi 1988, 18).

† "L'art c'est la force de faire dire à la réalité ce qu'elle risquait de passer volontairement sous silence"(Sony Labou Tansi 1985, 11).

women results in a new woman who refuses accepted gender limitations. Not only does Estina Bronzario issue decrees, such as the strike against sexual relations, she envisages a new type of woman whose role begins with replacing the men. "There are no more men in this country, I'll make the women work."* Honor and pride make Estina Bronzario "la dure des dures" [the hardest of the hard]. Authority and power pass to the women who alone demonstrate strength to resist. The resentment and pettiness of the men is measured against the qualities of the women. The figurative becomes literal as the crime of the bizarre Lorsa Lopez, the murder of Estina Bronzario, springs from the frustrated attempt of the men to stop the women from assuming their new role: "Now that the women play at becoming men (it's the fault of the Whites; they came and mixed everything: the place of the puppet, the epileptic, the simpleton) nothing works any more."† The "mélange" or mixture to which Lorsa Lopez refers, however, is not simply one of new cultural or social values; it is a sign of the more completely phantasmagorical world that the women and their dreams usher in. The end of male power does not denote a replacement, but a transformation in which the apocalyptic shift of fool and invalid to center stage has already occurred: "puppet, epileptic, and simpleton" are all validated.

The point at which this change takes place bears on the concepts of subject and identity, and Sony Labou Tansi pushes the fluidity of the boundaries of the subject by expanding the limits of language. Thus, whereas Henri Lopes has his dissident Colonel Haraka, in *Le Pleurer-rire* (1982), disguise himself as a woman when he tries to escape, leading to an *ironic* situation when he is taken to be an easy prey to the soldier's sexual advances, Sony Labou Tansi goes one step further, actually dismantling the gender boundaries. When the supermale Sarngata Nola explains that his intention in freeing the prostitutes and marrying them was to save them, he describes his action as a birthing: "I have always borne into the world those that even history would have been afraid to invent."‡ His noble intentions are caught in the contradiction he creates for himself— contradictions inseparably linked to gender identities. Thus, he would assume the responsibility for freeing those whose shame consisted in accepting constraints placed upon them by others instead of having them

---

* "Il n'y a plus d'hommes dans ce pays, je fais fonctionner les femmes" (20).

† "Depuis que dans cette ville les femmes s'amusent à devenir des hommes (c'est la faute aux Blancs; ils sont venus tout mélanger: la place du pantin, celle de l'épileptique et celle du niais) plus rien ne va plus . . . " (28).

‡ "J'ai toujours mis au monde ceux que même l'histoire aurait eu peur d'inventer" (68).

assume their own autonomy of action: "Today and *thanks to me* they understand that the genitals are not a panic machine"[*] (my stress).

One consequence of this reorientation of gender is the reformulation of gender identities. Estina Bronzario's new rule is based on a new being: "Women are also men;"[†] and she decrees that the women in the future will pass on not only their yeast infections, but their names as well. Estina Bronzario salutes Sarngata Nola with the same words she has used before: "Hello, Sarngata Nola! We come to tell you that in Valancia women are also men."[‡] Eventually we are not surprised to learn that the voice of the muezzin, the quintessential symbol of male authority, is also subject to the new powers of transformation. The new "crieur de prières" [caller of prayers] has a woman's voice and is thus nicknamed the man-woman of Nsanga-Norda.[**]

But if the line between life and death, man and woman, is effaced, so, too, is that which provides each individual with an identity, one's name. Sony Labou Tansi defines his role, his honor, as being the one who names, and the name of each chapter in *Les Sept Solitudes* is based on each of the principal characters, the first being the victim of Lorsa Lopez, Estina Benta. However, when an attempt is made to memorialize Estina Benta by naming the public square in her honor, it is revealed that Estina Benta is not her actual name: "in fact, Estina Benta was not the real name of the deceased."[††] The narrator's explanations become more and more extravagant, and in the final analysis there is no possibility of consistently assigning a name to the person. Even the meaning of the words with which her new name is constructed are indeterminate: "She had won it [her name] in a dance contest organized in Nsanga-Norda by the authorities, because all during her performance the head authority never stopped exclaiming, his arms raised, 'Benta Estina,' which means flesh of dreams or flesh of celebration."[‡‡] The name sticks, ironically, despite the fact that Estina Benta detests it, reminding us of the colonial practice of assigning official

---

[*] "Aujourd'hui et *grace à moi,* elles savent que le sexe n'est pas un engin de panique . . . " (68).

[†] "Les femmes aussi sont les hommes" (44).

[‡] "Salut, Sarngata Nola! Nous venons te dire qu'à Valancia les femmes aussi sont les hommes" (62).

[**] "l'homme-femme de Nsanga-Norda" (132).

[††] "En fait, Estina Benta n'était pas le vrai nom du défunct" (42).

[‡‡] "Elle l'avait gagné lors d'un concours de danse organisé à Nsanga-Norda par les autorités, parce que tout au long de sa prestation le chef des autorités n'avait cessé de s'exclamer les bras au ciel: 'Benta Estina', ce qui signifie chair de rêve ou chair de fête" (42).

names in Francophone African colonies. The words that define and signify, that identify the basic reality of the subject, enter the comic "chahut" [hubbub] of life.

This theme is pushed even further in *Les Yeux du volcan* where the hero-protagonist, the colossus around whom the action of revolt is centered, lacks a consistent name or identity. His role and his past are repeatedly called into question, just as our introduction to him is marked by narrative speculation that undermines any consistency of identity. As it is the people who stubbornly insist on giving Estina Benta her name in *Les Sept Solitudes,* so, too, is it the common knowledge of the people that provides contradictory information about the colossus: "We wondered if it wasn't the famous Colonel Benoît whom privately the Authorities nicknamed 'the angel with eyes of lead' " (my trans.).* However, absurdly, the man resembles none of the versions of the colonel known in the region:

> neither the one who came from the legends (he had no teeth since his tenderest youth; he was tiny, like his ancestors from the regions of the Delta and of the Kongo); nor the one proffered by the Authorities, according to which the colonel was a hippopotamus, a meter forty-seven tall, huge from head to tippy toe, bald like a crocodile egg, with a row of canines in his bottom jaw, and who, since his childhood, wore nothing but the ancestral toga of the Gogons.†

In the first improbable instance, the colossus ("with him everything becomes immense")‡ is likened to a toothless Pygmy—a type who appears in semi-idealized form in *La Vie et demie* as a natural denizen of the forest, victim of the more aggressive non-Pygmy neighbors who seek to domesticate and dominate the Pygmies. Their size is a disguise for their generosity of spirit, an overflow of natural interdependencies that leads them to achieve perfect integration with the environment. However, when it is a question of others in need, the dimensions of their spirit are reduced. The narrator's view of the colossus is tinged with a similar exaggeration, related to the unreality of legend that corresponds not only to a special world of its

---

* "On se demandait si ce n'était pas le fameux colonel Benoît qu'en privé les Autorités surnommaient 'l'ange aux yeux de plomb'" (Sony Labou Tansi 1988, 16. All translations of this text are my own.)

† "ni à celui qui venait des légendes (il n'avait pas de dents, et cela depuis sa tendre enfance; il était minuscule comme tous ses ancêtres des régions de l'Embouchure et du Kongo), ni à celui que donnaient les Autorités et selon lequel le colonel était un hippopotame d'un mètre quarante-sept, massif de la tête à la pointe des orteils, chauve comme un oeuf de crocodile, une rangée de canines sur la mâchoire inférieure, et qui, depuis l'enfance, ne savait se vêtir que de la toge ancestrale des Gogons."

‡ "avec lui toute chose devient immense" (16)

own, but also to a special discourse—one all too simply labeled oral or traditional literature. Here this discourse is identified with the literature that derives from the ancestors upriver, from the traditions and the past of purely African origin.

The second alternative description of the colossus is even more preposterous; it could be said to have its origins with the Uncles, a term employed by Henri Lopes and occasionally Sony Labou Tansi to designate the whites, and especially the white colonialists. The term "les Autorités" refers to those who assumed the mantle of rule upon Independence, and who are often depicted—as in *La Vie et demie* and *L'Etat honteux*—as dependent on the military forces of the Uncles to remain in power. The Uncles' view of the colossus, whose name legend preserves, fits in with that of a grotesque, Babar-the-Elephant universe. The menacing visage of "Africa" is exaggerated and caricatured: it is all teeth and crocodiles; its unnaturalness given in a row of canines on his lower jaw; its grotesqueness in a massive hippo; and, finally, its ugliness and impotence in the baldness of an egg. All these elements are synthesized in the mock anthropological description of the "authentic," "ancient," unpolluted African, of an Africa in its "Gogon" toga, one step from the Dogon sage.

These two views of the colossus, incompatible with each other and with the "actual" appearance of this "unnamed marvel," are joined in the *métissage* of gender in which the only "established" fact is in effect the least apparent of all, that the colonel "was not a man, but an incorrigible woman."* Having escaped the traps of legend or colonialist fantasy, s/he is free to take flight into the realm of Sony Labou Tansi's own universe, supercharged with all the by-now familiar signs of those stubborn adherents to mouth-to-mouth life: "as stubborn as steel wire" (or bronze); an "unrestrained consumer of cola nuts and of citronella brandies, a fanatical supporter of the regional team of Hozoronte and the apostolic con men of Yorzango. . . ."† The existence of these teams and their locations may be only imaginary; their particular spirit, the wild flavor they impart to this fantastic female supporter, imposes a figural dimension on life, a force that demands a new reading not only of subject and of text, but of the newly shaped context of African literature upon which the writings of Sony Labou Tansi insist.

---

* "n'était pas un homme, mais une femme indécrottable" (Sony Labou Tansi 1988, 16–17).

† "têtue comme un fil d'acier [or bronze] . . . consommatrice sans réserve de la cola et des alcools de citronelle, supportant comme une folle l'équipe régionale d'Hozoronte et les magouilleurs apostoliques de Yorzango . . ." (17).

Conclusion
▼▼▼▼▼▼▼▼▼▼▼

Esu at the Crossroads

The literary history and patterns of change that I have been attempting to delineate could themselves be read as a text, as a construct whose structure and patterns are the product of a particular reading, one that makes no claim to an objective, fixed, Absolute "Reality." This reading resists the totalizing call for classical realism as the only legitimate form of literature for Africa, just as it resists the authenticizing impulse with its xenophobic rejection of foreign influences on African culture—the Bolekaja fallacy. On the one hand, I argue that the culture has always been *métissée,* and is now more than ever the product of Western, traditionally African, Islamic, Christian, Marxist, and even colonialist influences, with a literature similarly influenced by written and oral, classical realist and magical realist traditions. On the other hand, I construct a particular genealogy, which traces the lineage from Camara Laye to Chinua Achebe to Sony Labou Tansi by way of Ferdinand Oyono, Wole Soyinka, Bessie Head, V. Y. Mudimbe, and others. The notion of a lineage may be deceiving. One could have disregarded the whoreson and taken only the legitimate heirs, choosing the upright *engagement* of Ngugi wa Thiong'o's or Mongo Beti's later fiction as the worthy successors of Negritude and anticolonial predecessors. But the whoreson would not be denied; the subversion of the language and texts, the revolutionary nature of the works of Oyono, Ouologuem, Soyinka, and Sony Labou Tansi have compelled recognition, as they stubbornly adhered to a program of defamiliarization that refuses to cast its wari pebbles quietly on the margins of a straightjacketed mainstream.

In fact, the mainstream of Declarative African literature, works grounded in a righteous self-assurance, has insisted on constraints that ultimately contradict their own aesthetic platform. To present the world as it really is, to sing the praises and damn the oppression of the people, is an admirable goal. But when unambiguous declarations of truth are necessarily married to discourses and visions that are easily accessible to all addressees, the result will be the perpetuation of familiar forms. These forms, in fiction, are variants of classical realism, and thus, as Catherine Belsey and Louis Althusser have shown, are grounded in a preexistent Order whose structure and patrilineage reinforce the status quo, even as their rhetoric is geared to calls for change. The problem is that, as the argument for realistic mimetic imaging is made, it marginalizes the very forces of revolt and subversion that it ostensibly aspires to affirm. The rhetoric of the argument operates as though the text were nothing but its mimetic function, and in so doing excludes the layers of subtextual and metatextual referencing and coding that reinforce the very order to which the surface meaning is opposed.

This forgetting of subtext and code is congruent with a deliberate failure to acknowledge the self-conscious dimension of discourse, an integral aspect of how ideology functions, according to Althusser. Belsey equates this suppression of the self-conscious with the fundamental project of classical realism, and we can further associate it with the patterns of resistance not only to change but also to all defamiliarization in literature. In Julia Kristeva's terms, the equivalent to this act of repression is the deliberate suppression of the awareness of the split in the subject, a painful awareness that accompanies the "thetic" break.* But the thetic break, the moment when the subject becomes aware of the separate existence of objects, of its separation as an independent being, of its own status as a subject and of its consciousness, brings simultaneously the painful recognition of division and rupture along with self-consciousness. This is the condition of possibility for language, coinciding with the moment when the self becomes aware of the split between self and other, and of the awareness of its own consciousness. The awareness is a painful experience, and so repression and sublimation immediately follow, along with the processes that rechannel basic natural drives and concomitant physical rhythms into the symbolic realm through which linguistic expression emerges.

---

* The thetic break is associated with Lacan's mirror phase, in which the child becomes aware of the separation between herself and the outside world, recognizes herself as separate from others, and from the mother in particular. Kristeva focuses on the impact of this break on the process of linguistic development: "The child's first so-called holophrastic enunciations include gesture, the object, and vocal emission. Because they are not yet sentences (NP-VP), generative grammar is not readily equipped to account for them. Nevertheless, they are already thetic in the sense that they separate an object from the subject, and attribute to it a semiotic fragment, which thereby becomes a signifier" (Kristeva 1984, 43).

Literature is the ultimate product of these processes. In opposition to Kristeva and Bakhtin, who set the epic text against the polysemic, polyphonic literature of the carnival—the contemporary novel with its roots in Menippean satire—I would argue that the African tradition, including its orature, its Europhonic predecessors, and its contemporary Europhonic heirs, has always exhibited the qualities of polyphonic writing. The reason the epic and oral traditions have been mistaken as monophonic texts is that their author-audience relationship has been subsumed under the all-embracing monoliths of Tradition and Community—the equivalent to Althusser's Absolute Subject. Of course, research from Ruth Finnegan (1970) to Robert Cancel (1989) has shown that neither the performer nor the texts are fixed or immutable, nor, more important, that they lack the basic requirement of double-voicedness. In fact, each performance is both a direct exposition of a familiar text within a familiar form, and simultaneously a play on that text and form, turned to the uses of the different performers, and received just as variously by the different members of the audience.

Similarly, just as Henry Louis Gates reads black American literature as a signifying process whereby the black author and reader signify on a prior white discursive practice, through the mask, as it were, of the white text, so, too, is the African literature of our times double-voiced in precisely the same way with respect to Europhonic discursive practice. The crossroads at which the two cultures find themselves are not the same. But the little figure of Esu who stands there is playing the same function—reminding the huge elephant, who thinks that all is clear before him, that the little figure forgotten behind him is in fact the very one meant to overthrow his reign. "Esu, little man," he is called:

Short diminutive man
Tiny little man.
He uses both hands to sniffle!
We call him master
He who sacrifices without inviting the manumitter
Will find his sacrifice unacceptable
Manumitter, I call on you.
Man by the roadside, bear our sacrifice to Heaven directly
Master, and son of the owner of Idere
Who came from Idere to found the town,
The son of the energetic small fellow
The little man who cleans the gates for the masquerade.
Elderly spirit deity!
(Ogundipe, quoted in Gates [1988] 1989, 65)

Both Gates and Kristeva call on Bakhtin so that the "elderly spirit deity" will free the texts from the constraints language wants to place on all communication, that is, the limitation of signification to direct referential meaning. But without the manumitter, the sacrifice is unacceptable, the discourse is enslaved by its readers' insistence on direct, unambiguous words, not to mention the author's claim to ownership of the meaning. In the final analysis, words, living language, spoken, mimicked by a voice, the product of the subject, can not be reduced to this level of directness. The speaker is two in one—both subject of the enunciation and subject of the utterance (*énoncé*), both observer and actor, while lurking behind both is the creator of the image of actor and observer. This simultaneity of function of the subject is mimicked throughout the process of signification, and is turned by Gates into "signifyin'." Thus, the critical discourse on "signal concepts" from "the black vernacular milieu" turns into a double-voiced discourse: "While critics write for writers and other critics, they also write—in this instance—for 'little' men and women who dwell at the crossroads" (Gates [1988] 1989, 65). This translates into the meeting of two languages created by the externalization of the project of a speaker addressing the other through the voice of a character, through the mask, as it were. Here is Gates's view of the critic of comparative black literature:

> [S/he] dwells at a sort of crossroads, a discursive crossroads at which two languages meet, be these languages Yoruba and English, or Spanish and French, or even (perhaps especially) the black vernacular and standard English. This sort of critic would seem, like Esu, to live at the intersection of these crossroads. (Gates [1988] 1989, 65)

Gates places Signification at this meeting of "two discrete discursive realms," thus echoing his subsequent use of Bakhtin's notion of hidden polemic when discussing Ralph Ellison. Here the key is the idea of a speech act that pretends to say one thing to one party while obliquely meaning something different in reference to another party.

> In hidden polemic the author's discourse is oriented toward its referential object, as is any other discourse, but at the same time each assertion about that object is constructed in such a way that, beside its referential meaning, the author's discourse brings a polemical attack to bear against another speech act, another assertion, on the same topic. Here one utterance focused on its referential object clashes with another utterance on the grounds of the referent itself. That other utterance is not reproduced; it is understood only in its import. (Bakhtin, quoted in Gates [1988] 1989, 111)

Hidden polemic as defined here is merely the special case of all poly-semic discourse in which the voice that is delivering a message puts on the voice of another and speaks in the tones of another. The presence of the two voices to each other is the source of all dialogism. It is fundamental to signifyin', to "Signification," to language, and to our notion of the relationships of intertextuality by which African literature, speaking to and through the voices of its predecessors, has evolved from literatures of *témoignage* to those of contradiction, ambiguity, and increasing antimimeticism.

The repression of plurality within the African voices that address us has proved futile. Not surprisingly, the project of a monological literature has attacked the very spirit of its own making, and like *nza* finds the redoubtable *chi* now at the point in the road where the passage forward would seem to lead.

That site I would like to call, after Kristeva, the place of a literature of subversion. This is the place where literature opens us onto the possibility of multiple meanings—simultaneously surface, subtextual, supratextual, and metatextual—onto the planes of polysemy:

> If one grants that every signifying practice is a field of transpositions of various signifying systems (an inter-textuality), one then understands that its "place" of enunciation and its denoted "object" are never single, complete, and identical to themselves, but always plural, shattered, capable of being tabulated. In this way polysemy can also be seen as the result of a semiotic polyvalence—an adherence to different sign systems. (Kristeva 1984, 60)

If any author would seem to fit this notion of a polysemic practice, it is Sony Labou Tansi. For Kristeva this is clearly the direction that twentieth-century European literature has taken after the monologic novels of the nineteenth century. Now we are accustomed to rupture and marginalized discourse. Indeed, her examples—from Joyce, for example, and Kafka—hardly seem revolutionary. The baseline definition of dialogism and polysemy, however, is not altered by the entry of "difficult" or "experimental" fiction into the canon—rather the canon and its standards have been altered, while at the same time a literature of the absurd and revolt is now familiar and even reassuring. The possibility of *transgression* as a condition for a literature of subversion is increasingly remote, even as the exigency of orienting the hidden polemic of current Congolese writers against political oppression becomes ever more pressing. I submit that we have reached the point where the demands for a literature of subversion are now as acute as the demands for an open polemic, so that we now *must* read the magical components of the works of Sylvain Bemba, Henri Lopes, and especially Sony Labou Tansi as the established order of postmodernist revolt.

The features Kristeva associated with that stance on subversion in her 1966 essay, "Word, Dialogue, and Novel," seem to have been written with a Sony Labou Tansi in mind. To begin, the two pillars on which the "challenge to past writing" rests are *dialogue* (in Bakhtin's sense) and *ambivalence*. We have seen how the literature of revolt, from Oyono's use of the mask to Sony Labou Tansi's double-voicedness, is dialogical. As for ambivalence, we have already noted how Sony Labou Tansi moves poetically across the divide that separates such opposites as life/death, male/female, day/night—not just so that the line is effaced, but so that the *presence* of the terms is fissured because of the pressure of antithetical possibilities. Sony Labou Tansi's "homme-femme" [man-woman] is one example, while the fluid lines that separate river from land, ocean from shore, are another. These shifting spaces are matched by the shifting positions of the principal characters—Chaïdana, Estina Bronzario, Sargnata Zola, and the colossus—leaving us with only one certainty, that no posture is apodictic. This frames our reading of all Sony Labou Tansi's fiction, challenging us not only in the certainty of our convictions, but even more in the comforting confidence of the widely accepted militant stance of resistance. This ambivalence over positions and postures is not what Kristeva calls 0-1, that is, all or nothing, but 0-2, an interval of uncertainty and most of all of "non-exclusive opposition."

Instead of stasis and fixity, the resultant texts give us fluid motility, a "becoming," as opposed to "the level of continuity and substance, both of which obey the logic of being and are thus monological" (Kristeva 1984, 42). Instead of a logic of causality, the rigidity of a law-abiding order, or even simply an order grounded in the deceptive rhetoric used to justify the regimes of force and terror, a logical leap is performed by the use of analogy and anomaly, where the slide along a border places one simultaneously on both sides of a position, a classical Möbius strip locus, the strip itself the classical figure of non-exclusive opposition.

In the postmodern, postrevolt African text, transgression finds its echoes on both fundamental metaphysical and on narrative levels. Just as *identity, substance, causality,* and *definition* are "transgressed," so is a new carnivalesque literature created in its play on *analogy, relation,* and *opposition,* all of which are the constituent elements of dialogism (Kristeva 1966, 56). The uncertain positions generated by ambivalence can not avoid marking the "psychic aspect of writing" as a "dialogue with oneself," as well as with another, can not avoid marking the first trace that every gesture of writing entails, the splitting of the subject of the enunciation and the subject of the *énoncé* (utterance) (Kristeva 1966, 44).

We come home with this split in the subject, returning to Laye and the initial classical realist deception of masking the split between the three "I"s, the pretense that one is not writing, or conversely, that one is not reading a composed text, but rather that the raw experience has been passed on as if through a clear pane of glass.

Yet, although Ouologuem, Oyono, Soyinka, Mudimbe, Lopes, Kourouma, Sony Labou Tansi, and the younger generation of writers led by Ben Okri and Calixthe Beyala have insisted that writing is not pure transparency, have highlighted the act of writing through repetition, parody, and hidden polemic, and have foregrounded dialogism, they could not have found the words for the King's Horseman to intone on his ride home without those words echoing, even from a distance, the earlier voices. No words arise in a vacuum, and nowhere more than in Africa, has there been a conscious awareness, as well as an unconscious inheritance, of the power and authority attached to the word and its master or mistress. If the uses to which the word has been put have changed, the gestures, flavor, and rhythm are still familiar. The voices are still enhanced by the palm-oil (or is it Murano's palm-wine?) with which, as at the beginning, words in Africa are eaten. The defamiliarized text stands in a relationship of dependency on a familiar predecessor whose progeny have nonetheless hewed out a recognizable tradition of their own, and can look, like Esu, simultaneously behind and ahead while standing at the crossroads.

Esu: "You who translate yesterday's words
Into novel utterances"
(Traditional Oriki Esu, quoted in Gates [1988] 1989, 3)

Notes

Chapter 1. Thresholds of Change in African Literature— The Emergence of a Tradition

1. See Robert Cancel's work with Tabwa oral narratives (1989).
2. Add to this the fact that Achebe's Ibo, in novels like *Things Fall Apart,* is not only regional, it is formal and antiquated.

Chapter 2. Literatures of *Témoignage*

1. Irele (1981, Chapter 10) has shown the place of Tutuola's work within the larger corpus of Yoruba literature in which D. O. Faguna's rank as predecessor, and preeminent creator, is noted.
2. For example, Robert Cole's assimilationist *Kossoh Town Boy* paints a portrait of the youthful student struggling to acquire an education and finally finding success after falling in love with the Metropolitan language and literature en route.
3. Cf. Hadyn White's *Metahistory,* which traces the central trope, as narrative model, from the earliest historical chronicles to the present.
4. In *Le Baobab fou* Ken Bugel presents what might be termed the breakdown of the form with the chaotic account of her youth in Africa and her "decadent" experiences in Europe. She generally employs picaresque devices in recounting her European adventures while reverting to a more conventional form of *récit* when focusing upon her African childhood. In *The African,* William Conton breaks out of the autobiographical open form after some eighty pages, and launches into an unconvincing classical realist narrative dealing with the life of an African politician. Robert Cole fails to incorporate some features generally common to the form, and so his autobiography, *Kossoh Town Boy,* is marginal.
5. "Le souci des traditions fait un devoir au romancier de recourir aux structures romanesques les plus simples, les plus sommaires. Jusqu'à ces dernières années—et aujourd'hui encore, la majorité des romans répondent à cette description—le récit l'emporte sur la narration et le roman se déroule de la façon la plus classique. On y relève une exposition, une action nourrie par des péripéties et qui évolue vers la fin. L'action, unique, se déroule de façon rigoureusement rectiligne. Ce sont là les caractéristiques de la littérature dont les romanciers dotent leurs oeuvres, spontanément. . . . Partout ailleurs, s'exerce la tyrannie du temps qui reste sans épaisseur, en ce sens que la simultanéité des actions ne joue aucun rôle. Les romanciers, par manque de maîtrise ou parce que prisonniers d'une tradition d'écriture, ne retiennent que la succession des événements. . . . Il est cependant évident que la linéarité du récit sert fort bien le souci de présentation. Dans un premier temps, le romancier ne s'embarrasse pas de révéler la complexité de l'âme africaine. Il se soucie avant

tout d'en faire ressortir l'originalité. Dans la description de cet univers, il procède partie par partie, avec un étonnant souci d'ordre. . . . L'intrigue semble n'avoir d'autre finalité que celle d'assurer la cohérence et la continuité du récit" (M. Kane 1982, 63–64). ("Concern for traditions obliges the novelist to have recourse to the simplest and most abbreviated of novelistic structures. Until the last few years—and still today, the majority of novels corresponds to this description—the narrative text counts for more than the narration and the novel unfolds in the most classical of manners. There is an exposition, an action fed by digressions and that evolves toward a conclusion. The sole action transpires in a rigorously rectilinear manner. These are the literary traits with which the authors spontaneously endow their works. . . . Everywhere one senses the tyranny of a temporality without any density in the sense that the simultaneity of actions plays no role. The novelists, due to a lack of mastery or because they are prisoners of a written tradition, present only a succession of events. . . . It is, however, obvious that the linearity of the narrative text serves well the requirements of the presentation. Initially the novelist showed no concern about revealing the complexity of the African soul. He worried above all about originality. In the description of this universe, he proceeded piecemeal, with an astonishing care for order. . . . The plot seemed to have no other closure but that of guaranteeing the coherence and continuity of the narrative text" [my trans.].)

6. Camus's apothegm from *L'homme révolté* would seem appropriate here: "Je me révolte, donc nous sommes." This is echoed in Fanon's (1965) depiction of the succession of passages, for the colonized, from an initial state of individual revolt to one that is grounded in a national consciousness.

7. These are the five levels mentioned in Chapter 1. "One might distinguish five levels of *vraisemblance,* five ways in which a text may be brought into contact with and defined in relation to another text which helps to make it intelligible. First there is the socially given text, that which is taken as the 'real world'. Second, but in some cases difficult to distinguish from the first, is a general cultural text: shared knowledge which would be recognized by participants as part of culture and hence subject to correction or modification but which none the less serves as a kind of 'nature'. Third, there are the texts or conventions of a genre, a specifically literary and artificial *vraisemblance.* Fourth, comes what might be called the natural attitude to the artificial, where the text explicitly cites and exposes *vraisemblance* of the third kind so as to reinforce its own authority. And finally, there is the complex *vraisemblance* of specific intertextualities, where one work takes another as its basis or point of departure and must be assimilated in relation to it" (Culler 1975, 140).

8. Kristeva (1984) goes to some pains to indicate that the term *intertextuality* denotes more than a simple relationship to a source. It is rather a question of one sign system being transposed into another: "The new signifying system may be produced with the same signifying material; in language, for example, the passage may be made from narrative to text. Or it may be borrowed from different signifying materials: the transposition from a carnival scene to the written text, for instance. In this connection we examined the formation of a specific signifying system—the novel—as the result of a redistribution of several different sign systems: carnival, court poetry, scholastic discourse. The

term *inter-textuality* denotes this transposition of one (or several) sign system(s) into another; but since this term has often been understood in the banal sense of 'study of sources,' we prefer the term *transposition* because it specifies that the passage from one signifying system to another demands a new articulation of the thetic—of enunciative and denotative positionality" (59–60).

9. Yacine's mother knew only Arabic, and Kateb attended school in French. He writes that he experienced "cette seconde rupture du lien ombilical, cet exil intérieur qui ne rapprochait plus l'écolier de sa mère que pour les arracher chaque fois un peu plus au murmure du sang. . . . Ainsi avais-je perdu tout à la fois ma mère et son langage" (this second rupture of the umbilical tie, this interior exile that ceases to bring the schoolboy closer to his mother except to tear him away, each time a bit more, from the murmur of the blood. . . . Thus did I lose at the same time my mother and her language [qtd. in Déjeux 1973, 212]).

10. Conventionally we have a form that resembles the European Bildungsroman, with the difference that the centrifugal action in the European text is often matched by a preoccupation with the protagonist's psychological or moral development, while its African counterpart more often gives emphasis to social development, even when it is focalized through an individual. Perhaps we might attribute this to the greater African sense of inhabiting a society in conflict and in flux.

11. This is Sartre's famous preface to Senghor's *Anthologie de la nouvelle poésie nègre et malgache* (1948).

12. Finnegan goes on to show how these misapprehensions have hindered the critical process: "It can be seen how both these assumptions have inevitably discouraged interest in the actual contemporaneous performance, variations, and the role of the individual poet or narrator in the final literary product. A related assumption was that oral literature (often in the context called 'folk-lore') was relatively undeveloped and primitive; and this derogatory interpre-tation was applied to oral literature both in completely non-literate societies and when it coexisted with written literary forms in 'civilized' cultures. This opinion received apparent confirmation from the appearance of bare prose texts in translation or synopsis, and people felt no need to enter into more profound analysis about, say, the overtones and artistic conventions underly-ing these texts, far less the individual contribution of performer and com-poser. There was thus no need for further elucidation, for it was assumed in advance that little of real interest could emerge from this 'inherently crude' oral medium" (1970, 14).

13. Harold Scheub (1985) contends that the oral tales lend themselves to a process of stitching, in which episodes are strung together, as in the *Thousand and One Nights*. Oral literature would seem to have had a greater impact on narrative voice and style than on form, mode and genre, though Mohamadou Kane argues for formal continuities here as well.

14. In this excellent study Jenny systematically develops Kristeva's notion of inter-textuality, using Arrivé and Tinjanov.

Chapter 3. From *Témoignage* to Revolt

1. A parallel model can be found in Bird and Kendall's essay (1987) on the Mande hero. There they outline the distinction between *fadenya* and *badenya*, terms that correspond roughly to distinctions Duerden is establishing between forces that tend to disrupt the established order and those that tend to reinforce it. *Fadenya*, meaning father-childness, indicates the value of establishing one's individual worthiness, often by competing with former models of greatness: "The *fadenya*-oriented actor regards obligations to the social group as impediments to his individual quest for reputation—impediments which he must overcome, actually or symbolically, to be recognized as special. In the Mande world *fadenya* is thus associated with centrifugal forces of social disequilibrium: envy, jealousy, competition, self-promotion—anything tending to spin the actor out of his established social force field." The opposing pattern, *badenya* or mother-childness, "is associated with centripetal forces of society: submission to authority, stability, cooperation, those qualities which pull the individual back into the social mass." This ideal is accomplished by subordinating the individual to the group, thus giving rise to "social solidarity, security, and assurances that members of a group will act in concert to defend their colelctive worth" (15).

2. Cf. Bjornson's (1989) statement about Kulu the tortoise who "copes with an inexorably harsh world of power relationships by resorting to ruses that are often quite cruel. . . . [T]he victims of Kulu's ruses generally lose the advantage of their superior physical strength when they succumb to illusions that are sustained by their own gullibility and pride. The moral of these tales revolves around the dual recognition that all creatures exist in a world governed by the interplay of competing forces and that those who adopt a false interpretation of reality render themselves vulnerable to exploitation by others" (3).

Chapter 4. The Margins of Autobiographical Literature of *Témoignage*

1. Cf. Dominique Zahan's similar formulation: "La psychologie africaine attribue au moi un contenu plus large et plus riche que nos traités classiques de la science de l'âme. Pour définir le moi, nous le séparons d'autrui, alors qu'en Afrique c'est le procédé inverse qui sert de règle: jamais et nulle part l'être psychique du Noir ne se limite à 'ce qui n'est pas autrui et ne vient pas de lui.' Bien au contraire, l'Africain porte en lui, physiologiquement et psychiquement, ses propres géniteurs et les lignées respectives dont ils relèvent. Son moi est donc plus 'social' qu''individuel'; il se définit justement par ce qu'à tout moment il reçoit des autres" (Zahan 1970, 19–20). [African psychology attributes to the ego [self] a larger and richer content than is found in our classical treatises on the science of the soul. To define the ego [self], we separate from the other, whereas in Africa it is the opposite rule: in no instances does the psychic being of the black limit itself to 'that which isn't the other and which doesn't come from him or her.' To the contrary, the African carries within, physiologically and psychologically, his or her own forebears and the respective lineages from which he or she descends. His or her self is thus more

'social' than 'individual'; it is defined precisely by that which is received at every instant from others (my trans.).]

2. "Devant les êtres et les choses, il nous semble, à nous autres Africains, qu'une source de l'existence s'ouvre, non pas un instant, mais constamment, et que (et non 'comme si') des profondeurs cachées dans toute vie se découvrent directement" (Laye 1978b, 78). [As we face beings and things, it seems to us Africans that a source of existence opens up, not for an instant, but continually, and that (and not 'as if') hidden depths in each life are directly uncovered (my trans.).]

3. Cf. Culler's discussion (1975, 144–45) of Derrida's use of the term "hymen" in *Dissémination* (1972).

4. This is my translation of the *Petit Robert*'s definition of "seuil": "Dalle ou pièce de bois, formant la partie inférieure de la baie d'une porte."

5. On the whole issue of revealed versus secret knowledge in *L'Enfant noir*, see Christopher Miller's chapter on Laye in his *Theories of Africans* (1990).

6. Christopher Miller's central thesis in his chapter on *L'Enfant noir* (1990) is precisely that Malinke aesthetic strategies, termed *nyamakala* art, form the unstated basis for Laye's work. His emphasis on Malinke tradition, though brilliantly argued, unjustifiably excludes Islamic traditions.

Chapter 5. Flying Without Perching—Metaphor, Proverb, and Gendered Discourse

1. Citing Aristotle, Paul Ricoeur defines metaphor as exhibiting these same qualities, stressing the idea of defamiliarization joined to instruction: "For this is the function of metaphor, to instruct by suddenly combining elements that have not been put together before: 'We all naturally find it agreeable to get hold of new ideas easily: words express ideas, and therefore those words are the most agreeable that enable us to get hold of new ideas. Now strange words simply puzzle us; ordinary words convey only what we know already; it is from metaphor that we can best get hold of something fresh. When the poet calls old age "a withered stalk," he conveys a new idea, a new fact, to us by means of the general notion (*genous*) of "lost bloom" . . .'" (Ricoeur, 1977, 33-34; citing Aristotle's *Rhetoric*, 1410b 10-15).

2. Metaphor's structure is based on a four-part relationship: two sets of images set in unaccustomed conjunction to each other comment or signify upon "nature" or "reality" whose structures or qualities are evoked and thereby, presumably, elucidated. Metaphor is thus viewed, from Aristotle on, as a verbal device that acts upon nature. But Ricoeur reminds us that "if mimesis involves an initial reference to reality, this reference signifies nothing other than the very rule of nature over all production" (Ricoeur 1977, 39). "All mimesis . . . takes place within the horizons of being-in-the-world which it makes present to the precise extent that the mimesis raises it to the level of muthos" (43). "But mimesis does not signify only that all discourse is of the world; it does not embody just the *referential* function of the poetic discourse. Being *mimesis phuseos*, it connects this referential function to the revelation of the Real as Act. . . . To present men '*as acting*' and all things '*as in act*'–such could well be the *ontological* function of metaphorical discourse. . . ." (43).

3. See Tzvetan Todorov's discussion in his "Language and Literature" in Donato and Macksey's *The Structuralist Controversy* ([1970] 1982).

4. "A story, a story. Let it go, let it come"—a Hausa opening (Abrahams 1983, 351).

5. Ricoeur's summation of Aristotle's differentiation between simile and metaphor is instructive: "Furthermore, Aristotle attributes the superiority of metaphor over simile to this same virtue of elegance. More concentrated and shorter than simile, metaphor astonishes and instructs rapidly. Here surprise, in conjunction with hiddenness, plays the decisive role" (Ricoeur 1977, 33-34). "Hiddenness" implies space, the unsaid space between two declarative phrases, between two unaccountably matched images that signify upon each other so as to produce "surprise" and "instruction."

6. Ramadan and Weinstock (1978a) take this tack, too, though their reliance on "universal" imagery weakens their argument; Innes sees Okonkwo's rejection of the feminine as encompassing a rejection of the "poetic" function of language.

7. Cf. comparable figures such as La Grande Royale in *L'Aventure ambiguë* (Kane 1961), Salla in *La Grève des battù* (Sow Fall 1979), arguably Laye's mother, Dâman, in *L'Enfant noir* (Achebe [1958] 1972). Conversely, more ideologically grounded attempts to empower female characters in male-authored texts often strike a false note, as in Mongo Beti's *Perpétué* (1974), in Achebe's *Anthills of the Savannah* (1987), or in Sembène's *Ceddo* (1976).

8. It is no surprise, then, to learn of the signs of prestige and wealth as having male attributes: the yam, "king" of crops, is a "man's crop" (Achebe [1958] 1972, 21), an attribute important enough to warrant repetition: "Yam stood for manliness" (Achebe [1958] 1972, 30).

9. As Scheub points out, "At the center of the African novel, as of the epic, is the hero, caught between past and future, forced to make decisions fateful to himself and, frequently, to his community as well. Inaction is not possible; a movement from one state to another is urgently called for. That transformation is the metaphorical and mythic core of the storytelling tradition. . . ." (Scheub 1985, 41).

10. See Achebe's essays, such as "The Novelist as Teacher," in Killam (1973).

Chapter 6. Of Fathers and Sons—A Cusp in African Literature

1. The "manly" Olunde berates the Elesin, his father, in *Death and the King's Horseman* by calling him an "eater of leftovers" (Soyinka 1975, 61).

2. The same pattern is to be found in *Le Vieux Nègre* with the emphasis on eyes, seeing, and on shifts in perspective. Meka looks to the cement for Father Vandermayer's "eyes of a snake" (Oyono 1969, 97) ["yeux de serpent" (Oyono {1956b} 1979, 108)]; as Father Vandermayer taps him on his shoulder, Meka senses his presence even "[b]efore he opened his eyes" (97) ["avant d'ouvrir les yeux" (108)], and the exchange of rebuffs between Meka and Father Vandermayer is accomplished through angry glances and looks. Father Vandermayer's reactions to Meka are described in terms of "noticing." We leap from gaze to glance, finding reason to share dismay, anger, and deception: how we see Meka is changing, just as Kelara's new view of him has caused her to

change radically: "She *saw* her husband his head gleaming in the sun, grin foolishly at the Chief of the whitemen. Something happened inside her and she could not understand. Meka seemed to her like someone she had never *seen* before" (Oyono 1969, 95; my stress). ["Elle vit son mari, le crâne luisant au soleil, sourire bêtement au Chef des Blancs. Elle ne sut ce qui se passa en elle. Meka lui apparut comme quelqu'un qu'elle n'avait encore jamais *vu*" (Oyono {1956b} 1979, 106; my stress)].

3. See pp. 31, 33, 34, 37, 38, esp. 40, esp. 44, 49, 51, esp. 54, esp. 55, esp. 67, esp. 68, 73, 74, 76, 79, and 80 of Oyono 1969.

4. Wole Soyinka would term this space the fourth stage, the stage of transition, the chasm between two realms, to be crossed by Ogun, the prototypical tragic figure (see "Appendix: the Fourth Stage" in Soyinka [1976] 1979).

5. This is, of course, the substance of Léon Damas's well-known, earlier poem "Solde" (in Damas [1937] 1962).

6. Except for one reference to Engamba's earlier feeling of elation, and that occurs only in a dream (Oyono 1969, 34; Oyono [1956] 1979, 41).

Chapter 7. The Ironic Limits of Revolt

1. "In the end . . . it is difficult to determine precisely what Ouologuem's intention is" (Dunton 1989, 438).

2. The definitive task of contextualizing the history of the novel has been done by Thomas Hale in his *Scribe, Griot, and Novelist* (1990).

3. Interview in *The Guardian* cited on the back cover of *Bound to Violence*.

4. Chris Dunton refers to Ouologuem's statement that the novel was intended to be printed with an apparatus of quotation marks and references surrounding its borrowings (qtd. in Whiteman 1972, 941).

5. It might be interesting to compare this caricature with Frobenius's often-cited reaction, in his *Histoire de la civilisation africaine*, to first seeing Kassaï-Sankuru: "En 1906, lorsque je pénétrai dans le territoire de Kassaï-Sankuru, je trouvai encore des villages dont les rues principales étaient bordées de chaque côté, pendant des lieues, de quatre rangées de palmiers, et dont les cases ornées chacune de façon charmante, étaient autant d'oeuvres d'art. Aucun homme qui ne portât des armes somptueuses de fer ou de cuivre, aux lames incrustées, aux manches recouverts de peaux de serpent. Partout des velours et des étoffes de soie. Chaque coupe, chaque pipe, chaque cuiller était un objet d'art parfaitement digne d'être comparé aux créations du style roman européen. Mais tout cela n'était que le duvet particulièrement tendre et chatoyant qui orne un fruit merveilleux et mûr; les gestes, les manières, le canon moral du peuple entier, depuis le petit enfant jusqu'au vieillard bien qu'ils demeurassent dans des limites absolument naturelles, étaient empreints de dignité et de grâce, chez les familles des princes et des riches comme chez celles des féaux et des esclaves. Je ne connais aucun peuple du Nord qui se puisse comparer à ces 'primitifs' pour l'unité de la civilisation" (qtd. in Schellens and Mayer 1962, 24-25). [In 1906, when I entered into the territory of Kassaï-Sankuru, I still found villages whose principal streets were lined on each side, for miles on end, with four rows of palm trees, and whose decorated houses, each in charming fashion, were veritable works of art. Every man carried sumptuous weapons of iron or

copper, their blades encrusted, their handles covered with snakeskins. Everywhere velvet and silk fabrics. Each goblet, each pipe, each spoon was an object of art, perfectly worthy of comparison with creations in a European Romanesque style. But all that was but the downy exterior, especially tender and glistening, that decorates a marvelous and ripe fruit; the gestures, the manners, the moral fiber of the entire people, from the smallest child to the elder, though residing within absolutely natural borders, were marked by dignity and grace–no less true for the families of the serfs and slaves than for those of the princes and the wealthy. I know of no people from the North who might compare with these 'primitives' with respect to the unity of their civilization.]

6. Consider how close to the spirit of *Devoir* Aimé Césaire, as predecessor, comes in this passage from his *Cahier*: "Au bout du petit matin, l'échouage hétéroclite, les puanteurs exacerbées de la corruption, les sodomies monstrueuses de l'hostie et du victimaire, les coltis infranchissables du préjugé et de la sottise, les prostitutions, les hypocrisies, les lubricités, les trahisons, les mensonges, les faux, les concussions–l'essoufflement des lâchetés insuffisantes, l'enthousiasme sans ahan aux poussis surnuméraires, les avidités, les hystéries, les perversions, les arlequinades de la misère. . . . Au bout du petit matin, la grande nuit immobile, les étoiles plus mortes qu'un balafon crevé" (Césaire [1939] 1983, 12-13). ["At the end of the dawn, the odd stranding, the exacerbated stench of corruption, the monstrous sodomies of the offering and sacrificer, the dauntless prows of prejudice and stupidity, the prostitutions, the hypocrisies, the lubricities, the treasons, the lies, the frauds–the concussions, the breathlessness of half-hearted cowards, the smooth enthusiasms of budding bureaucrats, the avidities, hysterias, perversions, the harlequinades of misery . . . . At the end of the dawn, the great motionless night, the stars more dead than a perforated *balafon*" (Césaire 1971, 39-41).]

Chapter 8. Change on the Margins

1. See Derrida's speculation on boundaries in "Living On: *Border Lines*" (1979a), "The Parergon" (1979b), and *Glas* (1974). He extends the concept of semipermeable membranes and margins with the figure of the hymen in *La Dissémination* (1972).

Chapter 9. Literature of the Oxymoron—The Crossed Lovers

1. In his *Francophone African Fiction: Reading a Literary Tradition* (1988, 11-12), Jonathan Ngaté points out Mudimbe's use of Foucault's formulation.

2. For the Minister, this freedom is evoked in response to the lawyer's condemnation of the nightclub scene, and to his dreams of sexual power, as vice. "[Le Ministre] releva légèrement sa taille, déconcerté. Du vice? Il se sentait au centre d'une harmonie parfaitement achevée, ne comprenait pas qu'à pareille ordonnance ne puisse pas répondre une entière liberté de vivre tous les rêves" (Mudimbe 1976, 67). [(The Minister) rose up slightly, disconcerted. Vice? He felt himself to be at the center of perfect harmony, did not understand how such an order (as the lawyer conceived) could not be answered by the complete freedom to live out all his dreams (my trans.)]

3. The term is, of course, Kierkegaard's, employed in *Fear and Trembling, and The Sickness unto Death* (1954). He develops the idea that neither a life lived after

beauty and pleasure, nor the ethical path, can escape the pathos and contradiction of the human condition, and that only the leap of faith will suffice. If Mudimbe's fiction is concerned with the various forms of human pathos, the despair associated with failure to find complete faith or love, it insists on broadening the issue so as to raise the question of the larger social/historical situation in which the protagonists find themselves.

Chapter 10. The Still Point of Transition

1. Where Scheub (1985), the scholar of oral literature, identifies such figures as epic heroes, the playwright Soyinka recognizes in them the features of the tragic protagonist.

2. In such popular market literature as *Veronica My Daughter* (Ogali 1980) the educated daughter and wife address the traditional paterfamilias in standard English, while he responds in pidgin. In Sembène Ousmane's *Xala* (1974), El Hadj expostulates with his daughter for insisting on responding in Wolof to his questions posed in French. In Soyinka's work the range is as variegated as his equally broad range of characterization. But instead of enhancing mutual comprehension, it increases the ways in which the lack of communication can be expressed.

3. This sense of a frustrated ritual is symbolically realized in much of African literature as the image of those failing to complete initiation rites (as in *Une Vie de Boy* [Oyono (1956) 1970], *The River Between* [Ngugi 1965], or even, in a sense, *Les Soleils des indépendances* [Kourouma (1968) 1970]); or of individuals caught between two realms, trapped in the spotlight in an unbearably uncomfortable position (*Le Vieux Nègre et la médaille* [Oyono (1956b) 1979]); or having successfully negotiated one phase without completing the passage (*Mission terminée* [Beti 1957a]).

4. This pattern of anticipation and regret over learning the new language is evident in *Weep Not Child* (Ngugi 1964) and *L'Enfant noir* (Laye [1953] 1973). Much of African literature makes reference to conflicting discourses by utilizing European figures, or "been-tos," in conflict with the older, illiterate, or more tradition-oriented figures. At times the reference is explicit: the end of *Things Fall Apart* (Achebe [1958] 1972), the voices of the colonialists in Achebe's fiction, the "rational" ending of *The Great Ponds* (Amadi 1969), and Pilkings opposition to Elesin in *Death and the King's Horseman* (Soyinka 1975) are obvious instances. Even without the deus ex machina in *The Great Ponds*, the dialectic would be present in the clash between the description of the events as relatively remote occurrences and the less credulous gaze of the audience *assumed* in the manner in which the novel is narrated. The inevitable conclusion is that *littérature pour autrui* is characterized by incomplete ritual, by transitions that are frozen in space, by languages that fail to complete the communication—by voices, as in *The Voice* (Okara 1964), that fail to make themselves heard, by wounds, as in *La Plaie* (Fall 1980), that fail to heal, by love, as in *Because of Women* (Dipoko 1969), that leads to death.

In contrast, the ritual is completed in those works closest on the continuum to a *littérature pour soi*. Thus, Tutuola's palm-wine drinkard will save the community, his hero in *My Life in the Bush of Ghosts* (1954) will successfully complete the initiation (in contrast to *L'Enfant noir* with its successive stages of alienation, instead of initiation and integration). When the protagonist is not the individual trapped in tragic circumstances, but the whole society dancing to its own music, the transition ceases to be a moment of anomaly and chaos, but a true passage. The world of forces that inhabit the Yoruba universe is the protagonist of Tutuola's fiction. No conflicting discourses lead to blockages—Westernized elements are present, but transformed into Yorubized objects, i.e., assimilated (TV-handed ghosts). Similarly Laye succeeds most in *Le Regard du roi* ([1954] 1982) in presenting the mystico-Islamic African world as the active agent in the novel, and by using a European as the protagonist acted upon by that world, is able to make the mystical discourse prevail. When the terms are reversed, and we have the African protagonist confronted with the new pressures of "learning the language" of "today's world," we pass over to ambiguity and incompleteness.

The almost universally negative reaction to colonialism that typifies the literature born of the 1950s, the epoch of anticolonialism, is carried through to the 1980s—not so much in the guise of anti-neocolonial literature (despite a few writing in the style of Ngugi's recent polemical works), but by a continuing exploration of the sense of unease, angst, frustration, anomy. Often old battles are chosen to dramatize these feelings (see, e.g., *Dalanda* [Sacko 1975], Bessie Head's *The Collector of Treasures* [1977] and the issue of forced marriage, or Mariama Bâ's works), but even when cast into more radical psychological terms (as in Head's *A Question of Power* [1974], Myriem Warner-Vieyra's *Juletan* [1982], Ayi Kweh Armah's *Fragments* [1970] or *Why Are We So Blest* [1972]), the angst is never portrayed as a universal existential despair, but as a particularly African phenomenon experienced by the writer as the battleground for the intersection of persistently incompatible cultural and linguistic realms.

Chapter 11. Crossing the Bridge of Change

1. Other examples of the multitudinous triads: "there was nothing real, solid or enduring here for Fama to rely on . . ." (Kourouma 1981, 73) ["Fama ne tenait pas sur du réel, du solide, du définitif" (Kourouma [1968] 1970, 110)]; "the magic charms, red, yellow, green" (Kourouma 1981, 47) ["les sortilèges rouges, jaunes, verts (Kourouma [1968] 1970, 73)], the colors that mark Salimata's excision, show the pattern giving stress to the ironic tone of the narration, or to the violence inherent in the scene. When a fourth term is added, it must be separated from the series of three–as if summing them up: "So the Malinke species, tribes, land and civilization, was dying: crippled, deaf, blind- . . . and sterile" (Kourouma 1981, 13) ["Et l'espèce malinké, les tribus, la terre, la civilisation se meurent, perclus, sourdes et aveugles . . . stériles" (Kourouma [1968] 1970, 21)].

With *Monnè*, the frequent use of triads is replaced somewhat by doublings or quadruplings. The first page is full of examples: the animals being sacrificed are "boeufs, moutons, poulets" (Kourouma 1990, 13) [beef, sheep, chickens] whereas the agents of the king are listed as "sbires et sicaires" [henchmen and hired killers]; for the effect of the sacrifice, a doubling is repeated: "Du sang, toute sorte de sangs! Des sacrifices, toute sorte de sacrifices!" (13) [Blood, all kinds of blood! Sacrifices, all kinds of sacrifices!]. After the sacrifice of three albinos, three sorts of magicians are then evoked: "Les pythonisses, géomanciens, jeteurs de cauris et d'osselets" (13) [Pythonesses, magicians, fortune tellers using cowries and bones.]

Kourouma also employs, by extension, ironic multiplication. Djigui's aggrandizement is described in increasingly grandiloquent terms—"ses paroles sont devenues multidimensionelles et, notre ignorance aidant, il a paru et s'est cru incommensurable" (Kourouma 1990, 99) [his words became multidimensional and, with the help of our ignorance, he appeared and believed himself to be incommensurable]—while events reveal his ultimate impotency. At the age of 125, Djigui is elevated to mythic proportions while his subjects remain preoccupied with "la misère, les réquisitions, et les conscriptions" (99) [misery, requisitions, conscriptions].

2. "Les romanciers négro-africains d'avant 1940 écriront donc d'abord, à un premier niveau, pour se prouver à eux-mêmes et ensuite à leurs mâitres que par la sorcellerie de l'écriture et de la lecture, eux, ils valaient des Blancs, ils étaient des Nègres aussi adroits que les Blancs, et, à un second niveau pour dénoncer le mensonge social, la mystification qui les blanchissait et reléguait au rang de sous-hommes leurs frères et pères qu'ils savaient aussi intelligents et aussi sensibles . . ." (Kourouma 1973, n.p.). [The black African novelists from before 1940 wrote, first of all, on one level, to prove to themselves and then to their masters that, by the magic of writing and reading, they were the equals of the whites, that they were blacks who were as adroit as whites and, on another level, to denounce social lies, the mystification that whitened and relegated their brothers and fathers, whom they knew to be intelligent and sensitive, to the rank of subhumans.]

3. N.B.: This triad mirrors the novel's title.

4. This interpellation of the messenger reads like a reiteration of the Islamic interruption of Malinke practice. As Christopher Miller (1990) explains, traditional Malinke practice holds that truth is maintained intact and pure when kept within oneself and that the verbal expression of truth entails the passage to a state of increasing untruth: "The journey of the word upward [through the body] and out of the mouth describes a fall out of authenticity and truth, which, in and of themselves, are synonymous with *silence*. Simultaneous with the appearance of the word in the world is the possibility of lying. . . . True knowledge is held in silence. . . " (81).

Here, Djigui's reading of the vultures' arabesques and his sacrifices of the albinos, etc., are all distinctly pre-Islamic Malinke practices whose subordination to the newly dominant discourse of Islam reads like the transposition of former truths into their opposites—morning songs into evensongs, truth to lies. Finally, this passage of conversion is completed with the image of the arrival of *al-rasulu*, the messenger—echoing the basic role and supreme title of Mohammed as harbinger and transmitter of the new faith/new word.

There is also a final irony here. It is not Malinke but Islamic prayer that Djigui is describing as passing from truth to lies, and it is not the messenger of God but of Samory whose arrival presages Djigui's demise. In fact, the messenger is the harbinger of the demise of Malinke rule and of the arrival of the new dispensation of the French signaling the subordination of Islamic truth to colonial "mensonges" and "btardises."

5. "[Q]uand on court sur les braises, on ne s'arrête pas pour voir où mettre le pied, on ne réfléchit pas, de même quand la répression est là, on ne l'analyse

pas, on ne cherche pas à la comprendre, on n'écrit pas de romans" (Kourouma, qtd. in Kane 1982, 58). [When one runs over hot coals, one doesn't stop to see where to put one's foot, one doesn't reflect; likewise when repression exists, one doesn't analyze it, one doesn't search to understand it, one doesn't write novels.]

Chapter 12. The Dance of the Creole

1. This view conflicts with the Formalists' notion that art presupposes a conflict between dominant and subordinated factors. At the same time, art is also viewed by them as the product of an interaction, as stated here by Tinjanov: "Mais, si la sensation d'*interraction* des facteurs disparaît (et elle suppose la présence nécessaire de *deux* éléments, le subordonnant et le subordonné), le fait artistique s'efface; l'art devient automatisme. . . . Ce qui importe ici, c'est qu'il s'agit d'une nouvelle interaction et non de la simple introduction d'un facteur quelconque" (Tinjanov 1965b, 118). [But if the feeling of *interraction* of the factors disappears (and that presupposes the necessary presence of *two* elements, the subordinating and the subordinated), the artistic effect is effaced; art becomes automatism. . . . What matters here is the issue of a new interaction and not the simple introduction of some kind of factor.]

2. In John Pemberton's description of a pair of Ogboni staffs, or *edan,* we read that the Oshugbo (devotees of the divinity Onile) "express their metaphysical conceptions in the simple statement: 'Two Ogboni, it becomes three. . . .' The third element seems to be the mystery, the shared secret itself. The union of male and female in the *edan* image symbolizes this putting two together to make a third. . . . The secret of the Oshugbo society is that its members know, and are in touch with, a primordial unity, which transcends the oppositions that characterize human experience" (Fagg and Pemberton 1986, 186).

   It seems particularly apposite that the Creole experience, fashioned from the position of a third term that is "neither a bird nor a mammal" is also one that transcends opposites, that refers to a primordial unity created from the union of male and female, and that is grounded in another "supplement" that forms the archiconcept of self.

Chapter 13. Wordplay at the Water's Edge

1. Victor Erlich discusses Shklovsky's examples of defamiliarization, focusing on those drawn from Shklovsky's discussion of Tolstoy: "Tolstoy's works, Sklovskij observed astutely, abound in passages where the author 'refuses to recognize' the familiar objects and describes them as if they were seen for the first time. Thus, while describing in *War and Peace* an opera performance, he refers to the setting as 'pieces of painted cardboard' and in the scene of the mass in *The Resurrection* uses the prosaic expression 'small pieces of bread' to designate the host" (Erlich [1955] 1981, 177).

Works Cited

▼▼▼▼▼▼▼▼▼▼▼▼

ABRAHAMS, PETER. [1954] 1970. *Tell Freedom.* New York: Collier.

ABRAHAMS, ROGER D. 1983. *African Folktales.* New York: Pantheon.

ACHEBE, CHINUA. 1960. *No Longer at Ease.* New York: Ivan Obolensky.

———. [1958] 1972. *Things Fall Apart.* London: Heinemann.

———. 1973. "The Novelist as Teacher." In *African Writers on African Writing.* Ed. G. D. Killam. London: Heinemann.

———. [1964] 1974. *Arrow of God.* London: Heinemann.

———. 1975. *Morning Yet on Creation Day.* London: Heinemann.

———. 1987. *Anthills of the Savannah.* London: Heinemann.

ADOTEVI, STANISLAS. 1972. *Négritude et négrologues.* Paris: UGE (10/18).

AIDOO, AMA ATA. 1971. *No Sweetness Here.* New York: Doubleday.

ALTHUSSER, LOUIS. 1971. *Lenin and Philosophy and Other Essays.* Trans. Ben Brewster. London: New Left Books.

AMADI, ELECHI. 1969. *The Great Ponds.* London: Heinemann.

ARMAH, AYI KWEH. 1968. *The Beautyful Ones Are Not Yet Born.* Boston: Houghton-Mifflin.

———. 1970. *Fragments.* Boston: Houghton-Mifflin.

———. 1972. *Why Are We So Blest.* New York: Doubleday.

AUERBACH, ERIC. 1953. *Mimesis.* Trans. Willard Trask. Princeton: Princeton University Press.

BA, MARIAMA. 1980. *Une Si Longue Lettre.* Dakar: Nouvelles éditions africaines.

———. 1981. *So Long a Letter.* Trans. Modupé Bodé-Thomas. London: Heinemann.

BAKHTIN, MIKHAIL. 1971. "Discourse Typology in Prose." See Gates [1988] 1989.

———. 1983. *The Dialogic Imagination.* Trans. Caryl Emerson and Michael Holquist. Austin: University of Texas Press.

BARTHES, ROLAND. 1970. *S/Z.* Paris: Editions du Seuil.

———. 1971a. "Authors and Writers." In *Critical Essays.* See Barthes 1971b.

———. 1971b. *Critical Essays.* Trans. Richard Howard. Evanston: Northwestern University Press.

———. [1953] 1972. *Le Degré zéro de l'écriture.* Paris: Seuil.

———. 1974. *S/Z.* Trans. Richard Miller. New York: Hill and Wang.

———. 1981a. "From Work to Text." In *Textual Strategies.* Ed. Josué V. Harari. Ithaca: Cornell University Press.

———. 1981b. *Writing Degree Zero.* Trans. Annette Lavers and Colin Smith. New York: Hill and Wang.

———. 1982a. "The Reality Effect." In *French Literary Theory Today.* See Todorov 1982a.

———. 1982b. "To Write: An Intransitive Verb." In *The Structuralist Controversy.* See Donato and Macksey 1982.

BEBEY, FRANCIS. 1976. *Le Roi Albert d'Effidi.* Yaoundé: Clé.

BELSEY, CATHERINE. 1981. *Critical Practice*. London: Methuen.

BETI, MONGO. 1954a. *Ville cruelle*. Paris: Editions africaines.

———. 1954b. Review of Camara Laye's *L'Enfant noir*. *Présence Africaine* 16:419–20.

———. 1957. *Mission terminée*. Paris: Buchet/Chastel.

———. 1958. *Le Roi miraculé*. Paris: Buchet/Chastel.

———. 1970. *Mission to Kala*. Trans. Peter Green. London: Heinemann.

———. 1974. *Perpetué ou l'habitude du malheur*. Paris: Buchet/Chastel.

———. [1956] 1976. *Le Pauvre Christ de Bomba*. Paris: Présence africaine.

BIRD, CHARLES S. AND MARTHA KENDALL. 1987. "The Mande Hero." In *Explorations in African Systems of Thought*. Ed. Ivan Karp and Charles S. Bird. Washington, D.C.: Smithsonian Institution Press.

BJORNSON, RICHARD. 1986. Preface of *Road to Europe*. See Oyono 1986.

BLOOM, HAROLD. [1973] 1981. *The Anxiety of Influence*. London: Oxford University Press.

BLOOM, HAROLD, PAUL DE MAN, JACQUES DERRIDA, GEOFFREY HARTMAN, AND J. HILLIS MILLER. 1979. *Deconstruction and Criticism*. New York: Continuum.

BOURGEACQ, JACQUES. 1984. *"L'Enfant noir" de Camara Laye*. Sherbrooke: Naaman.

———. 1991. "Laurent Owondo's *Au bout du silence*; or, The Age When the Masks Give Up Their Secrets." *Research in African Literatures* 22(2):71–82.

BROOKS, GWENDOLYN. 1980. *A Primer for Blackness*. Chicago: Brooks Press.

BUGEL, KEN. 1982. *Le Baobab fou*. Dakar: Nouvelles éditions africaines.

CAMUS, ALBERT. 1952. *L'Homme révolté*. Paris: Editions de la rue.

CANCEL, ROBERT. 1989. *Allegorical Speculation in an Oral Society: The Tabwa Narrative Tradition*. Modern Philology 122. Berkeley: University of California Press.

CARTEY, WILFRED. 1969. *Whispers from a Continent*. New York: Vintage.

CARY, JOYCE. [1939] 1962. *Mr. Johnson*. New York: Time Inc.

CESAIRE, AIME. [1939] 1971. *Cahier d'un retour au pays natal/Return to My Native Land*. Trans. Emile Snyder. Présence africaine.

CHRAIBI, DRISS. 1954. *Le Passé simple*. Paris: Denoël.

COLE, ROBERT. 1960. *Kossoh Town Boy*. New York: Cambridge University Press.

CONTON, WILLIAM. 1960. *The African*. London: Heinemann.

CULLER, JONATHAN. 1975. *Structuralist Poetics*. London: Routledge and Kegan Paul.

———. 1982. *On Deconstruction*. Ithaca: Cornell University Press.

DADIE, BERNARD. 1955. *Le Pagne noir*. Paris: Présence africaine.

———. 1957. "Le Rôle de la légende dans la culture populaire des Noirs d'Afrique." *Présence Africaine* 14–15 (June–Sept.): 165–74.

———. 1970. *Monsieur Thôgô-Gnini*. Paris: Présence africaine.

DAMAS, LEON. [1937] 1962. *Pigments*. Paris: Présence africaine.

———. "Solde." In *Négritude*. See Shapiro 1970.

DEJEUX, JEAN. 1973. *Littérature maghrébine de langue française*. Ottowa: Naaman.

DE LEUSSE, HUBERT. 1971. *Afrique et occident. Heurs et malheurs d'une rencontre. Les Romanciers du pays noir*. Paris: Orante.

DE MAN, PAUL. [1971] 1983. *Blindness and Insight*. Minneapolis: University of Minnesota Press.

DERRIDA, JACQUES. 1972. *La Dissémination*. Paris: Seuil.

———. 1974. *Glas*. Paris: Editions Galilée.

———. 1978. *La Vérité en peinture*. Paris: Flammarion.

———. 1979a. "Living On: *Border Lines*." In *Deconstruction and Criticism*. Ed.

Harold Bloom et al. New York: Continuum.

————. 1979b. "The Parergon." *October* 9:3–40.

————. 1982. *Of Grammatology.* Trans. Gayatri Spivak. Baltimore: Johns Hopkins University Press.

DIA, MAMDOU. 1980. *Islam et civilisations négro-africaines.* Dakar: Nouvelles éditions africaines.

DIALLO, BAKARY. 1926. *Force Bonté.* Paris: Rieder.

DIALLO, NAFISSA. 1975. *De Tilène au plateau.* Dakar: Nouvelles éditions africaines.

DIOP, BIRAGO. 1947. *Les Contes d'Amadou Koumba.* Paris: Fasquelle.

————. 1958. *Les Nouveaux Contes d'Amadou Koumba.* Paris: Présence africaine.

DIOP, DAVID. 1957. Review of *Mission terminée,* by Mongo Beti. *Présence africaine* 16:187.

DIPOKO, MBELLA SONNE. 1969. *Because of Women.* London: Heinemann.

DONATO, EUGENIO, AND RICHARD MACKSEY, eds. [1970] 1982. *The Structuralist Controversy.* Baltimore: Johns Hopkins University Press.

DUERDEN, DENNIS. 1975. *African Art and Literature: The Invisible Present.* New York: Harper and Row.

DUNTON, CHRIS. 1989. "Homosexuality in African Literature." *Research in African Literatures* 20(3):422–48.

EKWENSI, CYPRIAN. 1961. *Jagua Nana.* London: Heinemann.

EMECHETA, BUCHI. 1979. *The Joys of Motherhood.* New York: Braziller.

ERLICH, VICTOR. [1955] 1981. *Russian Formalism: History-Doctrine.* New Haven: Yale University Press.

FAGG, WILLIAM, AND JOHN PEMBERTON 3D. 1982. *Yoruba Sculpture of West Africa.* New York: Knopf.

FALL, MALICK. 1980. *La Plaie.* Dakar: Nouvelles éditions africaines.

FANON, FRANZ. 1965. *The Wretched of the Earth.* New York: Grove Press.

FERAOUN, MOULOUD. 1954. *Le Fils du pauvre.* Paris: Seuil.

FINNEGAN, RUTH. 1970. *Oral Literature in Africa.* Oxford: Oxford University Press.

FLANNIGAN, ARTHUR. 1982. "'The Eye of the Witch': Non-Verbal Communication and the Exercise of Power in *Une Vie de boy.*" *French Review* 56(1):51–63.

FOUCAULT, MICHEL. 1973. *The Order of Things.* New York: Vintage.

FRYE, NORTHROP. 1957. *Anatomy of Criticism.* Princeton: Princeton University Press.

GATES, HENRY LOUIS, JR. 1984a. *Black Literature and Literary Theory.* New York: Methuen.

————. 1984b. "The Blackness of Blackness: A Critique of the Sign and the Signifying Monkey." In *Black Literature and Literary Theory.* See Gates 1984a.

————. [1988] 1989. *The Signifying Monkey.* New York and Oxford: Oxford University Press.

GBADAMOSI AND ULLI BEIER. 1959. *Yoruba Poetry.* Ibadan: General Publications Section, Ministry of Education.

JEAN GENET. [1958] 1960. *Les Nègres.* Décines: L'Arbalète.

HAMILTON, VIRGINIA. 1985. *The People Could Fly.* New York: Knopf.

HALE, THOMAS A. 1990. *Scribe, Griot, and Novelist.* Gainesville: University of Florida.

HARARI, JOSUE V., ED. 1981. *Textual Strategies.* Ithaca: Cornell University Press.

HARROW, KENNETH W., JONATHAN NGATE, AND CLARISSE ZIMRA, eds. 1991. *Crisscrossing the Boundaries in African Literature.* Washington, D.C.: Three Continents Press.

HAZOUME, PAUL. 1938. *Doguicimi.* Paris: Editions Larose.

HEAD, BESSIE. 1974. *A Question of Power*. London: Davis Poynter.

———. HEAD, BESSIE. 1977. *The Collector of Treasures*. London: Heinemann.

HRUSHOVSKI, BENJAMIN. 1984. "Poetic Metaphor and Frames of Reference." *Poetics Today* 5(1):5–43.

INNES, C. L., AND BERNTH LINDFORS, EDS. 1978a. *Critical Perspectives on Chinua Achebe*. Washington, D.C.: Three Continents Press.

———. 1978b. "Language, Poetry, and Doctrine in *Things Fall Apart*." In *Critical Perspectives on Chinua Achebe*. See Innes and Lindfors 1978a.

IRELE, ABIOLA. 1981. *The African Experience in Literture and Ideology*. London: Heinemann.

IYASERE, SOLOMON O. 1978. "Narrative Techniques in *Things Fall Apart*." In *Critical Perspectives on Chinua Achebe*. See Innes and Lindfors 1978a.

JABBI, BU-BUAKEI. 1978. "Fire and Transition in *Things Fall Apart*." In *Critical Perspectives on Chinua Achebe*. See Innes and Lindfors 1978a.

JAKOBSON, ROMAN. 1963. *Essai de linguistique générale*. Trans. Nicolas Ruwet. Paris: Editions de minuit.

———. 1965. "Vers une science de l'art poétique." In *Théorie de la littérature*. See Todorov 1965.

———. 1971. "Two Aspects of Language and Two Types of Aphasic Disturbances." *Selected Writings*. Vol. 2. The Hague: Mouton.

JENNY, LAURENT. 1982. "The Strategy of Form." In *French Literary Theory Today*. See Todorov 1982a.

JULIEN, EILEEN. 1989. "Dominance and Discourse in *La Vie et demie*; or, How to Do Things with Words." *Research in African Literatures* 20(3):371–84.

KANE, CHEIKH HAMIDOU. 1961. *L'Aventure ambiguë*. Paris: Julliard.

KANE, MOHAMADOU. 1974. "Sur les 'formes traditionelles' du roman africain." *Revue de Littérature Comparée* 3–4 (July–Dec.):10–38.

———. 1982. *Roman africain et tradition*. Dakar: Nouvelles éditions africaines.

KARP, IVAN, AND CHARLES S. BIRD, EDS. [1980] 1987. *Explorations in African Systems of Thought*. Washington, D.C.: Smithsonian Institution Press.

KILLAM, G. D., ED. 1973. *African Writers on African Writing*. London: Heinemann.

KONE, AMADOU. 1976. *Jusqu'au seuil de l'irréel*. Dakar: Nouvelles éditions africaines.

KOUROUMA, AHMADOU. [1968] 1970. *Les Soleils des indépendances*. Paris: Seuil.

———. 1973. "Les Années de silence du roman francophone." In "Culture et Côte d'Ivoire." Special supplement to *Le Soleil* (Dakar), December.

———. 1981. *The Suns of Independence*. Trans. Adrian Adams. New York: Africana.

———. 1990. *Monnè, outrages et défis*. Paris: Seuil.

———. 1993. *Monnew*. Trans. Nidra Poller. San Francisco: Mercury House.

KRISTEVA, JULIA. 1966. "Word, Dialogue, and Novel." In *The Kristeva Reader*. See Moi 1986.

———. 1984. *Revolution in Poetic Language*. Trans. Margaret Waller. New York: Columbia University Press.

KUHN, THOMAS. [1962] 1970. *The Structure of Scientific Revolutions*. Chicago: University of Chicago Press.

LAUDE, JEAN. 1971. *The Arts of Black Africa*. Berkeley: University of California Press.

LAYE, CAMARA. 1966. *Dramouss*. Paris: Plon.

———. [1953] 1972. *L'Enfant noir*. Paris: Plon (Livre de Poche).

———. 1978a. *The Dark Child*. Trans. James Kirkup and Ernest Jones. New York: Farrar, Straus and Giroux.

————. 1978b. *Le Maître de la parole.* Paris: Plon.

————. 1981. *The Guardian of the Word.* Trans. James Kirkup. Glasgow: Fontana/ Collins.

————. [1954] 1982. *Le Regard du roi.* Paris: Plon (Presses Pocket).

LEJEUNE, PHILIPPE. 1982. "The Autobiographical Contract." In *French Literary Theory Today.* See Todorov 1982a.

LEMON, LEE T., AND MARION J. REIS, EDS. 1965. *Russian Formalist Criticism: Four Essays.* Lincoln: University of Nebreska Press.

LEVI-STRAUSS, CLAUDE. 1969. *The Raw and the Cooked.* Trans. John and Doreen Weightman. New York: Harper and Row.

LINDFORS, BERNTH. 1968. "The Palm-Oil with Which Achebe's Words Are Eaten." *African Literature Today* 1:3–18. Rpt. in *Critical Perspectives on Chinua Achebe.* See Innes and Lindfors 1978a.

LOPES, HENRI. 1982. *Le Pleurer-rire.* Paris: Présence africaine.

————. 1990. *Le Chercheur d'Afriques.* Paris: Seuil.

LUKCS, GEORG. 1964. *Studies in European Realism.* New York: Grosset and Dunlap.

————. [1920] 1983. *The Theory of the Novel.* Trans. Anna Bostock. Cambridge, Mass.: MIT Press.

MANGIER, BERNARD. 1985. "Je ne suis pas à développer mais à prendre ou à laisser." Interview with Sony Labou Tansi. *Notre Librairie* 79 (Apr.–June):5–7. Issue entitled "Cinq ans de littérature africaine, 1979–1984."

MERNISSI, FATIMA. 1987. *Beyond the Veil.* Revised edition. Bloomington: Indiana University Press.

MILLER, ARTHUR. 1955. *A View from the Bridge.* New York: Viking.

MILLER, CHRISTOPHER L. 1985. *Blank Darkness: Africanist Discourse in French.* Chicago and London: University of Chicago Press.

————. 1990. *Theories of Africans.* Chicago: University of Chicago Press.

MOI, TORIL. 1986. *The Kristeva Reader.* New York: Columbia University Press.

MOORE, GERALD, AND ULLI BEIER, EDS. 1965. *Modern Poetry from Africa.* London: Penguin.

MOSER, GERALD. 1991. "Childhood Memories in Lusophone Africa: Are They a Literary Genre?" In *Crisscrossing the Boundaries in African Literature.* See Harrow et al. 1991.

MPHAHLELE, EZEKIEL. 1959. *Down Second Avenue.* London: Faber and Faber.

MUDIMBE, V. Y. 1973. *Entre les eaux.* Paris: Présence africaine.

————. 1976. *Le Bel Immonde.* Paris: Présence africaine.

————. 1978. *L'Ecart.* Paris: Présence africaine.

————. 1982. *L'Odeur du père.* Paris: Présence africaine.

————. 1988. *The Invention of Africa.* Bloomington: Indiana University Press.

————. 1989. *Before the Birth of the Moon.* Trans. Marjolijn de Jager. New York: Simon and Schuster.

NGATE, JONATHAN. 1988. *Francophone African Fiction.* Trenton: African World Press.

NGUGI WA THIONG'O. 1964. *Weep Not Child.* London: Heinemann.

————. 1965. *The River Between.* London: Heinemann.

————. 1967. *A Grain of Wheat.* London: Heinemann. Ngugi wa Thiong'o and Micere Mugo. 1976. *The Trial of Dedan Kimathi.* London: Heinemann.

NZEKWU, ONUORA. 1961. *Wand of a Noble Wood.* London: Heinemann.

OGALI, OGALI. 1980. *Veronica My Daughter and Other Onitsha Plays and Stories.* Washington, D.C.: Three Continents Press.

OGUNDIPE, AGODELE. 1978. *Esu Elegbara, the Yoruba God of Chance and Uncertainty: A Study in Yoruba Mythology.* See Gates [1988] 1989.

OHAEGBU, A. E. 1978. "An Approach to Ouologuem's *Le Devoir de violence.*" *African Literature Today* 10. London: Heinemann.

OKARA, GABRIEL. 1964. *The Voice.* London: André Deutsch.

O'TOOLE, L. M., AND ANN SHUKMAN, EDS.. 1977. *Formalist Theory.* Vol. 4 of the Russian Poetics in Translation series. Oxford: Holdan Books.

OUOLOGUEM, YAMBO. 1968. *Le Devoir de violence.* Paris: Seuil.

———. 1977. *Bound to Violence.* Trans. Ralph Manheim. London: Heinemann.

OYONO, FERDINAND. 1960. *Le Chemin d'Europe.* Paris: Julliard.

———. 1969. *The Old Man and the Medal.* Trans. John Reed. London: Heinemann.

———. [1956a] 1970. *Une Vie de boy.* Paris: Julliard (Presses Pocket edition).

———. [1956b] 1979. *Le Vieux Nègre et la médaille.* Paris: Julliard (10/18).

———. 1982. *Houseboy.* Trans. John Reed. London: Heinemann.

———. 1989. *Road to Europe.* Trans. Richard Bjornson. Washington, D.C.: Three Continents Press.

PALMER, EUSTACE. 1972. *An Introduction to the African Novel.* New York: Africana.

———. 1979. *The Growth of the African Novel.* London: Heinemann.

PAULME, DENISE. 1976. *La Mère dévorante.* Paris: Gallimard.

RAMADAN, CATHY, AND DONALD WEINSTOCK. "Symbolic Structure in *Things Fall Apart.*" In *Critical Perspectives on Chinua Achebe.* See Innes and Lindfors 1978a.

RAY, BENJAMIN. 1976. *African Religions.* Englewood Cliffs, N.J.: Prentice-Hall.

RICOEUR, PAUL. 1977. *The Rule of Metaphor.* Toronto: University of Toronto Press.

———. 1979. "The Metaphorical Process as Cognition, Imagination, and Feeling." Trans. Robert Czerny. In *On Metaphor.* Ed. Sheldon Sacks. Chicago: University of Chicago Press.

ROUCH, JEAN. 1953. *Les Maîtres fous.* (Film)

RYAN, MICHAEL. 1984. *Marxism and Deconstruction.* Baltimore: Johns Hopkins University Press.

SACKO, BIRAM. 1975. *Dalanda.* Dakar: Nouvelles éditions africaines.

SACKS, SHELDON, ED. 1979. *On Metaphor.* Chicago: University of Chicago Press.

SADJI, ABDOULAYE. 1953. *Maïmouna.* Dakar: Les Lettres faciles.

SALIH, TAYEB. 1968. *The Wedding of Zein, and Other Stories.* Trans. Denys Johnson-Davies. London: Heinemann.

SCHELLENS, JEAN-JACQUES, AND JACQUELINE MAYER, EDS. 1962. *Le Dossier Afrique.* Marabout University Collection. Verviers, Belgium: Gérard.

SCHEUB, HAROLD. 1985. "Review of African Oral Traditions and Literature." *African Studies Review* 28(2–3):1–72.

SCHOLES, ROBERT. 1974. *Structuralism in Literature.* New Haven: Yale University Press.

SCHOLES, ROBERT, AND ROBERT KELLOGG. 1981. *The Nature of Narrative.* London: Oxford University Press.

SELLIN, ERIC. 1976. "The Unknown Voice of Yambo Ouologuem." *Yale French Studies* 53:137–62.

SEMBENE OUSMANE. 1957. *O pays, mon beau peuple.* Paris: Le Livre contemporain.

———. 1960. *Les Bouts de bois de Dieu.* Paris: Le Livre contemporain.

———. 1962. *Voltaïque.* Paris: Présence africaine.

———. 1964. *L'Harmattan.* Paris: Présence africaine.

———. 1965. *Le Mandat et Véhi ciosane; ou, blanche genèse.* Paris: Présence africaine.

———. 1971. *Emitai.* (Film)

———. 1974. *Xala.* (Film)

———. 1976. *Ceddo.* (FIlm)

———. 1988. *Camp de Thiaroye.* (Film)

SENGHOR, LEOPOLD SEDAR. 1948. *Anthologie de la nouvelle poésie nègre et malgache.* Paris: PUF.

———. 1958. Preface of *Les Nouveaux Contes d'Amadou Koumba,* by Birago Diop. Paris: Présence africaine.

SHAPIRO, NORMAN, ED. AND TRANS. 1970. *Négritude.* London: October House Ltd.

SHKLOVSKY, VIKTOR. [1925] 1929. *On the Theory of Prose.* Moscow: n.p.

SOCE, OUSMANE. [1935] 1964. *Karim.* Paris: Nouvelles éditions latines.

SONY LABOU TANSI. 1979. *La Vie et demie.* Paris: Seuil.

———. 1981. *L'Etat honteux.* Paris: Seuil.

———. 1983. *L'Anté-peuple.* Paris: Seuil.

———. 1985. *Les Sept Solitudes de Lorsa Lopez.* Paris: Seuil.

———. 1986. "Réinventer la logique à la mesure de notre temps." *Equateur* 1:33–35.

———. 1988. *Les Yeux du volcan.* Paris: Seuil.

SOW FALL, AMINATA. 1979. *La Grève des battù.* Dakar: Nouvelles éditions africaines.

SOYINKA, WOLE. 1965. *The Interpreters.* London: André Deutsch.

———. 1967. *Idanre and Other Poems.* London: Methuen.

———. 1972. *The Man Died.* London: Rex Collins.

———. 1973a. *Collected Plays.* Vol. 1: *A Dance of the Forests, The Swamp Dwellers, The Strong Breed, The Road, The Bacchae of Euripides.* London: Oxford University Press.

———. 1973b. *Season of Anomy.* London: Rex Collins.

———. 1974. *Collected Plays.* Vol. 2: *The Lion and the Jewel, Kongi's Harvest, The Trial of Brother Jero, Jero's Metamorphosis, Madmen and Specialists.* London: Oxford University Press.

———. 1975. *Death and the King's Horseman.* New York: Hill and Wang.

———. [1976] 1979. *Myth, Literature, and the African World.* Cambridge: Cambridge University Press.

———. 1981. *Opera Wonyosi.* Bloomington: Indiana University Press.

———. 1984. *A Play of Giants.* London: Methuen.

———. 1985. *Requiem for a Futurologist.* London: Rex Collins.

SPIVAK, GAYATRI. 1982. "Translator's Preface." In *Of Grammatology.* See Derrida 1982a.

STEINER, PETER. 1984. *Russian Formalism: A Metapoetics.* Ithaca: Cornell University Press.

TINJANOV, JURIJ. 1965a. "De l'Evolution littéraire." In *Théorie de la littérature.* See Todorov 1965.

———. 1965b. "La Nation de construction." In *Théorie de la littérature.* See Todorov 1965.

TODOROV, TZVETAN, ED. 1965. *Théorie de la littérature.* Paris: Seuil.

———. 1968. Introduction to *Le Vraisemblable. Communications* 11:1–4.

———. 1981. *Introduction to Poetics.* Minneapolis: University of Minnesota Press.

———. , ed. 1982a. *French Literary Theory Today.* Trans. R. Carter. Cambridge: Cambridge University Press.

———. 1982b. "Language and Literature." In *The Structuralist Controversy.* See

Donato and Macksey 1982.

TOMASHEVSKY, BORIS. 1965. "Thematics." In *Russian Formalist Criticism: Four Essays.* See Lemon and Reis.

TOWA, MARCIEN. 1971.. *Léopold Sédar Senghor: négritude ou servitude?.* Yaounde, Cameroon: Editions Clé.

AMOS TUTUOLA. 1954. *My Life in the Bush of Ghosts.* London: Faber and Faber.

————. 1967. *Ajaiyi and His Inherited Poverty.* London: Faber and Faber.

VIEIRA, JOSE LUANDINO. 1980. *Luuanda.* Trans. Tamara L. Benda and Donna S. Hill. London: Heinemann.

WARNER-VIEYRA, MYRIEM. 1982. *Juletan.* Paris: Présence africaine.

WESTCOTT, JOAN. 1962. "The Sculptures and Myths of Eshu-Elegba, the Yoruba Trickster." *Africa* 32(4):336–54.

WHITE, HAYDEN. [1973] 1979. *Metahistory.* Baltimore: The Johns Hopkins University Press.

WHITEMAN, KAYE. 1972. "In Defense of Yambo Ouologuem." *West Africa* 2875 (21 July):941.

ZABUS, CHANTAL. 1991. *The African Palimpsest: Indigenization of Language in the West African Europhone Novel.* Amsterdam: Rodopi.

ZAHAN, DOMINIQUE. 1970. *Religion, spiritualité, et pensée africaines.* Paris: Payot.

Index

▼▼▼▼▼